FINANCIAL MANAGEMENT
An Analytical Approach

FINANCIAL MANAGEMENT

An Analytical Approach

J ROBERT LINDSAY, PH.D.
Professor of Finance

ARNOLD W. SAMETZ, PH.D.
Professor of Finance

both of

Graduate School of Business Administration
New York University

Revised Edition • 1967
RICHARD D. IRWIN, INC.
Homewood, Illinois

Revised Edition

First Printing, February, 1967

Library of Congress Catalog Card No. 66–29192

PRINTED IN THE UNITED STATES OF AMERICA

For Two Helens,
an Agnes,
and a Natalie

PREFACE

This revised edition retains the basic themes of the first edition, and the same flavor. Large chunks of it, however, have been rewritten—to introduce fresh ideas, or to introduce ideas at a different point, or to develop them in a different manner.

The central purpose is still twofold. Our fundamental aim is still to explore business finance as an analytical subject, and the main map of exploration continues to be the organizing device known as sources and uses of funds. Moreover, the book is still directed at the needs of two groups of students—(1) students of finance in business schools and (2) liberal arts majors who have an interest in finance and economics.

For the business school student, we have had in mind the general course in corporate or business finance. Before reaching such a point, students in a commerce program normally will have had an introductory course in economics. The general corporate finance course thus catches the commerce student after he has been exposed to general economics issues but before he has plunged into his professional specialty. This book is, in part, aimed at students crossing this critical bridge. It can, in fact, be that bridge, both to get students across this boundary, and to connect directly the general economics and analytical ideas with the specific practice.

For the liberal arts student, the problem is likely to be the other way around. He often finds that, even for a general understanding of business finance, he must discover a place in his schedule for courses in accounting, corporation finance, and perhaps several other commerce subjects. Often, there is simply not time for these courses. And even when they can be fitted in, they are likely to include a great deal of detail that is useful only to students who are preparing directly for careers in financial management. By the same token, such courses typically skirt, for lack of time, many of the interesting analytical questions that are inherent in the subject matter. As a result, the liberal arts student—whether or not he takes such courses—is generally left to discover the economics of business finance as best he can, on his own.

vii

To meet the needs of both commerce and economics students this book attacks the issue on two fronts:

1. It presents a general body of business practice in the area of finance, at the same time avoiding the swamp of detail sometimes offered in textbooks in this field.

2. Using this general body of material as a backdrop, it attempts to relate business practice to the larger issues of economic policy and economic theory, and to an analytical approach in general.

As is apparent from these two objectives, the book is designed to give the reader a general understanding of corporate financial behavior. That is to say, it is in no sense a "how-to-do-it" book. Nevertheless, for those who will one day themselves be financial managers, we have tried to give the feeling of what that job will involve. On the other hand, for those who will attempt only to fathom business behavior in the aggregate, we have felt it important that they understand something of practice at the level of an individual firm. To be at all useful, any general interpretation of corporate financial patterns, taken in the round, must be consistent with the likely behavior of individual firms taken one by one. The two objectives are thus closely related, and are, so far as possible, treated equally throughout the progress of the book.

As noted, the changes from the first edition have been far-reaching. Any overhaul of a textbook should accomplish two things—it should update the numbers used in the earlier version, and it should update the thinking.

New numbers are relatively easy to find. New thinking is the bigger job. In the several years since the earlier edition of this book, the field of financial analysis has continued to grow and spread at a rapid pace. New ideas have flowed into the journals. New analytic techniques have spilled over from mathematics and operations research and other places. New problems have moved to center stage, as older problems either were solved or were seen to be less important than people had thought before.

Also, the moment a book is in cold print, things happen to the thinking of its authors. They see the book at a greater distance. Their child abruptly becomes an adult, on his own and responsible for himself. In addition, other readers are soon heard from. Teachers who try the book question a conclusion here, protest an exposition there. The muttering of students grows more audible at some passages than at others. Reviewers work like a dentist looking for cavities, moving quickly past the sound tissue and digging in at the weak spots, probing for larger weaknesses underneath.

A revision thus gains from the efforts of all these workers, direct and indirect. We have listened carefully and thought hard. The principal changes that emerge are as follows:

1. A more explicit development of stockholder wealth maximization as the goal. This means development of the idea earlier than in the first edition, followed by more consistent references through the rest of the text.

2. A considerable reorganization and expansion of the material on short-term sources and uses. Inventory management is joined with the other short-term elements, and the whole subject is moved nearer to the front of the book. All the material is then handled as suboptimization in the short run—that is, it takes as given a number of cost and earnings considerations.

3. Reorganization of the sections on capital budgeting and the cost of capital.

   a) To develop early in the book the fundamental concepts of discounting and uncertainty and opportunity cost, so as to show their relevance to all areas of decision making, not just to plant and equipment investment.

   b) To put the deeper development of these concepts further along— so student understanding can build over a longer period of study.

   c) To achieve a somewhat more systematic discussion of capital budgeting than in the first edition.

   d) To expand the formal treatment of uncertainty.

   e) To draw the dividend decision more closely into the cost of capital analysis.

The book falls into six major parts. In the opening section, the first chapter is offered as a rough and elementary substitute for an accounting background. But it serves a further purpose. It develops the interrelationships of balance sheet and income statement that give shape to the rest of the book. The idea of stocks and flows is thus introduced early and implanted firmly, and the central place of cash budgeting is driven home. The other chapter in this section lays out, in general lines, the theory of finance of the firm—the ultimate goal of stockholder wealth maximization, the emphasis on cash flow, the quantity and quality of these flows, and the tie with economic theory.

In Part II, short-term sources and uses are taken up in seven chapters.

Part III turns to the long-term uses—four chapters on capital budgeting, one on the problem of uncertainty, and one sketching some economic theories of capital investment and some of the relevant data. Part IV takes us to the long-term sources and the whole analysis of the cost of capital. Part V tackles the question of capital structure—again a matter of long-term sources. Part VI takes a closer look at the details of security instruments, and at the markets for these instruments and the machinery for getting them sold.

We are under no illusions that the correction of earlier errors has produced a new book free of error. We have almost surely made mistakes of our own. And unwittingly we have doubtless also gathered here some common mistakes of the profession, those present truths that time will show to be false, or slightly askew at best. The subject of financial analysis is boiling with ideas and imagination these days. To give the reader the sense of change associated with this wide-ranging exploration, we have included a number of recent articles and books in the suggested readings at the ends of chapters. There are also questions and problems at chapter-ends, some of them designed to stir the student up again about matters he might have thought were settled in the chapter itself.

There are no deliberate mistakes of course, and many people have helped us in the hunt for inadvertent error. We received much thoughtful advice from Professor A. E. Grunewald of Michigan State University, and Professor Sidney Jones of the University of Michigan, both of whom read the manuscript with great care and offered many penetrating and helpful suggestions. We are indebted also to Professor Alan Heston of the University of Pennsylvania, Professor Victor L. Andrews of Harvard University, and Professor William W. Alberts of the University of Chicago, all of whom wrote journal reviews of the first edition which proved very valuable in our thinking. Indeed, our debt in general is heavy and our creditors many. We have borrowed working capital from many earlier writers, and in some cases have taken over bodily the assets developed by the many people who have come before us. Among these intellectual lenders, however, special mention should be made of the written work, now approaching two decades ago, of Norman Buchanan, Ruth Mack, and Friederich and Verz Lutz. Also, for the special encouragement he gave us, early and later, we owe a virtually permanent debt to Thomas Norton of New York University. We are also grateful to friends and colleagues at New York University and at the Federal Reserve Bank of New York, although of course they bear no responsibility.

Finally, there is our very great gratitude to Mrs. Ruth Burnett and Mrs. Ligija Roze, who performed many wonders in preparing the manuscript, and our appreciation to William Schneider and Earl Foster, who made the index.

New York, N.Y.   J. ROBERT LINDSAY
December, 1966   ARNOLD W. SAMETZ

TABLE OF CONTENTS

PART I: BACKGROUND AND FOREGROUND

PART III: LONG-TERM USES OF FUNDS

OF CORPORATE FINANCE IN THE SEVERAL INDUSTRIAL SECTORS: A STUDY OF
COMPARATIVE CAPITAL STRUCTURES: Cyclical Variations in the Sources of
Funds. EXTERNAL SOURCES AND SECURITY ISSUES.

PART VI: LONG-TERM EXTERNAL SOURCES

INDEXES

Part I

BACKGROUND AND FOREGROUND

Chapter 1

FINANCIAL FLOW AND THE
POOL OF CASH

This is not a book about lobster fishermen. But to see just what it is about, suppose we take such a fisherman as an example. Following this man around for a while, we can begin to see what his financial problems are. We can also see how these problems give rise to a framework, or rather several frameworks, for thinking about the problems.

At one level or another, these frameworks will be familiar to many readers. They serve so admirably as organizing ideas that they are almost universally the tools for analyzing business endeavor. Nonetheless, precisely because the ideas are so fundamental, it is well to make sure they are firmly in our grip.

In particular, we can make good use of the *statement of sources and uses*. To make that set of ideas securely our own, we start with the two organizing devices from which it is usually derived—the *income statement* and the *balance sheet*. With these tools in hand, we will be ready to take up the major tasks of financial management.

THE INCOME STATEMENT (OR PROFIT AND LOSS STATEMENT)

As we first come upon our lobsterman, he has not yet become one. He is a young man with a yearning to be master of his own lobster boat. To his great good fortune, one of his uncles, who owns a boat and a large number of traps, decides to run for Congress. Since the uncle will be busy campaigning throughout the summer, during the heaviest part of the lobstering season, he makes his nephew an offer. He proposes to turn over his entire operation—boat, traps, and all—to his nephew for the season,

3

if the young man will agree to pay for any incidental expenses and to give his uncle one third of whatever profits he makes.

The First Year

The young man's business life begins. He works very hard. The uncle also works very hard, and is elected by a large majority. It is so large, in fact, that the uncle concludes he can make a better living at politics than at lobstering. Thus, soon after the election, he makes the nephew another offer. He will *sell* him the boat and all the traps for a total of $10,000.

At this point, the lobster season is over, and our young man sits down to draw up an income statement. He must not only compute profits for the season in order to pay the uncle his share, but before deciding whether to buy the rig, he must determine just how well he is doing at the business. What he seeks now is an accounting device that will reveal to him (1) how much money he took in from the year's operations, (2) what costs were involved in producing that revenue, and (3) how much remained in profit after subtracting the costs from the revenue. After considerable searching of his memory and digging around for various receipts and other slips of paper, he arrives finally at the account of the year shown in Table 1–1.

TABLE 1–1

INCOME STATEMENT FOR FIRST YEAR

Total revenue from sale of lobsters		$5,600
Cost of gasoline	$1,100	
Cost of repairs to traps	250	
Paint job for boat	300	
State fishing license	50	
Total Cost		1,700
Total Profit (total revenue minus total cost)		$3,900
Uncle's share (one third)		$1,300
Nephew's share (two thirds)		$2,600

Studying this statement and remembering blue, sunlit days on the water, the nephew resolves his few remaining doubts. He will buy the boat and the traps. He has a little money saved, and the banker in the village, it turns out, has heard good reports of the lad. A loan is made; the young man buys the boat and traps; a faintly perceptible swagger enters his walk. (We shall ask in later chapters whether this kind of decision should be made in such a fashion.)

The Second Year

In the second year, he works still harder. His skill grows, and he gets more lobsters. At the end of the year the young man finds his total revenue from the year's operations has increased from $5,600 to $6,200.

Computing his costs for the year, he finds that his gasoline bills add up to $1,000, slightly less than last year, as he has learned ways to avoid idling the motor. All the other items carried over from the previous year's statement are unchanged. He has once again paid out $250 for repairs to traps, $300 for a new coat of paint, and $50 for his annual fishing license required by the state. There are also the interest charges on the bank loan. These come to $600.

But there is still another new cost item. The nephew has paid out $10,000 for a boat and traps, and since they will not last forever, he must assume that part of them was used up during the year. He might, of course, count the full cost of the boat and traps in this year's statement. After all, he did pay for it all during this accounting period. But as our young man begins to realize, it is not the purpose of an income statement to record all *cash outlays* made during the year. It is rather to assign to that period all the *costs* involved in producing the revenue received during the period. Our young man must distinguish between *expenditures* or cash outlays and *assignable costs*. Since he did, in fact, pay out a considerable sum of money to his uncle, this amount must be classified as an expenditure. The assignable cost, on the other hand, was only a part of that expenditure. For in buying the boat, the nephew has acquired an asset that will contribute to his livelihood over a number of years.

The boat and traps can be thought of as bundles of services, ingrained in the wood and steel, that will gradually be used up in the steady rounds of lobster fishing. As those services are consumed, they make it possible for the young man to catch lobsters and sell them for money. Accordingly, in one single year the assignable cost will be measured by the services used up. The cost incurred will be equal to that part of the assets' total lives that were lived during the year.

Our young man has arrived, after much puzzling, at what is called an *allowance for depreciation*. An even better term would be *capital consumption allowances*. Spreading the total cost of the boat and traps over several years will give him a more reasonable picture of the cost of doing business year in and year out. Equally important, it will prevent the distortion of his profits record. For if the total cost of the boat and the lobster traps should be subtracted entirely from *one* year's sales receipts, the nephew's profits history would soon begin to look very unstable.

The first year's statement, carrying the full burden of the purchase of the boat, would show an abnormally low profit or an actual loss. The second year, by contrast, would be shown as completely free of this sizable outlay, so that the difference between revenue and costs would jump sharply. Yet such a jump would have no real meaning at all. The young man might have sold exactly the same number of lobsters, for exactly the same price, after exactly as much hard work. The big leap in his profits in the second year would thus be quite misleading. And so, for that matter, would the low level of earnings shown in the first year.

Anxious not to mislead himself, the nephew focuses closely on his computation. Lobster boats of the class he now owns generally last about 15 years, given good treatment and reasonable good luck. The uncle, who treated it well, had bought the boat new and had used it about five years. Therefore, the remaining life of the craft could be approximated at ten years. The traps, let us say, are also expected to give service for another ten years. Since the young man had paid his uncle $10,000 for the full rig, the average consumption of the services left in them could be figured at $1,000 for each of the next ten years. Our young man turns this over in his mind for several days, and then enters it on his ledger.

This decision made, he now completes his income statement for the year. In its final form, it takes the shape shown in Table 1–2.

TABLE 1–2

INCOME STATEMENT FOR SECOND YEAR

Total revenue from sale of lobsters		$6,200
Cost of gasoline	$1,000	
Cost of repairs to traps	250	
Paint job for boat	300	
State fishing license	50	
Interest on loan	600	
Allowance for depreciation	1,000	
Total Cost		3,200
Total Profit		$3,000

The summing-up for the year reveals that total costs have been $3,200. When these are subtracted from total sales of $6,200, the remaining profits are $3,000. This is a somewhat smaller figure than in the first year, but since the nephew does not have to share any of it with his uncle this year, his returns from the enterprise have risen. He realizes, of course, that these are not strictly "profits," since they include an element of wages in them.

The Thirty-fifth Year

Many years pass. The young man becomes middle-aged, and his business acumen grows. By the time he is 50, he has amassed a fleet of lobster boats. He rarely gets on the water himself any more, and complains about it, but he is now the president of a firm that is incorporated and that employs almost one hundred men and women. These men and women fish for lobsters out of several towns and operate several restaurants for the tourist trade.

Quite naturally, the man no longer keeps his own books. His accounting is done by accountants; and at the end of his thirty-fifth year as a businessman, they draw up for him the income statement shown in Table 1–3.

TABLE 1–3

INCOME STATEMENT FOR THIRTY-FIFTH YEAR

Total revenue	$1,000,000
Costs and expenses	906,000
Net profit before federal income taxes	$ 94,000
Provision for federal income taxes	44,000
Net profit after federal income taxes	$ 50,000
Cash dividends	20,000
Net Profit Retained in Business	$ 30,000
Memorandum: Depreciation allowances shown in costs ...	$ 25,000

This is, of course, only a short form. The internal records of the company will be much more detailed than this, with the amount of detail depending on what is most useful to the managers of the firm.

Nonetheless, all the essentials are to be found in the income statement of Table 1–3. The item for total revenue is substantially what it was before. And the same is true for the entry called costs and expenses, which is now just a summary of the cost items that were spelled out in detail in the accounts of earlier years. For reasons that will become evident later on, however, we are especially interested in the depreciation allowances that are lumped in with the other costs. In order not to lose sight of this information, it is entered in a special memorandum item at the bottom of the statement.

The difference between *total revenue* and *costs and expenses* is shown in the third line as *net profit before federal income taxes*. Fundamentally, the taxes are themselves a cost, and a large one. They are based, however, on the net income of the company, and hence can only be computed after net income has been determined. Moreover, with the income tax taking so large a bite, it is useful to show it separately. Hence, the entry labeled *provision for federal income taxes*, which is subtracted to give *net profit after federal income taxes*.

With the next entry, *cash dividends*, we must remind ourselves that the once-modest lobster business of our hero has been turned into a corporation in the course of its rise to great renown. This change in legal structure has, among other things, transferred ownership of the company to a group of stockholders. The nephew who started the firm may continue to be the major owner, but if he is, it is through his holdings of stock and not in his earlier status of proprietor.

The stockholders thus have the claim on profits that once belonged solely to the founder, and their thirst for a share in these earnings is partially satisfied through the payment of dividends. This thirst is sometimes mitigated, if not quenched, with what are called stock dividends. As we shall see later, this is nothing but a paper change, although the income statement will record these dividends too.

After taking account of these deductions, we are left with the final entry, *net profit retained in business*, which is often referred to as *retained earnings*. This is one of the sources of finance that will enable the company to grow over the years. We will return to these funds later.

To consolidate the discussion thus far, we can reconstruct the income statement in diagram form. The flow chart shown in Figure 1–1 does this. Entering from the left, we have the *total revenue* from sales. The revenue, soon after entering, is reduced by the subtraction of all assignable *costs and expenses*, including depreciation. However, because the depreciation charges are not paid to "outsiders," they are shown breaking off in a separate stream.

With costs drained off, the portion of the revenue stream that continues to move to the right is *profits before taxes*. The stream is then narrowed again by the draining-off of the *provision for federal income taxes*, reducing the flow still further to *profits after taxes*, which in turn is diminished by the payment of *cash dividends*. What remains finally, to flow out of the diagram to the right, is *net profit retained in business* or *retained earnings*.

FIGURE 1–1

INCOME STATEMENT

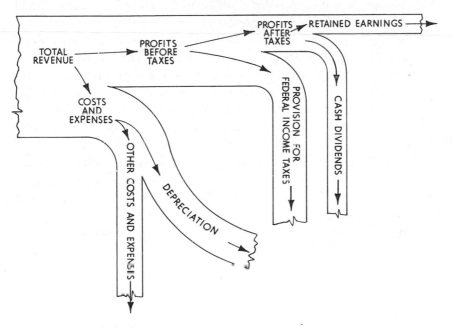

THE BALANCE SHEET

The information on an income statement is quite useful and indeed indispensable to a clear understanding of the continuing health of the firm. But this information is not enough. In the first place, it relates only to one accounting period—a single year or month. We have no way of knowing, for example, what becomes of the retained earnings after the year is over. The story ends abruptly with the close of the accounting period, and we are left hanging in midair. Similarly, it gives us no inkling of where the company stands at a given point in time. It fails to reveal the well-being (or ill-being) of the company at a single moment—to show the *things* the company owns and the things it owes. Nowhere is there an entry, for example, that tells us the value of the boat the nephew has bought from his uncle. Nor is any information given on what the nephew owes to the bank.

To present these things, we need another accounting framework, the balance sheet. With this invention, information can be organized into two columns. In one are all the things of value that the company owns; in another column, all the claims against those things. The balance sheet affords a snapshot of the firm's status, as if time had stood still for just that moment. It is thus in sharp contrast to the income statement, which describes the experiences of the company over the course of time.

Indeed, pursuing this idea a little further, we can make a very useful conceptual distinction between *stocks* and *flows*. The balance sheet describes the *stock of values* that a company has at a particular time. The income statement, on the other hand, deals with a *flow of values* during a period of time or, as we shall see further on, with certain selected flows.

In a balance sheet, all of the firm's possessions that have any value are called its *assets*. These items of value are not always tangible, as they include all the things owned by the company on which a dollar value can be placed, whether a sturdy machine or a famous trademark. When a balance sheet is set up in two columns, the usual listing puts the assets on the left-hand side.

Opposite the assets, on the right-hand side, are the claims on the firm's assets. Claims held by "outsiders" are called *liabilities*, and they are measured by the quantity of debts the company has—the amount of money it owes. Typically, however, the claims of these outsiders are not as large as the total assets of the company. That is, assets exceed liabilities by some margin. This margin is known as *net worth*. The total assets might be called the *gross* worth. But if the firm owes money to someone, we adjust for this by subtracting that amount from the total worth, or total assets, and arrive at *net worth*. This, in a manner of speaking, is the claim the firm has on its own assets. The modern corporation, of course, is treated by the laws as if it were a separate person. The owners of the corporation are the stockholders, and the net worth is the measure of their claim on the company. Another name for net worth is *equity*.

It is very important to understand, however, that this equity claim is a residual claim. If some of the assets were to burn up in a fire and there were no insurance, the left-hand side of the balance sheet would thus become smaller. The company's obligations to its creditors, on the other hand, would be absolutely unchanged by this destruction of assets. Thus, automatically, the net worth would shrink. The total worth has shrunk, the outsider claims are the same, and so the net worth must decline. By the same token, if assets should somehow be increased, with no change in liabilities, then the net worth would go up. Net worth will also change if liabilities move up or down while assets remain constant. The point is that a rise or fall in net worth must be associated with movement in assets or liabilities.

It also bears stressing here that the claims, whether held by outsiders or owners, are usually only general claims against the firm. Except for a few special cases, they attach to the assets as a body, and not to specific parts of the total. Some claims rank ahead of others; but unless otherwise specified, it may always be assumed that the obligation to pay is supported by the combined value of all assets added together.

And still another point to emphasize is that the residual claim may have a *book value* that differs from its *market value*. The book value reflects the dollar value placed on assets and liabilities by the accounting process. But obviously, in the marketplace where these residual claims are bought and sold—the stock market—the buyers and sellers may assess the worth of a company differently than the accounting record has assessed it. For good and sound reasons, accountants stick close to the historical cost of assets in determining their book value. The book value of equity claims is thus dominated by these earlier circumstances. By contrast, the market value reflects the actual and expected earning power of these assets, which may give them quite a different value than the price paid for the assets at the time they were acquired by the firm. Further along, we shall see that the market value can be pivotal in financial management.

The First Year Again

All these points about balance sheets will take on greater clarity if we look at specific examples. When our hero, the lobsterman, first tried his hand at lobstering, he had some cash on hand, and that was about all. If he had known enough to strike a balance sheet at that point, it would have looked like Table 1–4.

TABLE 1–4

BALANCE SHEET AT BEGINNING OF FIRST YEAR

ASSETS		LIABILITIES AND NET WORTH	
Cash	$500	Liabilities	$ 0
		Net worth	500
		Total Liabilities and	
Total Assets	$500	Net Worth	$500

The nephew's assets consist entirely of the money he has. Since he has no debts, there are no outsiders with claims on the cash, and his net worth is equal to his total worth. He has full claim to his own assets.

It is well to realize at this point that the cash represents in full his *tangible* assets. As we know, he is endowed in addition with certain skills that are important to lobster fishing. He is also possessed of enthusiasm, a strong back, and an urge to succeed at his trade. These attributes, in a very real sense, might be considered to be assets, and perhaps as important as the cash he owns. For after all, they increase the likelihood that he will earn income as a lobsterman. His special talents and determination give him a decided edge over any less talented and less ambitious rivals. In a fundamental sense the nephew must be said to have assets that these other persons do not possess.

In practice, however, these considerations will leave no trace on the balance sheet—for the important reason that they are almost impossible to evaluate in a clear-cut fashion. We cannot measure them in dollar signs. Even those who know the man most intimately could make only an arbitrary guess at the dollar value of his chances of success as a lobsterman.

The inherent difficulty of fixing a monetary value for the nephew's skills points up, in fact, a problem that accountants face continuously in all assets, even the tangible ones. What is the proper measure—in dollars—of the worth of an asset? In order to have accounts at all, accountants have settled on a convention, a standard working rule. They have decided that with only a few special exceptions, assets shall be valued at their historical cost. The price that a business pays when it acquires the asset will establish its value on that firm's books.

In some special cases the valuation of an asset will be altered if the market value deteriorates after the asset was purchased. And in rare instances a rise in market value will also lead to a change in the value assigned to an asset on the balance sheet. The predominant rule, however, is to show the asset at its original cost. In this way the temptation to overstate a company's worth is put carefully beyond reach.

The Second Year

As our young lobsterman begins his second year at the trade, he has more to show. He still holds some cash, and he now owns the boat and all the lobster pots and other gear. As may be seen in Table 1–5, his cash has shrunk to $300, but acquisition of the boat and traps has increased his assets by $10,000. (Since he has just bought them, they are shown at cost, with no depreciation charges yet made against them. These will be entered after he has gotten another year's use from the equipment.) Accordingly, his total assets are now $10,300.

But it must be recalled that he has borrowed from the bank in order to

TABLE 1–5

BALANCE SHEET AT BEGINNING OF SECOND YEAR

ASSETS		LIABILITIES AND NET WORTH	
Cash	$ 300	Payable to bank	$ 9,000
Boats and traps	10,000	Net worth	1,300
		Total Liabilities	
Total Assets	$10,300	and Net Worth	$10,300

buy the boat. Since he had been able to pay his uncle partly out of cash he had already accumulated, he did not have to borrow the full amount, and the bank is due $9,000. This is a claim from the outside, which makes it a liability, as shown in Table 1–5. Thus, when the nephew's total assets—his total worth—is adjusted for this debt, we get his net worth. As shown on the right-hand side of the balance sheet in Table 1–5, this net worth is $1,300, the difference between total assets of $10,300 and total liabilities of $9,000. The young man's cash has gone down, and his debt has gone up; but because he has plowed back $800 of the $2,600 he had received during the first year as his share of the earnings, his net worth has increased over what it was a year earlier (see Table 1–4).

The Third Year

With the passage of still another year, there have been more changes in the balance sheet. Table 1–6 shows the account at this point. With the addition of the $3,000 earned in profits during the preceding year, cash holdings have expanded sharply to $3,300. A year's allowances for capital consumption have been charged against the physical assets and put into a so-called "reserve" for depreciation. This brings the residual value of the physical assets down to $9,000. On the opposite side the bank loan has been reduced, and this outsider claim now stands at $8,000. The residual

TABLE 1–6

BALANCE SHEET AT BEGINNING OF THIRD YEAR

ASSETS			LIABILITIES AND NET WORTH	
Cash		$ 3,300	Payable to bank	$ 8,000
Property, plant, and			Net worth	4,300
equipment	$10,000			
Less: Reserve for				
depreciation ...	1,000			
Net property		$ 9,000	Total Liabilities and	
Total Assets ...		$12,300	Net Worth	$12,300

claim, the net worth, is thus $4,300. The rise in net worth may also be seen as resulting from the complete retention of the $3,000 in earnings from the previous year.

The Thirty-fifth Year

We may now return to our lobsterman in his thirty-fifth year. His business has grown into a large corporation with many more varied activities than in the early days and many more types of assets and claims on assets. The greater complexity of the thirty-fifth year is evident at once in the balance sheet shown in Table 1–7. All three groups of entries—assets, liabilities, and net worth—have grown more complicated.

Assets.   Starting with assets, it will be noticed first that they have been grouped into two classes—*current assets* and *noncurrent assets*. The object in doing this is to separate those assets that will or can be turned into cash within a short period, usually meaning within one year. The first two items, for example, are *cash* itself and *U.S. government securities*. The cash entry represents currency on hand and readily available bank deposits, and both of these are obviously spendable within a matter of minutes. The firm's holdings of government securities are almost as liquid, since the market for these securities is highly organized and they can be sold for cash on very short notice.

The remaining three items in current assets—*accounts receivable, inventories,* and the *other current assets* group—cannot be liquidated quite so readily as government securities, but they can be sold if necessary. More importantly, they can be expected *automatically* to turn into cash within the near future.

The accounts receivable represent the credit that the firm has extended to its customers. Quite often, this trade credit will be repaid in as short a time as ten days, and rarely does it run beyond a few months. If the company continues to sell its products, it continues to extend new credit, so that at any given point in time there is likely always to be money owed to the firm on accounts receivable. But in each case the debt will be payable within a very short period, thus making these current assets. Moreover, when a firm gets impatient at waiting for these debts to be repaid, it can sell them to other businessmen who specialize in this sort of thing.

Inventories are accumulated to aid in carrying on the primary business of the firm. Inventories thus include any goods that may be required in the enterprise and are not consumed immediately upon purchase. In the

TABLE 1-2

BALANCE SHEET AT BEGINNING OF THIRTY-FIFTH YEAR

ASSETS			LIABILITIES AND NET WORTH		
Current Assets:			*Current Liabilities:*		
Cash		$ 225,000	Short-term bank loans		$ 80,000
U.S. government securities		100,000	Other notes and accounts payable		250,000
Accounts receivable		375,000	Federal income taxes accrued		145,000
Inventories		650,000	Instalments due in a year or less on a long-		
Other current assets		40,000	term debt		27,000
			Other current liabilities		98,000
Total Current Assets		$1,390,000	Total Current Liabilities		$ 600,000
Property, plant, and equipment	$1,570,000		Long-term debt due in more than one year ..		280,000
Deduct: Reserve for depreciation	620,000		Other noncurrent liabilities		20,000
Net property, plant, and equipment ..		950,000	Total Liabilities		$ 900,000
Other noncurrent assets		160,000			
			Net Worth:		
			Capital stock	$700,000	
			Earned surplus	900,000	
			Total Net Worth		1,600,000
Total Assets		$2,500,000	Total Liabilities and Net Worth ...		$2,500,000

usual case, inventories of any sort will be transformed into end goods and sold to customers within the space of a year. Thus, they too are readily classified as current assets.

The noncurrent assets consist chiefly of items we have already encountered. *Property, plant, and equipment* is just what it claims to be, and the net figure is the portion of the original cost that has not yet been written off in capital consumption allowances. The *other noncurrent assets* are of course a mixed bag. They include, among other things, securities other than governments, prepayments such as rental charges paid in advance, and the intangible values that stem from patent holdings or the good repute of the company in the minds of its buying public.

Before leaving the asset side, there should be a brief reminder of the problem of valuation. Most of the items we have just discussed will be carried on the books at their original cost, although in some circumstances this historical value may be written up or written down, in response to changing market conditions. The property, plant, and equipment are of course being consumed as the years go by, and this exhaustion of value is cumulated in the reserve for depreciation. Nevertheless, the original cost is entered, and it is not changes in current market prices that reduce the value on the books of the plant and equipment. It is their continued employment and the passage of time. In the case of receivables, there may be adjustments as debtors default on their obligations and the company abandons hope of collecting them. But some amount of this is anticipated, and the total entry is partially written down at the outset.

Hence, all things considered, it is only inventories and security holdings whose value on the books is much altered by current market changes. They are generally carried at original cost, but if the market price falls below this level, the company's book entries may be marked down accordingly.

Liabilities. Moving now to the right-hand side of the balance sheet in Table 1–7, the *current liabilities* include all known obligations of the company that will fall due within the near future, usually defined as one year. For some basic stratum of these liabilities, the old ones as they mature will be replaced almost automatically by new ones. In this sense, such liabilities are permanent and the firm will never be free of them. Nonetheless, particular debt obligations must be met. Their expiration will thus offer both the borrowing firm and the lending firm an option to change the relationship.

Short-term bank loans refers to any such loan whose original maturity was one year or less. *Other notes and accounts payable* includes short-term borrowing from any other source than banks and is made up principally of credit issued to the company by its suppliers. Such loans from suppliers are of course the exact counterpart, conceptually, of accounts receivable. They represent the funds that this company owes to other firms from which it has purchased goods that have not yet been paid for. This entry is thus the opposite side of the accounts receivable shown on the books of the other firms, and hence is an obligation that will probably be met within a few weeks or months at the most.

For the next entry, *federal income taxes accrued,* it must be pointed out that business corporations do not have to pay all of their federal income taxes in the same period in which the income is earned. The balance sheet must show, however, that this obligation is still outstanding—that the federal government has a claim that must be met in the near future. The entry for federal income taxes accrued is therefore used for recording that future obligation to the government.

The balance of current liabilities consists of *instalments due in a year or less on long-term debt* and finally an *other current liabilities* category.

The noncurrent liabilities are very simply dealt with. They refer to debts that need not be paid within the coming year; and they may take a wide variety of forms, including bonds and debentures sold to the public, special long-term loans from banks or from insurance companies, and even long-term credit extended by the firm's suppliers.

Net Worth. The *net worth* part of the balance sheet will typically show great variety, too, but in Table 1–7 it is divided into only two sections—*capital stock* and *earned surplus.* The capital stock refers usually to the dollar valuation placed on the equity shares sold to the ultimate owners of the business—the stockholders.

While practice differs somewhat, the entry for capital stock is often adjusted to show the actual amount of money received by the firm when the shares were issued. That is, such shares are usually given a face value, but they may have been marketed initially for more than this, or sometimes for less. In some balance sheets, this adjustment is shown separately and may be called *capital surplus.* In Table 1–7, it is simply included with the capital stock.

This leaves one final item, *earned surplus,* which represents income that has been plowed back into the business. This is where profits not paid out in taxes or dividends finally come to rest and become available to the company for the acquisition of further assets or the paying-off of outstanding debts. This is the point at which the stockholder's equity in the company grows without the stockholder having to supply any further funds. Equity can be increased again by the sale of additional shares of stock, but an expansion of earned surplus increases a stockholder's claim on the company independently of any additional shares he might purchase. It should always be kept in mind, of course, that corporations can suffer losses as well as profits, with resultant declines in earned surplus and in net worth generally.

Many useful comparisons can be made with a single balance sheet, and many are made. For example, current assets are quite commonly compared with current liabilities. The margin by which current assets exceed current liabilities is given the name *net working capital* and provides a measure of the firm's ability to meet all its near-term obligations. Similarly, we get an indication of the firm's ability to meet these obligations in a very short time by comparing its cash and government security holdings with its total current liabilities. These measures, and many others, can be computed with only one balance sheet, and we shall have occasion to refer to them again.

It will usually be found, however, that a single balance sheet is not enough. It soon becomes evident that even such measures as those just mentioned are limited in their usefulness unless they can be contrasted with similar "still pictures" taken at other points in time. As a matter of fact, through much of the discussion of the last several pages, the notion of change has regularly crept in. The business firm is a continuing endeavor, and time is always passing. It is perhaps only natural that we are dissatisfied with a measure of the firm's wealth at a single point in time, and that we seek ways to observe how that wealth changes.

In any case, we would find it difficult to combine the balance sheet and the income statement into one consistent body of information if we left each one in the state in which they now stand. The balance sheet gives us information for a *point* in time, while the income statement refers to a *period* of time. Without some sort of adjustment, the stocks of the balance sheet cannot be compared directly with the flows of the income statement. One of the two must be altered to accommodate the other.

THE STATEMENT OF SOURCES AND USES

For our purposes, the best way to bring the balance sheet and income statement together is to state them both as flows. Moreover, it is important for our needs that these flows be stated as *cash* flows. Let us take up these two matters one at a time.

Converting Stocks into Flows

Since the income statement is already expressed as a series of flows, it is the balance sheet that must be converted. But before doing this, we might ask why flows, and not stocks, should become the common denominator. Why, that is, should we not restate the income statement to fit the form of the balance sheet?

The answer lies in the presumption that the values of stocks are rooted in the values of flows, rather than the other way round. An asset has value only as it promises to yield some kind of return. The return may take different forms—it may be money, or pride, or the special satisfaction of owning a large collection of books or paintings or postage stamps. For a business firm, the major reward will usually be money, even if some satisfaction also springs directly from being the biggest retailer in town or the only movie house with box seats. The point is that the expected flows from an asset are what make it desirable to own that asset. It thus makes sense to reconcile stocks and flows by making flows the common parlance of the two.

To convert the balance sheet for this purpose, we must show the *change* in each balance sheet item between one point in time and a later point. Table 1–8 gives us this information, and it is restated diagrammatically in Figure 1–2.

In the diagram the net effect of all changes is registered by a rise or fall in the pool of cash held by the firm. To the right of the pool are the channels by which cash is drained out or used, and it will be seen that

FIGURE 1–2

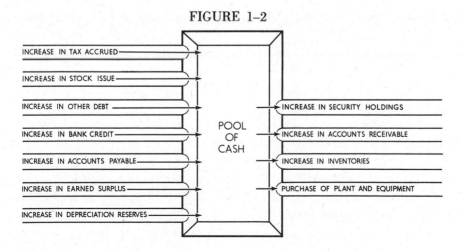

INCREASE IN TAX ACCRUED

INCREASE IN STOCK ISSUE

INCREASE IN OTHER DEBT

INCREASE IN BANK CREDIT

INCREASE IN ACCOUNTS PAYABLE

INCREASE IN EARNED SURPLUS

INCREASE IN DEPRECIATION RESERVES

POOL OF CASH

INCREASE IN SECURITY HOLDINGS

INCREASE IN ACCOUNTS RECEIVABLE

INCREASE IN INVENTORIES

PURCHASE OF PLANT AND EQUIPMENT

TABLE 1–8

CHANGES IN BALANCE SHEET DURING THIRTY-FIFTH YEAR

ASSETS	Beginning of Year	End of Year	Change (Dollars)
Cash	$ 225,000	$ 210,000	− 15,000
U.S. government securities	100,000	95,000	− 5,000
Accounts receivable	375,000	385,000	+ 10,000
Inventories	650,000	670,000	+ 20,000
Other current assets	40,000	40,000	......
Property, plant, and equipment ...	1,570,000	1,670,000	(+100,000)
Reserve for depreciation	620,000	645,000	(+ 25,000)
Net property, plant, and equipment	950,000	1,025,000	+ 75,000
Other noncurrent assets	160.000	160,000	......
LIABILITIES			
Short-term bank loans	80,000	90,000	+ 10,000
Other notes and accounts payable	250,000	270,000	+ 20,000
Federal income tax accrued	145,000	150,000	+ 5,000
Instalments due in a year or less on long-term debt	27,000	27,000	......
Other current liabilities	98,000	98,000	......
Long-term debt due in more than one year	280,000	300,000	+ 20,000
Other noncurrent liabilities	20,000	20,000	......
NET WORTH			
Capital stock	700,000	700,000	......
Earned surplus	900,000	930,000	+ 30,000

these are increases in assets. Cash leaves the company's possession, for example, when additional plant and equipment are purchased, or when the firm acquires additional security holdings. Although the diagram does not indicate the fact, it is important to realize also that these various flows can reverse direction, with the reverse impact on the pool of cash. For example, a decrease in security holdings through selling them will add to the cash pool, not drain it.

The pipes leading into the pool from the left represent sources of funds. As may be seen in the diagram, they are either (1) increases in liabilities or (2) increases in net worth. An increase in bank loans, for example, quite obviously adds to the cash holdings of the company, as does any other expansion of debt. Similarly, if more stock should be issued, the flow of cash into the firm would be heightened, as it would also by an increase in earned surplus, representing the money plowed back into the business during the year. Again reverse flows are possible, this time turning sources into uses.

Summing up, the sources and uses shown in Figure 1–2 are as follows:

SOURCES	USES
A. Increase in tax accrued	H. Increase in security holdings
B. Increase in stock issue	I. Increase in accounts receivable
C. Increase in other debt	J. Increase in inventories
D. Increase in bank credit	K. Purchase of plant and equipment
E. Increase in accounts payable	
F. Retained earnings (or increase in earned surplus)	
G. Depreciation allowances (or increase in depreciation reserves)	

When the pool of cash is drawn down, then cash balances might be shown as a source of funds. And of course, when the level of the pool rises, cash has been added, and the cash balance constitutes a use of funds.

Cash versus Accrual

About half of the items listed above are self-explanatory. There are at least five of them, however, that require some spelling-out. On the sources side, these are A, E, and G, the increases in tax accrued, accounts payable, and depreciation reserves. The uses calling for special attention are I and J, the increases in accounts receivable and inventories.

The special handling required of these items points up a very basic distinction in accounting practice. This is the distinction between cash statements and accrual statements. If a company is recording only cash transactions, it is the actual receipt or surrender of cash that enters the record books. But if an accrual system is used, the company will record its obligations and revenues at the time they are contracted for, regardless of when the transfer of cash will take place.

These comments underscore our decision to state all flows as *cash* flows. What do we mean by this, and why do we choose to do it? We mean essentially that we will consider a flow to have occurred when some change occurs in the pool of cash. This means, in turn, two things—all developments are both measured by their impact on the cash pool and dated by their impact on the cash pool.

Cash is taken as the *measure* because it is the one item that has universality. It alone has direct convertibility with all other assets. It is the common language for stating any flow and any change in stocks.

Given this commonalty of cash, it follows somewhat naturally that flows should be *dated* by their impact on the cash pool. This, as we shall see in later chapters, does not banish the idea of accrual. Rather, it draws attention to the particular timing of an expected inflow or outflow. The role of time—perhaps the most profound subject in all of financial management—is thus brought into play. With the focus on cash rather than accrual, the powerful influence of time can be seen more clearly, and dealt with more effectively.

At the moment, our problem lies in the five flows mentioned above, and the simplest way of clarifying their role is to take the next big step and reintroduce the income statement. For this, we go back to the earlier diagram, shown in Figure 1-1, and bring it forward to be joined to the flows shown in Figure 1-2. When these two flow diagrams are put together, they produce the chart shown in Figure 1-3.

This diagram will repay close study. The largest inflow of cash to the firm appears in the form of total sales, at the far left. Large amounts are sluiced off, however, in the form of operating costs, taxes, and dividends, so that what finally enters the pool of cash from the initial income stream are (1) retained earnings and (2) depreciation allowances. Both of these items have also been shown as balance sheet changes; but as such, they were called (1) increase in earned surplus and (2) increase in depreciation reserves.

The flow, retained earnings, can now easily be understood as an increase in earned surplus—i.e., as a change in a stock. It also becomes clear why the increase in depreciation reserves shown on the balance sheet was treated as a source of cash (item G in the list above). This change in stock is the same as the flow on the income statement, which was shown there as a cost deducted from current revenues. However, this cost represents cash held for the company's own use rather than paid out immediately to outsiders.

These depreciation funds may be spent in replacing that portion of plant and equipment that was consumed during the period. However, since most companies aspire to growth, their spending on plant and equipment may sometimes exceed their depreciation inflows, in which case the pool of cash will be drawn down unless the inflow from some other source is increased or the anticipated outflow to some other use reduced. Of course, if the firm does not spend all its depreciation allowances on new capital assets, the level of the pool will rise, making cash available for some other uses.

The effect of a change in inventories (item J above) must also be

FIGURE 1-3

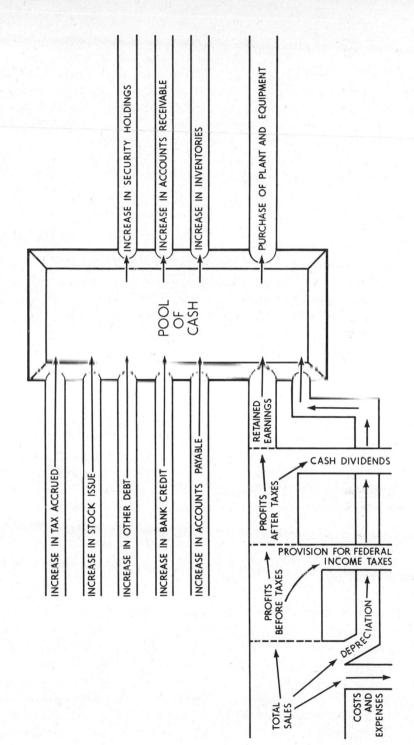

related back to current operating costs. The almost universal practice is to maintain some inventory stocks at all times and to replace those stocks as they are drawn down. As a result, actual expenditures are made during the year for the acquisition of materials that may not be used until a later period.

Costs, on the other hand, are based on the value of the stocks actually used up during the year. If, however, the expenditures for new materials serve to keep the level of inventories exactly even at all times, then the actual payments will be exactly equal to the costs computed for the year. What is drawn down will be replaced, and what is computed as cost will equal what is actually spent.

It is only when inventories are not kept level that they figure as a use of cash in our diagram. When inventories are increased, they absorb funds in addition to those shown as being drained off with other operating costs. By the same token, a decrease in inventories, though not shown here, would act as a source of funds.

We may now also see how accounts receivable and accounts payable (i.e., items I and E in the list above) influence the cash pool of the company. Their effects relate, in both cases, back to the income and cost flows. In the case of accounts receivable, it must first be noted that the total sales shown at the far left are not all made for cash. Some part of them is made on credit. In effect, our corporation receives the cash and then lends it back to the buying customer. In time, of course, the customer returns the funds. But if the amount of such credit outstanding should rise during the year, it must be counted as an outflow of cash—a use of funds. The increase in credit sales is shown coming in at the far left, along with all other sales, then moving through into the pool of cash, only to go out again as an increase in receivables outstanding. In actuality, the cash is not received and not paid out, but the fiction of its movement through the pool of cash helps us to understand the relation between the balance sheet change and the income statement.

The treatment of an increase in accounts payable is exactly analogous. It is as if the corporation had paid for its purchases and then borrowed the funds directly back from the seller. Hence, a part of the funds siphoned off as operating costs, which reduce the flow into the pool, is replaced by an increase in trade payables. This increase thus appears as a source of funds. These movements, of course, are also fictitious; but as in the case of receivables and sales, their influence on the level of cash in the pool is precisely the same as it would have been had the movements actually taken place.

We come finally to the increase in federal income tax accrued (item A), which is shown as a source of funds leading into the pool from the left. This also may be understood by relating it to one of the flows developed from the income statement. That flow, as might be guessed, is the provision for federal income taxes. This provision registers on the balance sheet as an increase in accrued taxes, which is followed by a decrease back to the former level when payment is actually made. But in the meantime the firm continues to have the use of the money. Hence, the expenditure of funds out through the "provision" flow pipe has been overstated, and funds must be added back through the increase in accruals.

One small technical point here. Assets, as mentioned earlier, are sometimes revalued in the light of changing conditions. In the 1930's, for example, many companies decided their fixed assets were no longer worth what they would have been in more prosperous times. Acting on this decision, some of these firms simply adjusted downward the balance sheet values shown for the assets and, by the same token, reduced some net worth account—say, earned surplus. Others put the write-down in net income, reducing the reported volume of that flow. Such adjustments would not be shown in our sources and uses framework as developed here, as they would have no effect, present or future, on the level of cash balances. They would, moreover, serve largely as a distortion, since the changes in earned surplus would not be equal to retained earnings during the period. All our subsequent discussion will abstract from such purely bookkeeping changes.

THE STEP TO CASH BUDGETING

The discussion thus far has served to weld together the income statement and the balance sheet, making a single instrument of them. But that instrument is still not as usable as one might wish. Its awkwardness becomes evident when the diagram of Figure 1–3 is expressed as a table with numbers in it, as in the left-hand side of Table 1–9. In particular, this expression reveals the large amount of activity in the cash pool that is not reported as such. Roughly a million dollars comes into the pool through sales, but ebbs and flows seen directly total only about a hundred thousand dollars. To record more of the action, we need a device with a much broader lens. We need, particularly, a device that will register the comings and goings of cash.

The very universality of cash means that every significant act of

business management has its expression in cash changes. As a consequence, a great variety of arrangements can be concocted. One such
concoction is shown on the right-hand side of Table 1–9. The entries grow
directly from the material on the left-hand side of the table, but perhaps
several of them require further explanation:

a) Total current sales were $1 million, but since accounts receivable rose
by $10,000, the sales have brought in *cash collections* of only $990,000.
The remaining $10,000 will be coming in later, when some customers
pay cash for goods already sold to them, but for the time being those
goods have been bought on credit.

b) *Purchases* during the period consist of costs and expenses, excluding
depreciation allowances, plus the expenditures that have increased the
stock of inventories on hand for later use. Thus $906,000, minus
$25,000, plus $20,000 gives $901,000.

c) Not all these purchases have required *cash payments* in the current
period, however, because some of them were made on credit. Of course
some cash probably was paid out during the period for credit purchases made in earlier periods, but accounts payable showed a *net*
increase of $20,000 during the current period. Hence in one way or
another, the company raised its borrowing from suppliers by another
$20,000, so that cash payments for supplies and labor were only
$881,000—i.e., $901,000 minus $20,000.

d) The provision for taxes included a rise in tax accrued. Thus the tax
charge on the left-hand side of Table 1–9 was associated with an actual
cash drain of only $39,000—i.e., $44,000 minus $5,000 put aside but
not yet paid out.

In general the move to a cash budget will put a firm in better position
both to control its financial activities in the present and to plan them for
the future. Indeed, the particular pattern of cash budgeting laid out in
Table 1–9 becomes a planning document for the near-term future. By
putting borrowing near the bottom of the list, it suggests that events
occurring elsewhere in the firm—the sales department, the purchasing
department—will find a buffer, if need be, in current borrowing and in
the cash pool itself. Planning for the longer range, however, can easily be
fit into the same format. Managers can project for succeeding periods.
Then, for example, if there promise to be continuing drains on the cash
pool and continuing need to go outside for funds, attention can turn to
changing the items further up the list—speeding up cash collections
through tighter policies on accounts receivable, or slowing down cash
payments by greater use of accounts payable, or other policy changes.

TABLE 1–9
(Thousands of Dollars)

	Sources (+)	Uses (−)		Sources (+)	Uses (−)
Total sales	1,000	...	Total sales	1,000	...
Cost and expenses ...	906	...	Rise in accounts receivable	10	...
Profit before taxes ...	94	...	Cash collections	990	+990
Provision for taxes ..	44	...			
Profit after taxes ...	50	...	Cost and expenses, excluding depreciation	881	...
Dividends	20	...	Rise in inventories ..	20	...
Retained earnings ...	30	+ 30	Purchases	901	...
			Rise in accounts payable	20	...
Rise in bank indebtedness	10	| 10	Cash payments	881	−881
Rise in accounts payable	20	+ 20	Provision for tax payments	44	...
Rise in tax accrued .	5	+ 5	Rise in tax accrued ..	5	...
Rise in bond indebtedness	20	+ 20	Cash payments for taxes	39	− 39
Depreciation allowance	25	+ 25	Dividends	20	− 20
			Rise in plant and equipment	100	−100
Rise in accounts receivable	10	− 10	Net cash change from operations		− 50
Rise in inventories ..	20	− 20			
Rise in plant and equipment	100	−100	Borrowing:		
			Bank	10	+ 10
Total sources		+110	Bonds	20	+ 20
Total uses		−130			
Net Change in Cash Pool		− 20	Net Change in Cash Pool		− 20

Or the focus can shift to a higher level of decision, at which, say, dividend payments are under discussion. In that case the expected drains on cash would not yet include dividends, and the analysis would center on the *decision* to pay dividends. A similar case is the entry for plant and equipment spending. That too must spring from a decision. The question will be whether in fact cash should be put to such a use.

Thus with the construction of the cash budget, the preliminary machinery is all in place. The sources and uses of cash as they ebb and flow through the entire business entity provide us with the basic framework for financial decision making. The next questions are the criteria for manipulating flows of cash—in particular, the ultimate aims of financial management and the guidelines for decisions carrying the firm toward those aims.

QUESTIONS AND PROBLEMS

1. Suppose that in the third year of lobstering, the young man's business had involved the following:

Total revenue	$15,000
Purchase of second boat and traps	10,000
Operating costs (including salary to his cousin)	7,000
Bank loan repayment	1,000
New bank loan	8,000
Depreciation	2,000

What would his balance sheet look like at the beginning of the fourth year?

2. Using the information of Question No. 1, develop a cash flow account of the kind illustrated in Table 1–9.

3. Would it be more useful to combine balance sheet information in the form of stocks rather than flows? Can you develop an example of using stocks as the common denominator?

4. Would you say that the thirty-fifth year (as depicted in Table 1–3, Table 1–7, and Table 1–8) was a "good" year or a "bad" year? Explain your answer.

5. Do you think the young man should have bought his uncle's boat, given only what he knew at the time? Should he have bought a second boat, given the experience of the first two years?

SUGGESTED READINGS

EDWARDS, EDGAR O. "Funds Statements for Short and Long-Run Analyses," *Journal of Business, July*, 1952. Reprinted in JOHN L. O'DONNELL and MILTON S. GOLDBERG (eds.), *Elements of Financial Administration*, pp. 179–203. Columbus, Ohio: Charles E. Merrill Books, Inc., 1962.

MACK, RUTH P. *Flow of Business Funds and Consumer Purchasing Power*, chap. i. New York: Columbia University Press, 1941.

PATON, WILLIAM A. "The Cash-Flow Illusion," *Accounting Review*, April, 1963.

POWELSON, J. P. *Economic Accounting*. New York: McGraw-Hill Book Co., Inc., 1955.

WALTER, JAMES E. "Determination of Technical Solvency," *Journal of Business*, January, 1957. Reprinted in JOHN L. O'DONNELL and MILTON S. GOLDBERG (eds.), *Elements of Financial Administration*, pp. 73–90. Columbus, Ohio: Charles E. Merrill Books, Inc., 1962.

Chapter 2

THE THEORY OF THE
FINANCE OF THE FIRM

What should the financial managers of a business take as their guiding star? Knowing all there is to know about the flows and stocks described in the previous chapter, what should managers aim to do about them?

A first suggestion might be to build the cash pool as high as possible. This suggestion, however, must be discarded at once. Although business-men sometimes behave as if they had this goal in mind, any prolonged pursuit of it would bring their business to a halt. If such a goal is to have any meaning, cash must be let into the firm but never permitted to leave it. For if cash *is* allowed to flow out, the managerial emphasis must shift to finding the proper relationship between the inflows to the pool and the outflows from it. The level of cash will of course be affected by these gains and losses, but the appropriate *level* becomes a by-product (or at least a joint product) of decisions about the appropriate *volume* of flows. Thus the managers will have lost the clear criterion based on the stock of cash alone.

A more familiar guideline, and a more reasonable one, is the maximization of profits—the earning of the greatest possible returns for the owners of the company. The owners may just pile up these returns in their own cash pools, outside the business walls, as it were. But presumably they will do so only to make possible the larger spending of cash at a later date, or to protect themselves against unforeseen expenditures at some future point. In any case, this decision is to be left to the owners. Following the rule of profit maximization, the duty of the managers is to achieve the highest possible flow of returns that will belong to the owners after all other obligations have been met.

Yet profit maximization as a ruling principle has its own shortcomings.

It is an improvement over cash maximization, but it is incomplete. In particular, it leaves unsettled three important matters:

a) It does not identify *which* returns are to be focused on—a somewhat mechanical issue but important nonetheless.

b) It says nothing of the *timing* of the returns being maximized. That is, it gives no aid in the managerial choice between an act that will produce profits of $10,000 in each of the next five years, and an act that will produce $60,000 five years hence but nothing in the meantime. Which pattern is maximal?

c) It gives no guide on levels of *risk and uncertainty* that might appropriately be accepted along with the profit forecast. Is a long chance at a million dollars preferable to a 50–50 likelihood of earning a thousand dollars? Which choice is maximizing?

Putting these three problems in other words, we can say that the advice to maximize the quantity of profits does not tell us (*a*) which quantity, nor (*b*) whether it is worth waiting for, nor (*c*) what chances we are willing to take to get it. Using still other words, the guideline underscores the *quantity* of profits, but is ambiguous about the *measure* of that quantity and completely silent about the *quality* of profits.

THE ULTIMATE GOAL—MAXIMIZATION OF THE OWNERS' WEALTH

The best remedy yet suggested for these problems is to set as the ultimate goal the maximization of the owners' *wealth*. Stating a goal does not of course tell one how to get there. By fixing its course on wealth maximization, management will not automatically find answers to the three problems we have just listed. This choice of ultimate aim, however, will automatically raise the questions.

Perhaps this can be seen most clearly by drawing again on the concepts of stock and flow. If management takes maximization of owners' wealth as its major end, it must ask what value the owners will place on a particular stream of returns. This necessarily will direct attention to the time pattern of that stream, and to the risks and uncertainty attached to it. Thus, the fundamental issue is the value of the claims on a stream of returns—the translation of flow value into stock value. Management must work to bring about those flows that in this translation provide the highest possible market value to the ownership claim on the firm.

To illustrate, suppose a rental building produces a stream of earnings over a period of years. If we let the symbol E represent annual earnings and assign the symbol V to denote the amount we would be willing to pay to acquire this building, we get the following relationship:

$$\frac{E}{V} = c .$$

This relationship is often referred as a "capitalization rate." It gives the capital value, or stock value, that is being ascribed to a flow.

The role of the capitalization rate becomes still clearer when the algebra is rearranged and stated as:

$$\frac{E}{c} = V .$$

Putting the relationship this way makes it still more evident that financial managers must not confine their attention to E alone. Though E, the quantity of earnings, may be raised by managerial acumen, care must be taken that the capitalization rate does not rise to offset, or more than offset, the gain in E. The capitalization rate represents the owners' assessment of the quality of the earnings. If the higher returns are achieved by delaying present earnings or taking greater risks, the owners —and the market for shares—will react to the decline in quality as well as to the increase in quantity. If, for example, E, rose from \$10 to \$12 with the adoption of a very risky project, the capitalization rate might rise from, say 0.10 to 0.15. The result would be a fall in V from \$10/0.10 to \$12/0.15—that is, a drop from \$100 to \$80. This is not to say that businessmen should, as a rule, shrink from delayed returns and risky ventures. It is only to say these attributes of quality must be assessed. The guiding principle is thus to seek the *combination* of E and c that yields the highest possible V.

Cash Flow as the Stream of Returns

With stockholder wealth as the ultimate aim, it becomes easier to decide the proper measure of the stream of returns. It is *that stream of cash that can be given to the stockholders, the owners.*

Notice that we do not speak of cash that *will* be given to the stockholders, but rather that which *can* be given them. In practice, the owners will rarely want to take all of the stream. For example, depreciation allowances could be paid out in dividends. But typically they will not be, for if this were done year after year the firm would find increasing difficulty in renewing itself, as old machinery needed replacing. Yet it should be very clear that replacement of worn-out equipment must not be an automatic step. It is an investment of cash that otherwise could be disbursed to stockholders. It is thus a use of cash that must be justified as a better employment of funds than the stockholder could make on his own, if the monies were put into his hands.

Indeed, stockholders will usually benefit from the reinvestment, not only of the depreciation allowances, but of some of the net profits of the company. As we shall see in later chapters, a business firm, particularly a corporation, can often put money to more profitable uses than the owner can, acting as an individual investor.

For financial management, then, and perhaps for all business management, the critical stream of returns is the *cash flow*. By this is meant *profits after taxes, plus depreciation allowances*. To be sure, *all* cash must be managed for the benefit of the owners. But cash flow, as defined, is what is left after all obligations to nonowners have been settled. It is what belongs to the owners, and must be paid to them, unless the managers can do better with the cash than the owners could do for themselves. Accordingly, the great bulk of this book will explore the two questions inherent in this position: (*a*) how can managers choose among the alternative uses of funds available to the firm, and (*b*) how can they ascertain that this is a better use than stockholders could find outside the company?

ECONOMIC THEORY AS THE TOOL OF ANALYSIS

We have settled on wealth maximization as the goal and on cash flow as the accounting entity to work with. What is needed now is a set of analytical principles to determine *how* the flow can be managed so as to maximize the stock value.

For this we may draw on the economic theory of the firm, sometimes called price theory. This vehicle of analysis will not carry us the last mile toward the goal, but it will prove enormously useful in organizing the trip up to that point.

In price theory, emphasis is put on output determination. That is, principles are sought to explain what output is best (most profitable) for a firm to produce. This branch of theory also has developed analysis of the other side of the coin—the ideal amount of factors of production for the enterprise to hire, the best pattern of inputs.

The basic concept in price theory is contained in the demonstration that business should produce that particular output where marginal cost and marginal revenue are equal. The firm should continue to hire inputs and extend output as long as the additional revenues exceed the additional costs. In other words, as long as *MR* exceeds *MC*, it pays to expand output, and this expansion should stop when *MR* equals *MC*, for then further production will reduce profits. Thus, the basic concept of the theory of the firm examines the implications of profit-maximizing behavior on production of output and on its distribution.

But the maximizing behavior of the firm or the businessman has other implications and other effects. For example, it may be asked: What are the implications of the rational (or maximizing) firm's behavior in terms not of optimum output but of *optimum assets and their finance?* The question can be framed in terms of the balance sheet: What is the ideal amount of assets and of liabilities plus net worth? Or in clearer language and in terms developed at the end of the last chapter: What is the ideal pattern of sources and uses of funds for any given firm?

Note that this approach, whether it be in terms of pools or stocks of assets and finance, or in terms of flows of funds to various uses from various sources, can also utilize the so-called "marginalist" technique of the traditional theory of the firm. Using this technique, the basic question in a theory of firm finance becomes: Will a given additional use of funds yield more in revenues than the additional required source of funds will add to costs? If so, it will increase the net returns if the firm taps the source and uses the funds as planned. Note, too, that given a particular use of funds, the firm should select the cheapest source of funds—that is, that source which adds least to total costs of finance—for comparison with that additional revenue-producing use. In such a theory of finance of the firm, then, the same marginal cost and revenue technique can be used as in the theory of the output of the firm.

However, in the theory of finance the comparison of marginal returns and marginal costs is restricted to *financial aspects* only. The prospective returns are the net returns after all costs (such as costs of production, marketing, etc.) except the cost of finance and depreciation, and these returns are compared with the payment that must be made to the source or supplier of funds. Quite simply, it will pay to expand *uses*, i.e., add assets, if the returns expected from those new assets are expected to exceed the cost of rewarding the additional *sources* of funds, i.e., add to liabilities or net worth.

In general, it pays to continue adding new assets—to expand investment in the firm—as long as acquiring new assets adds to returns left after all cash costs, including costs of financing those assets. Clearly, the limit to profitable expansion of assets comes when the cost of finance equals, and is about to exceed, the net returns expected to be obtained from the expansion.

By contrast with the theory of the output of the firm, in the theory of the finance of the firm we use not marginal costs of production but only the marginal costs of finance. And, instead of marginal revenues of sales, we use marginal return (or efficiency) of investment—that is the cash flow before deduction of finance costs. In this way, we can highlight finance costs and thus transform the theory of *optimum output of the firm* to the theory of optimum investment or *finance of the firm*.

Total Costs and Total Revenues

In making use of the theory of the firm, however, we want to set the financial analysis in the broadest frame possible. While it is very important to be able to identify the financial decisions among the welter of other considerations in running a business, it is equally important not to lose sight of the interrelationships between financial management and nonfinancial management.

To give us this broadest gauge, the theory of the firm can be restated in terms of *total* revenue and costs, as distinct from marginal revenue and costs. As it typically makes its appearance in price theory, this wider frame can be depicted as Figure 2–1. In this form, the emphasis is on profit maximization.

The revenue comes from sales, and is a result of the number of items sold and the prices charged for them. This pair of decisions—how many units the firm should try to sell and what price tag it should put on them—need not concern us here, but the total revenue curve in Figure 2–1 has been drawn on lines usually supposed to represent the facts of the real world. The firm is assumed to be able to sell some quantity of goods without a reduction in price per unit. At some level, however, sales can be increased only with lower prices. The curve of total revenue thus rises in a straight line, then rises less and less rapidly as larger quantities are offered for sale.

Total costs appear in Figure 2–1 under three headings—variable cash costs, fixed cash costs, and fixed noncash costs. The first type includes all those costs that vary directly with the level of output. They are best illustrated by the hourly wages of an assembly-line worker, which are not paid if the assembly line is shut down. Hence, the level of these expenses, as shown in Figure 2–1, is zero when output is zero, and rises with the level of output.

FIGURE 2–1

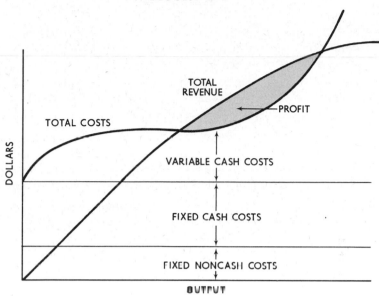

The costs in the second group—the fixed cash costs—are also paid to outsiders, as it were, but they are constant amounts, which do not vary directly with the number of units produced. They are represented by such obligations as interest payments on a firm's bond issue. Once such a commitment has been made, these costs continue regardless of output. For this reason, the chart shows them as a band that neither widens nor narrows, but instead adds a constant amount to expenses throughout the range of output shown on the chart.

In the third group, we have expenses that are fixed in total but are not owed to outsiders. Thus, no cash is involved, only bookkeeping. The chief, and perhaps only, item in this band is the depreciation allowance. It, too, appears in Figure 2–1 as a band of constant width.

The difference between total revenue and total cost is, of course, profit. To maximize profit, the firm should produce at the point where total revenue exceeds total cost by the widest margin. This, incidentally, will be exactly the output at which marginal revenue equals marginal cost. The marginal measures are simply the changes in total revenue and total cost resulting from the production of one more unit of output. Thus if one further unit were produced and the cost of that increment (which is the marginal cost) exceeded the additional revenue it would bring, then total profit would be diminished. Moving to a higher level of production would have increased costs by more than it increased revenue.

But all this applies to *profit* maximization. We must move on to cash flow maximization, and ultimately to wealth maximization. To turn Figure 2–1 into a cash flow framework, we need to take out the third type of cost—the fixed noncash cost. By doing this, we charge only the *cash* costs, and the total cost curve is lower than in Figure 2–1. Once the noncash cost is sliced away, we get the different picture shown in Figure 2–2.

With this broader focus, the problems of financial management can be seen in the perspective of all the money flows that wash over any part of the company. At the same time, those flows are conveniently organized for financial analysis itself. Thus the *determinants* of cash flow stand out in plain view, making it clear that financial management has much of its job handed to it by developments in marketing and in wage levels and the like. Yet the center ring, as it were, features the resulting cash flow, the stream that is the heart of financial management. And, indeed, as we shall see, the conclusions of financial management can send impulses riding out of that center ring, taking messages back to change decisions in the marketing department and production department and personnel department.

Coping with the Quality of Cash Flows

But how does the *quality* of cash flow get analyzed in this setting? How is the question of the time pattern of these flows to be taken account of, and how are risk and uncertainty to be dealt with?

The problem of time can be met by treating time as a cost of waiting. If $100 is promised for five years hence, it is not as attractive as $100 promised next year. Nor is a sum promised next year as appealing as the same sum paid in the present. Thus, the management of cash flow requires one of two steps: Either (*a*) future expected receipts must be systematically discounted to convert them to a *present value*, or (*b*) the future expected costs must be systematically increased to include the cost of waiting for the receipts. In the first option, the terms of analysis are made compatible by stating them all in present value. In the second, compatibility is achieved by stating all elements in terms of a given point in the future year. As these matters come up in later chapters, the techniques will be developed in detail.

To deal with risk, we must now call attention to its two component

FIGURE 2-2

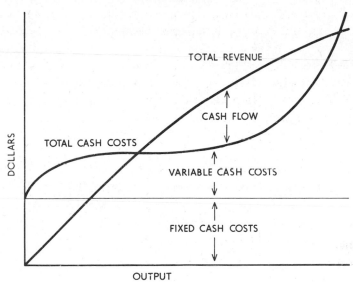

parts—business risk and financial risk. The first type covers all the variability that the firm itself is heir to. Disturbances that affect the whole economy, problems in the industry, the impact of rivalry in the local market—any disruption that hits the company as a company—are business risks. The second type, the financial risk, falls peculiarly on the stockholders and is an outgrowth of debt financing. That is, for firms with no debt at all business risk and financial risk are one and the same. But if a company of given size has financed with debt rather than equity alone, then the cash flow to stockholders is smaller than if there were no creditors to be paid. And yet the *variability* in cash flow will be just as great. Fluctuations of $10 above and below an expected cash flow of $100 become fluctuations of $10 around an expected flow of, say $75, when debt has been substituted for some of the equity. Where balance sheets show both debt and equity, the stockholders come second in line, and will suffer greater uncertainty about the earnings that will be left for them after the payments on debt.

The first component of risk—business risk—will enter the analysis much as the adjustment for time is to enter it. That is, the cash flows will be adjusted not only for the cost of waiting but also for the impact of uncertainty. By simple techniques to be developed as we go along, the future cash flows will be restated as mathematically expected values.

For the analysis of financial risk, we must go outside of our cash flow framework entirely. And as noted earlier, the established economic theory of the firm will not do this job, at least not as that theory is stated in the cash flow diagram of Figures 2–1 and 2–2.

To put these matters differently, we may turn again to the concept of a capitalization rate. As it was stated earlier, it is the rate that translates one year's cash flow into the market value of a claim on the full stream of cash flows. And with this rate, we get the market value

$$\frac{E}{c} = V \, .$$

If the cash flow is now examined *after* adjustment for both futurity and business uncertainty, then E has become something else—say, A. As a consequence, the capitalization rate will also have a changed content. Previously it carried the full burden of accounting for (a) futurity, (b) business risk, and (c) financial risk (along with, of course, the generally prevailing translation of any flow into stock form). Now with two of these elements—(a) and (b)—moved up into the numerator, the new rate becomes largely the depository of financial risk. If this new capitalization rate is denoted as k, we get:

$$\frac{A}{k} = V \, .$$

PLAN OF ATTACK FOR THE REST OF THE BOOK

From this point, the chapters of this book are grouped into three major sections, for each of three components of the algebraic expression just above. In the first two sections, we will focus on the A of that expression, and in the third section we will come to the k.

In looking at A, we will be asking how best to maximize the *expected present value* of cash flows. That is, the framework of total cash revenue and total cash cost will be taken from the theory of the firm. It will be altered to show the effects of time, either as a cost of waiting or as an adjustment to arrive at present values. And it will incorporate business uncertainty by restating the uncertain flows in the form of their certainty equivalents, a process to be explained as we go along.

Looking at all the financial decisions inherent in A is a large undertaking. To keep the task from growing unwieldy we shall first concentrate on the *short-run sources and uses* of cash. The seven chapters of Part II take on that task. In Part III, the *long-run uses* of cash—essentially the decisions to acquire plant and equipment—will move to the fore.

But then to analyze the k, including particularly the role of financial risk, we turn to the six chapters of Part IV, which treat the *long-term sources* of cash. The central concept here is the cost of capital. A final clump of seven chapters will examine in some detail the empirical development in corporate sources of funds.

Only when we have arrived at the last two sections will we be dealing with financial management at its highest level of *optimization*. For only then will the analysis focus directly on policies for maximizing the stockholders' wealth. Prior to that point, we will be dealing in what can be called *suboptimization,* and it is well to be fully aware of this. The framework of total cash revenue and total cash costs—i.e., Figure 2–2—is clearly suboptimal, since it points the way to cash flow maximization. For example, a completely optimal policy within the boundaries sketched by Figure 2–2 could nevertheless fail to maximize shareholder wealth. If the expected present value of cash flow is pushed up by a large debt financing, the stockholder might be worse off than before, despite a greatly enhanced cash flow. The role of financial risk must be added before we can know whether the optimal policy has in fact been found.

A similar point may be made about the relationship between optimal short-run policies and longer-run policies. The management of inventories, for example, may take quite a different course if the firm decides to add new plant and equipment. For expositional ease, however, we will first look at the short-run problems as if the larger structure were fixed and given. Hence this too is a form of suboptimization.

Summing up, then the reader will now board a raft designed to take him past turns in the river as follows:

Short-term sources and uses, and their management
    —suboptimization on a small scale;
    —through maximization of cash flow, within a fixed plant capacity;
    —with adjustments for futurity and business uncertainty.
Long-term uses, or capital budgeting for plant and equipment
    —suboptimization on a larger scale;
    —through maximization of cash flow, with plant capacity variable;
    —with adjustments for futurity and business uncertainty.
Long-term sources, or the cost of capital
    —the ultimate optimization;
    —through maximization of stockholder wealth;

—combining financing decisions and financial
uncertainty with the maximization of cash flow from
the first two stages.

But one last word before departure. Through pages behind us, and many that lie ahead, the reader may find himself wondering about the realism of maximization as a goal—the maximization of anything. In recent years, organization and decision theory have suggested that managerial behavior be analyzed around the assumption of "satisficing" rather than "maximizing" behavior. There is much to be said for this approach, because under conditions of uncertainty—the realistic conditions under which management makes its decisions—it may be impossible to maximize. But although satisficing may be a more realistic behavior assumption for a theory of corporate financial management, it is unmanageable as a first approximation to that theory, for it lacks precision and does not lend itself to simple predictions of how managers should behave.

Thus, even those who would prefer to erect a corporate finance theory on the satisficing basis must be content at first to explore the implications of maximizing behavior; this extreme but precise and clear analysis then can be relaxed to allow for more realistic satisficing behavior. Satisficing seems in essence some safe *degree* of maximizing. But the latter—the *optimum optimorum*—must be known before the more realistic optimum can be described and adopted. In other words, the maximum solution must be known before relaxing its rigor. Thus, we shall make many concessions in the following chapters to the satisficing mode of behavior but only after a close look at what is implied by the ideal maximization.

SUGGESTED READINGS

BODENHORN, DIRAN. "A Cash-Flow Concept of Profit," *Journal of Finance*, March, 1964.

CHAMBERLAIN, NEIL W. *The Firm: Micro-Economic Planning and Action.* New York: McGraw-Hill Book Co., Inc., 1962.

GORDON, MYRON J. *The Investment, Financing, and Valuation of the Corporation*, chap. ii. Homewood, Ill.: Richard D. Irwin, Inc., 1962.

MARRIS, ROBIN. "A Model of the 'Managerial' Enterprise," *Quarterly Journal of Economics*, May, 1963.

ROBICHEK, ALEXANDER A., and MYERS, STEWART C. *Optimal Financing Decision*, chaps. i and ii. Englewood Cliffs, N.J.: Prentice-Hall, Inc., 1965.

SOLOMON, EZRA. *The Theory of Financial Management*, chaps. i and ii. New York: Columbia University Press, 1963.

QUESTIONS AND PROBLEMS

1. Why should there be any doubt about profit maximization as the goal of a business firm?
2. Since the economic theory of the firm emphasizes flows, how can it assist in the analysis of wealth maximization—i.e., the maximization of a stock?
3. Why is it necessary to subdivide risk into financial risk and business risk?
4. Explain the special relevance of *cash* returns in financial management.

Part II

SHORT-TERM SOURCES AND USES

Chapter 3

WORKING CAPITAL AND
SHORT-TERM FINANCE

The short-term tasks of financial management center around those balance sheet items that are called *current*. The assets among them are often referred to as working capital, or circulating capital, since they represent funds that move in a short period from cash to noncash, and back around to cash again. Taking the assets and liabilities together, the current items give rise to two major uses of funds (inventories and accounts receivable) and two major sources (accounts payable and short-term borrowing of other types). The remaining entity is the pool of cash and other short-term liquid assets which play the role of buffer, serving sometimes as source of funds, sometimes as use.

If one takes a narrow view of the financial manager's job, it relates entirely to this buffer role. His assignment, in this view, is to get up cash when the pool is running low, and to find short-term employment for cash when the pool is brimming over. Sooner or later, however, someone in the firm must look beyond this residual role as manager of cash and securities. Indeed, ultimately, financial management must cope with all sources and uses. Since this broadening of focus can best be understood if done in stages, the next seven chapters will concentrate on the management of sources and uses springing from *current* assets and liabilities.

The nature of this undertaking can most readily be seen by a close look at Table 3–1. In that table, the sources and uses statement for the firm is organized to pull together all the pieces of short-term financial management. They are shown in the center box of the table. The flows that lie outside this group also are given (above the box), to remind us that they are interrelated with the short-term flows. But they are grouped apart and taken as something established elsewhere, beyond the influence of short-term financial management.

TABLE 3–1

SOURCES AND USES OF CASH, AND CLOSING LEVELS (SOURCES [+], USES [−])
(Thousands of Dollars)

	Periods			
	1	2	3	4
Total sales	+1,000	+1,100	+1,200	+1,400
Cost and expenses excluding depreciation	− 881	− 900	− 950	−1,000
Cash payments for taxes	− 39	− 80	− 90	− 100
Dividends	− 20	− 40	− 20	− 40
Change in common stock outstanding	0	0	0	0
Change in long-term borrowing	+ 20	0	+ 200	0
Change in plant and equipment	− 100	− 100	− 100	− 100
Change in inventories	− 20	− 300	− 800	− 200
Change in accounts receivable	− 10	− 100	− 150	− 300
Change in accounts payable	+ 20	+ 150	+ 300	+ 150
Change in short-term borrowing	+ 10	+ 15	+ 10	+ 20
Subtotal of sources	+1,050	+1,265	+1,710	+1,570
Subtotal of uses	−1,070	−1,520	−2,110	−1,740
Net change in cash and other liquid assets	− 20	− 255	− 400	− 170
Closing level:				
Inventories	1,500	1,800	2,600	2,800
Accounts receivable	1,100	1,200	1,350	1,650
Accounts payable	900	1,050	1,350	1,500
Short-term borrowing	400	415	425	445
Cash and other liquid assets	1,000	745	345	175
Current assets	3,600	3,745	4,295	4,625
Current liabilities	1,300	1,465	1,775	1,945

The four columns of figures in Table 3–1 refer to four different periods of time. We could think of them as a record of four periods already finished, but let us assume that here they are a forecast of developments over future periods. (The first column of figures simply puts in a different order the information contained in Table 1–9, back in Chapter 1.)

What should the manager's response be to such a forecast? His attention may be drawn first to the continuous drain of cash and securities that is anticipated. What should be done about this drain? New borrowing? A high level meeting to reassess the policy on accounts receivable, which promises to be a considerable drain on funds? Or perhaps a new look at inventory management, which promises to absorb even larger amounts?

But then again, should anything at all be done to head off the expected decline in cash and securities holdings? Maybe they *should* decline. In the bottom tier of Table 3-1 the first figure given for cash and other liquid assets is 1,000. Maybe this is too high to begin with. But what is *too high?* What is the optimal level of cash, or any of these current assets and liabilities?

The reader may wonder about this apparent emphasis on stocks when up to now we have insisted on the greater relevance of flows. The explanation is, first, that stocks are the underground wells from which some of the future flows will spring. Hence they too must be studied. For example, when the stock of cash has swindled to zero, there can be no further outflow unless the stock is somehow rebuilt.

Moreover—and this is especially significant—the flows that concern us most are the *flows of earnings and costs*. And these stem heavily from stocks, as it is often the existence of stocks that makes earnings possible and costs inevitable. Inventories on hand, for example, have money tied up in them. There is an interest cost to this money, and hence week by week the inventories standing there are giving off a stream of costs. At the same time, the availability of these inventories contains the hope of sales. Thus, they have the potential of producing earnings.

To give just the flavor of this kind of thinking, figures for two particular manufacturing industries have been pulled together in Table 3-2. For metalworking machinery and tobacco manufacturers, sales are compared with costs and expenses other than depreciation, to give a figure for net earnings before taxes. Hypothetical carrying costs on inventory holdings are then computed by assuming an annual rate of 8 percent for the cost of capital—a rate that probably comes close to the actual cost for these industries during the period reported.

In the bottom line for each industry in Table 3-2, the computed carrying cost is shown as a percent of the net returns before taxes. This percentage suggests the increase in earnings that would result if the firms could eliminate entirely the carrying of inventories and still meet production schedules and customer demands. Few firms have that alternative, of course, but the figure indicates the heavy impact that carrying costs had on the net returns that were experienced. For producers of metalworking machinery, the inventories generated a carrying cost equal to roughly one seventh of net earnings before taxes. And for the tobacco companies, the cost of carrying inventories ran as high as one third of net earnings. These are large costs, and to make sure they are justified the financial management must look at the revenues produced by having these inventories.

Occasionally one sees attempts to make these judgments about optimal stocks with what is called ratio analysis. Various pairs of figures of the kind given in Table 3–1 are looked at together, in ratio form. For example, the ratio of current assets to current liabilities, known as the *current ratio*, falls in Table 3–1 from 2.77 to 2.37. The quick ratio—cash and securities over current liabilities—drops much more sharply, from 0.77 to 0.09. Many other relationships can be developed, using other entries shown in Table 3–1 as well as figures not given there.

TABLE 3–2

(Millions of Dollars)

	1965				1966
	1Q	2Q	3Q	4Q	1Q
Metalworking Machinery					
Sales	1,269	1,388	1,430	1,467	1,512
Costs and expenses (other than depreciation)	1,104	1,188	1,233	1,278	1,296
Net before taxes	165	200	197	189	216
Inventories	1,134	1,180	1,243	1,272	1,320
Carrying cost:					
At 8% p.a.	22.7	23.6	24.9	25.4	26.4
As % of net returns before taxes	14	12	13	13	12
Tobacco Manufacturers					
Sales	1,384	1,529	1,561	1,532	1,484
Cost and expenses (other than depreciation)	1,224	1,343	1,360	1,350	1,315
Net before taxes	160	186	201	182	169
Inventories	2,766	2,591	2,594	2,826	2,862
Carrying Cost:					
At 8% p.a.	55.3	51.8	51.9	56.4	57.2
As % of net returns before taxes	33	28	26	31	34

Source: Federal Trade Commission and Securities and Exchange Commission, *Quarterly Financial Report for Manufacturing Corporations.*

As a way of getting a quick handle on a mass of data, such ratios can be quite helpful. They make it possible to keep an eye on developments without watching all the figures all the time. If a key ratio departs significantly from its expected level, it may call attention to a possible problem underneath.

But what must be avoided is any tendency to attach fundamental meaning to ratios. They contain no magic. Without analysis, we cannot know whether a current ratio sliding from 2.77 to 2.37 is a good thing or a bad thing. Perhaps it ought to fall further. Thus it takes careful analysis of sources and uses—and the costs and returns they imply—to determine what kind of behavior in a ratio can be read as a useful signal. It takes further analysis to be sure that the ratio has not given a false signal. In particular, the average of the rest of the industry should not be taken automatically as a norm. To be sure, if the ratios of a given firm depart significantly from those of other companies of a similar nature, managers in the divergent firms may expect questions to be raised. But if the departure from industry norms has been taken deliberately, after analysis of revenues and costs, the wisdom of the departure should be evident in the earnings figures. There is no necessary virtue in following the crowd.

In the six chapters coming up we will explore ideas for analyzing costs and revenues in the three major areas of short-term financial management—inventories, trade debt and credit, and the buffers of cash and other short-term financing. At various points we will also examine briefly the interrelationships among these areas.

To give perspective in advance, Table 3–3 records the levels and net changes in level for selected short-term items for all nonfinancial corporations over the eight quarters of 1964 and 1965. Because the figures for changes show only the net changes, they mask a large part of the ebb and flow that actually occurred. Even so, the volatility of the entries is marked. For example, inventory stocks continued to rise over the period,

TABLE 3–3

SELECTED SHORT-TERM STOCKS AND FLOWS, NONFINANCIAL CORPORATIONS
(Billions of Dollars, Not Seasonally Adjusted)

| | Stocks | Flows | | | | | | | |
| | End of 1963 | 1964 | | | | 1965 | | | |
		I	II	III	IV	I	II	III	IV
Inventories	110.0a	2.2	1.0	0.3	1.1	3.2	1.4	0.6	1.7
Trade debt	85.5	−0.7	−1.5	2.9	1.7	0.1	0.8	2.9	2.9
Trade credit	122.5	2.1	1.4	6.0	−0.4	4.1	3.0	4.9	1.6
Net Credit	37.0	2.7	2.9	3.1	−2.2	4.0	2.2	1.9	−1.4
Bank loans not otherwise classified	36.1	−1.2	1.2	0.7	2.8	1.5	2.7	1.2	4.5
Demand deposits and currency	29.4	−5.5	1.5	0.3	1.1	−4.8	−0.5	−1.2	3.1
Time deposits	12.2	1.6	0.4	0.4	0.8	2.1	1.7	0.9	0.3
Government securities	19.8	0.7	−1.2	−1.1	0.1	−0.7	−2.0	−0.6	1.1
Open-market paper ...	4.4	0.7	0.5	0.2	0.1	0.4	0.2	0.1	...

a —Inventory stock at end of 1963 is estimated, as Federal Reserve figures give stock figures only for financial assets and liabilities.

SOURCE: Board of Governors of the Federal Reserve System.

making all the changes positive, but the increments ranged from $0.3 billion to $3.2 billion—a multiple of more than ten. All the other items fluctuate significantly also, with the widest swings occurring in demand deposits and currency, the ultimate buffer stock.

QUESTIONS AND PROBLEMS

1. If you were applying ratio analysis to Table 3–1, what would you make of the behavior of accounts receivable? What about inventories?
2. Looking at Table 3–3, do you see any pattern in "bank loans not otherwise classified"? In inventories? In time deposits?
3. Again looking at Table 3–3, assume that the behavior of inventories and of accounts receivable is explained by events beyond the control of financial managers. Can you see possible patterns of "residual response" in the other items in the table?

SUGGESTED READING

GOLE, V. L. "The Management of Working Capital," *The Australian Accountant,* June, 1959. Reprinted in JOHN L. O'DONNELL and MILTON S. GOLDBERG (eds.), *Elements of Financial Administration,* pp. 57–72. Columbus, Ohio: Charles E. Merrill Books, Inc., 1962.

Chapter 4

INVENTORY MANAGEMENT:
THE INDIVIDUAL FIRM

Viewed as stocks, inventories are the second largest single item of either current assets or current liabilities. Potentially, they offer one of the greatest hopes of earnings, among short-term items, and one of the greatest threats of cost. This prominence leads us, in this chapter and in the one following, to ask several questions. First, why do inventories exist at all? We are interested in this question because an answer to it will help us settle a second major question, namely: What should determine the quantity of inventories that businesses hold at any one time? In addition, we should like to know the cyclical pattern of these holdings and the theories offered to explain the pattern.

WHY ANY INVENTORIES AT ALL?

It is possible to conceive of productive enterprises that get along with no inventories. But very few come to mind, and they seem farfetched. The reasons for carrying such stocks must be compelling. What are they?

The reasons will be more readily evident if we ask what inventories consist of. It is clear, to begin with, that they are goods, not services. This means that, unlike inputs of labor man-hours, they can be accumulated, should there be any reason to do so. They can be owned; they can legitimately grace a balance sheet. They are, moreover, "real" assets rather than financial assets.

Unlike other real assets, however, the time inventories spend with a firm will be short. Within a few months, any given unit is likely to disappear entirely—be burned up, painted over, fitted with wheels, handed on to the firm's customers. In this characteristic, inventories are

51

set apart from that other major clump of capital assets—plant and equipment. These others are likewise real goods, but they will not be wholly consumed in a single cycle of production and sales, or in a single accounting period. Indeed, with only minor license, capital assets of long life may themselves be thought of as bundles of inventories. They have long life only because the bundles cannot be physically broken apart, except at great cost.

The essential nature of inventories thus lies in these two traits—tangibility and short-livedness. They distinguish inventories on the one side from services, which cannot be accumulated, and on the other side from plant and equipment, which can be accumulated but which will not be entirely used up within a single accounting period.

We can take another step toward understanding the basic need for inventories by looking at the major stages through which these tangible assets pass during their short tenure with a firm. This tenure is commonly broken into three stages, with inventories classified progressively as *purchased goods* (or "raw materials"), *goods in process*, and *finished goods*.

Taking these in reverse order, it seems likely that under any circumstances, a firm will find itself holding some of its *finished goods*. For some companies—say, producers of electronic computers—a product reaching this stage will already be headed for a specific customer, since, as a matter of policy, production will only be started when a detailed order arrives. But even in this case the finished goods cannot all be whisked away the moment they emerge from the productive process. Time is required to assemble the order, attach the bills of lading, and so forth. For some few hours, at least, even the most efficient firms in these industries will have finished goods on their hands.

For most industries, this sort of forward planning is not practicable at all. They must keep finished goods on hand to be sold when the customer calls, or else lose the sale to a competitor. If these customer inquiries are received in an uneven pattern, as they almost universally are, the firm will find it impossible to predict the pattern with such accuracy that its flow of output can be matched exactly to its flow of sales. Moreover, short-run fluctuations of this sort in the level of output may drive up sharply the cost of the operation. Or alternatively, the production process may have a rhythm of its own, as in the case of a farming business, in which crops become finished goods when the harvest moon rises, whether or not the customer comes around.

Moving backward, we come to *goods in process*. For the retailer and wholesaler, inventories will consist in the main of finished goods. But in the world of manufacturers, it is impossible to think of a venture that can altogether avoid holding goods in process except by closing down. The level of these inventories will depend on many elements. But by the very nature of the productive process, there will always be some goods that are, so to speak, in the mill, goods that are in the pipeline. And the more complex the operation, the greater the likelihood that there is not one pipeline but several, with all the attendant problems of matching their differential flows to one another, and thus the greater likelihood of goods in process that are, in fact, waiting to enter the next process.

With *purchased goods,* we take the final step backward. Businessmen have tried at times to pursue hand-to-mouth policies at this stage, buying raw materials only at the last possible minute before they were to be used in the productive process. But the mouth may open by surprise, or the hand falter. While the electronic computer can greatly improve inventory control, the exact moment at which raw materials will be required cannot be forecast, as it will be influenced by all the elements that occasion changes in the stocks of finished goods and goods in process. These difficulties would not be overwhelming if a company could have absolute confidence in the ability and willingness of its suppliers to come through at a moment's notice. But obviously, it cannot take this risk. As a result, it holds inventories of purchased materials.

At this point, we can draw some rough conclusions. The existence of inventories can be explained, first, by the fact that *time* is required to move economic goods through the long process of production and distribution. This is obviously true of an economy as a whole, and would be equally true if the economy were organized into one big firm. Regardless of the social system or form of economic enterprise, time must elapse before completed goods can emerge into the hands of the final consumer of those goods. In a system made up of many different decision-making units, each individual company simply shares in this process. Each has the goods for a time before handing them on, in some changed form, to the next in line.

Secondly, the very smallest of economies is marked by diversity. There is never just one continuous process. There are many processes, many flows, many pipelines of many sizes that cannot be fitted exactly together. There are, in a word, *discontinuities.* For both technological and administrative reasons, it is impossible to plan with such precision that goods move steadily through the process without having to stop a while at some points to await transfer to other pipelines, larger or smaller or otherwise different. Thus, within the economy as a whole, or within a single firm, the managers of the process will want to hold in readiness some stock of goods to be fed into the next stage when the moment arrives. Extra goods will be kept available to prevent the fundamental discontinuities from becoming actual breaks in the availability of goods.

Finally, not all the decisions in an economy can be made by a single person, and this gives rise to *uncertainties*. This also is true regardless of the social organization. But in a society of free enterprise the individual firm must constantly be guessing at decisions made outside its own walls. To begin with, natural discontinuities exist at either edge of the individual company, as well as within the process over which the company itself has jurisdiction. In addition, an individual firm is always uncertain regarding the volume of finished goods that will be required by its customers and the volume of raw materials that can be readily delivered by its suppliers. Hence, it must keep buffer stocks of raw materials and finished goods partly because there are natural points of discontinuity for the economy as a whole, but also because the company has no direct control over the pipelines on either side of itself. Indeed, it has only limited knowledge of what may be required for those pipelines.

For these three reasons—the necessary passage of time, the discontinuities of the economic process, and the need to expect the unexpected—any business firm that hopes to stay alive will hold some quantity of goods in inventory. Our problem now is to discover what that quantity will be.

WHAT INFLUENCES THE LEVEL OF INVENTORIES?

The task of explaining the actual volume of business inventories can be tackled from two directions. One might examine the advice given to businessmen in managerial textbooks of the last several decades (and now sold to them by operations researchers). Alternatively, one might consult economists who, seeking to unravel the business cycle, have developed their own theories of inventory behavior. The two approaches do not, however, war against one another. The advice given directly by consultants, in textbook or in person, will not always be listened to, and cannot always be followed, anyway. And the economist, thrashing about in his own thicket of ideas, must arrive at some view as to what individual businessmen aim at. He must then probe further to see how far, and under what influences, the acts of businessmen in the aggregate fall short of this ideal.

In this chapter the emphasis is on the individual firm and the systematic management of inventories. It seems fair to assume that the same general influences will be at work in any well-run firm, even if only unconsciously, particularly in view of the deep inroads that professional business school graduates have made into American companies over the decades. The efforts of economists on the question will be examined in the next chapter.

THE BUSINESS-EYE VIEW

A. The Costs to Be Considered

Managers working with inventories have two decisions to make. They must decide the *quantity* of materials to be acquired in any one order. And they must decide *when* the order for this quantity should be placed. If they are to make good decisions, however, they must first examine the relevant costs.

1. *Acquisition Cost.* This expense cannot be avoided so long as any materials are being acquired. The supplier must be paid his price. Even so, this cost will sometimes influence inventory decisions. For example, if the supplier offers a quantity discount, it may pay to order a larger volume than otherwise. Or, if there is reason to expect price increases in the near future, it may be prudent to lay in a larger supply before the price advance.

2. *Carrying Cost.* Once a firm has decided to carry some quantity of materials in stock, it has in the same step decided to let some funds be tied up in that stock. The firm thus incurs, at the very least, an opportunity cost—a yield it might be earning by employing those funds elsewhere. If the funds have been borrowed for the purpose, they bear an outright *cash* cost in the form of interest due the lender. In addition, inventory stocks generate expenses of their own. They take up warehouse space, they require insurance coverage, and so forth. All things considered, it costs money to hold inventories, and the more you hold, the more it costs.

The existence of carrying costs argues for keeping inventory stocks as small as possible. This, in turn, is a recommendation to keep individual orders down to the smallest quantity possible. It is advice that favors small orders, placed with great frequency. Followed to its extreme, this advice would have the firm ordering only what it will need today, with a new call to be sent out tomorrow.

3. *Procurement Cost.* There is another set of costs, however, that push the decision in exactly the opposite direction. These are payments incurred in the process of acquisition, but independently of the acquisition cost. They are payments to cover the preliminary negotiations with suppliers, the ordering process, the bookkeeping and handling of invoices. If the item is highly standardized, the suppliers few and much alike, and prices highly uniform, the procurement effort may be very routine and relatively cheap. But if placing an order requires some shopping around, the drawing up of particular specifications, the solicitation of alternate bids, a research analysis of the bids offered—then obviously it can produce many hours of detail and paper work and telephone talk.

Whether the procurement cost is large or small, it will tend not to vary with the quantity ordered. Buying one million widgets requires much the same paper work as buying three million widgets. As a consequence, the firm will save by placing large orders. This will reduce the frequency with which procurement costs must be paid, without raising the expense of each of these orders. Two orders a year, rather than three, will shove down the total cost of procurement for the year. Hence the advice, on this front, will be to make orders both large and far between.

4. *The Cost of Being Caught Short.* This is also referred to as *stockout* cost, or *understock* cost. Several possibilities exist here. A customer may turn up unexpectedly, checkbook in hand, and go away dispirited when the shelves are found to be bare. His disappointment over the firm's inability to meet his present need may mean he is permanently lost as a customer. The cost of failing to have stocks on hand when he called for them must then be measured by all the future sales that might have been made to him, discounted to present value. Though such a cost is difficult to measure, it is no less real.

Alternatively, the customer may be able to wait a day or two longer, but not as long as it would take to get delivery of the item in the normal schedule. The sale is not lost, but to save it the firm will have to make hurry-up calls to its own supplier, assume the cost of overtime runs, arrange for special transportation and handling crews. The effect will be to increase both the acquisition cost and the procurement cost, per unit of material acquired.

Another, and happier, possibility is that customers expect to have to wait. It may be normal practice in the industry to take "back orders." Where the product is tailor-made, or where the demand for it is not significant in the overall offerings of the firm, it may make little sense to carry it in stock. There may still be a cost, however, even if only a small one. Reasonably prompt delivery may be thought of as a quality of the product. Customers will not be patient indefinitely, and if the delay is a long one the firm must expect lower prices for its product. Ultimately, it can expect frustration to send the buyer to another source entirely—i.e., an unwillingness to pay this firm any price at all.

Notice that in the cost of being caught short a new element has entered. With each of the two costs considered just previously—the carrying cost and the procurement cost—the manager had to make a choice between size of order and frequency of order. This new cost does not deal with any such trade-off. It concerns instead the total amount of inventory for which the firm might anticipate a need. It thus deals with the basic relationship between the firm's sales and the level of stocks it maintains on average. We shall see, further along, the implications of this difference.

5. *The Cost of Being Caught "Long"—or Overstocking.* There are two possibilities here. The first occurs when the goods are not sold as expected and have to be carried in stock into the next period. The cost of such overstocking is the extra carrying cost. The funds invested in the goods are tied up just that much longer, the display space or warehouse stalls remain occupied, and so on.

The second type of long cost is rather special, but real enough for those who bear it. Think of a fish peddler before the days of refrigeration. His inventories suffered a distinct decline in appeal a day or so after acquisition. Fortunately for the fish man, and for his neighborhood, refrigeration has become commonplace. But perishability is still with us. Some goods have a seasonable demand only, and, what is worse, some pass out of style forever at the end of that season.

The cost of being caught long is measured by all the funds invested in the goods and not recovered through sale of them. If the little-girl look in women's dresses is moved down to the bargain basement, the cost incurred is measured by the gap between the markdown prices and the funds tied up in the dresses. Notice that the gap is *not* measured from the price tags originally attached to the dresses, but instead from "cost of goods" before any potential profit was figured in. If the goods have become completely worthless by their failure to sell during the period in question, the cost of overstocking is the full cost of having acquired those goods and carried them up to the point of disposal.

These are the five costs that inventories give rise to, and it is useful to note how they grow out of the reasons cited earlier for having any inventories at all. Those reasons, it will be recalled were three—the passage of time, the discontinuities of the economic process, and the uncertainties of economic life. If we add that few material goods in this world are free, we have all the costs accounted for, as follows:

Cost	Reason for Cost
Acquisition	Rarity of free goods
Carrying	Time
Procurement	Discontinuity
Long and Short	Uncertainty

Special attention should also be called to the particular choice that has been made for the handling of time. As mentioned earlier, there are two options—revenues and costs can be stated to make them comparable as of the *present* moment in time, or they can be stated for a particular point in the *future*. By choosing to work with a carrying cost, we choose the second of these options. The two approaches are two sides of the same coin, but as will become more evident as we go along, the use of carrying cost offers greater convenience in the analysis of short-term finance.

B. Making the Decision

1. *When Demand Is Constant and Certain.* To see how these different costs interact with one another, let us start with a simple set of circumstances. Let us assume first that we are examining a wholesale firm whose function is to bring together goods for retail distribution. That is, nothing is done to the goods to change them physically. Let us also assume—and this is more significant—that the demand facing this firm is unchanged day in and day out, and further that this demand pattern can be assumed with confidence by the decision-makers. They live in a world of certainty, with demand for their product constant. Finally, let us suppose that delivery of goods to this firm is not instantaneous. The lag between placing the order and receiving it is known and constant, but it does run into days and weeks.

With these assumptions, we can focus our attention on the first three of the costs listed earlier. With demand known and constant, we need not worry about short costs or long costs. They will be dealt with later.

The acquisition cost will turn on the demand the firm faces. Over a given period, it will buy the same number of goods it sells, regardless of how it resolves the inventory management questions of size of order and frequency of order. This acquisition cost will depend on D, the number of units demanded, and C, the price paid to the supplier for each unit. Total acquisition cost will then be CD.

The first management decision is the size of the order to place in acquiring these goods—the so-called *economic order quantity*. We can designate as Q the size of order actually placed. The most appropriate size of Q will depend, as we have seen, on the balance between the procurement cost and the carrying cost, the one favoring a large Q and the other a small Q.

The procurement cost for the full year will be the number of orders placed times the cost of making each such order. The number of such orders we can denote as D/Q. For example, if the annual demand is for 100,000 widgets, and they are ordered 20,000 at a time, then five orders must be placed each year. The cost of placing each such order—the bookwork, the telephone calls, all the rest—we can simply label as S. Thus, the total outlay for procurement in a year can be stated as D/Q times S.

The carrying cost will also depend on two elements. First, it will turn on the *average* amount of inventory carried during the year. This average will be exactly half the size of each order, since for half the time the amount of inventories in stock will be higher than this and for the other half of the time the amount will be lower. This is perhaps more clearly seen in Figure 4–1 which shows the drawing down of three successive orders over the three time periods OA, AB, and BC. The average holding during each of the three periods, and during the three taken together, is shown by the dotted horizontal line at the level X.

In the terminology we have just been developing, the average holdings during the year—the X in Figure 4–1—would be designated as $Q/2$. To get the carrying cost, these would be multiplied by the per annum interest cost relevant for the money tied up in these average holdings. The money value of each item in the average is C, the price paid in acquiring each

FIGURE 4–1

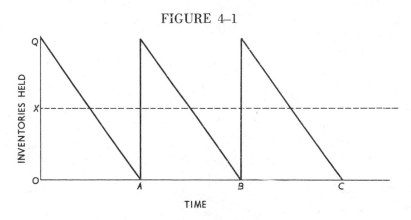

unit. The carrying cost for each unit will then be this unit value multiplied by the interest rate, I—or IC. And the total carrying cost will be the carrying cost per unit, IC, times the average number of units carried. $Q/2$. This gives us $Q/2\,IC$.

Putting these three cost expressions together, we arrive at the total cost of an inventory policy.

$$\text{TOTAL COST} = \text{ACQUISITION COST} + \text{PROCUREMENT COST} + \text{CARRYING COST}$$

$$TC \quad = \quad CD \quad + \quad \frac{D}{Q}S \quad + \quad \frac{Q}{2}IC$$

What we seek, of course, is the smallest possible total cost. Hence, using calculus to find the minimum TC, we can establish the optimal order size as

$$Q^* = \sqrt{\frac{2DS}{IC}}.$$

That is, the most appropriate Q (marked with an * to identify it as the optimum choice) will be higher as demand (D) is higher and as the cost (S) of placing an order is higher—just as we would expect. Also, the best size of order will be higher as the carrying cost (IC) is lower—again as we would expect. What we might not have expected, however, is the square root formulation. We shall have more to say of this later, but it can be seen straight off that a rising demand over time will not mean that orders for inventory stock should rise at the same rate. This has implications for decisions by individual firms, as for example in forward planning for warehouse space. And as we shall see, it will color the interpretation of data measuring business behavior in the aggregate.

Notice, further, that this answer tells us not only how much to order, but also when to place the order. We have assumed we know how long it takes for the supplier to make delivery. Thus, since the appropriate size of the order also establishes the date at which a new supply will be needed, the new order is placed the necessaary number of days prior to that date. Or the signal to reorder can be tied directly to the inventory stock itself by indicating a level of inventory on hand that will trigger the reorder. Suppose the lag is ten days, designated by the label m in Figure 4–2. As the diagram shows, the reorder date is $A - m$ and the inventory level signaling time to reorder is the amount R. This level of inventories, R, is called the reorder point.

It will be noted that the decision rules we have just been discussing set out first to answer the question of how much the order should be. The

FIGURE 4-2

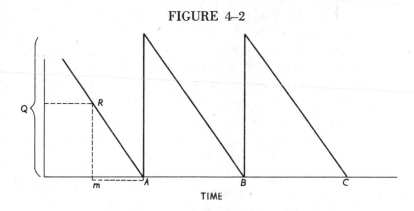

TIME

answer to the second question—the optimal time of ordering—follows as a consequence. This approach is sometimes called the two-bin system. When the bottom of the first bin is reached, the manager knows he has reached the reorder point. The second bin is stocked with just enough widgets to carry him until the new order is delivered. The new order then replenishes both bins, and needs are once again met from the first bin, until it again becomes empty and the next order goes out. The size of each order is fixed, and any variation in need is met by variation in the frequency of orders—not in the size of orders.

A quite acceptable policy could be developed from working the other way round. The constant star might be the reorder *period,* with the order size varying with the need. For example, it may be easier for everyone concerned to remember that the stock room is to be checked over at the end of the month, just before payday. The particulars of such a policy will not be developed here, and indeed the outcome will usually not differ much from the system we have been looking at. For some administrative purposes, however, the difference may be important. In a given situation some attention should be paid to the choice between the two approaches.

2. When Demand Is Not Certain. Now we march into the woods to grapple with our other two relevant costs—the cost of being caught short and the cost of being caught long. To keep to fundamentals, we can continue to look at a wholesale firm. Also for simplicity, we can largely ignore the peculiar case of being caught long—the fish peddler of olden days.

What kind of uncertainty could rise to trouble the inventory manager? What could happen to catch him with fewer inventory goods than he wishes? In general, his trouble may spring from two sources. His suppliers may deliver *later* than expected, and his customers may come to buy *more* than expected. We may note right away that the problem centers on the variation that occurs after the reorder point. It is in that period, after the manager has placed the order and before it is delivered, that he is most exposed to the winds of chance. For expositional ease, let us concentrate on possible variation in demand and leave aside slowdowns in delivery. We can see his exposure in Figure 4–3.

In a world of certainty and constant demand, our man can reorder the amount R at the point in time, t_1, with complete confidence that the new supply of widgets will arrive just as the last handful is being scooped from the second bin. What he faces in a world of uncertainty is the possibility that demand will pick up after the order R is placed, and goods in the second bin will move out more rapidly than anticipated. This more rapid decline, shown by the lower of the two dotted lines, will put him out of stock for a time. Alternatively, he may suffer a falling off in sales during the reorder period, so that stocks in the second bin are drawn down less rapidly than expected, as shown by the higher dotted line. Both before and after receipt of the new goods, his average holdings will be higher than they otherwise would have been. He will have overstocked.

Again the issue is one of opposing costs. Too small a quantity in the second bin will bring frequent stockouts, with the penalty of disgruntled customers and future sales lost forever. If this threat is countered by so large a second bin as to serve all possible comers, the stockout cost is avoided but the carrying cost is pushed skyward. Thus once more we seek

FIGURE 4–3

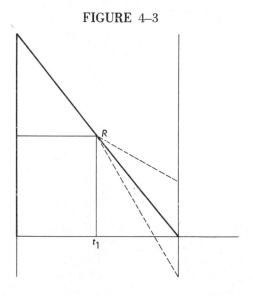

a balance. This time it is between (*a*) the extra carrying cost times its likelihood of occurring and (*b*) the stockout cost times *its* likelihood of occurring.

To find this optimum point, the manager will need information of two sorts. He needs some notion of the variation in customer demand during the reorder period, and some measure of the cost of overstocking and understocking.

a) Developing the Options. For the variation in customer demand, let us suppose first that the minimum demand during the reorder period is for 10 widgets. Suppose further that the maximum demand during this period is 13 widgets. The manager's problem is to decide the most appropriate capacity for that second bin—10, or 13, or something in between.

This gives the firm four different strategies to consider—i.e., 10, 11, 12, or 13. In assigning costs, let us assume that the short cost is $10 a widget and carrying costs are $4 a widget.

Combining this information gives the various possible outcomes shown in the matrix of Table 4-1. For example, look at the top row. This gives the possible consequences of adopting the first strategy and building no extra capacity in the second bin. If demand does not exceed the minimum, the cost will have been held to zero. No extra inventories were there to run up carrying costs, and no surprise customers appeared to generate stockout costs. If demand is greater than the minimum, however, the stockout cost rises with the demand. For a demand of 1 above minimum, for example, the cost having adopted this strategy is $10—the short cost for one widget.

TABLE 4-1

Strategy	Possible Demand 10	11	12	13
10	$ 0	$10	$20	$30
11	4	0	10	20
12	8	4	0	20
13	12	8	4	0

Or look at the upshot of a decision to prepare for a demand of 11 units—shown on the second line. Should the demand not rise above the minimum, the cost of this strategy will be $4, the carrying costs on the extra item that was stocked. With a demand of 11, the cost of the strategy drops to zero. The forecast has been perfect, and the strategy has avoided both stockout cost and any extra carrying cost. For a demand of 12, the strategy becomes expensive again—$10, the penalty for understocking by one unit. And so on.

But the story need not end here. If we assume a profit of $5 on each widget sold (before carrying costs or short costs), we can turn our cost matrix into a payoff matrix, as shown in Table 4–2. This matrix shows, for example, that if the firm has a perfect forecast, it will get the full $5 on each widget stocked. If it acquires 10 and sells 10, the payoff is $50. Acquiring 11 and selling 11 gives a payoff of $55. These happy outcomes appear on a diagonal running from upper left to lower right—$50, $55, $60, and $65.

TABLE 4–2

Possible Demand Strategy	10	11	12	13
10	$50	$40	$30	$20
11	46	55	45	35
12	42	51	60	50
13	38	47	56	65

When the demand is *less* than expected, however, the carrying cost eats into the payoff. Look for example, at the first column in Table 4–2 where the demand is for 10 widgets. When the firm anticipates a demand for 11, it is carrying one too many, and the payoff falls by the $4 of carrying cost. It drops from $50 to $46. The rest of the column shows further declines in payoff, reflecting strategies still more wide of the mark.

If the demand should run ahead of expectations, the firm would suffer the short cost. A company prepared to sell 12 widgets when customers wanted 13 would make $5 on each of the 12 it had available—a payoff of $60. But the cost of not having the thirteenth is $10, reducing the payoff to $50. This may be seen by looking across the row for the strategy in question.

b) Making the Choice. How does the manager know what to do? Several decision rules are available to him, but one widely supported rule tells him to guess as well as he can the probabilities of these different levels of demand. Then he can use those guesses as weights, to arrive at a single value for each of the strategies.

For example, his studies of the records, his knowledge of the business, and his hunches about the current state of the market might suggest to him a probability distribution as follows:

Demand	10	11	12	13
Probability	0.10	0.20	0.40	0.30

With these estimates, our manager can figure the mathematical expectation of each strategy. By applying these weights to each row of the matrix in Table 4–2, and then getting the total for each row, he has a new matrix, Table 4–3.

TABLE 4–3

Possible Demand / Strategy	10 (0.10)	11 (0.20)	12 (0.40)	13 (0.30)	Expected Total
10	$5	$ 8	$12	$ 6	$31
11	4.6	11	18	10.5	44.1
12	4.2	10.2	24	15	53.4
13	3.8	9.4	22.4	19.5	55.1

Running his eye down the "Expected Total" column, our manager finds that a decision in favor of 13 units produces the highest figure. That becomes his strategy. A policy that prepares for a demand of 13 will carry the highest expected payoff. There will be occasional overstocking with consequent carrying costs. But for all other strategies, the mathematical expectation is that such costs will be higher.

With this issue settled, our manager now has his inventory policy. From the earlier analysis of the economic order quantity, he knows how much to order. With the analysis just finished, he knows when to place that order. For he has established the expected need for inventories during the time that will elapse between the placing of the new order and the delivery of it. He knows he will be best off if the new supply is ordered when the existing supply has fallen to 13 widgets. This figure represents the minimum demand of 10 to be expected while the new order is on the way, plus the additional quantity of 3 indicated in the matrix of mathematical expectations.

Should he wish to take account of uncertainty in delivery time, he would proceed to make probability guesses about the delivery lag. These estimates would be combined with the probability distributions he used for variations in customer demand. Together, they would give the joint probabilities of overstocking and understocking. The computations get more complicated than in the matrix seen above, but the principle is the same. The manager is working toward the highest probable payoff from inventory management that can be mathematically expected in an uncertain world.

3. When Production Enters the Picture.   Up to now, the problems of inventory management have been illustrated by a wholesale firm. As we have defined such a firm, its essential characteristic has been that the goods it sells are the goods its buys. Its inventories of purchased materials are not distinguishable from its inventories of finished goods. And with no production process, there are no goods in process.

When we introduce manufacturing, the effect is to break apart this single stock of inventories. It becomes two stocks (purchased materials and finished goods), with a third stock (goods in process) inserted between. And with this change, the management of inventories comes into a much wider web of interrelationships.

One might suppose, for example, that the costs of holding finished goods could be analyzed as if these were the inventories of a separate firm. An optimal policy for finished goods, however, is likely to involve only periodic "purchases" from the manufacturing department. If as a result the manufacturing department must produce in broken runs, there will be extra expenses of stopping and starting, and the extra cost of idle men and idle machines. Hence for a grand design there must be a *joint* determination of production and inventory policies.

This is not the place to develop the complex analysis needed for these problems of joint management. What can be conveyed is a quick sampling of interrelationships. For example, Figure 4–4a gives an idea of the inventories a firm might hold if demand were constant, production were constant, and deliveries of raw materials were always made on time. The stock of purchased materials would fall steadily until replaced by a new order just as the old supply was disappearing. The volume of goods in process would never vary. Production would always move at the same pace, day after day consuming precisely its alloted quota of purchased materials and disgorging precisely its alloted quota of finished goods. Nor would the supply of finished goods ever vary. Losses to the steady appetite of demand would be continuously restored by the steady flow from the factory room. Indeed, in so smooth a world, the stock of finished goods probably could be held to zero.

If goods were produced in batches, instead of in a continuous stream, the pattern might look like Figure 4–4b. Purchased materials in stock would fall while the mills were running, and the supply would just fill the need. While the mills were down, no purchased materials would be needed, and the stock would not be replenished until production got under way again. Assuming the mills could achieve full production immediately and could close without delay, goods in process would be measured by the flow of materials moving through the mills while they were running. Once the run was over, all goods in process would have

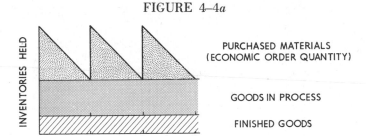

FIGURE 4-4a

FIGURE 4-4b

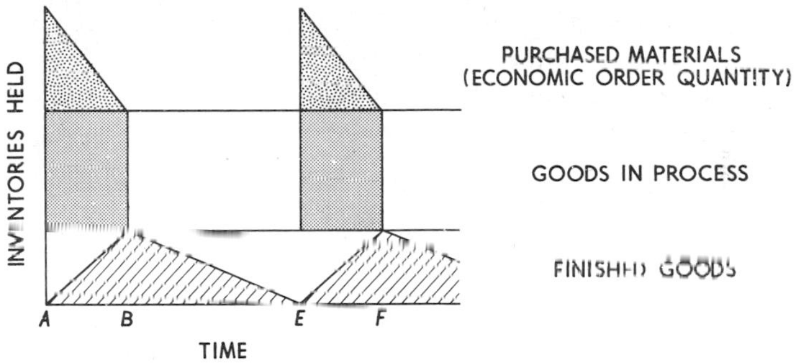

turned into finished goods. The stock of finished goods would be drawn on all the time, from the steady press of consumer demand. While production continued, however, more finished goods would be entering the stock than leaving it. Hence the stock would rise. With the run past and the machines down again, the finished goods inventory would decline.

It must be remembered that Figures 4-4a and 4-4b describe only two of an infinite variety of possible patterns. They do suggest, however, the *types* of interrelationships that must be examined for any given possibility.

QUESTIONS AND PROBLEMS

1. Explain why firms hold inventories of purchased materials. Will they automatically hold smaller amounts under certainty than uncertainty?

2. Suppose that in a world of certainty, demand for your product has been averaging about 1,600 units a week when you land a major new account that raises average demand to 2,500 units a week. Procurement costs continue to run at $50 an order, carrying costs at 10 percent a year, and acquisition costs at $5 a unit. (*a*) What was the optimal order quantity

before the change in demand and (*b*) what is it now that demand is higher?

3. If the change in demand described in Question No. 2 is part of a general rise in demand, it may be accompanied by a rise in carrying costs. (*a*) What is the optimal size order under these conditions? (*b*) What would be the effect if acquisition costs rose to $5.50 a unit? (*c*) And if procurement costs moved to $55 an order?

4. In each of the various circumstances of Questions No. 2 and No. 3, (*a*) What would be the effect on the average inventory held by the firm? and (*b*) How often should reorders be placed?

5. You must place your order now for a special variety of spruce tree that turns silver on the morning of December 24. You know from experience that these are bought by husbands who want nothing else but who forget until the last minute. The trees will cost you $1 each (they are very small), and you can sell them to the husbands for $5 each. If you have any left after Christmas, you can sell them for 20 cents apiece to commercial artists who design wallpaper.

   From earlier years you estimate a 0.60 probability that the demand will be for 100 trees, a 0.25 probability for 110 trees, a 0.10 for 120 trees, and 0.05 for 130 trees. If you run short of trees, it is usually possible to find another 30 or 40 of them in a neighboring town at a cost of $3.50 each.

   a) Assuming you will avoid completely the loss of goodwill, show how you would use a payoff matrix to choose your strategy.

   b) On the same assumption, show how you might find the answer with a cost matrix.

   c) Suppose you did not act to avoid all of the goodwill loss. What range of cost estimates for this loss would give the same choice among strategies?

   d) How does this decision relate to the ultimate aims of financial management? Be sure to explain fully your answer.

SUGGESTED READINGS

FETTER, ROBERT F., and DALLECK, WINSTON C. *Decision Models for Inventory Management.* Homewood, Ill.: Richard D. Irwin, Inc., 1964.

SNYDER, ARTHUR. "Principles of Inventory Management," *Financial Executive,* April, 1964. Reprinted in JAMES VAN HORNE (ed.), *Foundations for Financial Management,* Homewood, Ill.: Richard D. Irwin, Inc., 1966.

STARR, MARTIN K., and MILLER, DAVID W. *Inventory Control: Theory and Practice.* Englewood Cliffs, N.J.: Prentice-Hall, Inc., 1962.

STOCKTON, R. STANSBURY. *Basic Inventory Systems: Concepts Analysis.* Boston: Allyn & Bacon, 1965.

Chapter 5

INVENTORY BEHAVIOR: CYCLE THEORIES AND EMPIRICAL EVIDENCE

In trying to measure the actual behavior of business inventories, it has been necessary to look at business firms as a group. That is the form the data take. Moreover, the chief investigators have been economists studying the business cycle in the economy at large.

By its nature, however, this probing of group behavior has led economists to form hypotheses about the response of individual companies when faced with change. In this way, economists have hoped to understand how the decisions of the many could emerge to make the mass performance that is evident in the figures for the business community as a whole.

As we shall see, most of the thinking on the subject has assigned the dominant role to customer demand. This is particularly true of attempts to explain *changes* in inventories. Bit parts are given to other possible determinants—interest rates, procurement costs, and the like. But by and large it is only in the most recent research efforts that these other forces are treated as anything but minor modifiers.

THE BASIC ACCELERATOR

The simplest model employed by economists in this quest has been the *acceleration principle*. In this formulation, businessmen are assumed to tie their inventory decisions almost entirely to the level of expected sales. They are assumed to have a target ratio of inventory stocks to sales, and to direct their fire at this target without wavering.

Accordingly, an increase in sales has a double effect: (1) it increases the flow of inventories needed to supply the new level of sales; and (2) it requires additional inventories to raise the stock up to the new, higher level needed to reach the target ratio of stocks to sales. The first effect is a continuing one, lasting as long as sales stay on the new plateau. The second effect soon fades away.

Suppose, for example, that sales have run along for a while at 100, and then suddenly move up to 120. A firm that attempted to keep its average inventories of raw materials at about double its sales would then require a stock of 240 instead of the former 200. Under these new circumstances, it could meet its need by stepping up its purchases of inventories by an additional 60—of which 20 would supply the sales increase and the other 40 would provide the enlargement of stocks now called for. That adjustment once made, however, the new level of sales would require purchases only 20 higher than before the change in circumstances. Thus, inventory purchases which had shot up from 100 to 160 (in order to supply the current higher sales of 120 and the inventory increase of 40) would drop back to 120.

1. Inventory Stocks and Inventory Flows

To see what the acceleration principle implies for patterns during a business cycle, we look first at the relationship between the stock of inventories and the flow of expenditures for inventories. This relationship is illustrated in Figure 5–1.

The top curve shows the movement of the stock of inventories over the cycle, and to make the example simple, it is both smooth and symmetrical. This top curve moves through four stages. It first rises at an increasing pace, then rises further but at a slower and indeed declining rate. For example, the numbers 1, 3, and 8 are moving up in ever larger leaps, while the numbers 12, 15, and 16 are still rising but by smaller and smaller increments. Then, in the third stage, the curve turns down and falls at an increasing rate and then at a declining rate. The ends of the first and third stages thus mark a change in the *rate* of movement without a change in direction.

The implications of this pattern are brought out in the lower half of the figure, which shows the *change* in the stock of inventories. That is, it measures the amount added to total inventories or subtracted from them at each step of the way. It makes clear that the amount being added to inventories rises during the first stage, but turns down as soon as the total curve is no longer rising at an increasing rate. The amount being added is

FIGURE 5–1

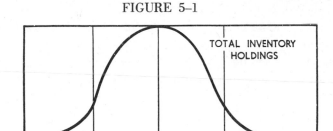

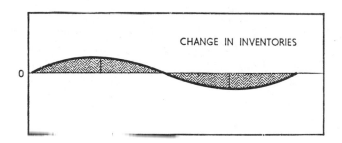

still positive in this second stage. It is, however, an increasingly smaller amount. When the total inventory reaches a peak and turns down, the curve showing changes breaks through the zero line and descends into the negative area. Inventories are being decumulated. With the passage of the total stock curve into the fourth stage, inventory holdings are still being reduced, but in steadily smaller amounts. Accordingly, the lower curve, while still in the negative area, moves back toward zero.

What does this process imply for the flow of spending for inventory acquisitions? It tells us that this pattern of spending will be *superimposed* on the flow of purchases necessary to supply current sales. What we have just examined are the purchases made to change the *stock* of inventories. All the while, *sales* have also been changing, and inventories have been acquired to fill these current needs as well. The economic impact of these current sales is simply passed through the business concern in question. It is the demand for *extra* inventories to maintain the firm's target ratio of stocks and sales that augments the initial change in customer demand.

2. The Timing of Inventory Change

The critical assumption at this point is the timing of the inventory response.

If businessmen are able to adjust instantly to changes in customer demand, their inventory stocks will move up and down in perfect congruence with fluctuations in sales. We can see what this implies by looking again at Figure 5–1 and supposing that the upper panel also represents the general business cycle in sales. The trough is at the far left, the peak and upper turning point at the center, and so on. This pattern of customer demand will be transmitted through the particular firm to its raw materials supplier in the form of demand for inventories for current use.

The firm will have, however, its own demand for inventories, in order to change the volume of its holdings. And the turning points of this demand will *precede* those of the demand that is simply passed through from customers. As Figure 5–1 makes clear, the extra flow of spending for inventories will lead by one quarter of a cycle. It will reach its upper turning point as the general cycle is still rising, and its lower turning point while the general cycle is still falling. Following this pattern, inventory spending will serve to stabilize the economy. It will dampen the general upswing and dampen the general downswing.

TABLE 5–1

	Sales	Stock	Purchases For Current Sales	For Change in Stock		Total
Trough	100	200	100	. . .		. . .
	101	202	101	2		103
	103	206	103	4	Peak	107
Peak	104	208	104	2		106
	103	206	103	−2		101
	101	202	101	−4	Trough	97
Trough	100	200	100	−2		98

To illustrate, suppose sales moved through the expansion and contraction shown in the column at the left in Table 5–1. A stock/sales ratio of two to one would give the patterns in purchases shown in the table. The peaks and troughs in purchases would come one period in advance of those in sales.

But all this assumes instant adjustment of inventory stocks. Suppose we abandon that assumption. It seems more likely, in fact, that businessmen will not respond immediately. An increase in customer buying, for example, may appear at first to be only a temporary surge. And even after the demand increase has been recognized, lags may develop in production and delivery of new goods.

If there is a lag in reaction, we may expect the patterns shown in

Figure 5–2. With the rise and fall of sales from four million to eight million and back, the desired level of inventories swings up from eight million to sixteen million and back. That is, the target ratio of stocks to sales is two to one. The effect of the lagged response, however, is to shift the curve of actual inventory holdings to the right of the desired curve. Moreover—and this is a major point—if the lag in inventories is about one quarter of the cycle, as assumed in Figure 5–2, the cycle of *extra* spending, aimed at the rebuilding of inventory stocks, will *coincide exactly* with the cycle of sales themselves.

(This is important to the general study of business cycles because it explains how inventory movements that might appear to be simply responding to changes in demand are in fact contributing directly to the overall cycle of economic activity. If the lag is *less* than one quarter of the cycle, then changes in inventories will occur ahead of the turn in sales. But if there is any lag, inventories which are laid up to help stabilize the activities of a single firm are likely to create instability for the economy as a whole and ultimately for that single firm as well.)

FIGURE 5–2

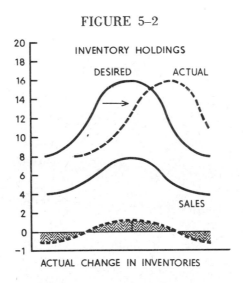

THE VARIABLE ACCELERATOR

The stiff rule of a fixed stock/sales ratio has long been a source of uneasiness among economists working with the acceleration principle. From this uneasiness has come the suggestion that the target ratio of stocks to sales is itself subject to change.

1. Deliberate Lag

In its pristine form, the variable accelerator model does not discard the idea of a fixed and constant target of stocks to sales. It assumes rather that business concerns will not try to achieve the target *immediately* after customer demand has changed. Instead, they will move to close only part of the gap between actual holdings and the new desired level of holdings.

When sales expand, for example, they will tolerate a decline in the ratio because an effort to restore the ratio immediately would bring its own problems. One of these problems is suggested by the need for what is called "production-smoothing"—avoiding the extra expense of sharply increasing output by letting the brunt of the changed demand fall on inventory stocks rather than on the production process. Also, if the economic order quantity is large, and hence infrequently placed, this may be another reason for businessmen not to try to adjust stocks immediately upon an increase in demand.

Indeed, as we have seen earlier, a carefully thought-out policy will enable a firm to absorb surprise changes in sales without hurry-up orders to replenish the second bin. Only when demand begins to average higher than the mathematically expected level will the policy need to be changed. For only then will cost minimization be achieved by larger holdings of inventories.

2. Change in Target

It may be, however, that the target itself will change over the cycle. This possibility, it should be realized, is very different from the pure form of variable accelerator which envisions only that businessmen are willing temporarily to let the stock/sales ratio drift away from the desired level. It is instead the suggestion that events will change the desired level itself. Several forces may bring this about:

a) The square root formulation developed in the previous chapter tells us that higher sales will not bring a proportional increase in desired levels of inventories. Thus, even after demand rises above the mathematically expected level—or after production has been increased in an orderly fashion—the new, higher level of inventories sought by management will not have increased as much as sales have.

b) The carrying cost may change over the business cycle. If it rises with the advance in sales—a typical business cycle pattern—it will press down the economic order quantity and, as a consequence, the average level of stocks desired.

c) The procurement cost may also move with the cycle. It probably will increase with the general upswing, but unless it rises fast enough to offset the advance in carrying cost the result will still be a decline in the desired ratio of stocks to sales.

d) "Speculative" increases in inventory holdings may occur in expectation of rising prices for the inventory goods in the supply market (or, what is essentially the same thing, in anticipation of shortages of these goods). Similar advance buildups may be undertaken when demand and prices are expected to move up in the customer market. In either case, when the rise in sales does come, it will not be accompanied by a rise in inventories. The stock/sales ratio will already have moved up in expectation, and with the advance in sales the ratio may actually fall.

WHAT ARE THE FACTS?

As is so often the case, the facts are ambiguous. Finding the truth underneath the data available to us is a task bedeviled by (*a*) the problem of changing prices, (*b*) the problem of aggregation and (*c*) the problem of interdependence.

Price changes make trouble because inventory figures are reported from accounting records. For reasons spelled out in the appendix to this chapter, a period of rising prices may create a picture of rising inventory holdings when in fact the physical amounts are being reduced. The difficulty is to find the appropriate deflators for such a conglomerate as the inventory holdings of a whole industry. The difficulty is great indeed.

The aggregation problem is simply that our theories are for individual firms, while our data are for large numbers of firms taken together. Since firms deal with one another, a rise in stocks at one company often stems directly from a reduction in another. Conditions in both companies will now be different, but the figures will show no change in inventory holdings. This becomes important because companies in one part of an industry will have one pattern of behavior and those elsewhere different patterns. These distinctions are not only lost to view but when mingled in the mass data they may suggest patterns that no one practices.

The problem of interdependence refers to the *inter*action between inventory investment and ultimate demand. The models we have examined concentrate on business response to customer demand. They take no account of new consumer demand created by business buying. Models have been developed, of course, to incorporate this feedback, but they require still other theories. This adds more complexity to the detective work and more ambiguity to the findings.

Looking at the empirical research that has been done, we find a large part of it centered on manufacturers' inventories. For one thing, these stocks account for three fifths or better of all inventories held by United States firms. Another reason for emphasis is the great volatility these stocks display over the business cycle, to point of being a major force in generating cycles.

The relative standing of manufacturing corporations as holders of inventories may be seen in the figures given in Table 5–2 for corporations in a recent year.

TABLE 5–2

CORPORATE HOLDING OF INVENTORIES,
END OF YEAR 1962–63
(Millions of Dollars)

Manufacturing	60,941
Trade, retail	16,776
Trade, wholesale	13,113
Transportation, communication, and utilities	3,112
Construction	2,559
Services	1,112
Mining	1,004
Agriculture	632
Finance	231
Total	100,327

SOURCE: U.S. Treasury Department, *Statistics of Income—Corporate Income Tax Returns.*

The special volatility of manufacturers' inventories is pointed up in Figure 5–3. In 1960, for example, the decline in inventory investment by manufacturers accounted for over three fourths of the cutback in total inventory investment.

In seeking an explanation of this strong cyclical tendency of manufacturing inventories, it is well to remember that we are speaking here of inventories in three different stages of fabrication. Some idea of the diversity introduced by these different stages—purchased materials, goods in process, finished goods—may be gained from looking at Figure 5–4, which shows inventory stocks, as distinct from the *changes* in stocks shown in the preceding chart. The difference between the inventory habits of producers of durable goods and those of producers of nondurables is striking. Note, for example, the contrasting importance of goods in process in the two sectors. The chart also makes clear the much wider swings in durable goods inventories at all stages.

Despite this heterogeneity of inventory practice, some generalizations can nonetheless be made about the cyclical behavior of inventories in

FIGURE 5–3

INVENTORY INVESTMENT, 1947–66

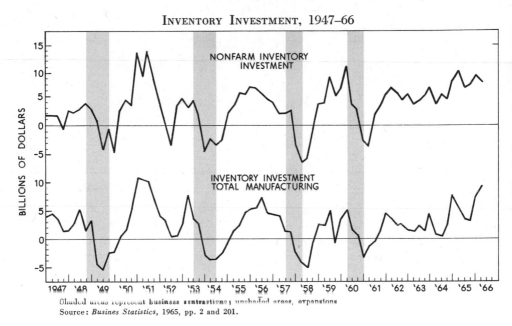

Source: *Busines Statistics*, 1965, pp. 2 and 201.

FIGURE 5–4

MANUFACTURING INDUSTRIES: INVENTORIES, BY STAGE OF FABRICATION

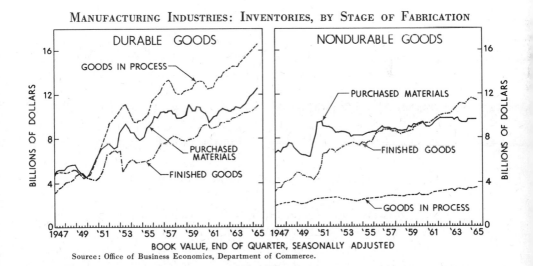

Source: Office of Business Economics, Department of Commerce.

different stages of fabrication. Keeping it simple, we can focus on inventory *investment*, i.e., on changes in the level of inventory holdings. The first generalization is that the cyclical turns in investment in goods in process tend to come before the turns in finished goods investment. This is what our earlier discussion would lead us to expect. The firm has its most complete control over goods in process. This is the thing it can change with least delay. Its finished goods, on the other hand, cannot be restocked immediately if sales should pick up. Nor are they likely to be unloaded quickly when sales fall off. Hence, it is only after the production process has been cut back for a while, or speeded up for a while, that finished goods inventories can begin to overcome the original surprise and then move to the new desired level.

The second generalization is that investment in goods in process tends to turn either at the same time as investment in purchased materials or somewhat in advance of it. This, too, we might have expected. The tendency for turns in purchased materials to lag behind goods in process has an explanation parallel to the one just offered for the lag in finished goods inventories. With a rise or fall in sales, and a consequent change in goods in process, orders for purchased materials can be stepped up or cut back. But there may be some delay in getting immediate delivery when orders are increased. Or it may be impossible to cancel some orders already placed but not yet delivered.

The occasions on which investment in purchased materials has *not* lagged behind goods in process require special explanation. They appear to reflect the backlog of unfilled orders at the firm under consideration. For many companies an important part of production is carried on to fill specific orders that customers have placed. As the book of unfilled orders begins to grow thin, the firm will begin to gear itself down toward lower levels of production. Hence, its investment in purchased materials will move closely with its investment in goods in process.

How do all these movements in the inventory investment of manufacturers relate to the turning points in general economic activity?

Taking all types together, manufacturing inventory investment has, in the postwar years, either coincided with the general turns or preceded them. This pattern is evident in Figure 5–3. Investment in goods in process has led in every case, but the delayed reaction of investment in purchased materials, and particularly in finished goods, has slowed the turn in total inventory investment.

Putting the record in terms of stocks rather than flows, we find that manufacturers' holdings of inventories of all kinds have lagged the cyclical turns in general business by one to eight months.

Does this overall cyclical pattern favor either of the models examined earlier? No. It is consistent with either one. In the basic accelerator model, a delayed response to changes in demand would generate the pattern observed in the figures. Thus the aggregate data do not rule out the possibility of a fixed accelerator either, since it too would show inventory stocks not rising and falling directly with sales. The possibility of a changing target ratio also remains in the running.

Perhaps the answer will never be definitive, but recent evidence has given the edge to the flexible accelerator. The U.S. Department of Commerce has been taking quarterly surveys of manufacturers' expectations and plans since 1957. From the evidence, it now appears that manufacturers as a group can forecast their sales with relatively small error. It also appears from these data that when sales outstrip their expectations, manufacturers can nevertheless adjust their production and procurement rapidly enough to meet the higher demand and to increase their stocks of finished goods after meeting the demand.

Consequently, it seems possible that when the economy is moving up, the failure of stocks to rise as rapidly as sales may not be so much a failure as it is a choice being made by the manufacturers themselves. They seem to be comfortable with a lower stock/sales ratio. They may even be seeking it. This, as we have seen, is the basic assumption of the flexible accelerator.

It is also relevant that after the upswing has continued for a while manufacturers push the stock/sales ratio back up again. That is, with sales continuing to rise, inventory holdings are increased at a more rapid pace. Moreover, since this rise in the ratio comes well in advance of the next downturn in the economy, it can be assumed to be intentional. These patterns may be seen in Figure 5–5.

Is there other evidence on the point? And is there evidence pointing out which forces have the greatest influence in restraining inventory accumulation and decumulation when sales are rising and falling? Again, we may note the several forces suggested earlier, and ask what the data show. And the handful of evidence we have suggests the existence of a variable accelerator:

a) The square root definitely seems to have been at work over the longer run (though hardly visible in the data shown in Figure 5–5). Some part of the trend is doubtless traceable to better record-keeping and better control procedures, but not all of it. In any case, the square root effect dampens swings in the desired level of inventory holdings during both the upsurge of sales and the dropping off of them.

b) The carrying cost has been much scorned as an explanation of inventory behavior. In particular, empirical studies of the effects of interest rates have largely rejected this explanation. More recently, however, it has been argued that the earlier studies were looking in the wrong

FIGURE 5–5

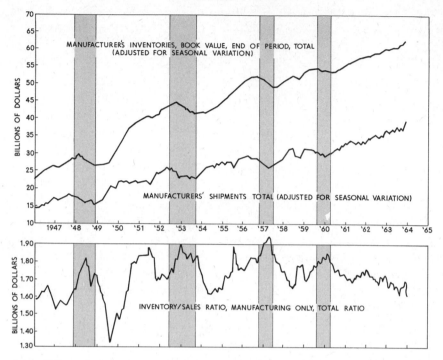

place. When the cost of capital is seen more broadly than in these earlier explorations, it appears to take on considerable influence.

c) The procurement cost has hardly been studied at all, and one can only theorize.

d) Price speculation as a determinant of inventory decisions has found very little support in econometric studies. Particular episodes have occurred, to be sure, but as a general phenomenon, responses to price expectation appear to have played a very minor role.

In any case, it seems hard to disagree with the observation that the "solo theme of sales, however enriched by accompaniment, needs to be recast as a duet in which expectations about market conditions and the entire complex of business choices may have an equal voice."

APPENDIX TO CHAPTER 5
INVENTORIES AND CHANGING PRICES

When prices are changing, should the inventory stocks put into production be valued at the old price or the new one? The answer can make quite a difference, since the value assigned to such stocks will influence the level of costs and expenses, which in turn will affect profits before taxes, and hence profits after taxes, dividends, and retained earnings.

In the actual workaday treatment of inventories, the question tends to be asked from the opposite direction. That is, it focuses on the proper valuation of the inventory goods remaining on hand at the end of the period, rather than on those consumed in the production process during the period. But the two views are only mirror images of one another, as the following equational identity makes clear:

Opening Inventories + Stocks Purchased during the Period = Inventories Used Up + Inventories Remaining at the End of the Period

The left-hand side of the equation gives, roughly speaking, the sources of the firm's inventories, and the right-hand side gives the uses to which they are put. Since the dollar value of both items on the left is simply a matter of factual record, the *total* value of the uses side is already decided. What has not been automatically established is the allocation of this total between the right-hand items, i.e., the flow that occurred during the period and the stock on hand at the end of the period. As noted, the emphasis typically falls on the proper valuation for the stock component, the inventories on hand when the accounts are closed.

The valuation of these closing inventories requires answers to two subordinate questions: (1) how to decide which of the inventories remain at the year-end and (2) how to ascribe a value to the stocks identified as still on hand at that time. Accounting theorists and practitioners have devised a number of ingenious answers to these questions; but in general, the systems they have invented belong either to a family headed by FIFO or to a second family headed by LIFO.

THE PRACTICE OF FIFO (FIRST IN, FIRST OUT)

Under this general family of practices, the stocks assumed to be on hand at the close of the period are, quite simply, those that were bought last. By the same token, inventory goods used up during the year are assumed to have been those that had been in the company's possession for the longest time. It is as if inventory goods were, upon arrival within the company walls, to be placed on a long conveyor belt that gradually fed them into the maws of production. The stocks entering the production process during the year would be those acquired at the earliest point in time. They would add to total operating costs whatever amount had been paid for them at the time they were first acquired and put onto the conveyor belt—however long ago that might have been and however much the purchase price of them might have changed in the meantime. The stocks still on the conveyor belt at year-end, whenever acquired, would therefore be regarded as the closing inventory.

This is the answer given by FIFO to the first question on valuation. It can be illustrated by the following example:

Suppose a company opened the year with 500 "widgets" on hand and purchased an additional 300 of them during the succeeding 12 months. Suppose further that out of this total of 800 widgets, it burned up 400 in the course of productive activities, thus leaving 400 others on hand at the close of the year. If there was no change in the purchase price of widgets during the time, there would be no problem of valuation. Therefore (in order to have a problem), let us assume that the 500 widgets held when the year began had all been bought for $1.00 each, while those acquired during the year cost $1.20 each.

Under these conditions, as shown in the equation below, the opening inventory would be valued at $500, and the goods purchased during the year would be valued at $360. The total for the left side of the equation would thus be $860.

To divide this amount appropriately between the two items on the right-hand side, the FIFO rules require that the cost of goods used during the year be figured first. Since the goods on hand at the start of the year are already on the conveyor belt, they are assumed to enter production first. The 400 widgets absorbed into production during the year are thus drawn from the 500 widgets held in the opening inventory. Since they cost $1.00 each, the cost of inventories burned up during the year thus becomes $400. This leaves in the closing inventory the remaining 100 of the original 500 widgets, plus the 300 new widgets acquired during the course of the year. At costs of $1.00 and $1.20 each, respectively, the inventories remaining at year-end are assumed to be worth $100 and $360, for a total of $460. The equation thus balances, with goods totaling $860 on either side. This whole example may be shown schematically, as follows:

Opening	+	Purchased	=	Used	+	Closing
500 widgets @ $1.00		300 widgets @ $1.20		400 widgets @ $1.00		400 widgets: 100 @ $1.00 ($100) 300 @ $1.20 ($360)
$500		$360		$400		$460

To carry the illustration a step further, suppose that prices rise more rapidly, with the result that purchased inventory is valued at $1.50 per widget. This will have two effects. It will increase the value of the purchased inventory. But since these more expensive goods will by assumption enter production *after* those acquired earlier, at lower prices, the changed situation will also increase the valuation of goods held in the closing inventory. This slight alteration in the example can also be made clearer in schematic form:

Opening	+	Purchased	=	Used	+	Closing
500 @ $1.00		300 @ $1.50		400 @ $1.00		100 @ $1.00 ($100)
						300 @ $1.50 ($450)
$500		$450		$400		$550

Now, notice carefully what has happened with the change in assumption. The value of the opening inventory has remained the same, and the purchased inventory now draws a different valuation, as an automatic result of the new assumption. But on the right-hand side the full brunt of the change is borne by inventories remaining at the end of the production period. None of the effect of the rising price of goods in the preceding period is carried into costs and expenses. These remain the same. Since the sales prices are also likely to be rising, so will sales revenues be advancing. The unchanged level of costs will thus mean a higher level of profits (and of taxes).

The FIFO path is followed chiefly in the name of conservatism, even if, paradoxically, it may tend to exaggerate a company's profits. It is a course directed toward cautious valuation of the balance sheet entry for inventories. It is a careful effort to avoid overstating the firm's assets; and as such, it is the product of highly responsible thinking.

Indeed, the most common forms of FIFO accounting go still another step in conservatism. For in answer to the second of the two subordinate questions posed earlier, the typical form of FIFO not only embraces historical costs in assigning values to the closing inventory, as was done in the examples. Playing things even safer yet, the usual practitioner of FIFO wants also to know the current market price of these goods, and will use either this or historical cost, whichever of the two is lower. The justification is again a concern for the balance sheet, where the fundamental rule is to anticipate losses, but never to count gains until they have been realized in actual revenues.

Without dwelling on the matter, it should perhaps also be noted that the value of closing inventories is colored as well by the manner in which "cost" is defined. There is little difficulty with goods purchased directly from outside. The problems arise with items already processed within the company's own operation, and carried as goods in process or finished goods. The matter rests essentially, however, in the hands of cost accountants. It is not easy, even working from a wealth of careful records, to assign overhead costs to a given time period, or to allocate such costs among the different activities occurring within any one period. Someone must attempt it, and it is often done with great skill; but quite obviously, there can be wide variations in practice. There are, accordingly, wide variations in the values ascribed to inventories not actually bought in the marketplace.

One should note further that the writing-down of closing inventory to current market value has two important effects. First, it throws more of the inventory cost back into current expenses. If prices are also falling in the market for the firm's finished goods, this conservative practice serves to push up expenses at the very time that revenues are drifting down. Conservatism thereby brings reported profits down an even steeper slope than would straight FIFO at cost.

The second effect is to ring in the new year with a lower valuation for the opening inventory. With a continuing slide in prices during the year, this effect would have little significance. With a turnaround in prices, it would hold down expenses and throw much of the increase in sales money into the profit column. In short, the practice of writing down to market level will exaggerate the roller coaster tendencies already inherent in FIFO accounting.

THE PRACTICE OF LIFO (LAST IN, FIRST OUT)

The essence of FIFO accounting is stated in the metaphor of a conveyor belt, and it seems a reasonable enough approach. As is the way of metaphors, however, one can think up others that have entirely different implications and yet seem equally persuasive. In a heavily stocked wine cellar, for example, the handiest bottles are those near the head of the stairs. As new bottles are acquired to replenish the stock, they go into these same racks. The basic, continuing supply thus remains untouched. The safety stock—the stock of bottles stored far from the top step—is not dipped into for year upon year.

In the wine cellar metaphor we find the essence of LIFO accounting. Yet a moment's reflection will make clear that it is fundamentally different from the notion of a conveyor belt. Under the LIFO system a firm's opening inventories consist of those bottles stored back under the building, plus any unused bottles in the caches along the stairwell. In the same way, the closing stocks include the stores far back in the shadow and anything not yet taken from the racks by the stairs. Accordingly, the inventories used during the year will be chiefly those that have moved into and out of the racks nearest the stair head. These will, of course, have been acquired at prices prevailing during the year. The inventory cost of operations will thus reflect price levels that are current or very nearly current.

This can be illustrated by shifting our widget maker over to LIFO. As before, the company has 500 widgets on hand at the beginning of the year, acquires an additional 300, uses up 400, and is left at the end of the year with 400 on hand. The opening inventory and the purchases during the year are valued just as before. As shown in the equation below, the 500 widgets are carried at $1.00 each and the 300 added during the year at $1.20 each.

The inventories consumed by the productive process during the year are regarded as having come first out of the new acquisitions. Accordingly, the 400 widgets used during the year consist of the 300 bought during the year at $1.20 each, plus an additional 100 valued at $1.00 each and held in readiness in the extra bin. The cost of all inventories used in production thus totals $460. The 400 widgets still left in the extra bin are the closing inventory. At $1.00 each they give a total valuation of $400.

Opening	+	*Purchased*	=	*Used*	+	*Closing*
500 widgets @ $1.00		300 widgets @ $1.20		400 widgets: 300 @ $1.20 ($360) 100 @ $1.00 ($100)		400 widgets @ $1.00
$500		$360		$460		$400

The difference between the two systems can be further pointed up by carrying the illustration through the same additional step as in the earlier example. Suppose, that is, that prices had risen more sharply during the year—to $1.50—and that all inventories purchased during the year had been acquired at that price. The opening inventory is of course carried at the same valuation, while the value of purchased stocks now rises to $450.

On the other side of the equation, the closing inventory is unchanged in value, but the figure for inventories used in production goes up by the full amount of the additional price rise. As a result—and this is the crux of the matter—current costs are made to reflect something very close to the current market cost of inventories. The firm thus avoids the emergence of "fictitious" accounting profits resulting from a failure to reflect recent changes in prices.

Opening	+ Purchased	=	Used	+	Closing
500 @ $1.00	300 @ $1.50		300 @ $1.50 ($450)		400 @ $1.00
			100 @ $1.00 ($100)		
$500	$450		$550		$400

In the tax laws as now written, the choice of valuing the closing inventory at the lower of cost or market is not open to a firm practicing LIFO. In the example at hand, the choice would be an empty one, even if granted. The market has already risen above the cost. If market prices were to turn down late in the year, however, and fall below $1.00 per widget, a revaluation of closing inventory to reflect this change would give the firm a further tax advantage. To shave down the valuation of these inventories would at the same time raise the valuation of inventories used in production. With this increase in expenses, reported profits would fall and so, of course, would the tax take. A company on LIFO would thus have had the best of both worlds. Its profits and taxes would have been damped down in years when FIFO firms were suffering a rise in tax payments. It would, in addition, enjoy much of tax decline experienced by FIFO firms as prices fell.

CHOICE BETWEEN LIFO AND FIFO

Inventory accounting on the LIFO model has been widely adopted. It appears, however, that the bulk of American corporations still favor FIFO. Even in those industries in which LIFO is most prevalent, a larger proportion of inventories is valued by FIFO than by LIFO.[1] What explains this choice?

The central disadvantage of FIFO relative to LIFO is that it permits large and disruptive swings in reported profits. For some businesses, this central fact about FIFO is sufficiently damning in itself. Profits reported by such a method may be misleading as a guide to management decisions. More cash is needed to replace inventories at rising prices. In fact, there

---

[1] American Institute of Certified Public Accountants, *Accounting Trends and Techniques* (New York, annual issues); Internal Revenue Service, U.S. Treasury, *Statistics of Income* (Washington, D.C., annual issues). See also J. Keith Butters, *Effects of Taxation: Inventory Accounting and Policies* (Boston: Graduate School of Business Administration, Harvard University, 1949).

may be extra cash coming in. But it gets labeled as profits and then is dissipated in other ways.

The apparent swelling of profits may, for example, induce an expansion of operations when, in fact, all the additional cash is needed just to maintain the old level of activity. The overstatement of profits may, in addition, stir up unfounded expectations among stockholders and employees. And other entrepreneurs may be induced to enter the competition for the apparently higher profits.

But the greatest harm from a fictitiously high profit report is the increased bite of income taxes. This is more significant partly because the bite is large at present tax rates, but perhaps even more because it is a certainty. Where stockholders and trade unions may be fought off, or at least negotiated with, the tax collector will automatically take his pound of flesh.

For some industries, none of these considerations is compelling. Some types of economic activity do not require a firm to hold much in the way of inventories. The differential costs of inventories are completely swamped by other costs. The differential impact on profits is too small to be worth the effort.

For other companies, even those with large inventories relative to total assets, there may be other objections to LIFO. Some firms decide against it because of real or fancied administrative red tape that it may involve. For others there are perhaps three main considerations. These are (1) their general expectations of price behavior, (2) the likelihood that their inventories might decline in some future period, and (3) permissibility by tax authorities of what is known as pooling.

If prices are expected to remain stable, then of course a company has little to gain from a shift to LIFO, particularly if its management feels there may be administrative difficulties. This reasoning presumably also holds when prices have gone up but are now expected to remain constant for an indefinite period in the future. Indeed, there may be unhappy transition effects if the price rise has now come to an end, even if it should level off thereafter. The adoption of LIFO would immediately carry into the cost of operation the inventories purchased at recent higher prices, instead of drawing first on opening inventories, which are valued at lower prices. The increased cost would of course not change the volume of revenues. Profits would be dampened, and perhaps even reduced, as a result of only an accounting change, not a different economic position.

If a rise in prices is expected to be followed by a long decline, again a firm might be ill-advised to adopt LIFO accounting. The damage done by adoption at such a time would not be to the income statement but rather to the balance sheet. The inventories still carried on the balance sheet—in effect, those in the second bin—would in time come to look quite excessive, suggesting a large glut of inventories and a poor management of assets. This distortion of the balance sheet might create serious difficulties in borrowing from banks or the public.

If prices are expected to rise and fall intermittently, however, LIFO will offer advantages, particularly if at the same time, tax rates are also expected to rise and fall. With a price cycle of this sort, companies on FIFO will show wider swings in profits than if they had used LIFO accounting. The good years will return to them what the bad years took away, and profits over the long run will be the same as under LIFO. But LIFO has advantages, even so.

To begin with, a wider swing in profits increases the chances of a negative profit, an actual loss. A loss is bad for morale and for the company's public image. Secondly, if the switch to LIFO is made in a year of advancing prices, the firm will retain the extra amount of cash immediately. Cash in hand is worth more than cash that *may* turn up later. Finally, history suggests some tendency for the tax structure to be notched upward in those years when prices are rising. A firm under LIFO is obviously more protected from the ravages of this pattern, since its profits will expand less at such times than will those of a FIFO firm.

The most favorable climate for the adoption of LIFO is a long unbroken spell of price advance. Profits will tend to rise, regardless of inventory accounting. But under LIFO the volume of profits exposed to the tax collector (and to other outsiders thirsting after them) will at all stages be lower than under FIFO.

Even in this most favorable case, a firm may hang back if there seems any possibility of a future cutback in its inventories. The difficulty here is a simple one. It is rooted in the law itself, which prohibits a corporation, once it has elected the LIFO method, from ever turning away. The embrace of LIFO is eternal (subject, of course, to repeal by Congress). Before stepping into anything as long term as that, a corporation must consider the consequences if at some time in the future it should find itself with less inventories at the end of the year than at the beginning. If this were to occur, particularly after a long and steep climb in prices, the cost of goods would suddenly plummet as inventories acquired long ago at much lower prices were drawn into current expenses. Profits, by the same token, would leap sharply upward. So would taxes, and so might dividends and wage demands.

It is this same feature of the law, and this risk attached to dalliance with the method, that gives importance to the question of pooling. If a separate computation had to be made for each type of item held in inventory, the chances would be very great that the stock of at least some items would decline in a particular year. On the other hand, if all items could be considered in a lump, the chances of the level being lower at the end of the year than at the beginning would be very limited. In practice, companies are allowed to take a position somewhere in between these two extremes, and over the years the rulings have permitted increasingly more generous grouping, or pooling, of otherwise disparate items of stock.

QUESTIONS AND PROBLEMS

1. Make up an example to explain how the acceleration principle emphasizes the change in demand rather than the level of demand.

2. Take the numerical example of Table 5–1 and assume that inventory adjustments are not instant as shown there, but instead lag by one period. What would this do to the cyclical pattern of *changes in stock* (the fourth column of Table 5–1)?

3. Again taking the example of Table 5–1, suppose that a variable accelerator was at work, with the target ratio moving down, and then up period by period, as follows:

Sales	Target Ratio of Stock to Sales
100	2.00
101	1.99
103	1.98
104	1.96
103	1.98
101	1.99
100	2.00

What would this do to the pattern of stocks, and of inventory purchases?

4. What would be the effect of combining the circumstances of Question No. 3 with those of Question No. 2—assuming both a lag in adjustment *and* a deliberate dip in the target ratio?

SUGGESTED READINGS

EISNER, ROBERT, and STROTZ, ROBERT. "Determinants of Business Investment," *Impacts of Monetary Policy*, see especially pp. 1–11 and 192–227. Commission on Money and Credit, 1963.

JOINT ECONOMIC COMMITTEE, CONGRESS OF THE UNITED STATES. *Inventory Fluctuations and Economic Stabilization*, Parts I–IV. Washington, D.C., 1961 and 1962.

KUZNETS, PAUL W. "Financial Determinants of Manufacturing Inventory Behavior: A Quarterly Study Based on U.S. Estimates, 1947–1961," *Yale Economic Essays*, Fall, 1964.

LOVELL, MICHAEL. "Determinants of Inventory Investment," *Models of Income Determination*, pp. 177–224. Studies in Income and Wealth, Volume Twenty-eight. New York: National Bureau of Economic Research, 1964.

Chapter 6

BORROWING FROM OTHER BUSINESSES: ACCOUNTS PAYABLE AS A SOURCE OF FUNDS

If a firm can postpone paying for its supplies, then for a time it escapes having to tie up its own money in these inventories. Someone's money will be frozen into those supplies, however, and the someone may exact a fee for the service. We shall discuss further along the nature and cost of this kind of service when supplied by financial institutions. Here, we want to look at the cost of such credit when offered by a nonfinancial firm as a side feature of its primary merchandise.

These credit costs are especially important because of the very large amounts of such borrowing and lending done by the business community. The practice of extending credit to other businesses is very widespread, and the volume of trade credit outstanding has come to account for fully half of all financial assets of business firms. In this chapter, we look at this important matter through borrowers' eyes, and in the next chapter we look through lenders' eyes.

THE STANDARD TERMS OF TRADE CREDIT

Sometimes, trade credit will take the simple form of a grace period following delivery of the goods. That is, the purchaser is not required to pay cash in advance or on delivery, but is expected to settle up within, say, 15 days. In such a case the cost of the credit is buried somewhere in the cost of the goods. It may even be coming out of the seller's profit.

In the more typical case the credit terms are more specific, and the cost to the borrower is easier to calculate. This cost will be determined chiefly by three elements of the arrangement—the rate of discount for early payment, the discount period, and the so-called "net" period. For example, a typical set of terms will (1) offer the buyer a 2 percent discount on the price of the goods if he pays within ten days, but will require him (2) to pay the full price thereafter and (3) to discharge the obligation completely within 30 days after the initial sale. In this illustration the discount is 2 percent, the discount period is ten days, and the net period is 30 days. At this point it should be noted that we are referring, and will be referring, to a trade discount and not a quantity discount—the one is granted for early payment, the other for large purchases.

When the terms are thus explicitly stated, the buyer is, in effect, being offered two commodities in the same package. He is being offered both goods and credit. The cost of the goods can be thought of as the quoted price minus the discount. The cost of the credit is the additional amount he must surrender if he does not pay until the end of the net period. Under the terms in the illustration above, a buyer may get a shipment of goods for $98 by paying within ten days. If he chooses not to pay until the end of the 30-day period, this decision will cost him an additional $2.

This seems little enough to pay for borrowed money—until we translate it into annual rates of interest. In effect, the buyer has borrowed $98 for an additional 20 days, the number of days left in the net period after the discount period has passed. For this 20-day loan, he has paid $2. To see what his *annual* rate of interest is, we ask how many 20-day periods there are in a year, and the answer is, roughly, 18. Hence, his annual rate of interest is not 2/98 but 18 times 2/98—36/98, or slightly more than 36 percent. This is obviously a very high rate of interest.

WHAT THE TERMS IMPLY

Several other important points now come into view.

First, if there is any discount period at all, the buyer can get credit during this period at no evident cost. He may, as noted above, be paying an interest charge that is hidden in the price of the goods. If these are the terms offered him, however, he has no way of avoiding this hidden cost.

Second, even as small a discount as 1 percent in the price of goods can be too expensive to be passed up. In the same example as above, but with a 1 percent discount, the cost would still be 16/99 per annum.

Third, if a firm nevertheless decides not to take the discount, then it should also not pay any of the bill until the very end of the net period. The dollar amount it will have to surrender in payment for the credit has already been fixed. Thus, the longer the firm can put off the final payment, the cheaper the credit will be.

Fourth, as a corollary to the point just made, the credit will grow less expensive to the user as the time lengthens between the end of the discount period and the end of the net period. If, for example, the terms were 1/10, net 90, then the firm that took the full line of credit extended would pay $1 in interest for an 80-day loan of $99. Since a full year includes only four periods of this length, the annual rate of interest would be only 4/99. Even at a discount of 2 percent, the annual rate would be only 8/-99, which is certainly much less frightening than the 36/98 encountered in the first example above. Indeed, a firm might be tempted to let the end of the net period slip past with the bills still unpaid, if it can get away with it. There is the possibility, however, that the supplier will get tough at this point and put the matter in the hands of his lawyers. He might also decide to make credit more expensive the next time, or even insist thereafter on cash in advance. This sort of reaction could raise sharply the cost of credit to the buyer in question.

Finally, something like the reverse of the point just made might be also true at times. A firm may get trade credit for a period longer than it would typically hold the purchased goods in inventory. If so, the trade credit will not only have financed the inventory of the purchasing firm, it will also have financed a part of the company's other expenses. Whether this is the cheapest way to finance these activities depends, of course, on the cost of trade credit and the cost of alternatives. But it is certainly a convenient way. And it may also be relatively inexpensive.

These various points about the cost of trade credit can be made to stand out clearly in a diagram. On the vertical axis of the diagram—shown in Figure 6–1—we measure the cost of credit at an annual rate of interest. Along the horizontal axis is the time elapsed after shipment of the goods by the seller. During the discount period the trade credit is supplied virtually free of charge. If there is any cost, it is hidden in the base price and cannot be avoided at all. This being the case, the purchaser might as well hold off payment until the last possible moment of the discount period, and earn whatever he can on the funds he would otherwise give up immediately.

Once this period has passed, however, the purchaser should be in no hurry to pay up, for the credit then reaches its most expensive point.

FIGURE 6–1

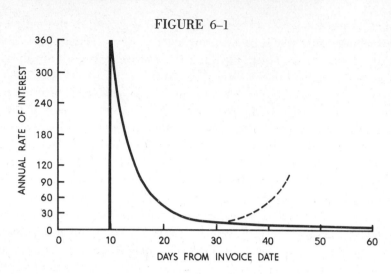

Assuming terms of 1/10, net 30, for example, the shipment that would have cost $99 the day before will now cost $100. If the buyer should pay now—i.e., on the eleventh day after shipment—he would be spending an additional dollar in order to use the funds for a single extra day. Since there are 365 such single-day periods in a year, the *annual* rate of payment for this credit would be $365. And this would be interest paid on a principal of $99, a high rate of interest indeed.

Payment on the following day, the twelfth day after shipment, would also be expensive, but the cost will already have dropped sharply. There are only 180-odd *two*-day periods in a year. The absolute size of the interest payment will still be only $1. The annual rate will thus be only $180-odd on a principal of $99. This is high enough but obviously a pronounced improvement over the one-day rate. As the diagram indicates, the passage of time will bring the rate down to a significantly lower level by the end of the net period of 30 days. As the diagram also makes clear, the rate will fall still further if the net period is stretched beyond this point. It will, in fact, fall indefinitely.

The business lender will of course move to prevent the cost curve from falling indefinitely. The existence of a net period is designed to halt the decline. The mailing of due notices and the placing of follow-up telephone calls and other, stronger reminders will turn the cost curve up again. To be sure, such measures do not raise the cost of credit to the borrower on the bill already outstanding. But failure to pay this bill on time will raise questions about the borrower's ability to pay, and perhaps about his good faith. These doubts will make the supplying firm, and probably other lenders, less willing to finance the delinquent firm in the future.

The rising segment of the cost curve thus represents future costs that will be levied against *any* amount of trade credit if payment is late on the current bill. This indirect cost is indicated in the diagram by the dotted line rising to the right, after a due date assumed to be the thirtieth day.

Thus, given this modification, the potential user of trade credit should pick one of two points on the curve—the end of the discount period or the low point around the end of the net period. His best choice between these two will be determined by the cost of credit from the cheapest alternative. If that alternative rate lies below the low point of the trade credit cost curve around the end of the net period, the best policy will be to take the discount and borrow from the alternative source in order to make payment on the tenth of the month. If, on the contrary, the rate at the other source is higher than the trade credit rate at the trough of the curve, the trade credit should be used. Any other policies will be more expensive.

IMPLICATIONS FOR A CONTINUING STREAM OF PURCHASES

We can push further into these relationships by looking at what happens to costs over a *series* of time periods. After all, a firm makes new purchases month after month, and each time it starts the credit process anew.

To illustrate, let us say that our firm buys supplies, month in and month out, at a total cost of $100, as listed on the invoices. The supplier offers a discount of 1 percent for payment by the tenth of the month, but our firm chooses not to take advantage of the offer. Instead it "borrows" $99 and pays another $1 in "interest" at the time of settlement.

To see what this decision will cost the firm, we must know the length of the net period. The effect of different net periods may be seen in the upper panel of Table 6–1, which shows the accounts payable that are outstanding at the end of each month. Goods bought in April must be fully paid for by the end of May—i.e., a net of 30 days. Hence the volume of accounts payable on the books as the end of May approaches is $100. As the last day passes, the payables are paid and go off the books. Similarly, the $100 of goods bought in May produce the $100 in accounts payable to be found outstanding at the end of June.

For shipments made during June, however, the terms are changed. For whatever reasons, the supplier has changed the net period to 60 days. The

TABLE 6-1

Accounts Payable Outstanding at End of Month

Net Period	Purchases Made by End of Month	May	June	July	Aug.	Sept.	Oct.	Nov.	Dec.
30 days	April	$100							
	May		$100						
60 days	June			$100	100				
	July				$100	100			
90 days	August					$100	100	100	
	September						$100	100	100
	October							$100	100
	November								$100
	Total A/P outs	$100	$100	$100	$200	$200	$200	$300	$300
	"Principal" repaid	99	99	0	99	99	0	99	99
	"Interest" paid on $99 borrowed: For 20 days — For 50 days — For 80 days	1	1	0	1	1	0	1	1
	Annual rate of interest paid 1/$99 times— $\frac{360}{20}$ (or 18)	$\frac{18}{99}$	$\frac{18}{99}$	0					
	$\frac{360}{50}$ (or 7.2)				$\frac{7.2}{99}$	$\frac{7.2}{99}$	0		
	$\frac{360}{80}$ (or 4.2)							$\frac{4.2}{99}$	$\frac{4.2}{99}$

accounts payable arising out of the June invoices are thus carried on the books through two months, appearing there at the end of July and at the end of August.

Then, with the coming of August, the terms are lengthened again (we dare not ask what is going on inside the supplying firm) and our company finds the August shipments will not have to be paid for until 90 days afterward. The August purchases will thus produce payables on the books at the end of September, at the end of October and again at the end of November. Likewise, for goods delivered in September, the payables will remain outstanding for the following three months. And so through the rest of the table.

Notice first what this changing pattern does to the total amount of payables outstanding at a given point in time. As may be seen in the middle panel of Table 6–1, payables on the books are $100 at the end of May, of June, and of July. With purchases made in June, however, the new policy begins and the associated payables remain on the books into August, while the payables generated by July deliveries have also entered the books. The total outstanding thus moves up to $200 in August—*with no change in actual deliveries*. The further lengthening of the net period, starting with deliveries made in August, has its expansive effect in November. Payables outstanding are pushed up to $300, again with no change in shipments of the goods themselves.

Notice also what has happened to the flow of repayments of "principal" and to the associated rate of interest on that indebtedness. In the example shown in the table, the principal to be repaid in May is $99, as a result of total invoices of $100 for goods delivered in April and not discounted. The interest paid for this credit is $1, and it is paid for the use of $99 for a period of 20 days. As there are 18 such time spans in a year of 360 days, the annual rate of interest being paid is 1/99 times 18, or 18/99. These entries may be seen by looking down the column for the month of May.

Moving across the table to look at successive months, it will be seen that in two of the months—July and October—there is neither principal nor interest to be paid. These two months mark the transition to longer net periods, a stretching action that in each case pushes one month's payments forever into the future. Had the policy been changing in the other direction, toward shorter net periods, each transition month would have seen a piling up of two months' payments into one.

Aside from these two transition periods, however, the principal falling due in any one month is always $99, despite the rising volume of indebtedness over the eight months. And, again with the two exceptions, the *amount* of interest also holds steady month in and month out. What does change is the length of time for which the funds are borrowed—20 days in the first phase, 50 in the second, and 80 in the third. Thus, the interest *rate* per unit of time goes down. As may be seen in the bottom panel of the table, the rate per annum falls from 18/99 to 7.2/99, and then to 4.2/99. This, it will be observed, is the same set of answers that turned up when we looked at the credit costs on a single month's purchases.

Looking at an example like this also reminds us of the frequency with which new "loans" are contracted when a business uses trade credit. It also calls attention to the rapidity with which failure to pay on time can make itself felt in the cost of future credit.

TRADE CREDIT AND INVENTORY THEORY

Does the formal analysis of inventory management developed in the preceding chapter have any bearing on the management of accounts payable? The answer is quickly stated. Accounts payable produce a carrying charge. They are a mode of financing an investment in goods or services acquired from a supplier. They are not the only source of finance, but if they are used at all they have an influence on the overall cost of capital which is a large part of the carrying cost to be calculated for inventory decisions.

If accounts payable cost no more than the cheapest alternative source of finance, they are justifiable, assuming of course that they can earn at least as much as they cost. The meaning of "cost" must be construed broadly, as will be analyzed further in later chapters. But in all our discussion of short-term finance we are in a world of suboptimization where these broader meanings are not a problem. If the credit terms of our supplier give us an annual rate of 4.2/99 (that is, about $4\frac{1}{4}$ percent) and our banker insists on an effective rate of 6 percent, we are better off financing with trade credit. Indeed, so long as we can earn better than $4\frac{1}{4}$ percent with the funds we should make maximum use of this source of credit.

It should be noted, however, that decisions about accounts payable also have implications for inventory policy as such. First of all, if a discount is offered, the acquisition cost of the goods is thereby lower—whether the firm takes the discount or not. If the firm does choose to take the discount, the carrying cost on those inventories is computed quite independently of the trade credit arrangement. If on the contrary the firm does not take the discount, the carrying cost becomes some combination of the cost of trade credit during the time it is extended and the cost of other financing for as long as the inventories are carried after the end of the net period.

For example, goods selling for $100 with terms of 1/10/60 have an acquisition cost of $99. Should the goods be resold on exactly the sixtieth day, the carrying cost will be exactly the cost of the trade credit—7.2/99 per annum. If the goods must be carried another 60 days before sale, and the firm must pay, let us say, 8.0/99 per annum for capital, then the carrying cost will be the weighted average of these two costs of capital— i.e., 7.6/99 per annum. On the other hand, if the firm can move the goods after, say, 30 days, the carrying cost will be reduced, because the funds can be reinvested during the remaining days of the net period.

What if no discount is offered, but immediate payment is not required? In this case, the acquisition cost is the nominal price of the goods. There is no other way to acquire them except by paying the full price. The carrying cost, however, will not begin until the day payment must be made. If, for example, the bill need not be paid until 15 days after the invoice date, then no money need be tied up in these goods during that time. Only when funds must be forwarded to the supplier does the carrying cost set in.

THE ACTUAL COSTS OF TRADE CREDIT

What are the terms that business firms meet in practice? The question is not easy to answer, partly because of the variety of practice and partly because of the scarcity of statistics on the subject. From various sample surveys, however, we can get some general impressions.

The first thing to note is that many firms do not offer a cash discount at all. Among wholesale concerns, something like a fourth of the firms give no discount, and among manufacturers the proportion may run as high as a third of the companies.[1] This does not mean that all purchases from these firms must necessarily be paid for in cash before delivery. The bulk of their customers will get credit automatically for periods that will typically run to 30 days, but may in some cases run as long as 90 days.[2]

These customers, then, are borrowing from their suppliers, and in some fashion they are paying for this credit. The cost is buried in the price of

---

[1] Roy A. Foulke, *Current Trends in Terms of Sale* (New York: Dun & Bradstreet, 1959), Tables 1, 2, and 3. See also H. Reinhardt, *Terms of Sale and Collection Practices in 32 Industries* (New York: Credit Research Foundation, 1955), p. 4.

[2] *Ibid.*, p. 2.

the goods, however, leaving us—and the buyer—no way of knowing whether the credit is cheap or expensive. The buyers have no choice but to pay the cost, as long as they continue to deal with these suppliers, and their rational course is to pay at the latest possible date. Moreover, they have no decision to make in choosing between this mode of financing credit and some alternative, such as a bank loan.

A second general observation is that when a credit discount is offered, many purchasing firms seem to take advantage of it. It appears, for example, that as many as a third of the retailing firms pay before the end of the discount period. Among manufacturers, over 40 percent of the firms do this; and among wholesalers, over half take the discount.[3] Thus, a very sizable portion of the business population receives trade credit for some period of time without paying the high interest costs discussed earlier.

The length of time for which this "free" credit is offered is typically ten days, particularly when the seller is a manufacturer. Under so-called "proximo" terms the discount period may run somewhat longer, perhaps as much as 15 days. With this arrangement the buyer who receives a shipment after the twenty-fifth of one month can take the discount if he pays by the tenth of the following month. In addition, many sellers apparently accept postdated checks and in general look the other way when their customers use devices to stretch the discount period a few days longer.

In some industries, there is also the special system called "dating" to meet the problem of a pronounced seasonal swing in buying. A manufacturer of sunburn lotion, for example, may want to encourage retailers to commit themselves to precise amounts and prices in February, so that he can get his production geared up well in advance of the summer season. The retailer's inventory is thus being built up for him, and carried for him by the manufacturer. The retailer, however, need pay nothing until his selling season is under way. Then, up to some agreed-on date, he may take a cash discount if he chooses.

Unfortunately, these various forms of free indebtedness are not broken out of the figures on total accounts payable, and we do not know whether the firms that discount are large or small. Hence, we do not know how large a portion of the dollar volume of trade debt is accounted for by this kind of free borrowing.

---

[3] Martin H. Seiden, "Trade Credit: A Quantitative and Qualitative Analysis" (unpublished Ph.D. dissertation; New York: Columbia University, 1962), p. 77.

As a third general point, it is clear that many other firms do not pay during the discount period. These businesses thus commit themselves to the higher cost of trade credit. How high a cost it is depends on (1) the rate of discount they have passed up and (2) the time that elapses between the end of the discount period and the time of final payment.

The predominant discount seems to be 2 percent, although in manufacturing about a third of the firms offering discounts offer only 1 percent.[4] In particular lines the rate is much higher.

The time for which credit is extended after the discount period is typically 20 days—the difference between a standard discount period of ten days and a standard net period of 30 days. However, since the purchasing firm might have been able to crowd a few extra days into the discount period, as mentioned earlier, it can be thought of as paying for, say, 17 days of credit rather than 20 days. This does not reduce the dollar amount it is paying in interest for that credit; hence, the annual rate of interest is pushed up.

The net period, however, may well be longer than the standard 30 days. The practice of dating, for example, implies a long net period.

A fourth general point is that the buyer who partakes of trade credit often pushes it beyond the due date. He makes the net period longer by not paying at the end of it. In one survey, half of the companies extending trade credit allowed customers to be persistently late in payment.[5]

The dollar amount of credit involved here seems to be large, though doubtless the degree of permissiveness will differ at different stages of the cycle and with different competitive pressures within the industry. Indeed, in recent years as much as 18 percent of the trade credit outstanding may have been past due.[6] For credit extended by wholesalers, the proportion past due may have been more than 25 percent. Moreover, a considerable part of the delinquent credit—perhaps as much as a third—appears to have been past due by 60 days or more. Finally, while the portion of past-due accounts that run so far beyond the due date seems relatively steady over the decade of the 1950's and perhaps longer, the past dues have accounted for an almost steadily rising share of total trade credit outstanding.

A fifth general point is that many buyers apparently receive trade

---

[4] Foulke, op. cit.

[5] Reinhardt, op. cit., pp. 6–9.

[6] Martin H. Seiden, The Quality of Trade Credit, Occasional Paper 87 (New York, National Bureau of Economic Research, 1964), pp. 33–35.

credit for a longer period than the purchased goods are held in inventory. This is difficult to establish with certainty, but it seems a reasonable inference from some figures offered in the next section, showing the ratio of payables outstanding to inventories outstanding. Where the amount of trade payables outstanding exceeds the amount of inventories held, it would appear that the firms in question have "borrowed" from their suppliers more than enough to pay for the purchased goods inventories they still hold.

Whether this extra trade credit is expensive or cheap, it is difficult to say. As we have seen, the buyer who does not take the discount should then wait, in his own best interest, until the latest possible date to make payment. This is the cheapest way, regardless of how long he keeps the purchased goods in inventory. The extra trade credit, however, will in effect be financing some other part of the firm's operation, and the question is whether alternative financing for that operation would be less expensive. And the further question is whether a lower interest charge on such alternative financing would offset the increase in interest charge that would result if the trade credit were repaid earlier than need be. It may, on balance, be less expensive to take the trade credit, despite the higher rates of interest associated with this form of borrowing.

Taking all these general observations together, we can summarize as follows:

1. For an important part of trade credit outstanding, the buyer has no chance to take a cash discount.
2. Another important part of trade credit outstanding represents credit that will be discounted.
3. Still another important part of the trade credit outstanding will not be paid until long after the discount period, thus diminishing the annual interest cost of the credit.
4. Still another important part of trade credit outstanding is more than enough to finance the materials purchased, and thus serves to finance additional activities of the firm, perhaps in a way cheaper than would otherwise be possible.
5. These four points together suggest that a considerable portion of the trade credit outstanding does not represent either bad arithmetic on the part of trade debtors or an inability to obtain alternative financing at moderate rates.
6. There doubtless remain, however, a large number of businessmen who pass up the savings of cash discounts as a result of their ignorance, their carelessness, or their limited access to other financing.

THE BORROWERS OF TRADE CREDIT

Far and away the largest corporate borrowers of trade credit are the manufacturing companies. They account for more than twice the amount owed by the next largest sector, as may be seen in Table 6–2. And they

TABLE 6–2

CORPORATE ACCOUNTS PAYABLE—
END OF YEAR 1961–62
(Billions of Dollars)

Manufacturing	27.3
Wholesale trade	10.5
Retail trade	7.3
Construction	4.5
Public utilities	4.3
Services	2.5
Mining	1.3
Agriculture	0.4
Total	58.2

SOURCE: U.S. Treasury, *Statistics of Income—
Corporate Income Tax Returns.*

and the two trade sectors together owe almost two thirds of the trade debt of all corporations. (The figures here are for one year, but the distribution of trade debt among the different sectors during the preceding decade was about the same as shown here. Also, while the figures are for corporations only, the addition of unincorporated firms would not significantly alter the pattern.)

This order of ranking does not, however, tell us much about the relative intensity with which different parts of the business community use trade credit financing. The order of magnitude shown here reflects instead the general importance of these sectors in the economy. A ranking of sectors by volume of sales, for example, would give us the same list shown above, and other measures of activity and size would give a generally similar picture.

To find where accounts payable have a special importance, we must relate them to such things as inventories, total indebtedness, size of firm, and profitability of firm.

Accounts Payable and Inventories

The link between inventories and trade debt is certainly a direct one. Accounts payable will be created when goods are purchased, and the goods will become part of the buyer's inventory. As a result, the ratios of payables to inventories for different industries indicate the intensity with which trade credit is utilized in different parts of the economy.

Unfortunately, the statistics available to us give only a crude approximation of this link, for reasons we can look at in a moment. But the approximation is helpful. The postwar record for the decade through 1961 is given in Figure 6–2.

What do these figures show?

They show first that, by this measure, manufacturing and the two trade sectors belong at the bottom of the list, instead of at the top, as in the

FIGURE 6–2

RATIOS OF ACCOUNTS PAYABLE TO INVENTORIES*

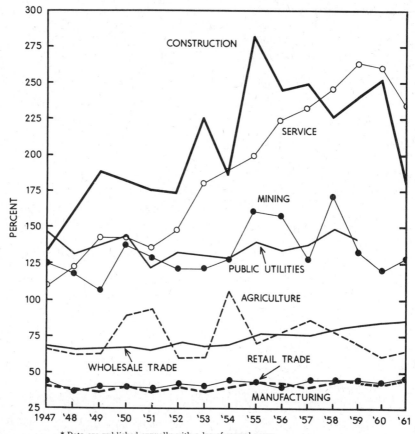

* Data are published annually with a lag of several years.
SOURCE: U.S. Treasury, *Statistics of Income—Corporate Income Tax Returns.*

figures given earlier. The most intense users of trade credit are now seen to be the construction industry and the service industry. These are followed by public utilities and mining.

The figures also show that for the four groups leading the list—construction, service, public utilities, and mining—the ratio has been greater than one—much greater than one—during most of the postwar period. This suggests that trade credit has financed all the inventories of these industries, with something left over to help finance other parts of their operations. If this is anywhere near the truth, it gives considerable point to the possibility suggested earlier—the possibility that trade credit might turn out to be relatively inexpensive if it more than covers the cost of inventories being held.

The picture suggested by these figures must be modified by two further considerations. But since these modifications work in opposite directions, they may cancel out.

The first problem is that the statistics on inventories include some inventories that are not relevant here. A producer of office furniture, for example, has three general kinds of inventories purchased materials, goods in process, and finished goods. In a discussion of accounts payable, it is obviously only the first type that ought to be counted. They are the inventories financed by the trade credit.

The adjustment thus has to be made for those businesses that process materials before passing them on to their own customers. The prime candidate for this adjustment is the manufacturing sector. And when rough allowances are made, the ratio of payables to purchased inventories for the manufacturing segment appears to have been about 1.20 in recent years, i.e., these inventories also are more than financed by trade credit. This process, in fact, would probably push up the ratios for all the sectors except the two trade groups. These two should not be influenced, however, because both wholesale and retail firms resell purchased goods in virtually the same form in which they receive them. Their purchased goods and their finished goods are one and the same, and there are no goods in process. In all probability, the correction of the ratios for an overstatement of the inventory component would leave only these two sectors with ratios less than one.

The second modification springs from the use of accounts payable for financing purchases that do not become a part of the buyer's inventory. A building contractor, for instance, may retain a law firm to help him get a zoning ordinance changed, making possible a new residential development. The bill sent by the law firm is not necessarily paid the day it arrives. The lawyers may be given half at the start and the other half when the new ordinance is passed. The contractor will have an account payable, but his inventories will in no way be enlarged.

This adjustment to the ratios will pull them down. We can only guess at how far they would have to be lowered, as there is no satisfactory way to make the adjustment. Hence, on balance, we are left with the very tentative assumption that the overstatement of accounts payable cancels out the overstatement of inventories. As a result, our highly tentative conclusion is that trade credit finances most, if not all, of the inventories of each group except wholesale trade and retail trade. It may thus be an important source of funds for other uses.

Accounts Payable and Other Sources of Funds

Indeed, for some industries, trade credit ranks very high as a source of external funds. But when the importance of trade credit is measured in this fashion, the pattern among the different users shifts again. Construction firms are still on top, but wholesalers and retailers move up near the head of the list, and the utilities drop to the bottom. For the years 1947–61, trade debt as a percent of total liabilities and net worth was as follows:

Construction	26%
Wholesale and retail	19
Services	12
Manufacturing	10
Mining	8
Utilities	3

And when, for the same years, we look at the share of payables in total *debt* (i.e., excluding equity as a source of external funds), the order is roughly similar, with trade debt playing an important role in every sector but utilities:

Wholesale and retail	41%
Construction	35
Manufacturing	27
Mining	22
Services	21
Utilities	7

The patterns of size and profitability would also appear to have some bearing on the importance of trade debt in different segments of the business community. It seems evident from other figures, for example, that unprofitable firms owe a larger portion of trade debt than would seem warranted by the portion of sales they account for. This is true not only for all corporations taken together, but also within each major sector.

The available evidence also makes clear that the smaller the firm, the more important is trade indebtedness as a source of external financing. The exceptions seem to be limited to the profitable firms in the construction and wholesale sectors. In those areas, payables gain an increasingly prominent place among external sources of funds as the firm size is larger. And since there seems to be a somewhat greater distribution of construction firms toward the larger sizes than is true for other sectors, this pattern helps explain the presence of the construction sector at the top, or near the top, of the several listings we have looked at.

QUESTIONS AND PROBLEMS

1. Reconstruct Table 6–1 on the assumption of a trade discount of 2 percent.
2. Suppose a firm typically carries goods 40 days before selling them. If this firm can get bank credit at 12 percent and trade credit at 2/10/60, how should it finance the purchase of these goods?
3. Discuss the relevance, if any, that trade credit has for computing the acquisition cost of inventories. Should trade credit terms influence the economic order quantity?

SUGGESTED READINGS

Andrews, V.; Friedland, S.; and Shapiro, E. "Who Finances Small Business?" *Financing Small Business*. Washington, D.C.: Federal Reserve System, 1958.

Meltzer, Allan H. "Monetary Policy and the Trade Credit Practices of Business Firms," The Commission on Money and Credit, *Stabilization Policies*. Englewood Cliffs, N.J.: Prentice- Hall, Inc., 1963.

Seiden, Martin H. *The Quality of Trade Credit*. Occasional Paper 87. New York: National Bureau of Economic Research, 1964.

Chapter 7

THE BUSINESS LENDERS: ACCOUNTS
RECEIVABLE AS A USE OF FUNDS

Among the users of trade credit, some considerable number appear to be paying a high rate of interest for the funds, as pointed out earlier. If this is so, can it be assumed that the lending firms are eager to extend the credit and would gladly extend more than they do? In fact, with such a high rate of return on their investment, why is the rate not bid down as the lending firms compete with each other to get more of this profitable credit business?

The answer lies in the cost to the lender. But in moving toward that answer, let us note once more that when trade credit is extended, the seller is offering two items. One is the good or service being sold, and the other is the credit.

Now it might happen that the seller offers the goods and the credit separately. An automobile dealer sells cars on one side of the room and installment credit on the other. In such a case, he might hope to make a profit on each. Or he might shade the price on one to encourage the sale of the two as a package. The joint profit might then be better than the profit on the two components if sold independently of one another.

But the case that interests us is quite the opposite. In our case, the seller will shade his price if assured that the buyer will *not* take the credit along with the goods.

Why should this be so? The answer seems to be that the costs of extending such credit are too high to make it an attractive line of trade in its own right. Bankers make money at it, to be sure, and so do factors and commercial credit companies and the "captive" finance companies of large manufacturers. But for the nonfinancial firm there are costs that a banker can avoid through specialization and economies of scale. The nonfinancial lender of this kind of money thus aims to lend as little of it as possible. He hopes to induce the buyer to pay earlier than otherwise. He prefers a claim on cash to a claim on the customer.

THE COSTS OF LENDING

Trade credit has three separate types of cost for the lender. These are the carrying cost, the routine collection cost, and the past-due collection cost. The first two of these costs will occur even under conditions of certainty. The third one—the cost of delinquency—will emerge only as we enter the world of uncertainty.

The lender, first of all, is tying up some of his funds. This means that he cannot put them to doing some other job that might increase his earnings. Notice also that he incurs the cost during the discount period as well as afterward. As a result, even when a customer takes the discount, the seller must find some way to recoup the cost of this "free" credit.

The second cost is an operating matter. A seller who extends credit must have a credit department to help identify the buyers who are bad risks and who should perhaps be made to pay cash. The seller also needs a collection department to keep track of shipment dates, invoice dates, end of discount period dates, and due dates, and to send out reminders. As the cost of having these chores done will be roughly the same for each shipment, it is in effect a lump-sum cost, regardless of the length of the net period.

The third cost emerges when, despite the careful work of the credit department and the stern reminders of the collection department, the buyer fails to meet the deadline. And because it is a cost that could be avoided if the seller could identify the poor risks ahead of time, it springs from uncertainty. As noted earlier, many lenders of trade credit allow their customers to be persistently overdue. But this is a disguised extension of the due date. The third type of cost begins to emerge when the selling firm begins to take serious steps to get the money collected.

At this point, costs can rise sharply. If the matter is turned over to a commerical collection agency, the fees are likely to be at least 12 or 15 percent of the account outstanding; and for smaller bills, they will be much higher than this. If, after that, it becomes necessary to retain a lawyer, there will be another fee running at least to 10 percent of the balance, and much more if litigation is necessary. If in the end the debtor company fails, the trade creditor stands well down the list of creditors. As a result, he will recover little, if anything, from final liquidation of the debtor's assets.

Some idea of the rapid increase in this cost may be gained from rough estimates made by the American Credit Indemnity Company, based on the cost of collection and the probability of recovery.[1] These suggest that an account that is 90 days past due will be diminished in value by 10 percent, an account four months past due 15 percent, and so on. This means that as a delinquency approaches 90 days, the seller of a $100 shipment can expect not only to lose the $2.00 in "interest" on the trade credit extended but also $8.00 of the $98 basic price of the goods.

Of course the risk of such a loss does not attach to all of the trade credit extended. Moreover, where such risk does apply, the high rates of return often charged for such credit might make the risks worth taking. As we saw earlier, however, delinquencies running well beyond the due date were sizable in some sectors. If, in addition, the interest charge on this credit is high, we may suspect that the customer borrowing the funds either has little astuteness or no alternatives. Either way, he may be foreshadowing failure. He may be a bad debt about to happen.

THE GAINS FROM LENDING

Must we then conclude that firms supplying trade credit are just as short on astuteness as firms borrowing it? Should all sales be made for cash? The answer lies in thinking of trade credit as part of the selling effort.

Lending without a Discount

Perhaps the simplest effort is to give the customer several weeks to pay—say, 30 days. For each unit of goods sold to him the cost of credit extended would behave as pictured in Figure 7–1.

The longer the buyer waits to pay, the higher will climb the total interest cost borne by the seller. To this will be added the collection cost, the lump-sum expenditure made necessary by having sold for credit rather than cash. After the due date, failure to pay will set in motion other machinery which adds extra collection costs.

In this simple situation, the price of the good is the same whether the buyer pays cash or takes the credit. Accordingly, before the cost of the credit is calculated, the profit on each unit of sales will also be the same. Once the due date arrives, however, and the bill remains unpaid, the

---

[1] American Credit Indemnity Co., *A Preface to Profits* (Baltimore, 1955), p. 12.

FIGURE 7–1

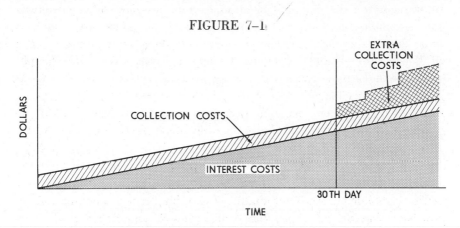

chance of collecting the full price begins to wane. And this will be true despite the special steps taken at that point.

The profit per item can thus be superimposed on the diagram in Figure 7–1 to show the net profit for varying lengths of credit period (Figure 7–2.) Obviously any extension of credit reduces the profit per unit sold.

The appeal of this credit policy, however, is that it tends to increase the *number* of units sold, even while reducing the net profit on each unit. Suppose, with only cash accepted, and with the price per unit given as p, the total quantity of goods sold is X. The total revenue associated with these sales would then be pX. With the total cost designated as cX, profit would be $pX - cX$.

Suppose now that credit is extended for 30 days, and that all customers choose to delay payment exactly that long. The effect of this extension will be to increase the quantity sold—say from X to Y. The total revenue will then rise from pX to pY. The total cost, however, will also be larger and

FIGURE 7–2

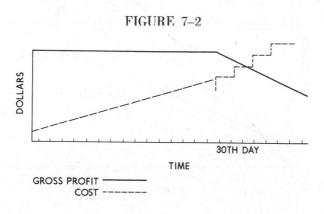

on two counts. First, the number of goods to be produced or acquired will have expanded, and second, the cost of credit for each good will now enter. If we label the credit cost per item as a, then our total cost at sales of Y will be $(c + a)Y$. Whether the firm is better off by offering the credit depends on whether the change in total revenue—$pY - pX$—is greater than the change in total cost—which is $(c + a)Y - cX$.

The happy outcome may be seen in Figure 7–3. The profit P_y is greater than the profit P_x. Suppose then that flushed with this success, the firm lengthened its net period, pushing it out from 30 days to 90 days. After all, if a little bit of credit will raise profits, a lot of credit ought to raise them a lot.

Thus is the deterioration of quality invited in. Firms headed for trouble now have time to get deeper into trouble before your bill is due, where under the old terms they had to put a higher priority on paying you. Your sales go up from Y to Z, but both your costs and revenues feel the strain.

Collections come harder now. Extra effort is required (call it eZ), and your total costs move up to $(c + a + e)Z$. As these are not enough to save some of the accounts, some of the expected revenue must be written off. Total revenues thus increase but some of them are never collected. The result is $pZ - (b)pZ$, with b the portion of sales that go sour. The new profit P_z, is thus $pZ - bpZ - (c + a + e)Z$. As we have shown it here, the new profit is less than when sales were at Y.

FIGURE 7–3

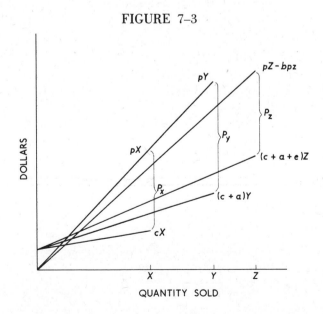

So the firm has gone too far in leniency. But let it retreat back toward the credit period associated with Y. At some point in between it will find that period that maximizes profit.

Lending with a Discount

Suppose it is suggested now that profit might be further enhanced by encouraging customers to pay early. Specifically, if they pay by the tenth of the month, they get a discount on the price. For each unit sold, the picture might look like Figure 7–4. As drawn in this diagram, the discount cuts into the profit per unit by a lesser amount than the saving in interest cost and collection cost—i.e., E is bigger than H. If this should be the case, the net profit will be enhanced each time a customer decides to take the discount. Thus, if any customers at all elect this option, the seller will benefit.

But what if customers can be induced to discount only by a discount that wipes out the saving on each item sold? Is it then a mistake to offer a discount? Again we must look to the impact on total quantity demanded.

Without the discount for cash payment, the customer has been buying two items in a package—the goods and the credit. He may have been interested only in the goods, but he had to pay the same price whether he took just the goods (paying at time of purchase) or took the goods and the credit (paying at the end of the net period). Since he was paying for the credit in any case, he was better off taking it, however little he wanted it.

Now we offer him a chance to buy the goods separately. Now he can

FIGURE 7–4

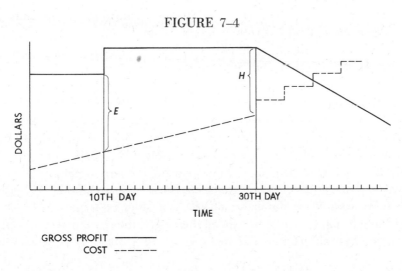

GROSS PROFIT ———
COST ------

put together his *own* package, buying goods from us and credit from someone else—and probably he can get a package that is cheaper. We may thus expect him to increase the volume of goods he buys from us. And it may follow—though not necessarily—that our total profit will rise, even if our profit per unit falls.

To see this more clearly, assume that the volume of sales is Y when payment is due in 30 days and when the price per unit is p, with no discount offered. This indeed is where we left matters in the discussion above. Total revenue then is pY and total cost is $(c + a)Y$.

Now we introduce a discount for payment by the tenth day—call that discount d—and we discover that some customers do not discount and some do. Those who do not are the buyers of nY and those who do are the buyers of $(1 - n)Y$. Our *revenues* from the nondiscounting customers are labeled as n times pY, and the corresponding *costs* as n times $(c + a)Y$.

For the sales that are discounted, the price goes down by the fraction d, making the price $(1 - d)p$. Since these customers account for $(1 - n)$ of total sales volume Y, the total revenues associated with these sales is $(1 - n)(1 - d)pY$. For example, with a price of $5 and total sales of 100 units, we may suppose a discount of 2 percent would induce all but 20 percent of sales to be discounted. Thus total revenues from the discounting customers would be $(1 - 0.20)(1 - 0.02)$5(100)$.

Because these payments are received earlier, the carrying cost on these sales will be less per unit than on the nondiscounted sales. The funds are tied up for ten days instead of thirty. The seller thus bears a cost of $0.33a$, rather than the full a. The total cost on the goods sold to customers taking the discount can be stated as $(1 - n)(c + 0.33a)Y$.

But there is a further effect of offering a discount for early payment— the expansion of the total volume of goods sold. If we assume, then, that buyers taking the discount will increase their purchases by the percentage m, the quantity of goods sold to them will rise to $(1 + m)Y$. Accordingly, the total revenue from these customers will be $(1 + m)(1 - n)(1 - d)pY$. And the associated total cost will be $(1 + m)(1 - n)(c + 0.33a)Y$.

Pulling all these expressions together, we get the algebra shown in the box at the top of Figure 7–5 and the diagram shown at the bottom. We start out with a policy that gives a sales volume of Y and a profit of P_y. This is a policy of 30 days' grace period but no discount for early payment. Now a discount is introduced. Some buyers continue as before, and they account for purchases of nY. The other customers, who previously bought $(1 - n)Y$, now expand their purchases by the proportion m. Their total purchases thus rise to $(1 + m)(1 - n)Y$. The revenue line

FIGURE 7–5

	Nondiscounted Sales	Discounted Sales
Revenue	npY	$(1+m)\,(1-n)\,(1-d)pY$
Cost	$n(c+a)Y$	$(1+m)\,(1-n)\,(c+0.33a)Y$

The net profit (P_w) will thus be

$$npY + (1+m)\,(1-n)\,(1-d)\,pY - n(c+a)Y \\ - (1+m)\,(1-n)\,(c+0.33a)Y$$

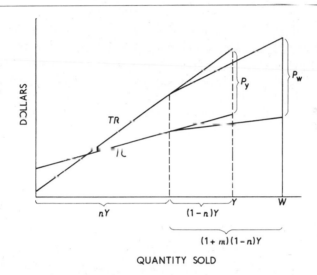

QUANTITY SOLD

(TR) for these accounts moves up less steeply, but so does the cost line (TC). The new profit of P_w thus may exceed the old profit of P_y. In the diagram as drawn here, the new profit is greater than the old.

To make the picture clearer, the diagram and the algebra ought to say something of the effects of delinquency and default. In the diagram, this would mean little more than relabeling the lines already there. In the algebra, three more terms need to go in. If we identify the delinquent customers as $q(nY)$, then there will be two costs associated with them— extra collection efforts and extra carrying costs. Designating these costs as e and f, we get $e(qnY)$ and $f(qnY)$, both to be subtracted from the profit. The customers who go bad entirely must also be subtracted. Since they will first have become delinquent, they will account for some portion, call it b, of the sales that were not discounted and were not paid for on time. They will be $(bq)(npY)$. This term must also be subtracted from profit. It should be clear, however, that even with these three costs, the profit might still be larger than before, as shown in the diagram.

The success from offering a discount may suggest offering a still deeper discount. This may have two effects. First, it should induce some customers to discount who formerly were not discounting. At the deeper discount, these customers will be paying a higher cost for the credit then before, and for some it will now be higher than the cost of their alternative sources. Second, for many who discount, the combined cost of (a) the goods and (b) the credit from other sources will be lower than before. Unless demand is completely insensitive to changes in combined cost, the quantity of goods demanded should thus grow larger.

In the diagram of Figure 7–5, this would appear as a redrawing of the cost and revenue lines for the discounted sales. These lines would start from points further to the left, as a smaller number of goods will now be sold to nondiscounting customers. And they would be still less steeply sloped, representing the further cut in price per unit and in cost per unit. Whether the new profit would climb still higher than P_w would depend on the facts of the case.

THE IMPACT OF UNCERTAINTY ABOUT SALES VOLUME

Up to this point, we have moved in a world in which uncertainty enters entirely as a product of customer delinquency. That is, we have included in the analysis the risk that sales proceeds might be much delayed and might be only partly collected or not collected at all. For a complete analysis we should also cover the uncertainty surrounding (a) the quantity of goods that will be sold in the first place, and (b) the distribution of those sales according to whether payment is made during the discount period, during the net period, or into the period of delinquency. We shall not undertake a discussion of the uncertainty about this latter distribution, as it would carry us well beyond the level of this book. Uncertainty about the volume of sales, however, can be tackled with some ideas already met in the chapters on inventories.

First, it should be realized that the offer of trade credit will complicate the inventory analysis even in a world of certainty. To begin with, if payment is not received immediately upon sale, funds are tied up in the inventories for a longer time. Some of the carrying cost will vanish, as shipment of the goods opens up storage space and as the insurance burden shifts to the buyer. But the opportunity cost on the funds themselves will continue to pile up until the account is settled. As a consequence, the added carrying cost may lead to a different Q^*, a different optimal order quantity for the selling firm.

But the problem goes deeper. When we looked earlier at inventory management, we assumed that the sales price to the firm's customers had been settled. By whom it was settled, and on what reasoning, we did not inquire. Now, with the introduction of trade credit, we come up against the same kind of issue. The terms of credit are terms of sale, modifying the list price and having a major impact on customer demand.

Thus, the credit terms will influence both the volume of sales and the timing of cash receipts in payment for sales. As a consequence, the credit terms will have a double impact on the inventory decision. Indeed, to find the optimal combination of all these decision variables would carry us around a loop, showing the feedback of inventory management on the cost curve, and on the optimum level of sales themselves. Then, when uncertainty enters such a system, the analysis will become enormously complex.

To incorporate all these relationships in a formal model for inventory management and for trade credit decisions would carry us much deeper than we can go in this book—especially if we were to attempt a solution for the world of uncertainty. We can get some insight, however, by looking at a suboptimum decision about inventories. Specifically, suppose we take as given the level of output, the offering price for that output, and the various terms of trade credit. We may then look at the effects of uncertainty on the choice of inventory buffer stocks, in the manner developed in our earlier analysis of inventories.

In looking at inventories, we assumed it might be possible to set down rough figures on probability distributions of the quantity demanded. Here the same assumption is made. And here it is further assumed that guesses can be made about the probable distribution of demand when the firm offers different sets of trade credit terms.

For example, in Figure 7–5, the profit P_w presupposes that under the terms offered the quantity sold will be exactly W. What if we now think of the quantity sold as likely to vary around W? Immediately we must focus on variations in total revenue and total cost, and hence in the profit itself.

To be more specific, the choice of trade credit terms will influence the probability distribution assumed in the inventory analysis. It will also influence the figures that go into making up a payoff matrix, changing (a) the profit per unit and (b) the carrying cost per unit. To illustrate, the number of units demanded might range from 10 through 13 when the discount is 1 percent, and from 12 through 13 when the discount is 2 percent. The probabilities over these ranges might be as shown in Table 7–1.

TABLE 7–1

Possible Demand Probability	10	11	12	13	14	15
d is 0.01	0.10	0.20	0.40	0.30	—	—
d is 0.02	—	—	0.30	0.40	0.20	0.10

As a start, we set up the cost matrix developed for inventory analysis. Using a short cost of $10 per widget and long cost of $4 gave us the figures in Table 7–2.

TABLE 7–2

Possible Demand Strategy	10	11	12	13
10	$ 0	$10	$20	$30
11	4	0	10	20
12	8	4	0	10
13	12	8	4	0

In the inventory chapter, we turned this into a payoff matrix by assuming a net profit of $5 per item (the difference, let us say, between $50 price and $45 cost). Let us assume now, however, that this general level of demand can be maintained only if the firm sells at credit terms of 1/10/30.

Thus, to get a payoff matrix, we must alter the net profit per item. We must take account of the changes in cost and revenue per item that result from the offering of trade credit and trade discounts.

Two computations are necessary here—one for the discounted sales and one for the nondiscounted sales.

For the customer who takes the discount, the price is cut from $50.00 to $49.50 (i.e., by 1 percent). The cost to the seller is being raised slightly because the customer is being loaned $49.50 for ten days, at the end of which the bill must be paid if he is to get the price saving.

Assume that increase in cost is $0.20. All told, the $5.00 net profit before the trade credit calculations is shrunk to $4.30, after $0.50 off for the discount and the $0.20 off for the ten-day loan.

For the customer not taking the discount, the price stays the same, but the cost rises. Funds are tied up in this customer's account for thirty days instead of ten. The cost is thus three times as much—$0.60 instead of $0.20. The net profit on his purchases is $4.40.

To get us into a payoff matrix, one more assumption is necessary. We must assume values for n and $(1 - n)$. To keep the arithmetic simple, say that the volume of sales divides half and half between discounters and nondiscounters. The *average* net profit per widget sold will then be $4.35, the weighted average of $4.30 and $4.40.

Putting this into a payoff matrix we get Table 7–3.

TABLE 7–3

Possible Demand / Strategy	10	11	12	13
10	$43.50	$33.50	$23.50	$13.50
11	39.50	47.85	37.85	27.85
12	35.50	43.85	52.20	42.20
13	31.50	39.85	48.20	56.55

Applying the probabilities noted earlier gives mathematical expectations as follows:

Strategy	
10	$24.500
11	37.015
12	45.860
13	47.365

But the analysis is only half done. The effects of a different trade credit policy must be considered. The cost matrix is set up as before, though it covers a different range.

The net profit per item will be different. A discount of 2 percent pulls the revenue per item down to $49. The cost per item will not change, however, and neither will the revenue or the cost on the undiscounted items. The net profit on discounted sales will thus stand at $3.80 (down another $0.50 from the $4.30 when the discount was smaller). On sales not discounted the net profit remains at $4.40.

The weighted average for net profit per unit thus slips down to $4.10. With this figure, the payoff matrix is computed as in Table 7–4.

TABLE 7–4

Possible Demand Strategy	12	13	14	15
12	$49.20	$39.20	$29.20	$19.20
13	45.20	53.30	43.30	23.30
14	41.20	49.30	57.40	47.40
15	37.20	45.30	53.40	61.50

Again, the probabilities associated with these conditions may be applied. The consequent mathematical expectations are shown in the left hand columns below. These may be compared with the earlier results, from the alternative trade credit policy, which are repeated in the right-hand columns:

With Discount of 2 Percent		*With Discount of 1 Percent*	
12	$38.20	10	$24.500
13	45.87	11	37.015
14	48.30	12	45.860
15	46.11	13	47.365

Thus, if customers are offered a discount of 2 percent, and if half of them take it (and if all the other specific assumptions hold), the best inventory policy will be to prepare for a demand of 14 widgets—even though the chances are twenty out of a hundred that the actual demand will be for 15 widgets. On the other hand, with a discount of only 1 percent, the firm will earn the highest profit, over time, by being prepared always for the very highest demand that might occur—in this case, a demand for 13 widgets. These are particular results of particular assumptions, but they make clear that different levels of discount may change the pattern of the inventory decision.

THE LENDERS OF TRADE CREDIT

The advantages of careful credit policies have a widespread significance for American business. For, as noted earlier, trade credit outstanding now accounts for half of all financial assets of business firms. As might be expected, the biggest corporate creditor is the manufacturing sector (see Table 7 5), although the rest of the list takes a somewhat different order than when the sectors are ranked by volume of payables.

TABLE 7-5

CORPORATE ACCOUNTS RECEIVABLE, FISCAL
YEAR–END, 1961–62
(Billions of Dollars)

Manufacturing 49.9
Wholesale trade 16.1
Construction 6.2
Mining 2.4
Services 1.9
Retail trade 1.3
Agriculture 0.6

SOURCE: U.S. Treasury, *Statistics of Income—Corporation Income Tax Returns.*

The only serious relocation is the standing of retail trade. The explanation is simple. By definition, most customers of retail firms are not other businesses. Hence, the lending to customers is not trade credit but consumer credit, which is not included in any of these figures.

Another general point should be noted. The total volume of receivables is almost half again as large as the volume of payables. This is true, moreover, of each of the sectors except retail trade and services, both of which sell in large measure directly to consumers. In some years, it is even true of the utility group, which also deals directly with the public much of the time. The essential reason for this is that each firm, whatever sector it is in, adds something of value to the materials it purchases. Hence, the dollar volume of its sales and receivables exceeds the dollar volume of its purchases and payables.

As was the case with payables, we must turn to some relative measure to determine the intensity with which the different firms offer trade credit to their business customers. The first relevant comparison here is with sales. What are the ratios of receivables to sales? As may be seen from Figure 7–6, the range is very wide. These figures do not tell us the proportion of sales that are made on credit, because they relate receipts to the volume of receivables outstanding at the end of that year. They do show, however, the relative importance of trade credit extension in different industries.

When we turn to the relative importance of accounts receivable among the total assets of different corporations, we find them accounting for about half in the construction sector, which is certainly consistent with the very large extension of credit per dollar of sales. But once more, the multiplicity of influences is evident. The wholesale trade group, which ranks well down the list when receivables are compared to sales, nevertheless has almost a third of its total assets tied up in accounts receivable. This reflects the vast difference in asset patterns in wholesale firms from those in, say, the manufacturing sector.

In corporate areas other than construction and wholesale trade, receivables are a much smaller part of total assets. In manufacturing, the sector of next greatest importance by this measure, the proportion is only about 15 percent.

RELATIONSHIP OF PAYABLES AND RECEIVABLES

All the discussion up to now has assumed, implicitly, that trade debt and trade credit are not very closely related to each other within an individual firm. This is accurate, within limits. Payables and receivables arise out of quite different activities, and the interconnection is more evident to the financial office than it is to the purchasing department, the credit and collection division, and the sales department, all of which have great influence on the volume of credit borrowed and the volume lent.

The relationship between payables and receivables is of interest, however, to the financial manager. It is also important for the student of business cycles and public policy. For both these groups, there is first the question as to who does the net lending of trade credit and who the net borrowing. Or put differently, in what manner is trade credit extension one of the channels through which funds flow to different parts of the economy? The other question is whether these flows tend to be altered by swings in the trade credit policies of lending firms. Do some firms try, for example, to stretch the period covered by trade credit so as to economize on their own cash holdings during times of expansion and boom? And are there other firms that typically accommodate them in this effort?

The evidence that large firms lend to small ones is not conclusive, but it suggests a strong tendency. When firms are grouped by size, the smaller groups seem to account for a larger portion of total trade debt than of total trade credit. This does not necessarily mean that small companies are always net debtors, or even that they are typically so. As we have already seen, most sectors, taken as a whole, are net lenders of trade credit because the flow of goods from the raw state to the final finished form tends to make every firm's receivables larger than its payables. The question, then, is whether the margin between amounts loaned and

FIGURE 7–6

Ratios of Accounts Receivable to Business Receipts*

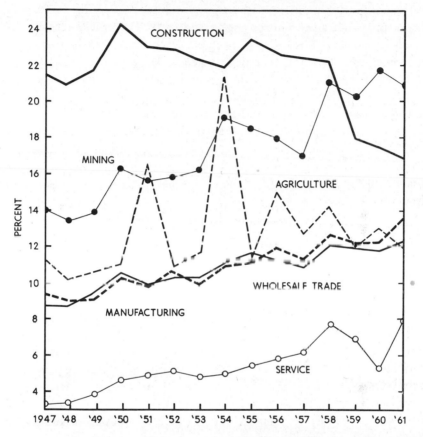

* Data are published annually with a lag of several years.
Source: U.S. Treasury, *Statistics of Income—Corporation Income Tax Returns.*

amounts borrowed is narrower for small firms than for others. The figures
we have suggest that this is the case.

In this same sense, trade credit seems to flow, on balance, from
profitable firms to unprofitable ones. Presumably, this is a natural consequence of greater delinquency in weak companies. The creditor firm,
seeing its customer on heavy seas, allows it to delay payment, hoping this
will help the debtor get home safely. Indeed, as we have seen, the creditor
has little choice in the matter. Forced collection is expensive, and
bankruptcy of the debtor firm is not likely to produce much salvage for
the trade creditor.

In addition, some part of the relationship between receivables and payables for individual firms, and for industries as well, is built into the basic institutional framework. Much of a company's trading is done with firms in a specific industry, with the same credit practices thus influencing the company's trade credit extension and its trade credit borrowing. The result is that the relationship of trade credit to trade debt is, in considerable measure, standard. It is determined in large part by what the firm buys and what it sells, and by the common credit practices in the markets in which it regularly buys and sells.

These more or less standard relationships are evident in Figure 7–7, which shows for each sector the ratio of receivables to payables. There is considerable volatility from year to year; but on balance, there seems to be no clear pattern. And for some of the sectors, neither the level nor the general order of ranking was greatly different at the end of the period from what it was at the beginning.

POLICY CHANGES?

What about the second question posed above—the possibility that trade credit policies are changed as the economy enters new phases of the business cycle?

To begin with, there is scattered testimony from businessmen themselves suggesting that when demand for their products falls slack, they may become more lenient with customers whose payments are past due. It may be also that they allow more customers to take the discount a few days late when business is not booming. As an offset to these various possibilities, however, it may be that sellers become more fussy about buyers' credit ratings when the economy generally is in a slump, and thus deny credit to customers who would have gotten it in better days.

Turning to the figures, we have only annual data to work with, outside of manufacturing. But from these, it seems evident, first of all, that both payables and receivables have some tendency to level off or turn down when the economy enters a recession, and then to pick up with a general recovery. This pattern was relatively consistent in the postwar period, through the 1950's. The only important exceptions were in the construction and service sectors, where the secular upward thrust was so powerful that both the payables and the receivables in these areas hardly slowed down at all.

The more pressing question, however, is the cyclical pattern of the

FIGURE 7–7

RATIOS OF ACCOUNTS RECEIVABLE TO ACCOUNTS PAYABLE*

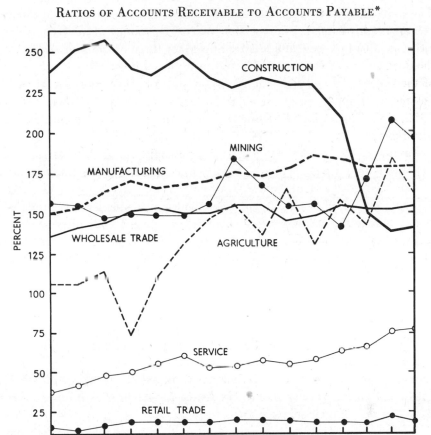

* Data are published annually with a lag of several years.
SOURCE: U.S. Treasury, *Statistics of Income—Corporation Income Tax Returns.*

receivables/sales ratios and the payables/inventory ratios. Do these suggest cyclical shifts in trade credit policy?

The ratios of receivables to sales do hint at a cyclical pattern. But the hint is too weak to be taken seriously. In the ratios of payables to inventories, there is virtually no pattern at all. This may of course reflect, as noted earlier, the inclusion in the figures on inventories of some matter extraneous to the relationship under discussion.

For further light on cyclical behavior, we have figures on net trade receivables, i.e., the dollar amount by which receivables exceed payables in each corporate sector. For the four important sectors that have more trade credit than debt (manufacturing, wholesale trade, construction, and mining), there is some semblance of a cyclical pattern. But here the evidence, albeit somewhat mixed, testifies against the proposition that credit is more readily extended in recession years. The volume of net receivables either declined or grew at a less rapid rate for three of the four sectors in the downturns of 1949 and 1953, and then picked up steam again in each of the succeeding years. In the recession year of 1957, however, the net volume in each case rose at least as rapidly as in the year before; and in 1958, it rose again for wholesale and manufacturing but dropped off for the others.

Taking all the evidence together, it gives only minor support for any hypothesis on cyclical swings in business policies regarding trade credit.

There is, however, one more straw in the figures suggesting that the management of trade credit has been blown by considerable winds of policy during the postwar years. That is the upward drift of the receivables/sales ratios and the payables/inventories ratios. It may have come about in some such sequence as this: As competition heightened, in boom and slump alike, individual firms sold increasingly larger portions of their goods and services on credit. This pressed them to shift the burden of financing this credit back onto their own suppliers. In this way, a gradual change in credit practice occurred, starting in one part of the business community, but in time spreading through the community. While individual firms might get ahead of the game at one time or another, whole sectors were not likely to. In time, most individual firms found their customers pushing as hard on them for easier credit conditions as they were pushing on their suppliers.

Whatever the process, the borrowing and lending of trade credit has become a larger force in business finance during these years. This probably could not have happened without considerable shifts in the policies of both borrowers and lenders.

QUESTIONS AND PROBLEMS

1. In a world of certainty, would the lender of trade credit have any collection costs? Explain your answer.
2. Explain how increasing the net period may add to profits, even while raising costs.
3. Figure 7–1 shows how profits may vary with different volumes of sales. The analysis assumes implicitly, however, that the variations in profit stem entirely from the effects of trade credit extension. Reconstruct the diagram

to include a cost of *production* that first rises slowly and then—say at output X—begins to move up sharply.

4. Suppose that in the numerical example starting on page 118, a discount of 2 percent had generated a larger demand with probabilities as shown here:

Possible Demand Probability:	10	11	12	13	14	15	16
d is 0.01	0.10	0.20	0.40	0.30	. . .	. . .	. . .
d is 0.02	. . .	. . .	. . .	0.10	0.20	0.40	0.30

Determine the optimal strategy.

5. What would be the outcome in Question No. 4 if the 2 percent discount induced 60 percent of the sales to be discounted?

6. Financial analysis sometimes focusses on the net trade credit position of a firm. Discuss the relevance of this measure for financial management discussions, and for assessing management from the outside.

SUGGESTED READINGS

BERANEK, WILLIAM. *Analysis for Financial Decisions*, chap. x. Homewood, Ill.: Richard D. Irwin, Inc., 1963.

COHEN, KALMAN J., and HAMMER, FREDERICK S. *Analytical Methods in Banking*, chaps. vi–viii. Homewood, Ill.: Richard D. Irwin, Inc., 1966.

CYERT, R. M.; DAVIDSON, H. J.; and THOMPSON, G. L. "Estimation of the Allowance for Doubtful Accounts by Markov Chains," *Management Science*, April, 1962.

FEDERAL RESERVE BANK OF CHICAGO. "Accounts Receivable Lending: Credit at the Margin," *Business Conditions*, March, 1958 (reprinted in JAMES VAN HORNE [ed.], *Foundations for Financial Management* [Homewood, Ill.: Richard D. Irwin, Inc., 1966]).

FEDERAL RESERVE BANK OF KANSAS CITY. "Forces Behind the Growth in Trade Credit," *Monthly Review*, October 1959 (reprinted in EDWARD J. MOCK [ed.], *Readings in Financial Management* [Scranton, Pa.: International Textbook Co., 1964]).

NATIONAL ASSOCIATION OF CREDIT MANAGEMENT. *Credit Management Handbook*, 2d ed. Homewood, Ill.: Richard D. Irwin, Inc., 1965.

Chapter 8

THE MANAGEMENT OF CASH
AND SHORT-TERM FINANCE

Is it useful to think of cash as an asset that behaves like inventories and can be managed with inventory-like ideas? Analogies can lead us astray, but they can also lead us to deeper understanding. With cash and inventories, the parallels turn out to be very useful.

First, it is clear that the two assets have much in common. Both may be thought of as stocks, without strain on the imagination. Both come in highly divisible units, making it possible to alter the level of the stock in the short term. In each case, decisions made beyond the walls of the firm may also raise or lower the stock in a very short span of time. And for both assets these changes from the outside may often come as a surprise.

But there are differences between cash and inventories. And the chief difference is that cash stands more nearly at the center of the action. All things turn into cash sooner or later, and cash can be converted into any of these things. "Converted," in fact, is the key word. Cash, with its universality, is interconvertible with all other stocks and flows a business may deal with. Thus, it moves in more directions, so to speak, than inventories do. The traffic in cash has greater variety.

Because of this universality, cash is likely to experience a greater variability in both its ebb and its flow. To see this clearly, think of inventory behavior. Inventories may flow out of a business at a more rapid rate than expected, or at a less rapid rate than expected, depending on the demands of customers. The flow of inventories *into* the firm, however, will only rarely occur at a *faster* rate than planned for. Mostly the problem, when there is one, will be an inflow at a *slower* rate than anticipated. Thus there is an asymmetry in the variability of inventory flows.

By contrast, the flows of cash are much more subject to variability both up and down, regardless of whether an inflow or an outflow. The *inflow* of cash is simply the outflow of finished goods inventories, after an interval spent in the form of accounts receivable. The cash inflow is thus subject to the variability up and down that has been experienced in the outflow of inventories. But the *outflow* of cash is not simply the other side of inventory behavior. It is the other side of *all* activities of the firm that require the spending of money. Hence cash outflow reflects all the fluctuations in all those uses. Where inventories suffer overages and underages mostly at the outflow edge of the firm, cash is subject to underages and overages in both its inflows and its outflows.

As we shall see, this can make the management of cash more complicated than the management of inventories. As we shall also see, however, it does not undermine the usefulness of the analogy.

THE RELEVANT COSTS OF CASH MANAGEMENT

In analyzing inventories, we worked with five types of cost—acquisition, procurement, carrying, short, and long. What can we carry over from this list into the analysis of cash management? The first two costs on this list will take some study, but the last three—carrying cost, short cost, and long cost—can be applied immediately.

Consider the carrying cost. If we hold any cash at all, we deny ourselves the earnings the cash would bring if invested. We pay the price of idleness, the opportunity cost. Hence cash has this carrying cost, just as inventories do.

Similarly, with the short cost. If a need for cash arises, and the coffers are empty, the firm may suffer the embarrassment of a payment run overdue. Or it will pass up a credit discount or a price reduction. Any of these choices will impose a cost. Sometimes the cost will be direct and easy to measure, sometimes only imputed and difficult to estimate. But one way or another the firm must bear some cost for running short.

If the firm avoids this by running "long" rather than short, we are back to the idea of a carrying cost. That is, cash is not perishable, nor will it go out of fashion, if the firm comes to the end of the planning period with more than it meant to have. Over long periods of time, of course, the value of cash may decline as the general price level moves up. But only in eras of wild inflation—as the Germans suffered after World War I—will changes in price be so rapid that money will "spoil" if carried over into the next month. The long cost is thus no different than the carrying cost.

When we turn to the idea of acquisition costs and procurement costs, we must look a little harder. To apply either one of these ideas to cash management seems to be forcing the analogy. Ultimately, of course, a firm acquires cash in one of two ways: It makes "payment" in the form of the goods and services it is selling. Or it makes "payment" in the form of debt or equity claims issued to creditors or owners. But with cash itself the universal coin, the very medium of exchange, the whole matter grows awkward.

At first thought, it might appear that acquisition cost of money could be measured by the cost of borrowing money. A moment's reflection, however, suggests that this is what we have already called the carrying cost. If we have in fact borrowed the money, one major alternative is to repay it. That is, repayment is certainly one important opportunity we are foregoing. Even if we have not borrowed the cash, we have the alternative of lending to some other borrower, which makes *his* borrowing rate the yield we are foregoing. As will perhaps be clearer at the end of our discussion, the only satisfactory way to handle the acquisition cost is to let it disappear into the carrying cost.

Procurement cost introduces the same awkwardness. Without acquisition, there is no procurement. But we have not said that cash is not acquired, only that the cost of getting our hands on cash is not separable from the cost of carrying it. And indeed cash acquisition may give rise to a cash procurement department—not for bringing in cash through the sale of goods, but for raising funds through the issue of claims against the firm. This is typically the corporate treasurer's function.

Claims may be sold as debt or equity, and the debt claims may be designed to fall due in the near future or the far future. As it happens our interest at this point is in debt claims of relatively short life. But, for all such claims, the activity of issuing them and retiring them will absorb the time and talent of some persons in the firm. This is our procurement cost. And, as in the case of inventory procurement, the cost will tend not to rise with the size of claim being issued. Indeed, if the firm is beyond a certain size, it will have a "money desk," a staff group that is kept in being even when no procurement is going on.

In sum, cash management involves fewer types of costs than inventory management does. There is a carrying cost, a short cost, and a procurement cost. The acquisition cost and the long cost both get absorbed into the carrying cost.

MAKING THE DECISION

How can the businessman put these several costs together to arrive at a cash policy?

To begin with, some concept of a planning period is needed. As with inventories, we need to consider some minimum unit of time, during which we leave ourselves at the mercy of events. Our goal is a plan that will maximize the goodness of that mercy. As a starter, we can assume simply that the firm has some natural unit of days or weeks, some rhythm that springs naturally from the flow of events in that firm.

As the planning period is about to start, we want to make decisions that will (a) meet our needs *during* the planning period and (b) leave us in some specified condition at the *end* of the period. Since the subject is cash, we seek to know the opening cash balance that will meet the requirements during the period and give us the desired balance at the end.

In general, for the beginning balance, we can use the symbol, C_b, and for the closing balance the symbol, C_c. For the net flow that occurs in between, we can use the symbol F. Thus $C_b + F = C_c$. For example, if the period begins with \$100 on hand, and the net flow is a drain of \$40, then the closing balance is \$60. Had the net flow been positive instead of negative—i.e., a net inflow of \$40—the C_c would have been \$140.

The Short Cost

At this point, enter the short costs. These will be associated with (a) the closing balance and with (b) the net outflow (if there be any). That is, the *short costs measure the damage done if the closing balance is, in some way, less than it ought to be. They also measure the cost of failing to meet payments during the period.*

We can look first at the short cost associated with the closing balance. In practice, the minimum level for C_c will be some positive amount, compounded of bankers' preferences and the company's caution. We shall see more of this idea further on. But even in logic alone there is the minimum of zero below which the closing balance cannot fall. (In some countries such as England, the practice of allowing overdrafts does make this possible, but we do not have the practice in the United States, and even in England there is a limit to which the overdraft privilege can be exercised.)

FIGURE 8–1

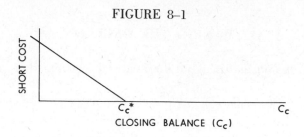

For the sake of exposition, let us assume the firm has set some positive amount as the desired minimum level for C_c. This desired level, then, we can denote with an asterisk, C_c^*.

In Figure 8–1, the horizontal axis measures the closing cash balance. For any balance to the left of the desired level—any shortfall from this minimum—there is a cost. And the greater the shortfall, the greater the short cost.

Now how can this relationship be applied to the *opening* balance (C_b)? Living in a world of certainty, we know what the net flow will be during the planning period. It is thus an easy matter to translate C_c^*, the desired closing balance, into an appropriate opening balance. We saw that $C_b + F = C_c$. Working back the other way, we can see that $C_c - F = C_b$. Since we know what we want C_c to be, and we know what F is going to be, we can tell what C_b *needs* to be if we are to avoid the short cost. Say that C_c^* is $20, and F is going to be an outflow of $70. Then $20 $-$ ($-$70) = $90, and it appears our opening balance should be $90.

At this point, the second kind of short cost becomes evident. It is a cost—or, better, a family of costs—that springs from failure to make payments because of insufficient cash on hand. In roughly ascending order of their importance to the health of the firm, the elements of short cost would be as follows:

a) Cost of passing up trade discounts.
b) Cost of passing up quantity discounts.
c) Cost of becoming delinquent at end of net period.
d) Cost of failing to meet payroll on time, or to make interest and principal payment when due.

If a firm has no funds coming in during the period, then sufficient cash must be held in the opening balance to provide both for meeting these payments on schedule (i.e., for an operating drain) and for producing the required closing balance. In such a case, the short costs associated with varying sizes of beginning balances could be depicted as shown in Figure 8–2.

FIGURE 8–2

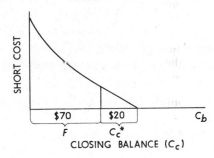

CLOSING BALANCE (C_c)

The right-hand segment of the curve measures the short cost arising from failure to end up with minimum required closing balance—the $20 minimum. And the left-hand segment shows the short cost that would occur if the outflows during the period could not be met. This second type of short cost—the F segment of the curve—would presumably rise much more steeply than the short cost stemming from too small a closing balance.

A moment's reflection will also suggest that the curve should not be smooth, as we have just drawn it, but instead should have a stepped pattern. Take, for example, the cost of failing to meet the minimum balance requirement of the bank. This cost is essentially an imputed one. It is more the glint in the banker's eye than an item in the monthly statement. As a consequence, it may be that a balance slightly below the minimum requirement is just as damaging as a balance well below the line. The other elements of the curve are lumpy. Passing up the discount for ten-day payment is an act that applies to the full invoice, the full shipment. Passing up a quantity discount refers to an entire chunk of purchases by its very definition. Similarly, delinquency may be regarded as applying to the full shipment. And so also with the weekly wage bill. If any workers have to wait for their pay, the imputed cost will be widespread, through the shock and loss of confidence that will spread among even those workers who were paid.

It must be admitted that *measurement* of the different items on the list is easier in principle than in practice. As noted, the cost of too small a closing balance may be mostly an imputed cost, not a direct accounting charge. The same must be said for the cost of failing to pay a supplier when payment is expected, and of failing to pay the work force when their wages and salaries are due. The costs of passing up a trade discount or a quantity discount, however, are much easier to measure. In both cases, the firm will have to pay an extra amount of money because of its inability to take advantage of the discounts. In both cases, taking the discount would mean a lower acquisition price for inventories, and this should lead to a lower total cost of inventories. To be sure, the quantity discount would require a larger purchase order. As a result, the higher carrying costs might outweigh the advantage of the quantity discount. But this will not always be the case. And, in any event, the important point is that the cost savings can be calculated rather precisely for both quantity discounts and trade credit discounts.

One other matter should be noted. We have so far drawn the short cost curve as if the firm experienced only outflows during the period. If there were in fact no inflows at all, the short cost curve would take the form shown in the upper panel of Figure 8–3, with a series of discrete points or steps to represent the lumpiness of the alternatives giving rise to short costs. Moving back to the left, these alternatives are the minimum desired closing balance and the four kinds of payments that will go unpaid if cash is not on hand (the four elements, [a] through [d] listed several pages back).

In many periods, however, there will be gross inflows to offset some or all of the gross outflows. For such periods the schedule of short costs will be unchanged, but the curve will shift back to the left. It is perhaps easier to see this by moving the vertical axis to the right, showing directly the magnitude of the cash inflow to be netted against the outflow. This is done in the lower panel of Figure 8–3. Here we show an inflow that partly offsets the outflow, leaving nonetheless a net outflow. There will of course be periods when the inflow exceeds the outflow and there is no short cost at all.

Carrying Cost

Does the firm necessarily want to avoid the short cost? Or, at any rate, does it want to avoid all of this cost? To answer the question we must introduce carrying costs. For, to escape the short cost, the firm will have to tie up funds at the beginning of the period. For example, in the net outflow case, there would be a carrying cost on $70 until it actually flowed out, and a carrying cost on the other $20 through the full period.

The carrying cost, however, will sometimes be an opportunity cost, and sometimes a borrowing cost. And we must look at them separately.

Opportunity Cost. Let us assume that a company has a certain quantity of cash on hand just before the planning period begins. If the firm continues to hold that cash as it goes into the planning period, it will

FIGURE 8–3

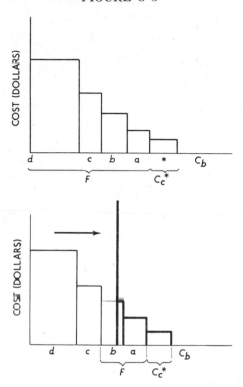

forego earnings the money would bring in if invested. The firm will thus suffer opportunity costs. These costs will arise from all the other assets that have been passed up in favor of holding the cash as cash. They will also arise from liabilities that continue to be outstanding because the cash is not used to pay them off.

What are these opportunity costs? Most of the time, in thinking about opportunity costs, a firm is well advised to consider the highest yielding alternative. That high yield is the hurdle that the present use of funds must clear if such present use is to be justifiable. To identify that high yield, a firm may want to scan a considerable list of possibilities. The search may move beyond short-term Government securities to accounts receivable which may promise higher yields. It may consider in passing the retirement of long-term debt, or short-term debt. Ultimately the choice may fall on a piece of machinery with long life and high returns.

In the management of cash, we rarely will look at all possibilities on this list. What we examine are only those opportunities relevant to the short-term decision we are making. The period we plan for now is short—

days or weeks, or occasionally months. This short period will be followed by another and another, each potentially different in its demands. This week brings a net cash inflow, but next week will see a drain, wiping out all we gained this week, and maybe last week as well.

The moral is this: The measure of opportunity costs will shift with changes in the opportunities we can let ourselves consider. Another way to put the matter is that we must link the current period to the periods coming after it. If we "need" the funds next week, we do not mean the need is absolute. We mean rather that the short cost of not having them next week will be high. To get deeper into the subject would thus require a dynamic analysis, linking us forward through many planning periods of different character. This we will leave for another day.

For now a general list of opportunities foregone may be drawn up as follows:

  a) Earnings on near-money instruments.
  b) Savings by repayment of short-term indebtedness.
  c) Earnings on additional inventories.
  d) Earnings on additional accounts receivable.
  e) Earnings on additional plant and equipment.
  f) Savings on long-term debt retirement.

The alternatives are ranked in what we may guess is roughly their order of attractiveness as short-term uses of funds. For example, at the head of the list are the near-money instruments. These would include Treasury bills, which can sometimes be a profitable use of cash for as little as four or five days. They would include short-term loans to Government securities dealers, which occasionally may be made for so short a time as 24 hours. Because of this flexibility, these are the opportunities most readily at hand, and most relevant as short-term alternatives to the holding of idle cash.

As a firm moves down the list, it makes a deeper and deeper commitment of its funds. The repayment of short-term bank loans, for example, may mean that getting the funds back again, through another loan, will require a new negotiation. Investment in additional inventories will reduce further the likelihood of early recovery of the funds, since the return flow of cash will not occur until the customer buys and makes payment. Only rarely will the customer be required to pay cash at the moment of sale. And if trade credit is granted him, the cash inflow is put that much further into the future. Skipping down to the last item—the

opportunity of retiring long-term debt—a firm will find it a major undertaking to get funds back again through this channel. If it makes sense to
finance with long-term debt issues in the first place, it is not sensible to
retire them early in order to use the funds for a short time, and then to
issue new long-term securities. The reissue will consume considerable time
in the planning alone.

On the other hand, moving down the list may also bring increasingly
larger earnings or savings. Indeed, a greater yield is probably necessary
to overcome the progressive loss of flexibility and liquidity.

The *measurement* of opportunity cost is not difficult to envision when
the alternative considered is a short-term security or the repayment of
short-term debt. Nor should there be conceptual difficulties with the
opportunity cost associated with plant and equipment or with long-term
debt retirement. Some comment is called for, however, when the cost
being measured is the forfeited opportunity to invest in inventories or in
accounts receivable.

Take inventories first, and assume certainty. The question is what
might be *added* to earnings by shifting funds into inventories instead of
holding those funds as cash. Put this way, we can see that some of the
carrying cost normally associated with inventory stock now becomes
irrelevant. Some part of that cost—perhaps we can call it pure interest
cost—is going to be incurred in any case if the firm would otherwise be
holding idle cash. The cost of additional inventories thus should not
include that charge. As a result, the *average* inventory can be larger. That
is, the economic order quantity will be larger and less frequently placed.
Hence the procurement cost will fall. Therefore, with the demand and the
sales price unchanged, the reduction in cost will add to profit. This is the
measure of opportunity cost for the inventory alternative to holding idle
cash.

Under uncertainty, inventory impact is partly on cost and partly on
revenue. As part of the carrying cost is dropped out of consideration, the
optimal level of inventory holdings will shift upward. It costs less to *hold*
additional units. Yet the cost of being short of those units has not gone
down. Thus revenue will tend higher, as the firm has more wares to sell.

The opportunity cost of additional trade credit may be analyzed in
much the same way. The availability of idle cash, at no *extra* cost, makes
it less expensive for the company to offer a longer net period. This is in
effect a cut in the price of the credit being offered. Hence it will increase
demand for the product and bring in additional revenue, without adding
pure money costs for the lending firm. The additional profit that could

FIGURE 8–4

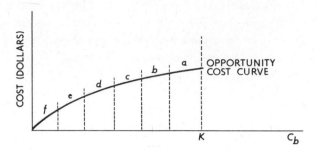

have been earned in this way is thus the opportunity cost of holding cash instead of investing in more accounts receivable.

Putting the various features of our list of relevant opportunities into a diagram, we get the picture shown in Figure 8–4. The firm is assumed to be holding cash of the amount K. The list of opportunities for alternative employment of this cash, in the short term, stretches back to the left of point K. In the diagram, the various potential outlets have been put in the order suggested in the list above. And they are identified by the letters used in the list. Moving to the left, each segment of the opportunity cost curve represents the next possibility the firm will examine as it chooses to hold less and less idle cash. Of course the diagram is only a suggestion, as the list is only a suggestion.

Borrowing Costs.   Closely associated with the opportunity cost curve is the schedule for borrowing or financing costs. This schedule will have two major segments—one for borrowing costs, the other for interest earnings forfeited on securities that are liquidated. Which of these segments is the first line of defense and which the second, we probably cannot say in general. The firm will sometimes find it cheaper to sell off Treasury bills. At other times the wiser course may be to borrow from banks and hold on to short-term liquid assets. In some instances, of course, the firm may not own any securities that can be sold.

Again, the diagram in Figure 8–5 is somewhat stylized. But we can assume tentatively that the selling-off of short-term assets is the nearest alternative. In this diagram, this course of action is labeled x. Borrowing at short term is labeled y, and it may be assumed that the cost of borrowing will rise as more and more of it is done.

One other quirk may be noted. The borrowing cost curve (to the right of K) is shown as beginning at a slightly higher point than the opportunity cost curve (to the left of K). This discontinuity reflects the cost of

FIGURE 8–5

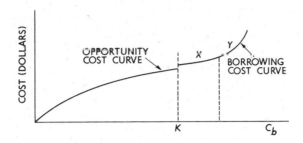

selling securities, either in the form of a commission paid to dealers or of a spread between bid and asked prices.

Procurement Costs

Now the role of procurement costs may be seen. The staff assembled for short term buying and selling of liquid assets (and sometimes for arranging loans) generates a fixed cost. They draw salaries and use space whether money is borrowed from the bank or not.

For this reason, the opportunity/borrowing cost curve will begin at some positive level on the vertical axis, not at zero. If that were the only impact of a "money desk" however, there would be no point in having one. The fruit of this specialization is in the flattening of that opportunity/borrowing cost line. By their vigilance and expertise the cost of borrowed funds is kept lower than it would otherwise be. The losses from liquid asset sales are likewise kept to a minimum by the specialization of a money desk.

PUTTING THE CURVES TOGETHER

It becomes a simple mechanical matter to put the two cost schedules together for a decision on the opening cash balance. The illustration could assume a firm to have no cash on hand when making the decision, or to have abundant cash on hand. It is only an illustration, but in the diagram in Figure 8–6 the company holds some cash (the amount K) though not enough to meet all short costs. Implicitly, this assumes also that the period will have a net outflow, thus giving rise to short costs.

The heavy dots, joined by a dotted line, indicate the short costs for the lumps of payments that will arise. The "x's" represent the summation of

FIGURE 8–6

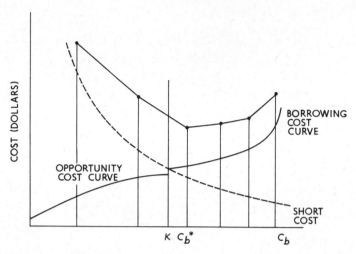

short costs and opportunity/borrowing costs. The optimum opening balance is thus shown by the lowest of these summary x's. It can be achieved by increasing the holdings of cash through selling off securities or by borrowing from banks or other short-term lenders. In another example, of course, the low point might come at the left of K. For that circumstance, the firm would reduce its cash holdings by investment or debt repayment.

CASH MANAGEMENT AND UNCERTAINTY

Where does uncertainty enter cash management? And how can the cash manager plan for it?

The reader should pause a moment and realize that in this discussion of cash management the short cost has already made its appearance in the world of *certainty*. In the inventory analysis, by contrast, nothing was heard of short cost until we had moved into the world of risk and uncertainty. This distinction is one more shadow cast by the universality of cash. If inventories are held to meet the known demand of customers, there is no competing demand for those inventories, urging that they be shifted into some other use. But, by contrast, if cash is held in one form, a decision has thereby been made *not* to channel the cash into some competing outlet. Hence cash faces opportunities in all directions, and what we choose to label as carrying costs and what as short costs is a matter of convenience. In the case of cash they are all opportunity costs.

The Impact of Uncertainty

A firm will aim of course to hold these costs to the cheapest combination possible. And in a world of *uncertainty*, its strategy for doing so will focus initially on the expected cash flows during the planning period. For it is this element—the *F*—that will produce the fundamental surprises.

Suppose a firm faces the following situation at the beginning of a planning period: An opening balance of $90 will cover in full a desired closing balance of $20 and an expected net outflow of $70. Assume that with the future known with certainty, the various cost schedules make $50 the optimal opening balance. The interjection of uncertainty will hit squarely at the $70 estimate for the net outflow and thus will raise questions about the choice of $50 as a proper beginning balance.

For example, if the net outflow turns out to be *more than $70*, then the short cost curve actually faced by the firm will lie to the right of the one that had been expected. The firm will have borne the expected carrying cost because the cash was carried. But the short cost will be higher. Putting it another way, the shift to the right of the short cost will push up the curve showing the combined short cost and carrying cost. Thus the opening balance, to be optimal, should not have been $50. This did not give the best counterbalance between the cost of being short the funds and the cost of carrying them.

In similar fashion, a net outflow of *less than $70* will shift the schedule of short costs back to the left. The curve showing the sum of short costs and opportunity costs will thus be lower than anticipated. This will not, however, mean that the opening balance should necessarily have been smaller than $50. The optimum is the low point on the combined cost curve, but since the two curves may have very different shapes, adding them together can give an infinite variety of forms. Sometimes the low point will be at a balance greater than $50, and sometimes a balance less than that. The significant conclusion is that the cost actually borne by the firm will be higher than has turned out to be necessary. The optimal trade-off between the two costs was not achieved, and a chance at cost savings was missed.

Coping with Uncertainty

In keeping down the costs of cash management in the real world of uncertainty, the businessman must give thought to three kinds of activities. There are first the steps he can take to reduce the cost of the optimal balance by shifting the schedule of short costs to the left. Second, he can act to limit the variability of net cash flows during the planning period. And third he can look to efficient ways of handling the overages and underages of cash that do occur.

The first two groups of activities bear on the basic uncertainties about F itself. The third group relates to the shape of the financing curve as a channel for short-term adjustments.

Shifting the Short Cost Curve to the Left.   The essential principle here is careful planning. With a little effort, a firm can arrange to have many of its gross cash outflows coincide with its gross receipts. This will make the net flow smaller than it otherwise would be. A smaller opening balance will then suffice to head off the short costs entirely or in part. In our diagrams, this would appear as a shifting to the left of the short cost curve.

To achieve this close matching of inflows and outflows, the firm must undertake cash forecasting. It must then explore ways to shorten the time and the distance that cash must travel in doing its work for the company.

Looking first at cash forecasting, it should be noted that the forecast sometimes will serve also as a control procedure.[1] Certain quotas will have been assigned the different divisions of the company, and the forecast becomes simultaneously a cash budget for those divisions. Under these circumstances, the forecast and budget will follow whatever form the company's organization dictates. They will be organized to show cash receipts and disbursements as they normally arise in different activities.

For example, the list of receipts might include collections on sales, repayments from subsidiaries, sales of fixed assets, and the like. Disbursements might list payroll, taxes, material purchases, dividends, and insurance. When the actual figures become available, they can be set down alongside the budget forecast figures, to show how good the aim has been. If the actuals are wide of the mark, then questions can be raised and tighter control exerted.

An equally common procedure, however—and often a parallel procedure—is the so-called "adjusted income" method. This is essentially the approach of our lobster fisherman in the opening chapter of this book. A forecast of this sort shows the projected income, expense, and profit. Then

---

[1] See Norman E. Pflomm, *Managing Company Cash*, Business Policy Study No. 99 (New York: National Industrial Conference Board, 1961).

it adjusts this flow for the various noncash items such as depreciation, change in receivables, and so forth. The result will be the net impact on the level of the cash pool, just as in Chapter 1.

With either method, many operating decisions and even quasi-financial decisions are taken as given. If a bond flotation has already been decided upon, the forecast will include its effect on the company's cash position. Expenditures on plant and equipment that have already been authorized will also be included. The two approaches are not really substitutes for one another and, as noted, are often used together in the same firm. Each in its own way helps clarify the amount of cash that will be moving in and out of the company, and the reasons for these flows and counterflows.

With this kind of information, the cash manager can identify those inflows and outflows that can be made to occur on the same date. Preferably of course that date should be later rather than earlier for the outpayments. Receipt of inflows should be not deliberately delayed, but if the outflows can be held off at no extra expense they can be paid with a later group of inflows.

Indeed, hastening the arrival of cash inflows may offer important efficiencies in cash management. For it will reduce the amount of cash tied up in idle form while it moves through bank collection processes or covers geographical distance. In terms of our diagram (Figure 8–6) this will make more of the firm's cash holding actually available for cash drains during the period, or actually in its bank accounts when the period ends. Hence it will shift to the left the cost curve associated with not being able to meet the drain or not having the minimum requirements at the close.

Most companies will have some opportunities to tighten up this gap of time and distance.

For example, except for purely retail establishments, most business firms have frequent occasion to ship their goods to some other place for final delivery to the customer. A good example is the automobile manufacturer. Plants are scattered over the nation, but automobile dealers are much more widely scattered. New cars have to be transported some distance to dealers' showrooms, and the sales money has to be collected and returned to the manufacturers' home office for deposit in a bank account.

Until this process is completed, the sales money cannot be used. To shorten the time during which funds are thus tied up, finance men in this industry have worked out special mailing arrangements, under which the check written by the dealer is put immediately into the mail upon delivery of the automobiles. The driver making the delivery is equipped with special envelopes, and special lockbox arrangements have been developed for getting the funds into a checking account immediately upon arrival at the bank.

Narrowing the Variability of Cash Flows.   By variability here, we mean departure from expectations. A careful forecast will produce more rational expectations, and should thereby reduce the number of surprises that a firm experiences. Its forecasts may miss the mark, but presumably it will less often suffer a large cash drain when it was prepared to enjoy an inflow.

Similarly, measures to synchronize receipts and payments should lower the absolute size of unexpected variations in net cash flow. An unanticipated outflow in one period followed by an unanticipated inflow in the next period will, instead, combine to give a net flow close to zero in the first period and a net flow equal to zero in the second.

Finally, steps to narrow the time and distance of cash in transit should give greater regularity to cash gains. In any case, they make it possible to plan with greater confidence. They also make it possible to find out where the delay has occurred, if it becomes necessary to revise the forecast.

Handling the Overstocking and Understocking of Cash.   Mistakes will be made, we can be sure of that. The firm must prepare for them.

If the drain is less than forecast (or the inflow greater than expected), the firm cannot avoid some of the extra carrying cost. But as the planning period wears on, and it becomes clear that the closing balance will exceed the minimum, the trade-off between short costs and opportunity costs can be reconsidered. The company can decide to meet some of the payments it had earlier decided to let pass. Or it can invest the excess funds for the remainder of the period. Or it can do some of both. In one way or another, the firm can capture some of the savings it might have had if it had forecast accurately the cash flow.

An understocking of cash may be more serious, for the reason that short costs may rise much more sharply than carrying costs. A greater outflow than anticipated (or a lesser inflow) may thus create an emerging pressure for extra funds. To avoid the unexpected short costs, the firm must get up the money by borrowing or by liquidating short-term assets. Thus, it must possess liquidity or borrowing capacity, or both. These form the parallel to safety stock in the management of inventories under uncertainty.

To meet this contingency—or other less drastic emergencies that threaten high short costs—the firm wants to make plans ahead of time. It wants to avoid having to face a very high short cost that can be alleviated only by a very high financing cost. Accordingly, many companies hold some sort of short-term earning assets that can be sold quickly with minimum loss of investment. And many firms develop some relationship with banks to insure at least a hearing when they need cash in a hurry.

Choosing the Opening Cash Balance.   We shall see, in the next chapter, what the character and cost of these emergency arrangements may be. But once they have been made, a firm can set down guesses about the shape of the financing curve it faces. With this information it can move toward selection of the beginning cash balance, using the same technique developed for identifying the inventory reorder point.

Estimates will have to be made for the cash flow during the period. Probability weights will have to be assigned for different possible levels of the cash flow. The information can then be put into a matrix showing the combined carrying cost and short cost for various beginning balances above and below the balance that would be optimal under certainty. The lowest mathematic expectation of combined costs will identify the best strategy.

QUESTIONS AND PROBLEMS

1. Discuss the similarities between inventory management and cash management, and the differences between the two.

2. It has been suggested that in cash management the short cost is simply a form of opportunity cost. Do you agree with this? Defend your position.

3. How might there be more than one opportunity cost?

4. The financial vice-president is much impressed with current yields on six-month time certificates of deposits. He is thinking of having the company buy about $20,000 of these liquid assets, and he has asked your advice. How would you respond (including questions you would ask in order to arrive at the best recommendation)?

5. Suppose a firm expects a net cash outflow with the following probability distribution:

$60,000	$70,000	$80,000
0.30	0.40	0.30

Making whatever additional assumptions you need, calculate the optimal opening cash balance for this firm.

SUGGESTED READINGS

BERANEK, WILLIAM. *Analysis for Financial Decision,* chap. xi. Homewood, Ill.: Richard D. Irwin, Inc., 1963.

BIERMAN, HAROLD, and McADAMS, ALAN K. *Management Decisions for Cash and Marketable Securities.* Ithaca, N.Y.: Cornell University Press, 1962.

PFLOMM, NORMAN E. *Managing Company Cash.* Business Policy Study No. 99. New York: National Industrial Conference Board, 1961.

ROBICHEK, ALEXANDER A., and MYERS, STEWART C. *Optimal Financing Decisions,* chap. vii. Englewood Cliffs, N.J.: Prentice-Hall, Inc., 1965.

TOBIN, JAMES. "Liquidity Preference as Behavior Toward Risk," *Review of Economic Studies,* February, 1958.

Chapter 9

THE BEHAVIOR OF CASH AND SHORT-TERM FINANCE—SOME FIGURES AND SOME THEORIES

Perhaps the most striking fact about the volume of cash held by nonfinancial corporations is that it is going down. For the better part of a decade, with the economic scale of almost everything else expanding enormously, business firms have actually reduced their holdings of demand deposits and currency.

This remarkable development may be seen in the first line of Table 9–1, which gives year-end figures for the 1950's and the first half of the 1960's. Through 1958, the cash balances of corporations moved up year by year, as one might expect in a growing economy. But thereafter, the absolute level of corporate cash balances leveled off, and since 1961 has drifted steadily down. By the end of 1965, balances were almost a third lower than in the earlier peak year.

As a part of the same story, the corporations' holdings of U.S. Government securities have also fallen during these years. This is part of the same story because debt instruments have great liquidity, approaching the liquidity of money itself. The market for them is highly organized and very widely based, and the risk of default is virtually nonexistent. The great bulk of Treasury issues held by business firms have original maturities of under one year, with many of them due in three months or less. This adds to their liquidity, since they will revert to cash automatically within a short time, and this in turn makes it easier to sell them without loss. A significant portion of these holdings are acquired as a way of accruing federal income tax payments. When these payables are netted out, the remaining corporate holdings of Government securities show an

TABLE 9–1

Selected Short-Term Assets and Liabilities of Nonfinancial Corporations End of Year, 1951–65

(Billions of Dollars)

	1951	1952	1953	1954	1955	1956	1957	1958	1959	1960	1961	1962	1963	1964	1965
Demand deposits and currency	27.9	28.7	28.8	30.9	31.9	32.1	32.1	33.5	32.5	32.0	33.4	32.8	32.0	29.3	27.4
U.S. Government securities	20.5	19.8	21.4	19.1	23.3	18.8	18.4	18.4	25.0	19.5	18.5	19.6	20.2	18.8	16.7
Adjusted for tax liabilities	−1.4	1.2	2.5	3.2	3.2	0.7	2.6	4.9	9.3	6.0	3.6	3.7	2.7	0.9	−3.7
Time deposits	0.9	0.9	0.9	1.1	1.0	1.0	1.0	1.9	1.5	2.8	4.6	8.4	12.2	15.4	19.2
All deposits and currency	28.8	29.6	29.7	32.0	32.9	33.1	33.1	35.4	34.0	34.8	38.0	41.1	44.2	44.7	46.6
All deposits, currency, and U.S. Governments	49.4	49.4	51.1	51.1	56.2	51.9	51.4	53.8	59.0	54.3	56.5	60.7	64.4	63.5	63.3
Open-market paper	0.9	1.2	1.4	1.3	1.3	1.5	1.8	1.8	2.3	2.8	2.9	3.7	4.4	5.9	6.6
All deposits, currency, U.S. Governments and open-market paper	50.3	50.6	52.5	52.4	57.5	53.4	53.2	55.6	61.3	57.1	59.6	64.6	68.9	69.4	70.0
Bank loans n.e.c.	17.6	19.2	18.8	17.9	21.3	26.1	27.3	26.6	29.8	31.1	31.1	33.5	36.1	39.2	48.4
Percent of total liabilities	12.1	12.5	11.7	10.8	11.3	12.8	12.8	11.9	12.3	12.2	12.1	12.0	12.0	12.4	13.8

Source: *Federal Reserve Bulletin.*

even sharper decline in recent years. These developments are evident in the second and third lines of Table 9–1.

With business holdings of time deposits at commercial banks, we have an entirely different picture. Indeed one of the fundamental shifts of recent years has been the rise in time deposits owned by business firms and the accompanying decline in their demand deposits. As the fourth line of Table 9–1 makes clear, the volume of time deposits had risen rather sharply in the late 1950's. The extraordinary climb, however, began in 1961, when major banks offered to issue *negotiable* certificates of time deposits—so-called "C.D.'s"—and securities dealers announced intentions to take part in market trading in these instruments. Interest rates on C.D.'s have been higher than on Treasury bills, banks have been willing to tailor maturity dates to the purchaser's requests, and the default risk to the holder has been regarded as minimal. All these features have made C.D.'s a very attractive form of short-term liquidity for business firms. At the same time, banks have seized on the new instrument as an opportunity to compete more vigorously for funds. The result has been an enormous outpouring of C.D.'s, with business firms becoming very large buyers, as may be seen in the fourth line of Table 9–1.

What the table also shows is that when time deposits are added to demand deposits and currency, the two together have *not* declined. The banks thus appear to have been competing partly with themselves, not only to lure deposits from each other, but also to lure them out of demand accounts into time accounts. This seems only part of the explanation, for if we now add gross holdings of Governments the new total declines, but only slightly. Thus some of the rise in time deposit holdings could represent shifts of funds that might otherwise have been invested in Treasury securities. The table also points up the considerable increase in corporate acquisition of open-market paper, which consists chiefly of the short-term notes of sales finance companies having national scope. When these are added to the money and near-money outlets already mentioned, the total moves up still more strongly during the last six or eight years. This development, taken along with the other changes, suggests that corporate liquidity holdings have undergone much more than a simple shift between demand deposits and time deposits. More fundamentally, there seems to have been a move away from demand deposits, which pay no interest, and toward other highly liquid assets that are interest bearing.

But liquid assets are not the only means of short-term financial adjustment. When business firms need cash, they may run down their short-term holdings, but they may also turn to short-term lenders, most notably the commercial banks. The degree to which they have done this is indicated in the last two lines of Table 9–1. Not all bank loans to corporations are shown here, because some take the form of mortgages, or the purchase of corporate bonds or open-market paper. The loans recorded in the table are those "not elsewhere classified" (n.e.c.). But the type of bank credit relevant to short-term financial management is given in these figures, and they make clear that bank loans have supplied funds on a magnitude fully equal to what could be provided by drawing down liquid assets. The much smaller role of this kind of bank credit among all sources of debt money is shown in the last line of the table. The apparently minor role it plays is a reflection of the large amount of bond financing, which of course is not relevant to short-term financial management.

THE SPECIAL PLACE OF BANKS

Digging further into these relationships, we may look first at the special functions performed by commercial banks. In any monetary economy, banks tend to be pivotal, particularly in a system characterized by freedom of enterprise. They are the chief depositories for the medium of exchange, they are the clearing mechanism for the flow of payments between buyer and seller, and they are a major engine of increased purchasing power. This central place of banks means that they will figure importantly in the financial management of most economic entities in the society, and we have just seen that this is so for business concerns.

In addition, just as banks occupy a rather special place in the lives of business firms, so do business firms loom large in the eyes of bankers. As depositors, business firms as a group are less important than households as a group, but individual business firms tend to hold much larger deposits than individual persons do. The decision of just one company to move its deposits may thus hit a bank much harder than a similar decision by several dozen households. And with the development of negotiable certificates, business firms have become large-scale holders of time accounts as well as of demand accounts.

On the other side of the banking business—the extension of bank credit—nonfinancial business concerns as a group are very significant, both singly and collectively. At the end of 1965, for example, all bank loans n.e.c. stood at $106 billion. And of this total, $73 billion were loans to nonfinancial businesses (including both corporate and noncorporate firms). When bank credit extended to households in the form of consumer credit and in the form of mortgages were added together, they still fell $10 billion short of the volume of business loans.

For many business firms and commercial banks, then, the relationship is a close one. The nonfinancial company borrows from a bank and, as depositor, lends to a bank—usually the same bank. For the bank, the relationship is a mirror image. The business borrowing is the bank lending, and the business lending is the bank borrowing. As a consequence, bankers with one hand beckon businessmen as customers and depositors, and with the other hand restrain them as debtors. Which of the two is the upper hand, if indeed either is, will depend on the relative bargaining power of the business firm in the loan market and in the deposit market.

Minimum Balances

This dual relationship has an important influence on interest rates and other terms of the loans that banks extend to businesses. In the clearest illustration, many business borrowers are asked to maintain their deposit balances above certain levels. In some cases the minimum is set as a percentage of a "line of credit"—i.e., an amount of credit the bank promises to make available to the firm on demand. Sometimes, deposits are not to be allowed to fall below the stated fraction of the line even though the line is not being used. And any firm that has a continuing relationship with a bank is likely to find the banker referring quite often to an "appropriate" level of balances.

This insistence on minimum deposits may not work any hardship on the borrowing company. A financial manager will scarcely ever let his company's cash holdings dwindle to nothing. He will keep some minimum amount in the cash pool at all times. If this amount is large enough to satisfy the bank's requirements, and if it resides chiefly in that one bank, the minimum balance requirement is of course no burden at all. In addition, the bank will almost certainly be supplying the borrower with services not mentioned in the loan agreement. It may offer advice on capital market flotations, or supply theater tickets for out-of-town sales managers. More importantly, the bank in times of tight money will probably supply credit first to those borrowers that have also been steady depositors. The corporation that is required to maintain balances can thus expect a receptive hearing when its borrowing needs rise sharply in a general expansion of the economy.

One widespread rule of thumb for minimum balance requirements is 10 percent of total negotiated lines of credit and another 10 percent for the portion of the line being used. Like most rules, this one varies with time and place, particularly with swings between tightness and ease in monetary policy. It also varies with the nature of the borrower, and with the size of the loan. Indeed, each arrangement tends to be negotiated between specific borrower and specific lender.

Not all bankers place heavy emphasis on the need for balances, and the minimum requirements are not usually written into formal agreements. But many bankers do feel the matter to be important, and the practice appears to have spread considerably since the early 1950's.[1]

Interest Rate Charges

The interest rate paid by a borrower doubtless depends on many things, as the level of any price does. Among the more important of these influences, however, one should certainly list the borrower's faithfulness as a depositor, the quality of risk that attaches to him, and the size of the loan he has requested. For short-term borrowers of the very lowest risk, the charge will be the so-called "prime" rate. Interest rates to other borrowers will range upward from that bench mark. The figures suggest that prime rate borrowers are also the larger customers with the larger loan demands. This means also that they are the more sizable depositors, the customers that banks are most anxious to keep. A borrower seeking a small loan may represent an excellent risk to the lender. But if he goes to a large bank, he cannot in the nature of things represent himself as a large depositor, which puts him at a disadvantage. And if he seeks accommodation at a small bank, he may run into diseconomies of scale in the banking industry.

In any case, rates charged for loans of $200,000 or more have been very close to the prime rate during the postwar years, while rates on smaller loans have remained well above the prime rate. As may be seen in Figure 9–1, however, the gap has narrowed somewhat as the higher rates moved near the usury rate ceilings, which in most states are set at 6 or 7 percent.

These figures show, of course, the nominal rates of interest. What they do not show are various devices for pushing up the *effective* rate of interest. The timing of interest payment, for example, can play an important

---

[1] See Caroline H. Cagle, "Credit Lines and Minimum Balance Requirements." *Federal Reserve Bulletin,* June, 1956, pp. 573–79; and Nevins D. Baxter and Harold T. Shapiro, "Compensating-Balance Requirements: The Results of a Survey," *The Journal of Finance,* September, 1964, pp. 483–96.

FIGURE 9–1

AVERAGE INTEREST RATES ON SMALL AND LARGE SHORT-TERM BUSINESS LOANS

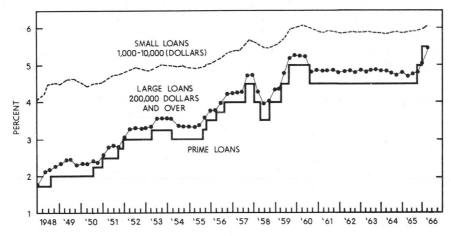

SOURCE: *Quarterly Interest Rate Survey* of the Board of Governors of the Federal Reserve System. Banks in 19 cities report rates on loans extended during the first 15 days of each end-of-quarter month.

role. Interest on short-term bank loans is typically taken in advance, as a discount. A business paying 6 percent is charged $6 for the actual use of $94—an effective rate of almost 6.4 percent. If, in addition, the balance must be repaid in monthly installments, then the effective rate is much higher. Moreover, the figures do not catch those business loans that have been handled as small loans under laws that permit the charging of nominal rates well above the usury ceilings.

Finally, one should add that total borrowing costs may exceed even the effective interest charge. If the borrowing company, at the bank's request, maintains balances above its own preferred working level, it avoids the bank's ill will and perhaps a higher nominal interest charge, but it forgoes potential earnings on the cash tied up thereby. Similarly, additional costs can be expected to arise out of some collateral requirements.

Security Terms

The best protection a banker has against default of loans is the continuing prosperity of the borrower. This is not always assured, however, and the borrower is sometimes required to put up collateral. The bank may actually take physical possession of the collateral, as in the case of marketable securities used to meet this requirement. In other cases, the borrower may give the banker a lien on some specific part of his assets, as, for example, a plot of real estate. Sometimes, a loan is secured by nothing more than the signature of a third party, who agrees to be held liable if the debtor fails to pay his debts. The range of possibilities is very wide.

For many borrowers the most prominent unpledged assets will be their inventories and their accounts receivable. These present some problems when offered as security, since putting them under bank control may interfere with the flexible operation of the borrowing company. To meet this difficulty, many ingenious devices have been invented. The notion of accounts receivable financing has been noted earlier. Another device of some importance is "field warehousing." If inventories can be kept in a public warehouse, the receipts issued by the warehouse can serve as collateral. But where the inventories are inextricably tied up with the production process, or where they are so bulky that transshipment between the warehouse and the producer's own premises becomes expensive, a warehousing company can set up a subsidiary at the producer's plant. This becomes a field warehouse, and it can create the necessary documents to provide collateral for the loan.

It appears that about one half of all business loans outstanding, including all maturities, are secured in some fashion. The smaller the borrower, the more likely it is that his loan will be secured. In fact, the proportion of loans secured ranges from about one fifth for the largest borrowers to almost four fifths for the smallest groups. When only short-term loans are considered, something less than half seem to require security, but the need to put up collateral is still much greater for the small firm than for the large.[2]

Maturity Terms

Loans tend to be described as either "short term" or "long term," with the dividing line placed by common understanding at one year. Loans made for longer than one year are called "term" loans, and have a closer kinship with stock and bond financing than with the short-term needs that concern us here.

It appears that the strictly short-term loan still accounts for the great bulk of business borrowing from commercial banks. It is important to add, however, that borrowers of short-term loans are sometimes able to renew them automatically at maturity. They can thus parlay a three-month credit into financing for a year or more. It should also be noted that patterns differ widely among industries. This is suggested in Table

[2] "Member Bank Lending to Small Business, 1955–57," *Federal Reserve Bulletin,* April, 1958, p. 403.

9–2, which shows for manufacturing corporations the amount of short-term bank indebtedness and the proportion of short-term to total loans from banks. Manufacturing firms as a group make greater use of term loans than some other sectors do, but the variation within manufacturing is considerable.

MONEY AND NEAR-MONEY AS SOURCES AND USES

Bank credit and bank deposits, however, are far from being the only channels through which short-term financial adjustments can be made. For one thing, there is apparently a significant portion of the business population that never borrows from banks at all. Some years ago, a study of widely distributed business firms turned up the surprising finding that a fourth of the companies interviewed had not been indebted to a

TABLE 9–2

SHORT-TERM LOANS FROM BANKS TO MANUFACTURING CORPORATIONS
(First Quarter, 1966)

	In Millions of Dollars	Percent of Total Bank Indebtedness
Durable Goods:	6,435	55
Transportation equipment	1,257	64
Electrical machinery	1,347	58
Other machinery	1,471	65
Other fabricated metal	680	55
Primary metal	369	42
Stone, clay, and glass	291	39
Furniture	154	53
Lumber and wood products	289	33
Instruments	291	58
Nondurable Goods:	6,001	53
Food	1,844	65
Tobacco manufacturers	447	98
Textile mill products	661	66
Apparel	719	73
Paper	222	34
Printing and publishing	238	42
Chemicals	720	36
Petroleum refining	534	30
Rubber	393	58
Leather	224	82
All Manufacturing	12,436	54

SOURCE: Federal Trade Commission and Securities and Exchange Commission, *Quarterly Financial Reports for Manufacturing Corporations*.

commercial bank in at least ten years.[3] Another third of the firms
reported that they borrowed only occasionally or rarely, leaving only
about two fifths that borrowed regularly. And for many of those that do
borrow there is the important alternative of selling off liquid assets
instead of turning to banks for credit.

One measure of the relative appeal of these various alternatives is the
interest rates that attach to the different options. For the firm seeking
additional funds, the cost of finance is suggested by the interest earnings
it must give up if it sells liquid assets and the interest payments it must
make if it borrows from banks. Conversely, if temporarily excess funds
are being put to work, they can earn the interest paid on liquid assets or
they can save the interest the firm is paying on bank loans that can now
be retired. As we have seen, interest rates are not the only terms of credit
agreements, and the nominal rates may not be the effective rates. Nonetheless, the list of rates reported in late 1966, and given in Table 9–3
suggests the rough order of relationship between these alternatives.

TABLE 9–3

	% p.a.
U.S. Government securities:	
Three-month bills	5.50
Six-month bills	5.80
Nine- to twelve-month bills	5.69
Three- to five-year issues	5.49
Finance company paper, 3–6 months	5.67
Negotiable time certificates of deposit:	
Three–six months	5.75
Six–twelve months	6.00
Prime rate	6.00

Probably the quickest way to see the interplay between money and the
various near-moneys is to examine the cyclical patterns. This is done in
Figure 9–2, which shows the *changes* in the selected current assets and
liabilities given earlier in Table 9–1. That is, the chart shows the flows
where the table had shown stocks.

In order to make them directly comparable, all the flows are stated so
that a positive change is a *use* of funds and a negative change a *source* of
funds. Thus when a curve moves above the zero dividing line, it indicates
that funds are being accumulated and put to a short-term use. That is,

---

[3] George Katona, *Business Looks at Banks* (Ann Arbor: University of Michigan Press,
1957), pp. 92–110.

FIGURE 9–2

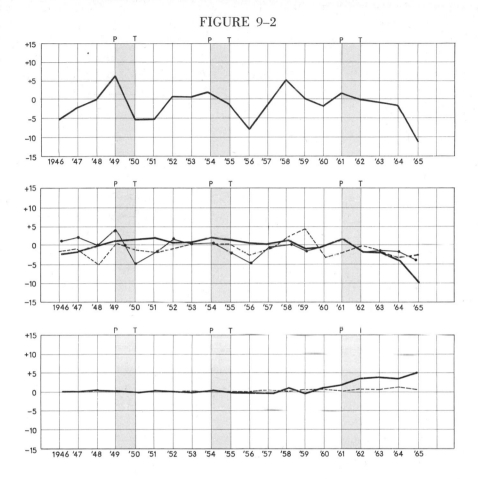

nonfinancial corporations as a group are (a) increasing their holdings of cash or (b) using cash to increase their holdings of liquid assets or (c) using cash to repay short-term bank indebtedness. Conversely, observations below the zero line refer to decumulation that brings cash into position for spending. These sources include (a) the direct drawing down of existing cash balances, (b) the liquidation of short-term financial assets, and (c) the increase in short-term bank indebtedness.

When these various strands are added together, we get the net uses of financial assets and the net sources of financial assets. Putting the figures together this way brings out very clearly that in recession years business firms tend to accumulate short-term funds, while in years of expansion and boom they decumulate funds. This pattern is unmistakable in the upper tier of Figure 9–2.

It is also clear that the greater part of this cyclical history can be explained by the swings in cash, bank indebtedness, and holdings of U.S. Government securities (over and above income tax accruals). The first two components—cash balances and bank credit—move very close together. The rise and fall of Treasury holdings is not exactly synchronized, but it follows a distinctly similar path. These fluctuations may be seen in the middle tier of Figure 9–2.

The two remaining financial assets are time deposits and open-market paper. They have taken on importance in the last five or six years—that is, since the last general recession. As a consequence, their record in the first half of the 1960's was more secular than cyclical. The impact they have made is shown in the bottom tier of Figure 9–2.

CASH MANAGEMENT IN THE LARGER SETTING

Before we risk losing our way in a maze of interrelationships, it is well to realize that we now stand at the border of a much larger country, a subject much broader than short-term cash management. That subject is the relationship of cash and other near-money to the full sweep of a firm's activities.

The role of cash is central to these activities, as it is to all economic analysis. We have in fact come to the major highway known as monetary theory. In particular, we seek understanding of the demand for money, and most especially the business demand for money.

In the discussions of a decade or so ago, this demand for money was often seen as falling into three classes. Using the distinctions proposed by Keynes, economists spoke of the transactions motive, the precautionary motive, and the speculative or investment motive. The first two, which most of the time got blurred together, were thought to be tied closely to the level of income. Balances held to meet this demand enabled the holder to make payments that might come due ahead of his receipt of income. They covered the time gap between outflows and inflows. The third demand, the speculative influence, was seen as acutely responsive to interest rates that might be earned on alternative uses of funds.

More recently, the discussion has shifted somewhat, putting more emphasis on measurement and less on motives, or at any rate, less on motives traveling under the Keynesian names.

An older school, somewhat modernized by its interest in new variants of the quantity theory of money, has denied the existence of a speculative motive for holding money. Interest rates do not enter into the demand for money, in this view. The demand stems entirely from the level of income. But it has also been proposed that the relevant measure is not observed income, but what is called permanent income. Others have suggested that the empirical measures of permanent income are really a partial measure of wealth. And using a more complete measure makes clear that wealth is (or is not) the governing force in the demand for money. Still others do give the interest rate a major role, but bring it into the analysis also as an influence on the transactions and precautionary demands, and not on the speculative demand alone. For these economists, the language of portfolio management has great explanatory power.

The preceding chapter, in analyzing the rational way for a firm to manage its short-term position, treated cash as an inventory in a manner similar to the portfolio approach.

The great bulk of the empirical work aimed at explaining the demand for money has centered on the household demand. The theory has been illustrated with individual persons and their decisions, and the data either exclude business firms or let them be swamped by other sectors that dominate the figures. A few studies have been aimed directly at the business demand for money. For the most part, these studies agree that interest rates play some sort of role. Some of the further suggestions from these studies are:

1. Given the level of interest rates, cash holdings are strongly influenced by the level of transactions, usually measured by sales. This might be interpreted as at least consistent with the existence of a short cost curve.
2. When the level of transactions changes from one period to the next, cash holdings change less than proportionately—i.e., the square root effect from inventory analysis.
3. When the level of transactions is higher because of larger sizes of firms within the same industry, cash holdings rise less than proportionately.
4. With increasing size of firm, there may be a wealth effect—i.e., total assets rise more rapidly than sales do, and since money balances are a part of assets they may rise as if they were a luxury good.
5. With increasing incidence of bank loans, cash holdings are relatively higher, probably reflecting compensating balance requirements in excess of what would be held if no balance minimum were set.

None of these matters can be considered settled. The different conclusions come out of different bodies of data, for different years and different numbers and kinds of companies. They use different definitions of cash, and different measures of transactions and of wealth. Thus on the theories themselves it is too early yet to choose.

ENVOI

At this point, the reader may suspect that he still would not know what to do if thrust behind a firm's money desk. We could go some further distance, but progress from this point would depend heavily on a knowledge of linear programming. That, we must assume, will come later in the reader's education.

It may also comfort the reader to know that he might climb the highest reaches of management science mathematics and not find a complete theory for short-term financial management. But those peaks will be conquered in time. For the present we can cheer the climbers on, and await their return.

Indeed, it is time that we left the world of short-term suboptimization. We have been treating the task of the money manager as a residual, a kind of catchall for the bigger decisions made elsewhere. This may be what often happens in fact, and it is what we mean by suboptimization.

We can also see, however, that even the best-run money desk may have an impact of its own. Heavy reliance on bank credit, for example, may suggest the need for funding these short-term debts by the issuance of bonds or new equity shares. Thus the question of appropriate capital structure is raised. And with it is raised the impact of capital structure on the cost of capital. These of course are much broader matters.

We must also realize that if new plant and equipment is acquired by the firm, the entire scale of operations may change. And because the firm will be larger, and perhaps somewhat different in nature, it will experience important new economies of scale, and perhaps diseconomies as well. These will ramify through its short-term financial management. New money and capital markets may open to the firm, and new specialization will become possible within the firm.

Accordingly, our attention will turn now to the broad plain of cash flow maximization for the firm's entire operations. After that, we will enter onto the still broader plain of maximization of stockholder wealth through the optimal combination of capital budgeting and appropriate capital structure.

QUESTIONS AND PROBLEMS

1. In 1965, the household sector increased its holdings of demand deposits by something on the order of $8 billion. In the same year, demand deposits

owned by nonfinancial business firms *declined* by more than $2 billion, repeating a pattern of several immediately preceding years. Against this background, why should much importance be attached to the relationship between banks and business firms?

2. If a dry-cleaning establishment must pay a nominal rate of 7 percent per annum for bank loans and maintain balances equal to 20 percent of the loan, what is the effective rate of interest? What is the rate if, in addition, the interest is paid in advance, as a discount?

3. Discuss the interrelations between short-term financial management and long-term financial management. Does it seem to you that short-term decisions should be thought of as essentially residual in nature? Explain your answer.

SUGGESTED READINGS

Heston, Alan. "An Empirical Study of Cash, Securities and Other Current Accounts of Large Corporations," *Yale Economic Essays,* Spring, 1962.

Hodgman, Donald R. *Commercial Bank Loan and Investment Policy,* chaps. x–xi. Urbana, Ill.: University of Illinois Press, 1960.

Meltzer, Allan H. "The Demand for Money: A Cross-section Study of Business Firms," *Quarterly Journal of Economics,* August, 1963.

———. "The Demand for Money: The Evidence from the Time Series," *Journal of Political Economy,* June, 1963.

Sorter, George H., and Benston, George. "Appraising the Defensive Position of a Firm: The Internal Measure," *Accounting Review,* October, 1960 (reprinted in E. Bruce Fredrickson [ed.], *Frontiers of Investment Analysis* [Scranton, Pa.: International Textbook Co., 1965]).

Whalen, Edward L. "A Cross-section Study of Business Demand for Cash," *Journal of Finance,* September, 1965.

Part III

LONG-TERM USES OF FUNDS

Chapter 10

MORE CASH FLOW MAXIMIZATION: CAPITAL BUDGETING

Up to this point, the focus of this book has been on short-term deci-sions. We have assumed that the basic plant and equipment of a firm were fixed. They have been seen as a framework within which managers operated. Given this basic structure, we have asked how managers should manipulate the elements of total cost and total revenue, so as to create the widest possible gap between the two. We have also asked how they can best insure that the firm is in fact operating at the point of widest gap between total cash cost and total cash revenue.

But time moves on. And as it moves, the framework itself will change. With the passage of time and the continued use of fixed assets, they age physically. They also become less relevant to the work of the firm, as time brings changes in taste and technique.

A firm thus faces two kinds of decisions regarding its plant and equipment:

—what action it must take, as time passes, to continue getting the same results out of fixed assets, and
—whether and in what manner it should restructure those fixed assets to enable itself to do things differently.

HOW THESE DECISIONS ARE DIFFERENT

Before looking more closely at these decisions it should be clear how they differ in character from the management activity taken up in preced-ing chapters.

The analysis of these problems dealing with plant and equipment is usually labeled as *capital budgeting*. This serves to distinguish it from *cash budgeting* and *working capital budgeting*, the subject matter of our earlier chapters. Capital budgeting is different in three respects:

1. The *long life* of the assets under consideration. These assets will yield their stream of returns over a period of years. As a consequence, the forecast of these returns flows is more uncertain, since the forecaster must peer further into the future. As another consequence, it is harder and more costly to reverse a decision of this kind. The commitment, once made, cannot be undone easily if the forecast proves to be wrong.
2. *Large outlays* are often involved. This is related to the long life of the assets. Long life means the asset cannot, or should not, be purchased piecemeal. In effect, a number of smaller assets are bundled into one larger one, and they must be acquired in a lump. Moreover, where outlays are large, the magnitude of financing will also be large.
3. The process of acquisition tends to be *unique*. Partly this stems from the infrequency of the decision. There is no weekly or monthly flow of closely similar decisions to make the decision a routine one. But partly also, the fundamental choices being made will fix the very character of the firm—the kind of output it sells, the kind of people it hires, the scale at which it operates, its essential mode of living.

These distinctions do not make short-term management less important. After all, poor inventory policies that go on too long can be just as damaging as a miscalculation in capital budgeting. The point is rather that *time* and *uncertainty* take on a deeper significance for capital budgeting. The uniqueness and longer life and larger lumps of outlays thus make capital budgeting an object of special attention at the upper levels of management. They also justify more elaborate techniques of analysis for coping with both time and uncertainty.

It must be noted that optimal decision making would require *all* asset acquisitions to be considered simultaneously so as to allow for interactions and net effects on returns and costs. Unfortunately, our analytical capacity and tools do not as yet permit us to approach asset management problems in this fashion. We compromise by assuming that working-capital decisions, being short run and therefore easily altered and not requiring sizable permanent finance, can be made "as if" the overall capital budgeting and capital structure problems had been solved.

HOW THE DECISION COMES UP

As we know, the short-term decisions can be organized within the framework suggested in Figure 10–1. This framework assumes the plant and equipment constant, with decisions made inside that setting.

FIGURE 10–1

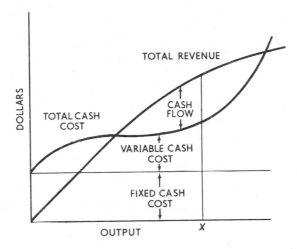

But when does the time arrive for *changing* the quantity and quality of plant and equipment? That is the question before us, and we may begin by noting five kinds of pressure that can threaten the level of cash flow enjoyed by the firm.

Maintenance and Replacement

To remain at the point of highest profit, the firm must continue to renew itself. Rust and decay must be headed off, worn cams and gears replaced. A great deal of this expenditure will be described as "maintenance," and will not show up at all as an outlay for plant and equipment. This flow of spending has some cyclical characteristics of its own, and peculiarities associated with the different habits of different companies. Whatever it includes in separate cases, maintenance is not a part of the expenditures we are most concerned with in this chapter. The focus here is on spending for any asset that is treated as depreciable by the company itself.

Replacement is less ambiguous. It refers to the depreciable assets that replace directly a piece of equipment or a building that has just been retired or passed on to someone else. The need for replacement, however, will not usually be suggested by a change in the fixed cost curves. Pressure will become evident, instead, in a gradual upward shift in the curve measuring *variable* costs.

These costs, it will be remembered, are determined by the quantity and quality of inputs required to get production with the existing plant and equipment. As those assets get older and crankier, they require more

FIGURE 10–2

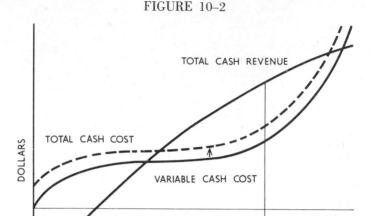

nursing and more repair. Frustrations mount; work has to be done over. All these developments cost money, and the variable costs for a given output creep steadily higher. This, of course, pushes the total cost curve higher and squeezes the cash flow, as suggested in Figure 10–2.

Cost Reduction: Changes in Factor Prices

The process just described might conceivably be labeled as "cost reduction," but firms find at least two other circumstances for acquiring plant and equipment in the hope of reducing their cost of operation. One of these springs from a change, or an expected change, in the dollars per unit that have to be paid for the inputs other than plant and equipment.

The most familiar examples involve rising wage rates. Companies that suffer rapidly growing wage bills, without much change in total output, look around for ways of substituting machines for men. If it is possible to add another machine to the row already at work, and thereby drop a dozen high-priced oilers or loom tenders from the payroll, the firm is under pressure to find a way.

This pressure may be envisioned in these diagrams as a gradual upward shift in the variable cost curve, much as in the case of a replacement need. For this, too, is a kind of replacement and can also be represented by Figure 10–2. The input to be replaced here is not the fixed asset but one or more of the factors being combined with it. Accordingly, the upward drift of the variable cost curve may trace out a somewhat different path than in the pure replacement case. The history of the two kinds of pressure, however, will often be closely intertwined. When a piece of old machinery has to be retired, this may also be the opportunity to retire some increasingly expensive loom tenders. The new machine may thus replace both old machine and old machinists.

Cost Reduction: Changes in Production Technique

The other pressure for cost reduction stems from the appearance of new techniques of production. New ways of carrying on the same old business may take many forms. They may appear in the shape of a new and cheaper raw material; or as new machinery that can do the old job in less time; or as new methods of handling the finished product, or of packaging it or storing it. Whatever the shape of the innovation, it offers the promise of lower costs for some given volume of output. This is not to say that it will permit cost savings at *all* levels of output. But if it gives promise of cost reduction over any significant range of output, the pressure for its adoption will mount.

Strictly speaking, this sort of pressure is not visible in these diagrams. Nonetheless, to the eye of the aggressive competitor (or the uneasy one), it is there if you seek it out. For the businessman looking ahead to greater profits, the existence of new techniques appears as a potential downward shift in the variable cost curve in its furthest reaches. Adoption of the new machine may simultaneously involve a somewhat higher fixed cost line, indicating a shift in the process toward greater fixed costs—as for example more specialized personnel, who will be kept on the payroll even in slack times. But while this puts a higher floor under the variable cost curve, it makes possible much smaller outlays for the variable inputs all along the way. As a result, total costs will actually be lower in the relevant range of output than under the old system. One possible pattern is shown in Figure 10–3.

For the uneasy management, fearful that its competitors will be in a position to undersell it by adoption of the new method, these fears take the shape of a flattening-out of the total *revenue* curve over the ranges of output at which the firm is currently producing, as in Figure 10–4. They are troubled that some part of the demand they now serve will be drawn away by the lower prices or better service offered by firms who have worked their cost structures down to lower levels. The lagging firm will then be able to sell its current volume of output only for a lower total revenue—i.e., lower prices—than before. If such a firm acts to forestall its

FIGURE 10–3

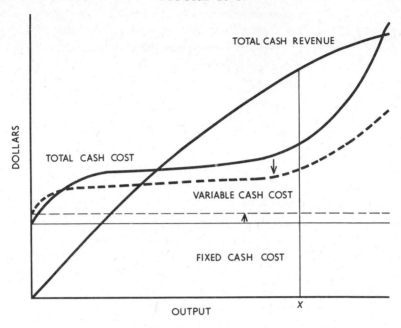

fears, its own total *cost* curve will shift downward, just as it would for the aggressive management.

When investment is carried out to take advantage of new techniques, the act may also reflect the other two pressures mentioned previously.

FIGURE 10–4

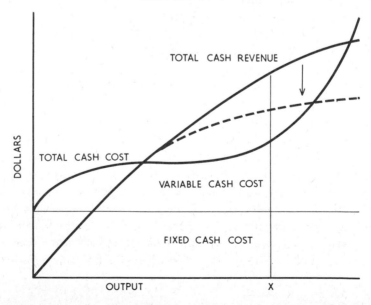

Adoption of a new process or a new machine is simply another kind of replacement. Moreover, the investment may be aimed at offsetting rising wages and other input costs, as well as at getting ahead or staying ahead of competitors. The three pressures we have listed so far may thus be rolled into one.

Expansion of Output

As time passes, the market for a company's product expands, and sales rise. The firm will increase its output, moving further to the right on its total revenue curve. Moreover, the curve may straighten up and rise steadily in the upper reaches of output, where formerly it had bent toward a horizontal line. With the growth in demand the firm no longer finds it necessary to shade its prices to move a larger volume of goods.

Cash flow, however, tends to be squeezed by this process. The impact can be seen in Figure 10–5. Output and sales that had once been at X_1 have grown to X_2, and total costs have begun to rise more sharply than before. The firm begins to consider expansion of its plant and equipment to meet the expanded market demand. In fact, it may take the occasion to increase its capacity beyond the present need, anticipating continued growth in the demand for its product—not too far ahead of current sales, but far enough to give it room for more growth in sales without a sharp run-up in costs.

For some firms the rise in demand may be inducement enough by itself, whatever the impact of expansion on total costs. These are firms seeking to maintain their "share of the market," a matter to which much prestige is attached. However, if such firms can produce and sell more only by expanding capacity, this is simply another way of saying that they find it too costly to operate at higher levels with their present capacity. Hence, they too are investing to avoid a squeeze on profit, and cash flow.

Again, the several pressures may converge. The firm may move at this point to replace old machinery, to shift the factor mix toward more fixed assets, to incorporate new techniques, and to expand total output capacity —all in one blow. The replacement feature would prevent the cost curves from shifting upward through age and fatigue. The change in capital intensity would raise the fixed cost line but flatten down the variable cost curve. The adoption of new kinds of equipment and methods would tend to reduce all forms of cost, at least over the relevant stretches of production. Finally, the installation of still larger amounts of fixed assets would make possible all these advantages at higher levels of output than before.

FIGURE 10–5

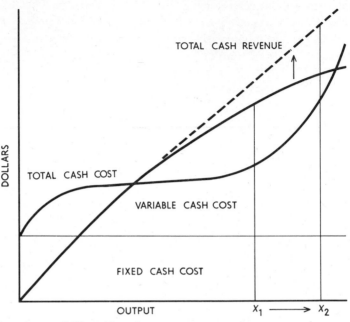

Introduction of New Products

The final kind of pressure for new plant and equipment is the decision to market products that the firm has not turned out before. These may consist of goods that the company's own research department has developed. They may, on the other hand, take the form of a new line of merchandise that competing firms have been offering at a tempting profit. Indeed, the easiest means of getting into production with a new line of goods will sometimes be to acquire control of another firm already in the business.

If the new product takes the place of an old one, there may be no net increase in the number of goods produced. The total revenue and cost lines would very likely change, however, reflecting the different market being served and the different process giving shape to the cost curves. If the new line of goods is added to the old one, the chart will again have to be altered. There may be savings in overhead costs that are common to both products—as, for example, the sales force or the advertising budget. There may be marketing advantages that serve to boost sales of both items. One can say only that all the curves are likely to shift.

When a firm is under pressure to introduce new products, it may also be experiencing the other kinds of pressure as well. The time may have arrived for replacing a worn-out piece of equipment. The company may feel that rising material costs, or wages, in its existing line of business make it profitable to shift into a new market. The perfection of a new technique in its own laboratories may now make possible the production of an item it has long wanted to manufacture. Thus, again, all the influences noted earlier may come to bear at the same time.

THE DECISION AS A CHOICE AMONG CASH BUDGETS

At this point, it is important to realize that capital budgets are also cash budgets, just as much as working capital budgets are. The difference is only that they stretch over a longer period of time.

This means that the various pressures just described can be seen as a comparison among alternative cash budgets. We could develop illustrations for each of the five types of pressure, but for our purposes two will do.

On some occasions the firm will be wondering whether to add a piece of equipment or a new building, with no change in its existing plant and machinery. This might be called the *pure expansion* case. Perhaps more typically the pressure will be for some form of *substitution*. In all five situations described above, there will probably be some element of substitution being considered—a new machine for an old one, a machine to replace workers, one mode of production instead of another, a new product for an old one, a new and higher scale of operation.

Taking pure expansion first, let us suppose a machine being looked at is expected to have a useful life of five years. Suppose also that during those years, the forecasts given in Table 10–1 have been made for the revenues, costs, and net cash inflow it will bring:

TABLE 10–1
(Thousands of Dollars)

	Year				
	1	*2*	*3*	*4*	*5*
Cash revenue	100	100	100	100	100
Cash costs:					
Variable	65	65	65	65	65
Fixed	10	10	10	10	10
Total	75	75	75	75	75
Net cash inflow	25	25	25	25	25

If the company must pay $80 thousand to get this machine, should it do so? The total cash return of $125 thousand is well in excess of the purchase cost. But not until four years from now will the firm recover all its original outlay and begin to gather in the funds in excess of that outlay.

This raises two fundamental questions: Is the return worth waiting for? And how should the firm deal with the element of uncertainty that naturally attaches to guesses about the future?

Before we begin grappling with these central questions let us look at the other major family of capital decisions—the substitution cases. For these we may assume that the new machine just discussed will, if adopted, displace some part of our present productive apparatus. To consider this possibility, we need a forecast of the cash budget behavior if *no* change is made.

As we have seen, the increasing pressure on cash flow can stem from pressures on either revenues or costs or both. Just for illustration, however, let us assume that variable and fixed cash costs are both expected to drift up over the next five years, if we do not acquire the new machine and retire an old one. Assume, for example the forecast in Table 10–2.

TABLE 10–2
(Thousands of Dollars)

	Year				
	1	2	3	4	5
Cash revenue	100	100	100	100	100
Cash costs:					
Variable	66	66	67	68	69
Fixed	10	11	11	12	13
Total	76	77	78	80	82
Net cash inflow ..	24	23	22	20	18

It is clear at once that the cash flow will be improved by buying the new machine and getting rid of the old one. But obviously the new machine is not free. We must push further.

We know that the new machine costs $80 thousand. Assume that the old one can be sold in the secondhand market for, say, $65 thousand. Then the net cost of the new machine will be $15 thousand. How does this compare with the improvement in cash flow the new machine will bring? The comparison can be set up as shown in Table 10–3.

Should the firm make the change? Again, the total cash flow will exceed the initial outlay—$18 thousand return for $15 thousand expenditure.

TABLE 10–3
CASH FLOWS
(Thousands of Dollars)

Year	With Old Machine	With New Machine	Improvement
0	—	−15	−15
1	24	25	+ 1
2	23	25	+ 2
3	22	25	+ 3 ⎫ +18
4	20	25	+ 5
5	18	25	+ 7 ⎭

But again the firm must wait a number of years for the cumulated inflows to match the initial outflow. Thus, again, the question: Is it worth waiting that long? And the further question: How should uncertainty be reckoned with?

Thus, whether the firm faces pure expansion or substitution, it needs a technique for coming to grips with time—both the passage of it and the uncertainty it brings. To this need we now turn.

QUESTIONS AND PROBLEMS

1. Why does the impact of time and uncertainty play a bigger role in capital budgeting than in working capital budgeting?
2. The acceleration principle discussed earlier in the inventory chapters was first used in analyzing the demand for capital equipment. How would you relate that principle to the discussion of capital budgeting in this chapter?
3. Are you sure you understand the statement that "capital budgets are also cash budgets, just as much as working capital budgets are"?

SUGGESTED READINGS

BIERMAN, HAROLD, JR., and SMIDT, SEYMOUR, *The Capital Budgeting Decision*, 2d ed., chaps. i, v, and vi. New York: The Macmillan Company, 1966.

MERRETT, A. J., and SYKES, ALBERT, *The Finance and Analysis of Capital Projects*. London: Longmans Green and Co., Ltd., 1963.

Chapter 11

CAPITAL BUDGETING
FOR SINGLE PROJECTS

How should management decide whether to go ahead with a proposed investment project?

Until quite recently, the economist offered little more than a fairly pat answer: "Go ahead with your investment project provided that it promises to yield a rate of return (after costs) greater than the interest rate." While this answer does focus attention on the central feature of capital budgeting—the comparison of expected revenues and costs of proposed investment projects—it does not provide a framework for the actual investment decision that management must make. Management might well ask the economist: "But how can we compute expected revenues or returns when the future contains so many uncertainties? And how can we figure the cost of raising the necessary money if, instead of borrowing it at a given interest rate, we use retained profits or sell stock?"

RULES OF THUMB

Payback Period

Not having received usable answers to these probing questions, management has tended to use rules of thumb to solve the problem. One of the most popular rules says: Adopt an investment proposal if it promises to "pay for itself" in five years. Managers feel some confidence in forecasting returns five years ahead. But feeling so uncertain about the more distant future, they play it safe by assuming zero returns after five years. Thus, management, using this rule of thumb too rigidly, might be led to pass up some profitable projects. Such rules of thumb are thus pessimistic.

This same rule of thumb has an overoptimistic side, too. It overstates the worth of the returns for the payback period of years in that it assumes that a cash flowback scheduled for later years—say year four—is as valuable as the cash flowback of the earlier years—say year two. In effect, this rule values the whole payback flow as if it were received on the day the investment outlay takes place. If the project in fact lasts no longer than the payback number of years, the projected rate of return by this method is seriously overstated.

Use of the words *optimistic* and *pessimistic* here really means that the rule yields wrong answers to questions about the volume of the cash flow returns and the present value of these returns. In the broad sense, the rule does not provide a reliable measure of the expected profitability of the projected capital expenditure.

Moreover, unthinking acceptance of any received rule of thumb neglects the *cost* of raising fresh funds. Thus, even if a firm uses a payback period rule on the revenue side, it must still calculate the comparative costs of raising the funds by alternative means.

Restricting Investment to Funds Available Internally: Plowback

When we do turn to the cost side, perhaps the most common rule of thumb is to restrict investment to the amount of retained profits generated internally. This so-called plowback rule frequently provides the cheapest financing. But this is not always so. For example, as we shall see, borrowing the funds may be cheaper when interest rates and the debt/equity ratio are low. Moreover, the supply of retained profits is not unlimited; alternative sources of funds must then be evaluated. And even if plowback were always the lowest-cost method of finance, a rule of thumb that called for capital expenditure whenever the funds were available within the company might at times preclude investments that ought to be made, and at other times lead to expenditures that ought not to be made at all. In fact, the rule assumes that the common stockholder would not be able to get a better rate of return by taking the dividends and investing them outside the corporation.

At a later point, we shall return to examine payback and plowback rules of thumb, since there are some cases where they may be used to good advantage. But it is not possible to know when such will be the case without a firm understanding of how business can estimate the expected flow of revenues from proposed investment projects as well as the anticipated flow of costs of financing them.

EXPECTED RATE OF RETURN ON INVESTMENT—
PROFITABILITY AND THE USES OF FUNDS

To determine whether a single piece of investment will be profitable requires that we first compute the rate of net return we expect it to yield. Then we can compute the cost of raising the funds needed to purchase the projected investment goods. If the expected rate of return exceeds the cost of capital, then the investment will benefit the stockholder and should be made; if not, the project should be abandoned.

Discounting for Futurity—The Internal Rate of Return Method

First, then, how can we compute expected rates of return? We know the cost of a piece of equipment. If we know the stream of returns that this investment will return to the firm, in principle there is no difficulty at all in deducing the prospective rate of return. But there are difficulties of computation and of coping with uncertainty as to *future* returns.

As we know from earlier discussions, expected returns are not profits in the traditional accounting sense. For these purposes, gross profitability is defined in terms of *net cash flow*, i.e, profits after taxes *plus depreciation*. The cash flowback to the owner consists of two parts: return on capital and recovery of capital. Owners' cash outflows or outlays are made in anticipation of obtaining a return on capital *while* it is invested as well as the return of the initial capital outlay itself. Moreover, we mean gross return before the cost of financing has been calculated, since we will want later to compare the cash returns with the financial cost of achieving those returns.

To see how cash flow can be stated as a rate, consider investment in a bond. With the purchase of a bond one is buying a claim to a stream of future returns (interest) plus the return of one's money at maturity. Take a bond that matures one year from now. Say that it can be purchased in the market for $1,000 and will pay $40 in interest at year's end. We know by inspection that the rate of return on this bond is 4 percent for the year.

This answer would be the same if we had turned the question around and asked for the rate of return on a bond that cost $1,000 and returned $1,040 at maturity one year hence. The 4 percent rate of return is the annual rate of discount that reduces the cash inflow ($1,040) to equality with the cash outflow ($1,000).

Finding the yield on a bond is perfectly analogous to finding the yield on *any* investment. In our simple example, we have the opportunity to invest $1,000 today in a machine that has a life of one year and that promises a return flow of $1,040 at the year's end. Thus we would say that the machine's yield or "internal" rate of return is 4 percent. That is, the investment will yield a flow of revenues that will return the fully depreciated value of the machine plus $40. After allowing for the return *of* investment ($1,000) there is a net yield of $40 *on* the investment.

Putting the matter generally, the "internal" rate of return is that rate which equates the smaller cash outlay with the larger, but lagged stream of cash inflows. This is *not* a rate of *profit* on the investment. Rather it tells us that if we can obtain the initial funds at any rate *less* than this rate of returns, we will earn a profit.

We should perhaps remind ourselves at this point that finding the rate we seek will sooner or later require an additional step. For the stream of cash inflows we are trying to evaluate is not only a *future* stream, but also an *uncertain* future stream. The rate that discounts the cash flow for futurity alone is not enough. There must be a double discount. We value the bird in hand because it is *surely* ours as well as because the sooner we have it the more eggs we get. In effect, then, the return on capital outlays is a combined reward for waiting and risk taking.

But for the balance of this chapter and for the next two chapters our concern will be the discount for waiting. The treatment of uncertainty will be taken up separately in Chapter 14.

Let us take a slightly more complex and realistic example which requires the use of the bond tables rather than arithmetic scanning to answer. Suppose our company is considering an investment project that will yield $1,000 a year for ten years but requires an outlay of $8,111. What is the expected rate of return from such an investment?

If we look at bond Table 11-1, "Present Value of $1 Received Annually at the End of the Year for N Years," we will find our answer by looking along the ten-year row to find a number close to 8.111 (for that number multiplied by $1,000 is $8,111) and then looking up the column to read off the percent. In this case, along the ten-year line the number 8.111 appears in the 4 percent column. This means that if we pay $8,111 today for the right to receive $1,000 a year for each of ten successive years, we will be earning 4 percent on the investment and getting the investment outlay back as well. In still other words, the present value (i.e., at time 0) of the future return—$1,000 to be received annually for each of the next ten years (i.e., over time 1–10)—is equal to $8,111

TABLE 11-1

Present Value of $1 Received Annually at the End of Each "Year" for N Years

Years (N)	1%	2%	4%	6%	8%	10%	12%	14%	15%	16%	18%	20%	22%	24%	25%	26%	28%	30%	35%	40%	45%	50%
1	0.990	0.980	0.962	0.943	0.926	0.909	0.893	0.877	0.870	0.862	0.847	0.833	0.820	0.806	0.800	0.794	0.781	0.769	0.741	0.714	0.690	0.667
2	1.970	1.942	1.886	1.833	1.783	1.736	1.690	1.647	1.626	1.605	1.566	1.528	1.492	1.457	1.440	1.424	1.392	1.361	1.289	1.224	1.165	1.111
3	2.941	2.884	2.775	2.673	2.577	2.487	2.402	2.322	2.283	2.246	2.174	2.106	2.042	1.981	1.952	1.923	1.868	1.816	1.696	1.589	1.493	1.407
4	3.902	3.808	3.630	3.465	3.312	3.170	3.037	2.914	2.855	2.798	2.690	2.589	2.494	2.404	2.362	2.320	2.241	2.166	1.997	1.849	1.720	1.605
5	4.853	4.713	4.452	4.212	3.993	3.791	3.605	3.433	3.352	3.274	3.127	2.991	2.864	2.745	2.689	2.635	2.532	2.436	2.220	2.035	1.876	1.737
6	5.795	5.601	5.242	4.917	4.623	4.355	4.111	3.889	3.784	3.685	3.498	3.326	3.167	3.020	2.951	2.885	2.759	2.643	2.385	2.168	1.983	1.824
7	6.728	6.472	6.002	5.582	5.206	4.868	4.564	4.288	4.160	4.039	3.812	3.605	3.416	3.242	3.161	3.083	2.937	2.802	2.508	2.263	2.057	1.883
8	7.652	7.325	6.733	6.210	5.747	5.335	4.968	4.639	4.487	4.344	4.078	3.837	3.619	3.421	3.329	3.241	3.076	2.925	2.598	2.331	2.108	1.922
9	8.566	8.162	7.435	6.802	6.247	5.759	5.328	4.946	4.772	4.607	4.303	4.031	3.786	3.566	3.463	3.366	3.184	3.019	2.665	2.379	2.144	1.948
10	9.471	8.983	8.111	7.360	6.710	6.145	5.650	5.216	5.019	4.833	4.494	4.192	3.923	3.682	3.571	3.465	3.269	3.092	2.715	2.414	2.168	1.965
11	10.368	9.787	8.760	7.887	7.139	6.495	5.937	5.453	5.234	5.029	4.656	4.327	4.035	3.776	3.656	3.544	3.335	3.147	2.752	2.438	2.185	1.977
12	11.255	10.575	9.385	8.384	7.536	6.814	6.194	5.660	5.421	5.197	4.793	4.439	4.127	3.851	3.725	3.606	3.387	3.190	2.779	2.456	2.196	1.985
13	12.134	11.343	9.986	8.853	7.904	7.103	6.424	5.842	5.583	5.342	4.910	4.533	4.203	3.912	3.780	3.656	3.427	3.223	2.799	2.468	2.204	1.990
14	13.004	12.106	10.563	9.295	8.244	7.367	6.628	6.002	5.724	5.468	5.008	4.611	4.265	3.962	3.824	3.695	3.459	3.249	2.814	2.477	2.210	1.993
15	13.865	12.849	11.118	9.712	8.559	7.606	6.811	6.142	5.847	5.575	5.092	4.675	4.315	4.001	3.859	3.726	3.483	3.268	2.825	2.484	2.214	1.995
16	14.718	13.578	11.652	10.106	8.851	7.824	6.974	6.265	5.954	5.669	5.162	4.730	4.357	4.033	3.887	3.751	3.503	3.283	2.834	2.489	2.216	1.997
17	15.562	14.292	12.166	10.477	9.122	8.022	7.120	6.373	6.047	5.749	5.222	4.775	4.391	4.059	3.910	3.771	3.518	3.295	2.840	2.492	2.218	1.998
18	16.398	14.992	12.659	10.828	9.372	8.201	7.250	6.467	6.128	5.818	5.273	4.812	4.419	4.080	3.928	3.786	3.529	3.304	2.844	2.494	2.219	1.999
19	17.226	15.678	13.134	11.158	9.604	8.365	7.366	6.550	6.198	5.877	5.316	4.844	4.442	4.097	3.942	3.799	3.539	3.311	2.848	2.496	2.220	1.999
20	18.046	16.351	13.590	11.470	9.818	8.514	7.469	6.623	6.259	5.929	5.353	4.870	4.460	4.110	3.954	3.808	3.546	3.316	2.850	2.497	2.221	1.999
21	18.857	17.011	14.029	11.764	10.017	8.649	7.562	6.687	6.312	5.973	5.384	4.891	4.476	4.121	3.963	3.816	3.551	3.320	2.852	2.498	2.221	2.000
22	19.660	17.658	14.451	12.042	10.201	8.772	7.645	6.743	6.359	6.011	5.410	4.909	4.488	4.130	3.970	3.822	3.556	3.323	2.853	2.498	2.222	2.000
23	20.456	18.292	14.857	12.303	10.371	8.883	7.718	6.792	6.399	6.044	5.432	4.925	4.499	4.137	3.976	3.827	3.559	3.325	2.854	2.499	2.222	2.000
24	21.243	18.914	15.247	12.550	10.529	8.985	7.784	6.835	6.434	6.073	5.451	4.937	4.507	4.143	3.981	3.831	3.562	3.327	2.855	2.499	2.222	2.000
25	22.023	19.523	15.622	12.783	10.675	9.077	7.843	6.873	6.464	6.097	5.467	4.948	4.514	4.147	3.985	3.834	3.564	3.329	2.856	2.499	2.222	2.000
26	22.795	20.121	15.983	13.003	10.810	9.161	7.896	6.906	6.491	6.118	5.480	4.956	4.520	4.151	3.988	3.837	3.566	3.330	2.856	2.500	2.222	2.000
27	23.560	20.707	16.330	13.211	10.935	9.237	7.943	6.935	6.514	6.136	5.492	4.964	4.524	4.154	3.990	3.839	3.567	3.331	2.856	2.500	2.222	2.000
28	24.316	21.281	16.663	13.406	11.051	9.307	7.984	6.961	6.534	6.152	5.502	4.970	4.528	4.157	3.992	3.840	3.568	3.331	2.857	2.500	2.222	2.000
29	25.066	21.844	16.984	13.591	11.158	9.370	8.022	6.983	6.551	6.166	5.510	4.975	4.531	4.159	3.994	3.841	3.569	3.332	2.857	2.500	2.222	2.000
30	25.808	22.396	17.292	13.765	11.258	9.427	8.055	7.003	6.566	6.177	5.517	4.979	4.534	4.160	3.995	3.842	3.569	3.332	2.857	2.500	2.222	2.000
40	32.835	27.355	19.793	15.046	11.925	9.779	8.244	7.105	6.642	6.234	5.548	4.997	4.544	4.166	3.999	3.846	3.571	3.333	2.857	2.500	2.222	2.000
50	39.196	31.424	21.482	15.762	12.234	9.915	8.304	7.133	6.661	6.246	5.554	4.999	4.545	4.167	4.000	3.846	3.571	3.333	2.857	2.500	2.222	2.000

Source: Robert N. Anthony, Management Accounting: Text and Cases (3d ed.; Homewood, Ill.: Richard D. Irwin, Inc., 1964), p. 743.

(paid in time 0), only when the rate of discount is 4 percent. Thus the definition of the internal rate is that rate which equates the present values of the cash outlay and the cash inflow.

Hence the procedure discounts expected streams of inflow to allow for futurity. Although the sum of the annual streams that will flow back to us from the machine during its lifetime totals $10,000, we know that the *present value* of that stream of returns is worth less than $10,000 to us because it is received only after the passage of time. If we had received the whole $10,000 stream at once in time 0, we could have loaned it out and earned 4 percent on it as if we had bought a 4 percent bond.

We can dig a little deeper into this illustration with the aid of Table 11–2. Where the first table showed the *combined* present value of a dollar of returns during each of the ensuing ten years, Table 11–2 shows the present value of a dollar of returns in *one* such future year. Thus, looking at the column under 4 percent, we see that a dollar received at the end of the first year will have a present value of slightly over 96 cents. That is, the investment of 96.2 cents now at an annual rate of 4 percent will produce 100 cents a year from now.

Moving down the column, the present value of a dollar to be received two years hence is 0.925. This is smaller than the present value one year from now, because after all it will take less money to grow to a full dollar when growth goes on for two years rather than one.

Copying off the column for the full ten years, and adding it up, we get the following:

One year hence is	$0.962
Two years hence is	0.925
Three years hence is	0.889
Four years hence is	0.855
Five years hence is	0.822
Six years hence is	0.790
Seven years hence is	0.760
Eight years hence is	0.731
Nine years hence is	0.703
Ten years hence is	0.676
	$8.113

Thus, for a stream of $1 for each of ten years we get a present value of $8.11. If the annual flows should be $1,000, then the present value obviously would be one thousand times larger—i.e., $8,113. With slight differences because of rounding, this is the answer we got from the first table. A ten-year flow with a face value of $10,000 has a present value of $8,111, assuming a 4 percent discount rate. Or, put the other way round,

TABLE 11-2

PRESENT VALUE OF $1 RECEIVED AT THE END OF THE "YEAR"

Years Hence	1%	2%	4%	6%	8%	10%	12%	14%	15%	16%	18%	20%	22%	24%	25%	26%	28%	30%	35%	40%	45%	50%
1	0.990	0.980	0.962	0.943	0.926	0.909	0.893	0.877	0.870	0.862	0.847	0.833	0.820	0.806	0.800	0.794	0.781	0.769	0.741	0.714	0.690	0.667
2	0.980	0.961	0.925	0.890	0.857	0.826	0.797	0.769	0.756	0.743	0.718	0.694	0.672	0.650	0.640	0.630	0.610	0.592	0.549	0.510	0.476	0.444
3	0.971	0.942	0.889	0.840	0.794	0.751	0.712	0.675	0.658	0.641	0.609	0.579	0.551	0.524	0.512	0.500	0.477	0.455	0.406	0.364	0.328	0.296
4	0.961	0.924	0.855	0.792	0.735	0.683	0.636	0.592	0.572	0.552	0.516	0.482	0.451	0.423	0.410	0.397	0.373	0.350	0.301	0.260	0.226	0.198
5	0.951	0.906	0.822	0.747	0.681	0.621	0.567	0.519	0.497	0.476	0.437	0.402	0.370	0.341	0.328	0.315	0.291	0.269	0.223	0.186	0.156	0.132
6	0.942	0.888	0.790	0.705	0.630	0.564	0.507	0.456	0.432	0.410	0.370	0.335	0.303	0.275	0.262	0.250	0.227	0.207	0.165	0.133	0.108	0.088
7	0.933	0.871	0.760	0.665	0.583	0.513	0.452	0.400	0.376	0.354	0.314	0.279	0.249	0.222	0.210	0.198	0.178	0.159	0.122	0.095	0.074	0.059
8	0.923	0.853	0.731	0.627	0.540	0.467	0.404	0.351	0.327	0.305	0.266	0.233	0.204	0.179	0.168	0.157	0.139	0.123	0.091	0.068	0.051	0.039
9	0.914	0.837	0.703	0.592	0.500	0.424	0.361	0.308	0.284	0.263	0.225	0.194	0.167	0.144	0.134	0.125	0.108	0.094	0.067	0.048	0.035	0.026
10	0.905	0.820	0.676	0.558	0.463	0.386	0.322	0.270	0.247	0.227	0.191	0.162	0.137	0.116	0.107	0.099	0.085	0.073	0.050	0.035	0.024	0.017
11	0.896	0.804	0.650	0.527	0.429	0.350	0.287	0.237	0.215	0.195	0.162	0.135	0.112	0.094	0.086	0.079	0.066	0.056	0.037	0.025	0.017	0.012
12	0.887	0.788	0.625	0.497	0.397	0.319	0.257	0.208	0.187	0.168	0.137	0.112	0.092	0.076	0.069	0.062	0.052	0.043	0.027	0.018	0.012	0.008
13	0.879	0.773	0.601	0.469	0.368	0.290	0.229	0.182	0.163	0.145	0.116	0.093	0.075	0.061	0.055	0.050	0.040	0.033	0.020	0.013	0.008	0.005
14	0.870	0.758	0.577	0.442	0.340	0.263	0.205	0.160	0.141	0.125	0.099	0.078	0.062	0.049	0.044	0.039	0.032	0.025	0.015	0.009	0.006	0.003
15	0.861	0.743	0.555	0.417	0.315	0.239	0.183	0.140	0.123	0.108	0.084	0.065	0.051	0.040	0.035	0.031	0.025	0.020	0.011	0.006	0.004	0.002
16	0.853	0.728	0.534	0.394	0.292	0.218	0.163	0.123	0.107	0.093	0.071	0.054	0.042	0.032	0.028	0.025	0.019	0.015	0.008	0.005	0.003	0.002
17	0.844	0.714	0.513	0.371	0.270	0.198	0.146	0.108	0.093	0.080	0.060	0.045	0.034	0.026	0.023	0.020	0.015	0.012	0.006	0.003	0.002	0.001
18	0.836	0.700	0.494	0.350	0.250	0.180	0.130	0.095	0.081	0.069	0.051	0.038	0.028	0.021	0.018	0.016	0.012	0.009	0.005	0.002	0.001	0.001
19	0.828	0.686	0.475	0.331	0.232	0.164	0.116	0.083	0.070	0.060	0.043	0.031	0.023	0.017	0.014	0.012	0.009	0.007	0.003	0.002	0.001	
20	0.820	0.673	0.456	0.312	0.215	0.149	0.104	0.073	0.061	0.051	0.037	0.026	0.019	0.014	0.012	0.010	0.007	0.005	0.002	0.001	0.001	
21	0.811	0.660	0.439	0.294	0.199	0.135	0.093	0.064	0.053	0.044	0.031	0.022	0.015	0.011	0.009	0.008	0.006	0.004	0.002	0.001		
22	0.803	0.647	0.422	0.278	0.184	0.123	0.083	0.056	0.046	0.038	0.026	0.018	0.013	0.009	0.007	0.006	0.004	0.003	0.001	0.001		
23	0.795	0.634	0.406	0.262	0.170	0.112	0.074	0.049	0.040	0.033	0.022	0.015	0.010	0.007	0.006	0.005	0.003	0.002	0.001			
24	0.788	0.622	0.390	0.247	0.158	0.102	0.066	0.043	0.035	0.028	0.019	0.013	0.008	0.006	0.005	0.004	0.003	0.002	0.001			
25	0.780	0.610	0.375	0.233	0.146	0.092	0.059	0.038	0.030	0.024	0.016	0.010	0.007	0.005	0.004	0.003	0.002	0.001				
26	0.772	0.598	0.361	0.220	0.135	0.084	0.053	0.033	0.026	0.021	0.014	0.009	0.006	0.004	0.003	0.002	0.002	0.001				
27	0.764	0.586	0.347	0.207	0.125	0.076	0.047	0.029	0.023	0.018	0.011	0.007	0.005	0.003	0.002	0.002	0.001	0.001				
28	0.757	0.574	0.333	0.196	0.116	0.069	0.042	0.026	0.020	0.016	0.010	0.006	0.004	0.002	0.002	0.002	0.001	0.001				
29	0.749	0.563	0.321	0.185	0.107	0.063	0.037	0.022	0.017	0.014	0.008	0.005	0.003	0.002	0.002	0.001	0.001	0.001				
30	0.742	0.552	0.308	0.174	0.099	0.057	0.033	0.020	0.015	0.012	0.007	0.004	0.003	0.002	0.001	0.001	0.001	0.001				
40	0.672	0.453	0.208	0.097	0.046	0.022	0.011	0.005	0.004	0.003	0.001	0.001										
50	0.608	0.372	0.141	0.054	0.021	0.009	0.003	0.001	0.001	0.001												

SOURCE: Robert N. Anthony, *Management Accounting; Text and Cases* (3d ed., Homewood, Ill.: Richard D. Irwin, Inc., 1964).

an outlay of $8,111 that yields $1,000 a year for ten years has an internal rate of 4 percent. That is the rate that will make the present value of the inflow equal to the present value of the outlay.

As one final example, let us look again at the investment decision left unsolved at the end of the previous chapter. In the pure expansion case, the firm was considering whether to add a machine that promised annual returns of $25,000 over five years, and cost $80,000 to acquire. Thus to get one dollar of annual return, it must make an initial outlay be $80,000 divided by $25,000—or 3.2 dollars. Taking this figure into Table 11–1, we look across the row for five years, in search of the number nearest 3.2. The search takes us to a point between 16 percent and 18 percent, and if the table were more detailed we would discover the answer to be almost exactly 17 percent. That is the internal rate of return on the machine up for decision at the end of the last chapter.

For the substitution case, the answer comes a little harder. The annual cash flow from substituting the new machine for an old one, it will be recalled, was not constant over the five years. This requires us to use Table 11–2 instead of Table 11–1, and to resort to trial-and-error methods. After some experimenting, we will discover that the answer is somewhere between 4 percent and 6 percent, as Table 11–3 will show.

TABLE 11–3

| Year | Improvement | Present Value with Discount of— | | | |
		4%		6%	
0	−15	1.000	−15.000	1.000	−15.000
1	1	0.962	0.962	0.943	0.943
2	2	0.925	1.850	0.890	1.780
3	3	0.889	2.667	0.840	2.520
4	5	0.855	4.275	0.792	3.960
5	7	0.822	5.754	0.747	5.229
			15.508		14.432

Using 4 percent we get a present value of future inflows that is higher than the outflow by 0.508. And using 6 percent we get an answer that falls short by 0.568. Without further computations, then, we can see that the correct rate lies almost exactly halfway between 4 and 6 percent, though slightly closer to 4 percent than to 6 percent. With more detailed tables, we would discover the true rate to be just short of 5 percent.

We still do not know whether to buy the machine or not. For that, we must know the cost of funds. Taking the substitution case as an illustra-

tion, if the cost of funds were exactly equal to the internal rate of return—
i.e., just under 5 percent—the firm would be at the point of indifference.
It could expect neither profit nor loss on the deal. If the cost of funds were
lower, say 4 percent, the firm would want to adopt the proposal. It could
raise funds at a cost of 4 percent and put them to work at a yield of almost
5 percent.

These same decisions could have been derived directly if, knowing the
cost of funds, we had discounted the future stream to find its present
value. If the cost of funds were just under 5 percent, the present value of
the future stream would be $15,000. But since the present value of the
outlays is also $15,000, there would be no *net* present value. There would
be no reason to go ahead with the investment.

By the same token, if funds could be raised for well under 5 percent—
say 4 percent—the project would add to the wealth of the owners and
should therefore be adopted. As we have just seen, a 4 percent discount
would yield a gross present value of $15,508. Since the outlay necessary
to generate those flows is $15,000, the project has a net present value of
$508. It thus should be accepted.

In all our discussion so far, the question has been whether to accept or
reject a single project, a procedure sometimes called screening. In such
cases, it makes no difference whether we judge by the standard that
internal rate of return exceeds the cost of capital or the standard that net
present value be positive. The internal rate method has the advantage of
separating the capital budgeting problem into two quite distinct stages,
thus helping our understanding of the process. But the answers will be the
same.

Difficulties begin to arise when we come to so-called "ranking" problems—the need to choose among *alternative* projects or the need to decide
how many projects to take. Were there no ranking problems we would not
even bother to introduce the net present value method. As we shall see in
the next chapter, however, when ranking rather than screening is the
issue, there may be times when the net present value method seems
preferable. We turn to those issues now.

QUESTIONS AND PROBLEMS

1. Looking back in Chapter 1, do you think the young lobsterman should
   have bought his uncle's boat? If you feel the need of information beyond
   that given in Chapter 1, make specific assumptions of your own.

2. In the substitution case discussed in this chapter and at the end of Chapter 10, the old machine could be sold in the secondhand market for $65,000. If funds could be raised at a cost of 4 percent, would you buy this secondhand machine? What if the cost of funds was 6 percent?

3. For a 15-year project that costs $56,000 and gives an annual cash flow of $10,000, what is the internal rate of return? If the cost of capital is 12 percent, what is the net present value of the project?

4. If a machine costing $50,000 has five years life in it and will produce a cash flow of $16,000, $14,000, $12,000, $10,000, and $8,000 over those five years, should it be purchased when the cost of capital is 10 percent? What is the highest cost of capital that will permit acceptance of the project?

5. Suppose a piece of equipment is expected to yield an annual cash flow of $10,000 a year for seven years at the end of which it will be sold for scrap for $4,000. If the cost of capital is 14 percent, what is the highest purchase price that should be paid to acquire the equipment?

APPENDIX TO CHAPTER 11
SOME OF THE MATHEMATICS
OF CAPITAL BUDGETING

The examples of capital budgeting discussed in this chapter were handled without any mathematics. All the information needed could be found in two simple tables.

Yet relying entirely on tables may leave us uneasy. It is much better to feel that we understand the relationships on which the tables are built. Fortunately, this understanding can be obtained with a few minor exercises in algebra.

The Basic Relationships

If a sum of money is invested now at a given interest rate, we know that with the passage of a year the original sum will have grown. It will equal the initial sum plus the interest on that sum:

Now	A Year from Now	
	Principal	Interest
$M \longrightarrow$	M	$+$ rM
	or $M(1+r)$	

If this new, larger amount is then invested again for another year, at the same rate of interest, the process continues:

Now	Two Years from Now	
	Principal Entering Second Year	Interest
$M \longrightarrow$	$M(1 + r)$	$+ \quad rM(1 + r)$
	or $(M + rM)(1 + r)$	
	or $M(1 + r)(1 + r)$	
	or $M(1 + r)^2$	

The value of our investment after two years thus comes out with an exponent of 2. If we pressed on to three years, the exponent would be 3. Four years would give us an exponent of 4, and so on.

From this we can make an important generalization. The future value of the initial quantity, when invested at a given rate for n years, can be stated as

$$F = M(1 + r)^n.$$

Then, using exactly this information we can shuffle it around to get

$$M = \frac{F}{(1 + r)^n}.$$

In putting the matter in this alternative form, we are simply looking through the other end of the telescope. We are asking, What is the *present value* (M) of an amount (F) to be received at the end of n years, given a discount rate of r? We are computing the present value when given the future value, where just above we were calculating the future value of an amount invested in the present.

Indeed, the basic relationship we have examined is an interlocking structure made up of four pieces—M, F, r, and n. Because they must all fit together, we can take any three of them and find the fourth. So far, we have set them up in two ways—first to find F, given the other three items; and then to find M, given the other three.

This is perhaps already evident to the reader in the use we made of Table 11–2. For that table is nothing more than the numerical expression of the formulation we have just developed. We used it to find r, given the other three variables. But it can just as easily be used to discover n, or M, or F, if any of them should be the one missing segment in the four-way structure.

Note with great care, however, that the discussion thus far has dealt only with a single future value—one sum at the end of a single, particular year in the future. What if we expect a *flow* of such sums to be received annually over a period of years? What are the interrelationships in this problem?

The answer is a direct extension of the same ideas. A series of sums is a *string* of the single future values we have already been working with.

That is

$$M_1 = \frac{F_1}{(1 + r)^1}$$

$$M_2 = \frac{F_2}{(1 + r)^2}$$

$$M_n = \frac{F_n}{(1 + r)^n} \cdot$$

The present value of this whole string is thus the sum of all the M's. If we call that sum P, we get

$$P = \frac{F_1}{(1 + r)^1} + \frac{F_2}{(1 + r)^2} + \cdots \frac{F_n}{(1 + r)^n} \cdot$$

This is sometimes written in a summary expression like this:

$$P = \sum_{j=1}^{n} \frac{F_j}{(1 + r)^j} \cdot$$

If the F's are all equal—as in the example called the "pure expansion" case in this chapter—then the present value of the whole string will boil down to this:

$$P = F \left(\frac{1 - \dfrac{1}{(1 + r)^n}}{r} \right) \cdot$$

Again we have four pieces to the puzzle. And again, once any three of them are put in place, the fourth one falls automatically into place. The process will be more difficult as the interrelationship is more complex. But again the relationships are worked out in tables. This, in fact, is exactly the structure expressed in Table 11–1.

When the F's, the annual cash flows, are not all the same—as in the "substitution" example in this chapter—the answers cannot be found in Table 11–1. For those problems, we must go back to the more open statement of the string of future sums:

$$P = \frac{F_1}{(1 + r)^1} + \frac{F_2}{(1 + r)^2} + \cdots \frac{F_n}{(1 + r)^n} \cdot$$

We must also go back to Table 11–2 and put together the string of M's one by one to arrive at the full string of them, which is what P is.

Finding the Internal Rate of Return

To find the internal rate of return, let us note carefully how it is defined. The internal rate of return is that rate that equates the present value of the inflows to the present value of the outflow. Thus the internal rate of return is that rate that will make P equal to what we shall call C, the present value of the outflows. And just to make clear what we are up to, any time that our formulation is used to find the internal rate, we shall use the symbol i instead of r.

That is to say C must equal P (which means $P - C$ must equal zero). This in turn means that if the F's are the same through each year in the future, then i must be such that

$$C = F \left(\frac{1 - \dfrac{1}{(1+i)^n}}{i} \right).$$

And, it means that if the F's are *not* the same through each year in the future, the i must be found so as to make

$$C = \frac{F_1}{(1+i)^1} + \frac{F_2}{(1+i)^2} + \cdots + \frac{F_n}{(1+i)^n}.$$

Once i has been established, the firm can make its capital budgeting decision. It compares the internal rate of return i, with the cost of capital which we can denote as k's. If i is greater than k's, the project should be accepted. Otherwise it should be rejected.

Finding the Net Present Value

The net present value method comes out of exactly the same structure. The difference lies entirely in which three variables we assume to be known, and thus which variable we solve for, as a residual. If we start out knowing the values of r, n, and F, we end up with P.

There is particular significance, however, in the r we take as given. That r represents the cost of capital to the firm. Thus, again to point up the special role assigned to this variable, we shall use the symbol k, instead of r, when the basic formulation is put to service in the present value method.

Hence, to solve for the present value of the stream of future flows, we get

$$P = \frac{F_1}{(1+k)^1} + \frac{F_2}{(1+k)^2} + \cdots \frac{F^n}{(1+k)^n}$$

and

$$P = F\left(\frac{1 - \dfrac{1}{(1+k)^n}}{k}\right)$$

But P is what might be called the *gross* present value of the future flows. To get the *net* present value, we must take out the capital expenditure necessary to produce these future flows. That is,

$$NPV = P - C .$$

For the capital budgeting decision, the rule is simple. If NPV is greater than zero, the project should be adopted.

The two approaches—internal rate and present value—will usually give us the same answer. Think of it this way. In the internal rate formulation, the rate i will make P equal to C. This is the very definition of i. We also know that if this rate, i, is greater than the cost of capital, k, the project should be accepted. Now, suppose in the same circumstances, we use k in the formulation. Since k is less than i, then the P given as a result of discounting the future flows with k will be larger than when they are discounted with the rate i. That is, P is greater than C—the net present value is greater than zero. Thus, this rule also says to accept the project.

Chapter 12

CAPITAL BUDGETING: RANKING PROJECTS

EXPECTED RATES OF RETURN IN GRAPHS: MARGINAL EFFICIENCY OF CAPITAL OR INVESTMENT

Thus far, our examples have considered expected returns from investment projects as if a firm had but a project or two to evaluate. But of course, it is frequently the case that management has before it not only alternative ways of investing to achieve the same general objective but also other quite different investment projects, with each of them affording several alternative technological methods of implementation. Fortunately, it is not difficult to generalize our approach to the single investment to cover all these other possibilities.

In principle, for each investment project, we can compute the rate of net return in the manner worked out in Chapter 11. Then all of these projects could be arranged in order of declining rate of return; such a schedule is usually called a schedule of the *marginal* efficiency (or productivity) of investment. The word efficiency refers to a rate of net return over cost—a time (and risk) discounted stream of revenues after subtracting all costs except depreciation and financing costs. It is marginal because it refers to the yield on net additions to total investment or capital, not the yield on all outstanding capital assets of the firm.

Suppose we were considering four separate projects as follows:

Outlay	Internal Rate
$25,000	16%
5,000	14
10,000	12
15,000	10

These are already ranked in order of yield. If we cumulate the list, it makes a schedule as follows:

$25,000 yielding 16%
　30,000 　　″　　14% or better
　40,000 　　″　　12% or better
　55,000 　　″　　10% or better

The result is the curve of marginal efficiency of investment and may be seen in Figure 12–1.

FIGURE 12–1

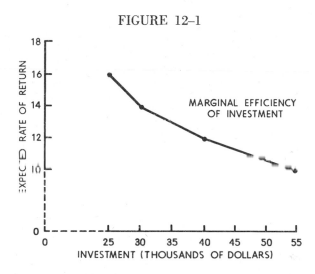

The Cutoff Point and Capital Budgeting

Now we can confront the curve of marginal efficiency of investment with a curve denoting the marginal cost of raising investment funds. Where the two curves cross, the last project just pays, but all higher yielding projects yield profits and should be adopted; all further projects where the cost of capital curve lies above the marginal efficiency curve will induce losses and should be rejected (Figure 12–2).

As we shall see shortly, however, it is likely that the marginal and average cost of funds to the firm will rise as the firm tries to raise more and more funds. Therefore, realistically, the cost of capital should be represented by a rising curve. For example, the cost of raising $30,000 may be 8 percent, but the cost of raising an additional $10,000 may be 20 percent. Clearly, the additional investment of $10,000 which yields 12 percent should *not* be compared with the *average* cost of capital which is

FIGURE 12-2

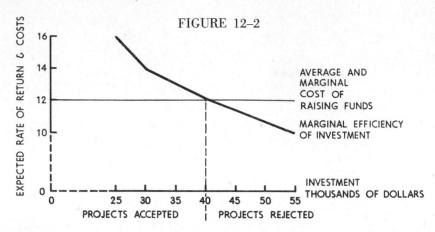

only 11 percent.[1] The additional investment of $10,000 should be considered on its own merits; it promises to yield 12 percent, but it will cost 20 percent to raise the additional funds. The project will add more to costs than to revenues and should be rejected. Thus, it is essential to use the *marginal* cost of funds in our schedules and diagrams, and this will be a rising curve. Where it crosses the marginal efficiency curve, we have the cutoff point.

The diagram in Figure 12–3 is analogous to those showing that the price and quantity taken of consumer goods are determined in the marketplace by the intersection of demand and supply of the consumer good in question. In our case the demand curve portrays the demand for investment funds as it is related to the rate of net returns expected from using the funds after discounting for both futurity and risk; our invest-

FIGURE 12–3

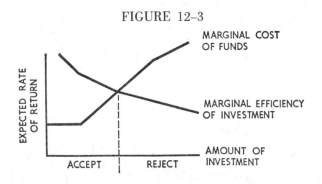

---

[1] The first $30,000 cost $2,400; the $10,000 additional funds cost $2,000; the average cost of $40,000 is thus $4,400, or 11 percent, but the cost of the last $10,000 addition is 20 percent.

ment demand curve is the marginal efficiency curve. The supply curve portrays the supply of capital or investment funds which is related to the rate *charged* for the funds; our investment supply curve is the marginal cost of capital curve. The intersection of these two curves gives the equilibrium amount of investment funds that will be offered and taken (horizontal axis), and the equilibrium cost or price and yield of that amount of funds (on the vertical axis).

Note that this is not a matter of arbitrarily choosing some cutoff cost above which all projects are rejected. Just as we rejected an arbitrary "payback" period because it implied (by inversion) an arbitrary percentage rate of net return below which no project would be adopted, so we reject the usual "cutoff" rule of thumb. There can be no rational capital budgeting that follows either a pure cost rule or a pure revenue rule. Capital budgeting, if it is to maximize profits, must consider *both* the costs of funds and net returns. For example, it is irrational for a profit-seeking firm to decide simply to invest all it can retain in profits each year. This is equivalent to assuming a zero cost of capital up to the volume of investment that can be financed from plowbacks, and an infinite cost thereafter. Note that even this procedure requires that investment projects be ranked in order of declining net returns, i.e., it requires the marginal efficiency of investment schedule curve. But it is an incomplete method because even before the arbitrary cutoff point some investment projects may yield less than the "cost" of retained profit financing. That precise cost we shall consider shortly; here, we merely note that the cost must be known if unprofitable investment projects are to be avoided.

It is similarly irrational to pick some point on the marginal efficiency schedule and include all projects that return that percentage or better. This assumes an unlimited supply of funds at a cost less than that rate of return. These are not matters to assume away but to examine carefully. (See below Chapters 16 to 19.)

The Declining Slope of the Marginal Efficiency Curve

Let us be sure we understand why the marginal efficiency curve as seen by the firm must be a falling one, i.e., why the rate of return is likely to fall as more and more investment projects are adopted. Another way to say this is that additional investment will add to returns but at a declining rate. Progressively smaller rates of cost saving are to be expected when the volume of such new investment is greater than smaller because the large cost-saving opportunities will be exploited first. And progressively smaller rates of return can be expected from the sales of the output of the proposed new investment, because with a given demand, more goods can only be sold at lower prices.

Investment tends, *as it proceeds*, to do away gradually with the incentives that promote it. Investment either cuts costs and in the process saturates further cost-cutting possibilities or expands output and in the process saturates the market and therefore the profitability of further output-expanding investment. In other, perhaps simpler terms, every firm has certain pressing investment projects (usually replacement types) which yield a very high rate of net return because *without* them the firm's total operations and returns would be jeopardized. Take, for example, investment in a generator that powers the entire plant. This investment places high on the marginal efficiency curve. On the other hand, firms usually have imaginative investment plans to expand output over the long term. Such investment may involve computation of sales 15–20 years hence, and these may be subject to such a heavy discount for uncertainty that the rate of net return in the final computation is very low. These projects will move *up* along the marginal efficiency curve should the future become more predictable or the fear of near-at-hand depressed demand be lifted. But currently, such projects would be low on the marginal efficiency curve. Investment in capacity to produce commodities with unpredictable or fluctuating demands is thus considered to be less rewarding in net returns than if the output were steadily demanded. Such projects will therefore fall at a lower point on the marginal efficiency curve of any multiproduct firm.

It is also possible to explain why one firm's investment plans for a given budget year run into diminishing net returns in terms of so-called "diseconomies" of scale or size. The firm's internal organization may become inefficient if spread over too many projects in the short run. Or looking outside the firm, if it becomes a very large purchaser of particular investment goods, the price or cost of those goods may be raised, thus lowering the returns over costs. But either way, when the firm invests great sums, it must be content with a lesser net return than when it invests a smaller amount: the marginal efficiency of investment slopes downward.

Ranking Strategic and Interdependent Investment Projects

It is only so-called "strategic" investments which appear to be difficult to fit into our method of appraising investment prospects through a schedule of rates of returns over cost or marginal efficiency. Strategic investments are those whose benefits in adding to profits or reducing costs are not strictly calculable. For example, investments in vertical integration of a firm may have the defensive aim of reducing risk of shutoff of supplies, or a stiff price rise; and investment in research and development (basic research) has the aggressive aim of trying to steal a march on competition a decade or two hence. In neither of these examples is a good quantitative estimate of the net returns over costs for such investment possible. "Their benefits are spread over many phases of the company's activities and stretch into the distant future."[2]

However, even in these cases a very rough estimate can be made so that such projects can be judged along with the other more predictable projects. Inability to judge accurately the net returns of some projects should not be allowed to stand as an excuse not to judge any investment accurately. It is well to remember, too, that not all investments in vertical integration are unmeasurable; projects that involve backward integration to get supplies at lower cost can be evaluated in terms of their cost-cutting benefits. And even "research and development" can be evaluated with accountants' records of net returns on past basic research.

In any case a rate of return approach is applicable to all these strategic investments taken as a group. Alternative strategic investments can be handled as competing with one another for a limited supply of funds arbitrarily set by managerial judgment at a specific cost of finance for such funds. After using such a method within the special sector of strategic investments to winnow out the best investment prospects, the surviving projects can then be added on to the marginal efficiency of investment schedule at the appropriate places. Then all investments can be exposed impartially to the rigors of the cost of finance.

The sequence of projects is also difficult to arrange if investment projects are *interdependent*, that is, if the net returns of investment are contingent to some degree on the simultaneous adoption of another project. For such problems of interdependent returns, the alternative investment choices are more numerous and cannot be handled by the simple marginal efficiency of investment approach. But the problem can be solved by our generalized method of making that choice of many possibilities that will maximize stock price. The difficulties involved in handling interdependent investment projects are similar to those the

2 Joel Dean, *Capital Budgeting* (New York: Columbia University Press, 1951), p. 140, and all of chap. ix, on which we have relied heavily for much of this section.

economist has to unravel when dealing with joint costs; after all, this is a problem of joint returns.

When we consider costs of financing investments, the jointness of the projects will not prove to be troublesome *unless* the finance is attached to a particular piece of investment. Generally, we assume that finance is available as a free flow, whether at constant or rising prices. For joint projects, this will only mean that if the cost of funds is rising, the joint project will have to include as a handicap a higher cost of funds. The problem of finance that is specialized—for example, funds that are *only* made available if mortgage-secured—is part of the problem of selecting an optimum capital structure.

PRESENT VALUE VERSUS INTERNAL RATE OF RETURN

Generally, in this chapter and the preceding one, we have used the so-called "internal rate of return" method for calculating the expected annual rate of return on alternative investments. This method involves finding that rate of discount that will equate the greater stream of expected returns from the investment with the smaller stream of expected outlays. The rate of discount so determined is called "internal" because it is independent of the external or market interest rate or other costs of capital. We have found it helpful to use this internal rate of return method because we have not yet considered the difficult issues of determining the cost of capital. We chose to study the returns side first and exclusively, for clarity and ease of comprehension. For the present, it has been enough to indicate that given this internal rate of return, we could plan to go ahead with the project if the cost of capital (at a rate) was lower.

However, we also have noted that there is another method of computing expected rates of returns—the so-called "present value" method. It is necessary to discuss this "external" rate of return method because in some cases, it—rather than the internal method—gives *the* correct ranking of alternative investment projects; in most cases, fortunately, both methods will rank the projects in the same order.

The present value method discounts the same stream of outlays and returns to find the yield of the proposed investment, but it does so by using the cost of capital—for example, the rate of interest at which funds may be borrowed or lent—as the rate of discount. This amounts to finding the *present value* of expected *net* cash flows.

For capital-budgeting purposes, it should be clear that the present value method can tell you in *one step* whether it pays to go ahead with the project. If the present value of expected cash inflows exceeds the present value of the investment outlay, the investment will be profitable. In the internal return approach a second step—to confront the expected returns with the cost of capital—is necessary. However, this "advantage" of the present value method is largely spurious, for it assumes that the supply of funds to the firm is infinite at some fixed rate of cost. If, as is usually the case, the supply of funds is limited or only available at a given time in increasing quantities at increasing cost, then it is useful to rank investment projects in a marginal efficiency schedule before finance costs and to introduce the schedule of these costs to show the cutoff point. The real issue then is whether the two methods will yield the same order of ranking of projects.

The answer is that in most cases the ranking will be the same. But for some investment projects—depending on the time pattern of the inflows—the two methods may give different ranking. The discrepancy is the result of the assumption made about the rate of return to be earned on net cash flow reinvested in the firm. In the internal return method, reinvestment is presumed to earn at the same internal rate as the original project, while in the present value approach the rate of return would be determined by the current cost of capital, e.g., the market rate of interest.

An example will make this clear.[3] Take two alternative or "mutually exclusive" projects, X and Y. The facts in the problem are as follows:

	X	Y
Cost of outlay	$100	$100
Expected return	$120 after 1 year	$174.90 after 4 years
Present cost of capital ...	10%	

The ranking by the two methods is:

	X	Y
Internal rate method	20%	15%
Present value method	$109.09	$119.46

Both methods show that each project is acceptable. The internal rate is higher in each case than the cost of capital, and the net present value is positive in either instance.

But the projects are mutually exclusive. The firm is choosing between,

---

[3] This example is taken from Ezra Solomon, "The Arithmetic of Capital-Budgeting Decisions," *The Management of Corporate Capital* (Glencoe, Ill.: Free Press, 1959), pp. 74–76.

say, a forklift and a loading platform. It cannot use both; it must choose one or the other. Yet the internal rate approach endorses project X as the superior investment and the net present value technique gives the nod to Y. Which is correct?

To resolve the problem, or at least to isolate the conflict, we must consider what happens in the second, third, and fourth years to the $120 returned from project X at the end of the first year. We can then compare it directly with the $174.90 provided by project Y in the fourth year.

By extending the shorter-lived project at some assumed rate of reinvestment and cost of capital over those future years to the length of the longer project, the two net terminal values may be compared and the larger one chosen.

Thus the heavy early returns of project X give it an advantage over project Y when it is assumed that the returns are reinvested at the higher internal rate of return. Project X's early returns on the other hand are handicapped when we assume reinvestment at the low cost-of-capital rate. To illustrate:

1. If the $120 is reinvested at the internal rate of 20 percent or at least at the 15 percent rate of the longer-lived project, then project X, selected by the internal method, promises the best yield. This may be seen in Table 12–1, showing compound interest. Looking at the column for 20 percent, and moving down to the third year, we can calculate that the $120 returned at the end of the first year would grow to $207.38 ($120 times 1.728) three years later. At 15 percent, it would expand to $182.51. By either standard the terminal value of $120, after reinvestment over three years, would exceed $174.90, the return from the alternative project that would first become available at that point.

2. If the $120 is reinvested at the cost of capital, i.e., at 10 percent, for the three remaining years, then at times 4 the company would end up with only $159.72 (that is, $120 times 1.331, the figure found in Table 12–1 in the column for 10 percent). Thus, on this reinvestment assumption, project Y is superior, for it will yield $174.90 at time 4.

Another source of conflict in ranking may arise, however, owing to shifts in market rates of interest or cost of capital for projects of equal duration but different time patterns of return flow. A project that has large returns in the early years and smaller returns in the later years will find its present value altered if the cost of capital rises, while, of course, the internal rate would be unaffected by this shift in market costs of capital. Thus, if projects differ in the time pattern of return flows, their ranking may be altered by shifts in costs of finance while the internal

TABLE 12-1

Compound Sum of $1

Year	1%	2%	3%	4%	5%	6%	7%	8%	9%	10%
1	1.010	1.020	1.030	1.040	1.050	1.060	1.070	1.080	1.090	1.100
2	1.020	1.040	1.061	1.082	1.102	1.124	1.145	1.166	1.188	1.210
3	1.030	1.061	1.093	1.125	1.158	1.191	1.225	1.260	1.295	1.331
4	1.041	1.082	1.126	1.170	1.216	1.262	1.311	1.360	1.412	1.464
5	1.051	1.104	1.159	1.217	1.276	1.338	1.403	1.469	1.539	1.611
6	1.062	1.126	1.194	1.265	1.340	1.419	1.501	1.587	1.677	1.772
7	1.072	1.149	1.230	1.316	1.407	1.504	1.606	1.714	1.828	1.949
8	1.083	1.172	1.267	1.369	1.477	1.594	1.718	1.851	1.993	2.144
9	1.094	1.195	1.305	1.423	1.551	1.689	1.838	1.999	2.172	2.358
10	1.105	1.219	1.344	1.480	1.629	1.791	1.967	2.159	2.367	2.594
11	1.116	1.243	1.384	1.539	1.710	1.898	2.105	2.332	2.580	2.853
12	1.127	1.268	1.426	1.601	1.796	2.012	2.252	2.518	2.813	3.138
13	1.138	1.294	1.469	1.665	1.886	2.133	2.410	2.720	3.066	3.452
14	1.149	1.319	1.513	1.732	1.980	2.261	2.579	2.937	3.342	3.797
15	1.161	1.346	1.558	1.801	2.079	2.397	2.759	3.172	3.642	4.177

Year	12%	14%	15%	16%	18%	20%	24%	28%	32%	36%
1	1.120	1.140	1.150	1.160	1.180	1.200	1.240	1.280	1.320	1.360
2	1.254	1.300	1.322	1.346	1.392	1.440	1.538	1.638	1.742	1.850
3	1.405	1.482	1.521	1.561	1.643	1.728	1.907	2.067	2.300	2.515
4	1.574	1.689	1.749	1.811	1.939	2.074	2.364	2.684	3.036	3.421
5	1.762	1.925	2.011	2.100	2.288	2.488	2.932	3.436	4.007	4.653
6	1.974	2.195	2.313	2.436	2.700	2.986	3.635	4.398	5.290	6.328
7	2.211	2.502	2.660	2.826	3.185	3.583	4.508	5.629	6.983	8.605
8	2.476	2.853	3.059	3.278	3.759	4.800	5.590	7.206	9.217	11.703
9	2.773	3.252	3.518	3.803	4.435	5.160	6.931	9.223	12.166	15.917
10	3.106	3.707	4.046	4.411	5.234	6.192	8.594	11.806	16.060	21.647
11	3.479	4.226	4.652	5.117	6.176	7.430	10.657	15.112	21.199	29.439
12	3.896	4.818	5.350	5.936	7.288	8.916	13.215	19.343	27.983	40.037
13	4.363	5.492	6.153	6.886	8.599	10.699	16.386	24.759	36.937	54.451
14	4.887	6.261	7.076	7.988	10.147	12.839	20.319	31.691	48.757	74.053
15	5.474	7.138	8.137	9.266	11.974	15.407	25.196	40.565	64.359	100.712

return method would not involve such shifts; therefore, the two methods might yield different orders of investment priority. But this conflict would only be serious if businessmen knew their costs of capital, acted on that knowledge, and assumed that prevailing costs of capital, once having shifted, would remain unchanged for the duration of the project.

What Reinvestment Rate?

It has been argued that the cost of capital is the "best available estimate" of the reinvestment rate because the additional return flows will make possible additional investment only at *marginal* rates of return. It is assumed, in other words, that since in any case the equilibrium amount of investment is set at the marginal cost of funds cutoff point, all that additional funds make possible is investment with a return in the neighborhood of that cutoff rate. Presumably all projects offering a return greater than the (marginal) cost of funds will have been adopted regardless of the return flow.[4]

This argument may be criticized from both the returns and the costs side.

1. *On the returns side*—the rate of return at the intersection does not tell us how to choose between two projects, both of which have internal rates of return above the marginal cutoff rate. In short, future *MEC* curves like current *MEC* are downward sloping.

2. *On the costs side*—If the cutoff point is achieved at some point on a *rising* cost of capital curve, the future availability of funds at relatively low cost will shift the whole cost curve and hence alter the equilibrium amount of investment. The return flow makes funds available at the low cost of internal funds, not at the cutoff cost rate, which may well be substantially higher.

3. Moreover, if the cost of capital from other (say, external) sources is changeable over time and less predictable than the internal rate of return expected from reinvestment, investment policy will be better scheduled via *IRR* than *NPV*.

Advantages of the Internal Rate of Return versus Net Present Value Approach

In summary, then, the possible mistakes in ranking when using the internal rate of return method rather than the present value or external rate method are likely to be rare and rather special cases. The advantages of using the internal rate, most of which we have already observed, are:

1. One can proceed step by step with the problem of capital budgeting because one can deal with expected returns without bringing in all at once the difficult cost of capital problem. Later we can confront the rate of return (discounted for time and business risk) with a *range* of costs of capital if we are unsure of the exact rate to use. It is wise to handle capital structure risk separately, for when costs of capital change

---

[4] See Ezra Solomon, *The Theory of Financial Management* (New York: Columbia University Press, 1963), pp. 134–35.

—rates of return unchanged—ranking as well as the cutoff point are altered in the *NPV* method.

2. It is easier to discount *IRR* for risk. *NPV* may be larger simply because the project is larger and more lasting and yet such a project may involve more risk. A project that requires one to commit resources for a longer period presumably entails more risk than if quick payoff and subsequent reinvestment were possible. Also, it is not possible to increase the rate of discount to allow for risk for that will penalize projects of different time pattern of flow differently though the risks are the same. We need rather to reduce uncertain returns to certainty equivalents and then consider cost of capital.

3. Internal rates of return are familiar to businessmen and students from their knowledge of how one capitalizes returns on securities. The *IRR*, being expressed in rate form, is easily compared to the cost of capital rate. It is also clearer to ask whether a project's expected return is worth the risk; one cannot simply reduce the present value index for risk.

In any case a more important issue is how to account for varying degrees of risk of competing investment projects. Strangely enough the problem of accounting for risk, which tells against *NPV* and in favor of *IRR*, if too difficult, tells against *all* discounting methods and in favor of the payback approach. For example, risk of sudden, total collapse of a project and dangerous illiquidity—risk of ruin rather than risk of greater or lesser profitability—may be essentially unmeasurable; short payback may be a way of allowing for such risks for it erects a high required rate of return barrier or large early return flows prerequisite for such investment. In general the riskier the project, the more the expected returns must promise to merit acceptance of the project.

QUESTIONS AND PROBLEMS

1. Graph the investment cutoff point from the following information:
   a) The cost of funds is 10 percent for any amount up to $50,000, 15 percent for further funds up to $150,000, and 25 percent for all additional finance.
   b) The investment projects under consideration in order of size are:

   $100,000 with an expected return of 5%
     75,000 25
     50,000 15
     25,000 10

2. Why is it realistic to assume that the marginal efficiency of investment is downward sloping?

3. For a single project—that is, for the accept-reject decision—one gets the same answer invariably whether one uses the internal rate of return method or the present value method of computing expected rates of return. Explain. Under what conditions is the method used to *rank* projects similarly a matter of indifference?

4. Assume that a company is considering two alternative projects, A and B, each of which requires an outlay of $200. The company's current cost of capital is 12 percent. The projects differ in that A has a life of one year and will return $250 at the end of that year while B will return $330 at the end of its life which is three years. Which project is the more profitable to adopt? Does your answer vary depending on the method used to compute a rate of return? If so, which method is preferable? Why?

SUGGESTED READINGS

BAILEY, M. "Formal Criteria for Investment Decisions," *Journal of Political Economy*, October, 1959, pp. 476–88.

CHENG, P. L., and SHELTON, J. P. "A Contribution to the Theory of Capital Budgeting—The Multi-Investment Case," *Journal of Finance*, December, 1963, pp. 622–36.

DUESENBERRY, J. *Business Cycles and Economic Growth,* chaps. iv–v. New York: McGraw-Hill Book Co., Inc., 1959.

HIRSHLEIFER, J. "On the Theory of Optimal Investment Decision," *Journal of Political Economy*, August, 1958, pp. 329–52.

LORIE, J. A., and SAVAGE, J. L. "Three Problems in Rationing Capital," *Journal of Business*, October, 1955, pp. 229–39.

SOLOMON, E. "The Arithmetic of Capital Budgeting Decisions," *Journal of Business*, April, 1956, pp. 124–29.

———. *The Theory of Financial Management*, chaps. i and ii. New York: Columbia University Press, 1963.

WEINGARTNER, H. M. "The Excess Present Value Index—A Theoretical Basis and Critique," *Journal of Accounting Research*, Autumn, 1963, pp. 213–24.

APPENDIX TO CHAPTER 12
DEPRECIATION METHODS AS A CHOICE BETWEEN MUTUALLY EXCLUSIVE PROJECTS

In this book, depreciation allowances gain their relevance chiefly from the effect they have on income tax payments. Our central concern is net cash flow—i.e., the cash left to the firm after all cash payments to outsiders. But the tax collector is one of those outsiders. And because the taxable base is influenced by the depreciation allowance, we must look at the different methods of depreciation allowed in tax accounting. What we want to see is the effect of these methods on the pattern of cash flow, on the internal rate of return, and on the net present value.

The federal tax laws offer business firms three basic methods to choose from. These are known as straight line, sum-of-the-years' digits, and double declining balance.

Under *straight-line* depreciation, the original cost of the asset being depreciated is spread evenly over the years of its economic life. For example, with a machine that costs $75 thousand and is expected to serve for five years, the annual depreciation allowance will be $15 thousand— i.e., $75 thousand divided by five. To see the impact of this method on net cash flow, we will assume an income tax rate of 50 percent and assume that revenues and costs other than depreciation and taxes are those shown in the top panel of Table A12–1.

TABLE A12–1

Year	Revenue	Cash Cost	Deprecia- tion	Profits before Tax	Profits after Tax	Net Cash Flow
			Straight Line			
1	100	65	15	20	10	25
2	100	65	15	20	10	25
3	100	65	15	20	10	25
4	100	65	15	20	10	25
5	100	65	15	20	10	25
Total	500	325	75	100	50	125
			Sum-of-the-Years' Digits			
1	100	65	25	10	5	30
2	100	65	20	15	7.5	27.5
3	100	65	15	20	10	25
4	100	65	10	25	12.5	22.5
5	100	65	5	30	15	20
Total	500	325	75	100	50.0	125.0
			Double Declining Balance			
1	100	65	30	5	2.5	32.5
2	100	65	18	17	8.5	26.5
3	100	65	10.8	24.2	12.1	22.9
4	100	65	8.1	26.9	13.45	21.55
5	100	65	8.1	26.9	13.45	21.55
Total	500	325	75.0	100.0	50.00	125.00

The internal rate of return with this method of depreciation is computed very simply from Table 11–1, back on page 180. With a net cash flow of $25 thousand annually for five years, as a return for an initial outlay of $75 thousand, the firm is getting an annual flow of $1.00 for every $3.00 invested. Looking at the table, and looking across the row for five years, we find the nearest thing to $3.00 is $2.991—at an interest rate of 20 percent. This then is the internal rate of return for this project using this method of depreciation. That is, it is the rate that makes the present value of the net inflows equal to the present value of the outflow incurred in acquiring the machine.

Before accepting or rejecting the project, however, the firm should realize that the internal rate will be different with different depreciation techniques, even though nothing else is different. The project can thus be thought of as three projects that are mutually exclusive.

This becomes clear when we turn to the method known as the *sum-of-the-years' digits*. This method is computed by first taking the number of years of expected life and adding them together. For the example here, the five-year assumed life means adding together the numbers one through five, which gives the sum of 15. The depreciation in the first year is then calculated at 5/15, in the second year as 4/15, and so on. The consequence is that depreciation is taken earlier in the life of the asset. And the more important consequence is that the taxes are paid *later* than they otherwise would be. The taxes are not avoided, but they are delayed. Hence the after-tax returns are higher in the earlier years, and the present value of the stream of returns is greater because of this time pattern.

Using the same revenues and costs other than depreciation and income taxes, the sum-of-the-years' digits depreciation gives the results shown in the middle panel of Table A12–1.

To find the internal rate of return with this form of depreciation, we must turn to Table 11–2 back on page 182. With different net cash flow for each year, a trial-and-error search is necesssary. Such a search will produce ultimately an internal rate of return of 21.613 percent.

This rate makes the sum-of-the-years' digits method clearly superior to straight-line depreciation. It may mean accepting a project that would be rejected under straight-line accounting. But the comparisons will not be complete without a look at the third technique—the double declining balance method.

The effect of the *double declining balance method* is also to push tax payments into the future, but the pattern is again different. With this method, the annual rate of depreciation is derived by doubling the straight-line rate and applying it, year by year, to the portion of the asset value still not depreciated. In our example of a five-year asset, the straight-line rate was thus 20 percent, and this is now raised to 40 percent. Hence the depreciation allowance in the first year will be $30 thousand instead of $15 thousand. Then, in the second year that will leave $45 thousand of the original $75 thousand of the asset, and the 40 percent rate will be applied to this remaining $45 thousand. This will give a depreciation allowance of $18 thousand for the second year. And so on, down the years. Because the method is always chipping off only a part of the remaining balance, the asset would never disappear entirely from the books. Thus, a company using this technique will find it necessary to switch back to straight-line accounting in the later years of the asset's life.

Applying the double declining balance method to the same project as above produces the results shown in the bottom panel of Table A12–1.

Now the pattern of cash flow is changed again. It is still superior to the straight-line result, but whether it is better than the sum-of-the-years' digits is not visible to the naked eye. To be sure, the returns are higher in the early years, which makes it advantageous. But the returns are also higher in the late years, which is a mark against it. To choose between the two methods, the internal rate must again be computed. And again using Table 11–2, we find the internal rate to be 21.952 percent. The double declining balance wins.

But two observations must be added. First, the difference is very small. And, second, different circumstances will find the sum-of-the-years' digits the winner between the two. The reader must take it on faith that the internal rates will never be far apart, but it might be helpful to demonstrate the second observation.

We may change any one of several assumptions in our example to show that a different outcome is possible. But let us suppose that the only change is in the expected life of the machine. Suppose that it will serve for ten years instead of five. With this alteration we get the patterns of depreciation allowances, tax payments, and net cash flows shown in Table A12–2. The calculation of internal rates, after much trial and much error, will be found to be 27.312 percent for the sum-of-the-years' digits and 27.086 percent for the double declining balance. Notice again how close the two are, but notice also that they have switched places. The double declining balance now falls behind the sum of the years' digits.

Summing up, once the firm has calculated its internal rate of return on each of these depreciation assumptions, it is ready to consider accepting

TABLE A12–2

Year	Revenue	Cash Cost	Deprecia- tion	Profits before Taxes	Profits after Taxes	Net Cash Flow
			Sum-of-the-Years' Digits			
1	100	65	13.636	21.364	10.6820	24.3180
2	100	65	12.273	22.727	11.3635	23.6365
3	100	65	10.909	24.091	12.0455	22.9545
4	100	65	9.545	25.455	12.7275	22.2725
5	100	65	8.182	26.818	13.4090	21.5910
6	100	65	6.818	28.182	14.0910	20.9090
7	100	65	5.455	29.545	14.7725	20.2275
8	100	65	4.091	30.909	15.4545	19.5455
9	100	65	2.727	32.273	16.1365	18.8635
10	100	65	1.364	33.636	16.8180	18.1820
Total	1,000	650	75.000	275.000	137.5000	212.5000
			Double Declining Balance			
1	100	65	15.000	20.000	10.000	25.000
2	100	65	12.000	23.000	11.500	23.500
3	100	65	9.600	25.400	12.700	22.300
4	100	65	7.680	27.320	13.660	21.340
5	100	65	6.144	28.856	14.428	20.572
6	100	65	4.916	30.084	15.042	19.958
7	100	65	4.916	30.084	15.042	19.958
8	100	65	4.916	30.084	15.042	19.958
9	100	65	4.916	30.084	15.042	19.958
10	100	65	4.916	30.084	15.042	19.958
Total	1,000	650	75.004	274.996	137.498	212.502

or rejecting the project. It also will know which of the depreciation methods it should adopt.

What if the firm prefers the net present value method of screening projects? The comparison can be made with the same information, simply by applying a discount rate to the net cash flow and computing its present value. Then the method that produces the highest present value relative to the original outlay is the best (assuming of course that it exceeds the original outlay).

But if the *NPV* method is to be used, there is another, perhaps more convenient route to the answer, which makes use of special tables devised for the different methods of depreciation. First, note how the net cash flow is arrived at. It equals:

Profits after taxes ¦ Depreciation

If we probe further, we see that profits before taxes are equal to:

Cash Revenues — Cash Costs — Depreciation.

Hence profits *after* taxes can be stated as:

$(1 - \text{tax rate})$ (CASH REVENUES $-$ CASH COSTS $-$ DEPRECIATION) ;

which can also be stated as:

$(1 - t)$ (CASH REVENUES $-$ CASH COSTS) $- (1 - t)$ (DEPRECIATION).

To turn this into net cash flow, we add depreciation, getting:

$(1 - t)$ (CASH REVENUES $-$ CASH COSTS) $- (1 - t)$ (DEPRECIATION) $+$ DEPRECIATION

Rearranging this, we get:

$$(1-t) \text{ (CASH REVENUES} - \text{CASH COSTS)}$$
$$- \text{DEPRECIATION} + (t) \text{ DEPRECIATION} + \text{DEPRECIATION}$$

which becomes finally:

$$(1 - t) \text{ (CASH REVENUES} - \text{CASH COSTS)} + (t) \text{ DEPRECIATION}$$

To get the present value of the net cash flow, we can take the two parts separately. In our example, the first expression becomes $(1 - 0.50)$ ($\$100 - \$65$) and the second expression (0.50) ($\$15$). Thus we are seeking the present value of $\$17.5$ thousand a year and $\$7.5$ thousand a year.

The first figure we can calculate straight out of tables as before. However, with methods other than straight line, the second figure will change from year to year. Hence to use special tables developed for the purpose, we look at the figure for the *total* amount of depreciation over the life of the asset, and find the present value of the total when it is spread over time in the particular pattern given by the depreciation methods. With double declining balance, for example, a 7 percent rate of discount gives a present value of 85.696 cents for one dollar of total depreciation spread over five years. In our case total depreciation over five years will be $\$75$ thousand. Accordingly the present value of the depreciation flow will be something over $\$64$ thousand.

Remember, however, that our only interest in depreciation is in the tax payments it will save. Hence to finish the calculation, we multiply the present value of the total depreciation times the tax rate. This will measure the taxes not paid because that amount of cash flow will have had a "depreciation shield." Adding this final figure to the present value of $(1 - t)$ (Cash Revenues $-$ Cash Costs), we arrive at the present value of the project, when the double declining balance technique is used. A present value for the sum-of-the-years' digits method would be calculated in the same fashion, using of course tables specially designed for this method. When these answers are compared with the original cost, they give the *net* present value, and tell the firm whether to adopt the project and which depreciation method to use.

SUGGESTED READINGS

CAPLIN, M. M., and KLAYMAN, R. A. "Depreciation 1965 Model," *Journal of Accountancy*, April, 1965.

DAVIDSON, S., and DRAKE, D. F. "Capital Budgeting and the 'Best' Tax Depreciation Method," *Journal of Business*, October, 1961, pp. 442–52.

DOMAR, E. D. "The Case for Accelerated Depreciation," *Quarterly Journal of Economics*, May, 1953, pp. 493–512.

EISNER, R. "Depreciation Allowances, Replacement Requirements, and Growth," *American Economic Review*, December, 1952, pp. 820–31.

MEIJ, J. L. (ed.). *Depreciation and Replacement Policy*, especially pp. 46–110 by E. O. EDWARDS. Chicago: Quadrangle Books, 1961.

Chapter 13

RULES OF THUMB VERSUS THE
RATE OF RETURN APPROACH

Most businessmen for most investment decisions use nondiscounting rules of thumb such as a payback formula and/or the average investment return as indexes of investment profitability. In general, as compared with internal rates of returns or net present value, these rules of thumb give demonstrably wrong answers. But under certain common circumstances they approximate the "true" rates of return quite closely. We must first demonstrate their fundamental weakness and then show their usefulness in given situations.

In the *payback* approach the emphasis is on *quick* cash return flow, and in the cutoff approach the emphasis is on restricting investment to internal funds, i.e., to cash on hand and available for outflow. In both cases, at bottom, there is an aversion to resorting to the capital markets for the needed funds. And in both cases, some profitable investment projects are forgone due to the fear of illiquidity. Note that the rate of return approach does not neglect these fears, for after all, they can be quite rationally allowed for in setting the discount for uncertainty. The two rule-of-thumb formulas allow for these fears in a crude fashion that seldom shows whether the allowance is correct in size.

PAYBACK AS A DECISION RULE

The payback formula neglects both the discount for futurity of the returns received *within* the payback period and the uncertain returns that may be received in the years *after* the payback period. It is true that this overstatement and understatement may be offsetting for investments with a real life of at least twice the life assumed for payback purposes. But it is also true that the formula gives very bad results for projects that have a real life close to that assumed for payback purposes.

Suppose, for example, a project costing $8,500 and promising cash flows of $2,000 annually for ten years. The internal rate of return on such a project will be 19.6 percent, a fact we can determine from tables. What will be the payback method say of such a project?

If we take the cash outlay ($8,500) and divide it by the annual cash inflow ($2,000) we get 4.25 as the number of years it will take to "pay back" the investment. If the firm has a rule that only investments that will pay for themselves in five years or less, then this investment is accepted on that basis. It is usually said that the *reciprocal* of the payback is the rate of return assumed—in this case, 1/4.25, or 23.5 percent.

In fact, that rate of return will be obtained only if the investment lasts forever. If the project really lasts only 4.25 years, the investment will only have returned the original outlay, and the yield is zero, or less than that if we allow for interest that might have been earned. That is, at the end of the payback period the return *of* investment is complete but there is no return *on* investment; the whole cash flow will equal depreciation. To find the true yield on such an investment one needs to know how long the *actual* life of the investment is likely to be *and* the rate at which to discount those future streams.

In practice, an investment need not be of *infinite* length to make the payback reciprocal approximate the internal rate of return. Using the present value table (Table 11–1, back on page 180) we can look at the present value of a dollar received annually at the rate of 20 percent (close to the actual 19.6 percent or *IRR* of our project) and at the rate of 24 percent (close to the 23.5 percent payback rate).

As the brief summary in Table 13–1 makes clear, a project that produced $2,000 a year for 50 years would give an internal rate very close to the one implied by the payback reciprocal. This similarity shows up in the present value column, at the far right.

TABLE 13–1

IRR	Assumed Life of Project	Present Value of	
		$1 a Year	$2,000 a Year
20%	10 years	$4.192	$8,384
24	50 years	4.167	8,334

Even if the table ran out to a thousand years, the multiple would not quite reach 4.250, the level necessary to give a present value of $8,500 to annual flows of $2,000. But the payback estimate is very close to the internal rate of return if the project lasts as long as 15 years. Inspection of the 24 percent column back in Table 11–1 (page 180) reveals that an actual life of 15 years yields a good approximation—4.001 × $2,000 = $8,002, or too low by about 1/17.

On the other hand the *average* investment return approximates the true or internal rate of return only for very short-lived projects. A common averaging formula is $\dfrac{\text{Annual Cash Flow}}{\text{Cash Outlay}}$. For example, a project that lasts just one year and returns $10,500 ($2,000 *net* cash flow) on an $8,500 investment can be said to have yielded roughly 23.5 percent.[1] Of course this is the result of so shortening the project's life that the failure to account for the time discount is of little moment. But if the project yielded its cash flow over a ten-year period, the average rate of return would yield a gross overestimate of the true yield. The average return would be $1,050/8,500 or 12 + % while the internal rate of return or true rate is around 4 percent—$1,050 received annually for ten years × 8.111 (the present value of $1 received annually for ten years at a 4 percent rate) = $85.15, or approximately the $8,500 outlay.

Thus the average investment return formula overestimates the "true" return from projects. Unlike the payback method which results in good approximations to true returns if the projects are long lived relative to the payback period assumed, the average investment formula yields worse and worse approximations the longer-lived the project. On the other hand if the average return is used as a cutoff point (as if it equalled the cost of capital), its use would lead the firm to pass up profitable investment opportunities. In either case, both "rules of thumb" are generally inadequate because of their failure to discount for futurity. To make the rules "work" requires laying down quite restrictive conditions. It is no more difficult to discount via the internal rate of return than to be certain that the restrictive conditions are being met.

Payback as a Rule for Ranking

Moreover, the rules of thumb are not only poor "screening" devices for investment projects, they are poor for "ranking" purposes as well. If funds were always available at a given cost, ranking of investment projects in order of profitability would not be necessary; financial man-

---

[1] In the 24 percent column the present value of $1 received at the end of the year is 0.806 which times $10,500 = $8,463.

agers would simply adopt *all* projects whose rates of return exceeded the given cost of capital. In other words a "screen" for profitability would suffice. But if funds are limited in supply or available only at increasing cost (for increasing amounts), it is necessary to *rank* projects in order of profitability to be sure that the limited funds are used for the more profitable projects. Even if funds were not limited in supply, ranking would be necessary to choose between two profitable but mutually exclusive projects. For example, two projects might meet the same payback requirement or have the same average return but differ in time pattern of cash flows. Neither of the rules of thumb allows for the advantages of projects that yield their returns more heavily in the early years of the life of the project.

For example, take two projects that both meet the requirement for a three-year payback: The outlay is $9,000, and the return flow sums to $9,000 in three years. But first, assume the different actual lengths of life and patterns of return flow shown in Table 13–2.

TABLE 13–2

Year	Project I	Project II	Project III
Year 1	$2,000	$4,000	$1,000
Year 2	3,000	3,000	2,000
Year 3	4,000	2,000	3,000
Sum at end of 3 years	$9,000	$9,000	$6,000
Year 4	$ 0	$ 0	$5,000

Note that although projects I and II both meet the payback requirement, it is clear that project II is the most desirable. Payback provides no method for such a ranking of alternative projects. Project II is superior to I because the same total sum is received at the end from both projects; but in II, you get more of the return earlier. Now consider project III, which is rejected by a three-year payback rule. This is an investment that yields its greatest returns late in its life rather than early. Is it clear that it promises a lower rate of returns than either I or II over the whole real life of the investment? We cannot tell without discounting the flows and finding the true internal rate of return. It is less safe than I and II, i.e., it does not provide a *quick* cash inflow; but it may well be more profitable.

THE APPEAL OF PAYBACK

Thus, the payback rule of thumb is subject to numerous criticisms which might well lead to serious errors in investment decisions both for single projects and for alternative projects. Why, then, does it remain the most popular method of "capital budgeting" even for well-managed concerns?[2]

A good part of the businessman's case *for* payback is a list of reasons why he cannot use the discounted flow method.[3] It is said that:

1. Some firms are so *liquidity poor* that they must concentrate on quick cash recovery. (But this applies only to *some* companies and in any case is a cost or supply of capital problem and should be handled as such. Remember, too, that the rule does not finally confront the payback rate with the cost of capital to see if it pays to go ahead. Presumably, in most cases the rate of returns required is so high that no normal cost of capital rate could conceivably cut it off. Moreover, the payback users are often the same companies that restrict themselves to internal funds.)

2. Returns are *so uncertain* beyond the selected payback period that no meaningful estimate can be made, and this is also true for estimates of the economic life of the investment. (But not all industries are subject to such uncertainty, e.g. the utilities; and not all projects within an industry or of a company are *equally* uncertain. Moreover, for long-lived projects, use of the payback formula would overestimate returns by failing to discount for uncertainty. That is, for projects that last, say, twice as long as the payback period, the rate of return by the payback method is quite close to the internal rate, but that rate should be decreased to allow for the uncertainty as well as the futurity of the returns stream.)

3. Since firms do not aim for *maximum* but only *satisfactory profits*, a rough gauge of returns is all that is needed. (But even if one does not maximize, using the discounted flow method assures that all the right questions are asked and all the important factors are considered.)

4. In general, the payback method is *easy to measure, compute, and explain* to others. (This is true, but the real issue is whether the time and cost of more perfect information are worthwhile in terms of additional returns. There is no way to find this out without trying the discounted-

---

[2] One survey shows that of 127 well-managed companies 66—or over half—used a payback formula and only 38—or 30 percent—used a discounted cash flow technique. Of course, many of those who used the payback method supplemented it with other techniques to remove its dangerous edges. See J. H. Miller, "A Glimpse at Practice in Calculating and Using Returns on Investment," *NAA Bulletin*, June, 1960, p. 73. For the even less widespread use of discounted methods among small firms, see Robert M. Soldofsky, "Capital Budgeting Practices in Small Manufacturing Companies," in Dudley Luckett (ed.), *Studies in the Factor Markets for Small Business Firms* (Ames: Iowa State University, 1964).

[3] For a good discussion, see N. W. Chamberlain, *The Firm: Micro-Economic Planning and Action* (New York: McGraw-Hill Book Co., Inc., 1962), pp. 270–78.

cash-flow method and thus evaluating its effects on returns after deducting all costs of solving the problem the longer and harder way.)

A second line of defense of payback is more acceptable but also makes more concessions to the discounted flow technique:

1. At least, payback calculating is superior to investment decisions made on a pure "hunch" basis.
2. Many businessmen say they use supplementary formulas in cases where payback gives possibly questionable answers.
3. Finally, businessmen are aware that in some cases, payback does give approximately the same results as discounted cash flow would.

In all these points, it is clear the businessmen are aware of and moving toward more precise methods of calculating estimated returns from investment. But the movement is slow, largely owing to the newness of the techniques, at least as applied to business problems, to the problem of making management aware of and skilled in the approach, and to the need for specialized personnel to carry out the calculations.[4] But the changes in the postwar economic system are tending to stimulate more careful planning of capital expenditures: The economy is more stable and therefore more predictable; cash management is becoming a more exact science; long-run investment planning has become more fashionable; liquidity crises are less feared than they once were, and less likely to be so pressing.

If, in fact, a firm has to consider all the data needed in the full calculation of net return to decide whether the shortcut formula is sufficiently accurate to use, it is difficult to see why efforts to work out the full net returns approach would not be rewarding. Even in its best use the shortcut formula gives but an approximate answer to the rate of returns question, and it does not solve the problem when there are two or more alternative investment mixes that meet the minimum requirement.

The prime reason for using the payback formula is management's fear of the uncertainty about future revenue flows back to the firm. But we have seen that this can be discounted for in the rate of returns approach, and in the next chapter we shall learn much more about the technique.

This fear can be rephrased as management's fear that it will lack cash (due to inadequate return flows) in some future year. This fear is reinforced if management has an aversion to going outside the firm for cash

---

[4] Cf. D. F. Istvan, *Capital Expenditure Decisions: How They Are Made in Large Corporations*, Indiana University Business Report No. 33 (Bloomington, Ind., 1961); and J. S. Earley, "Business Budgeting and the Theory of the Firm" *Journal of Industrial Economics*, Vol. IX, No. 1, pp. 23–42.

by borrowing it or selling additional shares in the equity. Further, this implies (1) that the firm fears debt either because of a fear of bankruptcy or it simply fears to rely on outsiders who may not make credit available at any price at the moment of need; (2) that the firm fears the need to sell new shares of stock either because of possible dilution of per share value or because of possible loss of control.

Finally, even if the reciprocal of the payback could be taken to be a good approximation of the internal rate of return, the rule still can not be a good guide to profit or wealth maximizing for it does not consider the cost of capital. Only if in addition the payback reciprocal were also the cost of capital in percentage form would that rule be a maximizing rule. But this raises the unexamined question as to how a firm decides upon its payback rule. It seems that the emphasis is not on the *cost* but the *availability* of funds; not on the *rate* of return (payback reciprocal) but on the payback *period*. The rule then is intended to ensure liquidity not profitability. As in break-even analysis, the emphasis is on recovering costs or outlays on investment within a short period of time; profit, if any, is then the extra cash flow (the "gravy") received back in the post-payback period.

AVAILABILITY OF FUNDS AS A DECISION RULE

The full implications, then, of the payback formula lead us quite naturally over to the other side of the equation, where the cost of funds enters the argument. It is here that the rule "cut off where retained profits give out" comes into focus. To see the full implications of the use of the this rule of thumb would require us to work through a full analysis of the various costs of funds. At this point, however, it should be clear that this shortcut, too, may involve the sacrifice of all but the most profitable investment projects out of fear of the uncertain future. But, at the other extreme, use of the cutoff rule may alternatively result in adoption of unprofitable projects just because the funds are available.

When internal funds are in limited quantity relative to the quantity of profitable investment projects, and investment is restricted to the amount of funds available internally, the result may be that unprofitable projects are avoided. Given that only a few of the many seemingly profitable projects can be adopted, only the very "profitable" ones will be chosen. These may be sufficiently profitable to remain truly profitable even after discounting them for time and allowing for the opportunity cost of funds. Profits are thus subjected to an arbitrary constraint for safety before they are maximized.

Instead of trying to measure the elements of uncertainty, this formula, like the payback formula, avoids them by taking few chances—even with the projects that have strong probability of success. The firm's profitability is likely to be reduced by such shortcuts for it is likely that profitable investment opportunities are passed up rather than traded off against risk.

On the other hand, to use funds for investment projects just because the funds are available is to assume that the cost of (internal) funds is zero and that any expected profit rate greater than zero justifies the use of such funds. This is just as irrational and potentially destructive of the firm as basing a plan of output on sales revenues alone with no consideration of the costs of production. Capital budgeting principles would require that funds be paid out rather than plowed back unless the firm's use of the funds would improve the stockholders' fortunes. But the hurdle is the marginal cost of funds which is assumed away by the (internal) cutoff rule of thumb.

In practice this rule of thumb is not so damaging, for business usually has more need for funds for projects than funds available and because in fact, as we will see in Part V, internal funds tend to be one of the cheaper alternative sources of funds.

Thus, like payback procedures, "plowback" financing also places a premium on liquidity or the availability of funds within the firm. Since no *out-of-pocket* costs are encountered in using retained earnings, many businessmen act as if such funds were costless. Combined with the fears of illiquidity and insolvency associated with borrowing funds, many firms end up using a payback period gauge with the cutoff determined by the availability of funds internally. Such a procedure is doubly inadequate: the management not only does not calculate the true *return* from using the funds, it does not determine the opportunity *cost* of using the funds. Such procedures obviously optimize liquidity and safety rather than profitability or owner's wealth. Insufficiently profitable investments might be adopted simply because funds were available or quite profitable projects might not be adopted because it would require going outside for funds and paying out-of-pocket rates for them.

THE RULES OF THUMB AND THE RATE
OF RETURN APPROACH

In criticizing such rules of thumb, no lack of understanding for management's fears of debt and dilution and so on is to be implied. These fears, however, can be more carefully weighed and accounted for as part of the computation of the cost of funds to the firm. Then we shall use the *cost* of funds to indicate the cutoff point rather than selecting some arbitrary fixed *sum* of funds as a limit to the volume of investment that is in the best interests of the company.

Thus, rules of thumb generally cannot be defended as shortcuts that do approximately the same job as full-scale analysis of rates of net return and cost of funds. The shortcuts overemphasize risk and underemphasize profit making. But the shortcut can be defended if the data required for the long method are unavailable or if the required calculations are too complex or too lengthy to be supported. And even the full returns/cost treatment involves practical simplification and the wide exercise of managerial judgment with respect to estimates of the length of life of the investment goods, the stability of the flow of returns, the discount for uncertainty, and so on. Nevertheless, if the complete analysis is attempted, it will at a minimum turn up the data needed for a careful execution and evaluation of the shortcuts.

Surely, rationality and precise pencil work are called for in planning investment projects, if not in all other aspects of business enterprise, for what is often involved are sizable amounts of money to be committed for lengthy periods of time. Much time and deep thought are well repaid here, for these decisions have perhaps the decisive influence on the future profitability of the company and the fortunes of management and the stockholders.

Of course, in practice, there are many other factors not considered here that determine the success of capital budgeting in a firm:

1. The ability of management to identify investment projects is critical: Our techniques will allow us to select the best alternative of identified investment projects, but what if the best potential project of all has never reached the desk of the man with the formulas?
2. Further, even if the best project has been evaluated by the best techniques we have, the outcome is still dependent on the quality of the data which are in many cases only "guesstimates."

But although we must caution that project discovery and information quality are very important and subject to vast improvement, it remains true that with *given* projects and *information*, the techniques outlined in Part III maximize the prospects of selecting those capital expenditures which promise the best rate of return.

QUESTIONS AND PROBLEMS

1. On your first job in the controller's department of a medium-sized manufacturer, your boss, weary of your critical comments about the firm's use of a four-year payback rule in its capital budgeting decisions, asks you to prepare a brief (1,500 words) critique of payback and to suggest a feasible alternative means of evaluating investment projects.

2. Impressed with your brief, the boss next asks you to demonstrate the superiority of your approach over the four-year payback for the following actual project facing the firm:

   Investment outlay—$10,400.
   Expected returns—$3,000 per year for 10 years.

   In this screening example why does the payback rule provide a reasonably good though partial answer? Make up an example of accept-reject where payback and the rate of return approach are in serious conflict.

3. Not discouraged by your inability to demonstrate the defects of the payback rule for the company's screening case, you extend the case with additional hypothetical examples to show that for ranking alternative projects and other cases where funds must be rationed, payback is an inadequate tool.

4. Your boss is impressed with the rate of return approach but would like to retain the simpler payback rule for cases where it is adequate. Provide him with a brief method of deciding whether or not payback needs supplementing by true rate of return analysis in order to make good investment decisions.

5. Although you are pleased to comply with the financial managers' request for guidelines restricting the use of the payback rule, you press still further by asking him why a four-year (rather than say three- or first-year) payback was chosen. In response he asks you to outline for him the factors which ought to enter into the determination of any particular payback rule. Although you present such an outline, you point out that the problem is fundamentally not soluble in these terms.

6. The "availability of funds" as a decision rule of thumb implicitly assumes that the cost of internal funds is zero. Explain. Why is this not a disastrous decision rule in practice?

SUGGESTED READINGS

CHAMBERLAIN, N. W. *The Firm—Micro-Economic Planning*, chap. x. New York: McGraw-Hill Book Co., Inc., 1962.

DOUGALL, H. E. "Payback as an Aid in Capital Budgeting," *The Controller*, February, 1961, pp. 67–78.

GORDON, M. J. "The Pay-off Period and the Rate of Profit," *Journal of Business*, October, 1955, pp. 253–60.

JOHNSON, H. W. "Measuring the Earning Power of Investments—a Comparison of Methods," *NAA Bulletin*, January, 1962.

SOLOMON, E. *The Theory of Financial Management*, chap. x. New York: Columbia University Press, 1963.

Chapter 14

DISCOUNTING EXPECTED RETURNS FROM INVESTMENT FOR UNCERTAINTY

In evaluating investment opportunities we have stressed the fact that the returns from investment are *expected* returns. As a consequence, we have found it necessary to discount those returns for futurity; that is, we have had to find the present value of expected returns. However, another important consequence of the fact that returns are expected is that they are *not certain* to be received in the fuure. We must learn therefore how to discount for risk as well as for futurity. A certain feature return has to be discounted for time; an uncertain future return has to be doubly discounted.

It is necessary to develop the treatment of risk in more depth than was necessary when considering working capital budgeting because the capital budgeting commitment, being longer, deeper, and generally more pervasive, carries with it danger and discredit to the firm from failure to receive returns as expected.

To this point we have learned that an investment that costs $8,500 and yields a ten-year stream of returns of $2,000 per year has an internal rate of return of 19.6. The annual rate of return is *not* 23.5 percent, or $2,000 /$8,500, the annual average return on investment, for such a formula does not account for the time lag between the outlay denominator and the inflow numerator. The time discounted rate of return is substantially less than the undiscounted rate—about one sixth less.

DISCOUNTING FOR UNCERTAINTY

But even the 19.6 rate of returns is too high, for it implicitly assumes that the future stream of income is certain to be $2,000 every year. Any businessman would tell you that he does not have perfect confidence in his forecasts of selling prices or volume of sales or even costs. Therefore, his estimates of future annual net cash flows are his best guess—or better put, *the most probable* results.

We can suppose that management forecasts future annual income in the form of a probability distribution. For example, in our case, management may figure that:

> There are 5 chances in 100 that annual cash flows will be $4,000
> There are 25 chances in 100 that annual cash flows will be 3,000
> There are 35 chances in 100 that annual cash flows will be 2,000
> There are 30 chances in 100 that annual cash flows will be 1,000
> There are 5 chances in 100 that annual cash flows will be   0

It is easy to see that the $2,000 annual net income is the most probable outcome in the sense that it is the modal value[1] and this can be used by management (as we have thus far assumed it would be) in its first rough calculations. But we have not yet allowed for the fact that this frequency distribution also provides us with a way to estimate and to discount for the likelihood that $2,000 will not be received. In fact, in this distribution, there are more chances (35 in 100) that less than $2,000 will be received than that more will be received (30 in 100). In other words, the distribution is skewed to the lower end; the mode ($2,000) is greater than the mean ($1,950).

If the entrepreneur had known that his expected returns comprised a *schedule* of probable outcomes weighted by their probabilities of occurrence as illustrated above, he would surely have used the weighted average—the mean—as the most probable outcome for it takes account of skewness, downward in this case. But even then the essential attribute of risk and uncertainty—dispersion around the mean—has still to be discounted.

To allow for uncertainty, then, we must correct our $2,000 estimated annual income downward to allow for the dispersion around the mode and the skewness. The wider the range of probable outcomes—the greater the variance—and the greater the downward skewness of the probable outcomes, the more the modal probability ought to be corrected downward. The question of just how to choose the proper rate of reduction for uncertainty is one we shall take up a little further along. For purposes of illustration, however, let us assume for the time being that management

---

[1] The class containing the greatest number of observations is the modal class. In this case, it is also the median class—the middle of the frequency range. The arithmetic mean is $1,950.

judges that expected receipts should be cut by 25 percent to allow for
uncertainty. This approach means that we are considering an *uncertain*
income ($2,000) to be equal in value to a smaller but *certain* income
($1,500).

Now, what is the rate of return on an investment of $8,500 when we
can certainly expect an annual cash flow of $1,500 for ten years? Again a
look at the ten-year line of the present value bond tables will provide the
answer. Here is a piece of Table 11–1:

Year \ Rate	8%	10%	12%	14%
10	6.71	6.14	5.65	5.22

What we are looking for in this table is a rate that will just equate the
certain annual flow of $1,500 for ten years and the investment outlay of
$8,500. To find it, we find note that for each $100 of annual revenue flow,
an investment of $5.67 must be made:

$$\$8,500 \div \$1,500 = \$5.67.$$

Then, looking across the ten-year line in the table, we can see that the
figure closest in size is $5.65. The rate of return is thus 12 percent. The
doubly discounted rate of return is not 23.5 percent nor even 19.6 percent but only 12 percent.

Why Uncertainty Requires Discounting

But let us be sure that we understand why uncertainty almost *always*
reduces the expected rate of return below the most probable outcome.
Thus far in our example, we have effectively stacked the cards against any
other position.

Even if the frequency distribution of probable profits had been perfectly symmetrical both above and below a very heavily marked average
or modal level, management would want to discount the most probable
profit. An even chance to make unusual profits is overbalanced by the
equal probability of making unusually low or negative profits. With
respect to net returns, businessmen have more to fear (bankruptcy) than
to hope for (spectacular profits). This is really a recognition that while
risk can be allowed for by probability distributions, business anticipa-
tions will nonetheless always involve some remaining uncertainty—that
is, the future contains unknowns that cannot even be estimated.

But it is not merely that greater dispersion around the central tendency increases the risk of ruin or the risk of heavy loss; greater dispersion is disliked because variability of returns per se is disliked. That is, the greater the variance, the less confidence one can have in the mean or expected return. It is generally presumed that business (management and its stockholders) have an aversion to risk. For example, it is assumed that for any given most probable rate of return, businessmen prefer less to more dispersion about that mean, even though the odds of making above-average returns are as good as the odds of making below-average returns. The general pervasiveness of risk aversion is well illustrated by the insurance industry which necessarily charges in premiums more than the expected monetary value of the policy's benefits to cover the costs (including profits). Self-insurance is cheaper (i.e., the "returns" are higher) but riskier; our aversion to risk leads us to trade off return for risk. We will pay to avoid (large) even-money gambles.[2]

Thus according to the general principles of risk aversion, when management is trying to choose between two investment projects which promise the same most probable profit but which differ in probable dispersion around that central value, obviously management would pick the project with the lesser dispersion. It is even more obvious that management would never even consider a project whose expected return was lower and whose risk was higher than an alternative project. However, most management decisions are more difficult, for risk and return tend to vary directly.

Projects with little dispersion usually involve investment in adaptable (flexible) equipment or in relatively shorter-run projects; it is such projects that offer more predictably stable future profits. It is also likely that the most probable profits on such projects tend to be lower than longer-run, more specialized ones. Therefore, management must be presumed to face the very difficult problem of choosing between projects that offer high average profits with large dispersions and low average profit projects with smaller probabilities of dispersion. Management can be visualized as trading off mean profits against variance, that is, asking the question: How much *average* expected profit is worth sacrificing to get less dispersion around that expected or only most probable average?

That is why it is necessary to try to measure risk: Risk must be quantified so that it can be set off against expected return.

---

[2] It is no rebuttal to cite widespread gambling at cards, etc., as an example of mass risk loving. The smallness of the stakes and/or the pleasure of the game itself in most cases will still allow us to assume that the mass of people (including businessmen) are not risk-lovers but risk-averters.

It is often difficult to separate management's aversion to risk from its aversion to the quantification of risk. There are certain risks that management may consider unthinkable or at least postponable; and quantification of risk might highlight possible differences between managerial risk preferences and those of the stockholders which should prevail. Many managements will not choose the high average profit project if it involves even a small chance of bankruptcy. Or in other words, it will place on such a project such a high discount for uncertainty that the net profit prospects are thus reduced *below* the project that has lower average profit but involves no chance of bankruptcy.

Management is also inclined to postpone investment projects when in doubt about the margin by which extra return offsets extra risk; a missed opportunity to profit is evaluated as less damaging (to prestige if not profit) than a real loss. A satisficing management's motivation *may* not be identical with that of the owners, preferring to take fewer risks than would be in the stockholders' interest.[3] Management may be primarily interested in assuring its own continuity in office at a relatively fixed salary. This objective would be endangered not only by a project that involves even a slight probability of bankruptcy but by projects that include the mere possibility of a few low earnings years; it is during poor years that managements are thrown out of office by either stockholder resentment or raids by outsiders. Thus, management may use a heavy discount for risk and uncertainty even when dispersion around the most probable profit is slight and symmetrical.

In most cases, then, it can be assumed that profit probability distributions will be seen as unfavorably skewed either because they are in fact so skewed or because risk aversion makes them so. Consequently, the discount for risk will be substantial. It is likely that these are the reasons why the quick payback rule of thumb is so often used to judge the profitability of an investment project. For example, a $10,000 project may only be accepted if it will pay for itself in three years; this is just another way of saying that the annual return must be $3,333 a year. Management may feel that profit possibilities beyond three years are *so* uncertain that it wishes to assume the worst—that they will be zero. But in fact, there is really only *some probability* that they will be nil; management's following such a role of thumb is a sign that profits are not likely to be maxi-

---

[3] On the other hand, management's and the stockholders' viewpoints on risk may coincide if stockholders place a high premium on stability of dividends, and therefore on earnings stability, too.

mized in that firm. To that end, the discount for risk must be quantified.

Summing up tentatively, it is necessary to discount expected returns for both futurity and riskiness. This can be done in several ways. In our example, we applied a 25 percent correction factor to the uncertain future stream of receipts ($2,000 × 0.75 = $1,500) and then found that the ten-year stream of certain annual receipts of $1,500 when discounted at a rate of 12 percent had a present value of $8,500. This was the equivalent of about a 12 percent net rate of return on the $8,500 investment. The payback approach also could account for uncertainty by reducing the number of years of expected life, and hence earnings, to be included in the profit calculation.

But a major question remains: How can business rationally decide on the size of the discount for uncertainty? Rough estimates of risk or simple inspection of probability distributions may suffice for most working capital decisions. But in capital budgeting, efforts to quantify risk allowances must be most carefully calculated, for the decisions are much larger in terms of money and irreversible for a long time to come.

Quantifying the Discount for Uncertainty

It would be permissible to use the average expected cash flow without discounting for the variability of expected cash flows around the average, *if*, for management and the stockholders, money were not subject to the law of diminishing marginal utility. Variability of cash flows around the average could also be disregarded even with diminishing marginal utility of money, if the variability in expected cash flow were small in absolute amount relative to individual or corporate total cash.

For example, consider your own attitude toward risk. Assume you have a total capital of $100 and are offered a speculative investment of $90 which promises *even* chances of doubling in a month or being completely lost. Would you take the chance? In pure monetary terms, it makes no difference whether you take the gamble or not, for you have equal chances of gaining $90 or losing $90. You would not *pay* for the opportunity to take such a gamble; that is, the monetary value of the gamble itself is zero just as is the monetary value of not gambling.[4]

But whether you take the gamble or not may make a difference in your total satisfaction or utility *if* you feel that additional amounts of money

4   $\dfrac{+ 90 - 90}{2} = 0 = \dfrac{\text{Possibilities}}{\text{Odds}}$ or $(0.50)\,90 - (0.50)\,90 = 0.$

are subject to a personal law of diminishing marginal satisfaction. That is, if you feel that the monetary value of an additional $90 is likely to add less to your satisfaction than would be sacrificed if you lost the gamble and thus the $90, then taking the even gamble will reduce your total probable expected satisfaction.

Even if the odds are *better* than even, if may not pay to take chances; it all depends on your feelings about the value of additions to and deductions from your total capital. For example, consider once more your own attitude towards risk. Assume you have a total capital of $100 and you are offered a speculative investment of $90 which promises even chances of tripling in a month or being completely lost. Would you take the chance offered? You must consider that at the end of a month, you will have either $280 or $10 or, if you do not gamble, the same $100. Now, if every dollar has the same value to you, regardless of the number you have, then rationally, although perhaps not ethically, you should take this gamble, for you have *equal* chances of gaining $180 and losing only $90. That is, the expected monetary value of the gamble is $+\$45$[5] and there is no charge for gambling, while the expected monetary value of not taking a chance is zero. If your feeling is that you would not take such a gamble, it must be because you feel that the additional $180 you may receive when you already have $100 is not more valuable to you than the $90 you will lose out of the $100 you have. The 2:1 odds in your favor are offset by your feelings that money has a strongly diminishing additional utility to you. This is a matter of individual preferences or differences, and one can only ask what these feelings are; one cannot assume them to be a certain value.

Take this example one step further. If you prefer not to take a chance of ending up with either $280 or $10, then you prefer the certainty of $100. Would your answer be the same if the gamble were for 90 cents rather than $90? That is, would you still prefer $100 for certain to the even chance of getting either $101.80 or $99.10? If your answer is that you would take the 90-cent gamble but not the $90 gamble, the difference is *not* due to a change in the monetary value of the gamble but to a shift in your feelings about additions to and subtractions from your cash balance. When *small* variations of your capital around $100 are involved, you may well feel that dollars added are of equal value to dollars lost and

---

[5] $\dfrac{(+\,180 - 90)}{2} = +\ \$45$ or $(0.50)\,180 - (0.50)\,90 = 45.$

therefore the greater odds of gaining make the gamble worthwhile. The chance of gaining $1.80 adds more to your well-being than you would subtract if you lost 90 cents. But this may not be true for a possible loss of nine tenths of one's income versus a chance to almost triple one's income.

It is along these same lines that one can see why business firms prefer investment "gambles" with narrow rather than wide dispersion. Take our previous example, where management's forecast of cash flows has the probability distribution:

$4,000	0.05	
3,000	0.25	The mode is $2,000.
2,000	0.35	The mean is $1,950.
1,000	0.30	
0	0.05	
	1.00	

Let us consider another project whose mode and mean are the same but whose variance is greater:

$4,000	0.15	
3,000	0.15	The mode is still $2,000.
2,000	0.35	
1,000	0.20	The mean is still $1,950.
0	0.15	

Would management be indifferent as to which of these projects it chose? Not likely; although the expected *average* monetary values are the same in both cases, the range of possible outcomes—the variance—is greater in the second case, i.e., the chances of complete success or complete failure are greater. If a firm has resources, and especially cash resources, which are quite limited relative to the size of the project, either because the firm is small or because the project is large, etc., the firm will prefer the less risky project, i.e., the project that has more chances of partial success and partial failure, although it has the same average probability of success. In other words, the firm's attitudes toward risk will help to determine its decisions. This decision, too, may be quantified, for the *different attitudes toward risk are in effect different feelings about the utility of probable additions to and subtractions from cash flow.* Conceptually, all that needs to be done is to weight all the probable money outcomes of the two projects by the firm's feelings about additional amounts of money, and then to apply these values to the different frequency distributions of the two projects.

THE UTILITY INDEX

In practice, it may be quite difficult to quantify the conversion of alternative dollar sums to utility. What we want to do is to get the businessman to describe to us his subjective attitudes towards risk in an "objective" or numerical way. One approach currently popular involves posing a varied sequence of lotteries or gambles to the businessman and deducing, indeed calibrating, his feelings about risk-taking as the process proceeds. For example, we can ask further questions of our businessman who has refused to gamble $90 with even chances of getting back $180 or $0. First we can point out to him that his unwillingness to take the gamble means that he prefers the certainty of $90 (Act I) to the chance of getting $180 or nothing (Act II). That is, the utility of Act I exceeds that of Act II. We next can find out what it will take to get him to take the gamble by reducing the certain amount he is offered when he does not gamble; this amounts to improving the odds if he does gamble. To illustrate, suppose we find that he would gamble if the certain alternative to +$180 or nothing were only $40 (Act III); and on pressing further we find that he is *indifferent* whether to take the gamble or not if the certain alternative is $60 (Act IV). Given this information, and assuming that the businessman acts to maximize utility, we can devise a utility index for this manager, for in telling us that he is indifferent between a pair of alternative cash flows, he is also telling us that the expected utility of the alternative outcomes is the same.

First, let us establish a scale or rules by which to measure the way expected utility would vary for alternative amounts of cash flow. We set the utility of $0 at 0.0, and $180—the largest possible cash flow in this case—is assigned a value of 1.0, the other extreme on the utility index. Our task is to develop the points (> 0.0 and < 1.0) on the utility index that correspond to alternative outcomes > $0 and < $180. In doing so, we will be measuring management's attitudes toward risk.

Second, on this scale, the even-money gamble of $180 or nothing (Act II) has a value of 0.5.

> The gamble—$\frac{1}{2}(\$180) + \frac{1}{2}(\$0)$
> The index weights—$180 = 1.0$ and $0 = 0.0$
> Substituting—$\frac{1}{2}(1.0) + \frac{1}{2}(0.0) = 0.5$

Third, Act IV—the certain receipt of $60—also has an index value of 0.5, for this management feels indifferent between (or equates the values of) the utility of a gamble of $180 or nothing, and the certain outcome of $60. Now we know a third point on our curve of utility or utility index: 0.5 and $60 are coordinates.

The utility of Act II—the gamble of $180 or
nothing—is worth ½(1.0) + ½(0.0) = 0.5.
The utility of Act IV—the certainty of $60—is 0.5.
Thus the utility of Act II = 0.5 = $60 =
utility of Act IV.

We knew that the utility of the gamble was less than $90; now we know that it is exactly $60. In similar fashion we can find other points on the utility curve. Such a curve would look as shown in Figure 14–1. It is *not* a straight line through the origin because $60 not $90 is the certainty equivalent of 50/50 odds of $180 or $0. Thus, such a utility function exhibits risk aversion with some precision. We knew that business generally required a premium to take an even money bet; now we know how to determine the exact size of that premium. (Note that the curve is drawn more as a straight line for small amounts of money; this is to remind you that we have little or no aversion to *small* even money gambles.)

Fourth, presumably we found the utility of $90 (Act 1) to be 0.75 when our businessman said that he would be just as happy with $90 certain as with the opportunity to play a lottery (Act V) in which he had a 50/50 chance of winning $180 or $60 (*not* $0). In this case

FIGURE 14–1

GRAPHING A UTILITY SCHEDULE

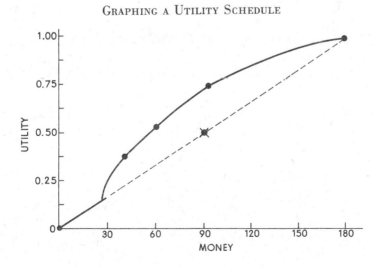

Utility of $90 = utility of ½ ($180) [6] + utility of ½ ($60) [7]
$$= ½ (1) + ½ (0.5)$$
$$= 0.75$$

And to complete our utility schedule, assume that our businessman tells us that he is indifferent between $40 certain and even odds of getting $90 or $0. Now we can find the utility of Acts VI and III as follows:

The utility of $40 = 50% chance of $90 + 50% chance of $0
$$= ½ (0.75) + ½ (0)$$
$$= 0.375$$

Putting all these observations together, we get the pattern shown in Table 14–1.

TABLE 14-1
Development of a Utility Schedule

				Utility Index	
	I	$ 90 certain	> 0.5	0.75	
	II	$180 or $0	0.5		
Acts	III	$ 40 certain	> 0.5		0.375
	IV	$ 60 certain	0.5		
	V	$180 or $60		0.75	
	VI	$ 90 or $0			0.375

AN EXAMPLE OF RISK QUANTIFICATION

Using the method of the previous section, let us develop a utility index for a firm which is considering two projects of identical mean expected returns but different dispersions. Then given the utility index of the firm considering projects I and II, we can weight the various probable monetary values by the firm's utility index and find the comparative expected utility of the two projects. Presumably by thus quantifying the comparative risks, we can select the project with the higher (doubly discounted) rate of return.

Let us assume for this example that the following represents firm A's feelings toward additional amounts of money returns. Thus, the marginal utility of money returns to firm A is:

$$\$ \quad 0 \text{ to } \$1,000 = 1.0$$
$$1,000 \text{ to } \quad 2,000 = 0.9$$
$$2,000 \text{ to } \quad 3,000 = 0.7$$
$$3,000 \text{ to } \quad 4,000 = 0.4$$

---

[6] As before, the utility index of $180 is 1.0.
[7] As deduced from the previous lottery, the utility of $60 is 0.5.

Note that these figures imply that the firm has a diminishing utility for additional flows of cash; the first additions are more highly valued per dollar than the later additions.[8]

From this information we can develop an index of utility for the various cash flows expected by firm A.

The utility of $1,000 cash flow is *1.0*.

The utility of $2,000 cash flow is an average of 1.0 for the first $1,000 and 0.9 for the second $1,000 or

the utility of $2,000 cash flow is *0.95*.

The utility of $3,000 is an average of 1.0, 0.9 plus 0.7 for the third $1,000 or

the utility of $3,000 cash flow is *0.867*.

The utility of $4,000 is an average of 1.0, 0.9, 0.7 plus 0.4 for the fourth $1,000 or

the utility of $4,000 cash flow is *0.75*.

Firm A's utility index then is:

$1,000	1.0
2,000	0.95
3,000	0.867
4,000	0.75

Now apply the nonlinear utility weights to the probable cash flows to find the expected utility of the two projects (Table 14–2).

The second project promises less utility ($1,705 versus $1,765), although the average expected monetary values promise to be the same. This results from the greater dispersion of project II—the greater probability of variance from the mean is viewed unfavorably by the decision-making firm whose utility index shows aversion to risk.

In order to find the internal rate of return on project I investment of $8,500, we should enter the present value tables not with $2,000 or even $1,950 but with $1,765—the certainty equivalent of $1,950. In the table along the ten-year row we find 4.833 (in the 16 percent column) which multiplied by $1,765 equals $8,530, quite close to our outlay of $8,500. Thus we can say that the IRR of project I, after *discounting for risk as*

---

[8] If the firm felt that additional amounts of cash flow were always of equal value, the equation would be linear, that is, each additional thousand dollars would be valued at 1.0 or any other constant figure, and the two projects' sums of expected utility would be equal, just as the sums of the expected monetary values were.

TABLE 14–2
EXPECTED UTILITY OF PROBABLE OUTCOME

PROJECT I

Conditional Cash Flows	×	Probability of Event	=	Expected Monetary Value	×	Index of Utility	=	Expected Utility of Probable Outcomes
$4,000		0.05		$ 200		0.75		$ 150
3,000		0.25		750		0.867		650
2,000		0.35		700		0.95		665
1,000		0.30		300		1.0		300
0		0.05		0				0
				$1,950	← 10.5% discount → for variance			$1,765

PROJECT II

$4,000		0.15		$ 600		0.75		$ 450
3,000		0.15		450		0.867		390
2,000		0.35		700		0.95		665
1,000		0.20		200		1.0		200
0		0.15		0				0
				$1,950	← 12.5% discount → for variance			$1,705

well as futurity, is 16 percent. (For alternative project II, the IRR is 15 percent.) It is also this rate (i.e., 16 percent and not the 19.6 percent or surely the 23.5 percent rate) that is compared to the cost of capital to determine profitability.

THE TRADE-OFF APPROACH

Although expected utility—the additional cash flows weighted for probability and utility—is the ideal approach for calculating the discount for risk, its operational usefulness will vary directly with management's ability to develop correct utility indexes. Indexing difficulties abound; it is not merely the necessarily subjective nature of the process. It is also that what really matters is stockholder attitudes towards risk and not management attitudes. To separate the more subjective *attitude* toward risk from the more objective *amount* of risk, and to develop the latter more intensively, another approach to quantifying risk has been suggested. Let us call this the "trade-off" method for it involves developing a precise measure of dispersion of expected cash flows as an index of risk and then considering that risk index as the price one pays for rate of return (also stated as an index). Firms can be thought of as trading off variance against mean cash flow.

Recall that as soon as we realized that the $2,000 annual cash flow was an expected rather than an assured amount we began to speak of $2,000 probabilistically, as only the "most likely" value within a range of probable cash inflows or outcomes. In fact, looking back at the probability distribution, the $2,000 value was "most likely," whether defined as the mode (most frequent value) or median (midpoint of the values). Neither of these central tendencies is as suitable as the mean for measuring risk, for they do not reflect the *range* of all possible outcomes. For this purpose we need the mean—the weighted average—which in our example was $1,950 and was called the Expected Monetary Value (*EMV*) of the project. But obviously the *EMV* or mean was still inadequate as a measure of risk for it had the same value for projects I and II although *dispersion* around the mean or the hazard of extreme results was more probable for II than I. In weighting extreme values relatively lightly, the utility index method both penalized the greater dispersion of project II *and* generated a certainty equivalent of the EMV in dollars. But we can rank projects I and II for risk without a utility index by taking the most common

TABLE 14–3

DISPERSION OF PROBABLE OUTCOMES

PROJECT I

Conditional Cash Flows	Deviation from $1,950 (The Mean or EMV)	(Deviation)^2 ×	Probability of Event =	
$4,000	+2,050	4,202,500	0.05	210,125
3,000	+1,050	1,575,000	0.25	393,750
2,000	+ 50	2,500	0.35	875
1,000	− 950	902,500	0.30	270,750
0	−1,950	3,802,500	0.05	190,125

1,065,625 Variance

$$\sigma = \sqrt{1,065,625} = 1,033$$

PROJECT II

$4,000	+2,050	4,202,500	0.15	630,375
3,000	+1,050	1,575,000	0.15	236,250
2,000	+ 50	2,500	0.35	875
1,000	− 950	902,500	0.20	180,500
0	−1,950	3,802,500	0.15	570,375

1,618,375 Variance

$$\sigma = \sqrt{1,618,375} = 1,272$$

measure of dispersion—the standard deviation or σ—of the probability distribution.[9] (See Table 14–3).

The greater risk of project II is objectively demonstrated by its greater variance and larger standard deviation. Measured by σ, project II is 23 percent riskier than project I in the sense that the probable outcome will be that much more dispersed. To choose between these two projects we do not need to go on to try to measure the dollar penalty of such risk because the two projects promise the *same* probable return. Assuming risk aversion as a general attitude, any rational decision maker will choose the less risky project among projects whose expected returns are the same. Similarly and in general, given equally risky projects, the project with the higher rate[10] of returns will be chosen.

For projects which differ *both* in expected rate of return and risk, the solution is more problematic for it requires (as in the utility index method) that we convert risk to a monetary or returns equivalent. For example, project I promised a 19.6 percent rate of return with a risk index of 0.53 and II a 19.6 percent return with a larger risk index of 0.65. To choose I over II was clear. But what if we had a third alternative, project III, which promises discounted returns of, say, 25 percent but has a risk index of 0.65? Project III is clearly preferable to II because for identical risk it promises a better return. But is project III preferable to I? Is the increased return on III worth the extra risk that must be incurred? To answer this question we must devise some measure of the stockholders' attitudes towards risk. For example, how much added return is just enough of a trade-off against added risk to leave the stockholder equally well off? But the method and its problems are precisely the same

----

[9] To find the standard deviation:
    A. For each probable cash flow:
        1. Take the difference between it and the mean of the whole distribution.
        2. Square it.
        3. Multiply by the probability of the event.
    B. Add up the results for each probable cash flow. This sum is the *variance* of the distribution.
    C. Take the square root of the variance—this is the σ.

[10] In generalizing it is necessary to shift to a rate of return from *absolute* returns because while our example compared projects of equal size in terms of investment and conditional cash flows, most comparisons will not be so conveniently arranged. To assure that mere size differentials do not affect the measure of risk although the size of the variance will be proportionally affected, it is customary to divide the standard deviation (σ) by the mean or the expected monetary value. σ/EMV is called the coefficient of variation and is a relative index of risk, that is, an index unaffected by mere size. In our example the risk relatives would be 1,033/1,950, or 0.53, for project I and 1,272/1,950, or 0.65, for project II—again a 23 percent difference.

as we have already considered in developing an index of the utility of money.

However, it is true that this "trade-off" approach provides a clarifying way to think about the aggregate riskiness of the enterprise as a whole rather than simply of the riskiness of each project considered one at a time. For example, when we seek to choose an optimum *group* of investment projects we realize that risk as measured by the coefficient of variation $(\sigma)/(M)$ need not be additive but may be *offsetting*. In short, a diversified portfolio of investments combines not merely high-risk–low-return projects but in the search for highest possible returns for any given risk level, projects of equally high but inversely correlated risk (or dispersion) may be sought. In other words, a high variance project may be added to a set or portfolio of investments without *adding* much risk (relative to what it adds to return) provided that the variance introduced is complementary in pattern and timing to the variance of the outstanding investments. For example, consider the old ice company that delivered coal in the winter.

On the other hand, the other major "company as a whole" influence on investment choice—the project that is very large relative to the size of the company—is more easily grasped via a utility index approach in which "risk of ruin" or bankruptcy possibilities can be severely handicapped. In the coefficient of variation or σ approach, the absolute size problem is deliberately buried. But of course a $1 million project with a given variance may be relatively riskless to General Motors and yet carry a heavy potential for ruin to a $1 million size firm; in this case it is not the odds or the probable dispersion but the stakes that inhibit the gambler. Concretely, firms will discount the average expected return sharply if the project involves risk of ruin or if its stockholders particularly value stability of cash dividends, which in turn are dependent on some stability of net cash flow. In these cases, given a sufficient number of chances or tosses of the coin, the average probability runs true; but a short streak of low cash flow or "heads" may well "end the game," i.e., bankrupt the firm, upset the stockholders, raise the cost of capital substantially, etc., before the game begins to run true to the expected average. Of course, the firm's or the individual's ability to "stay in the game" depends on cash position and access to cash relative to the probable cash drains of the investment projects.

All this is to say that liquidity or even cash-budgeting considerations enter into capital-budgeting decisions owing to the uncertainty of expected cash flow or returns from investment projects. Once again, it is clear why the quick payback approach to capital budgeting is so appealing to businessmen.

RAISING THE RATE OF DISCOUNT AS A METHOD TO ALLOW FOR RISK

If probabilistic information about expected cash flows is available, risk is better allowed for by discounting the flows themselves because raising the *rate* at which the flows are discounted penalizes projects whose cash flows are heaviest in the later rather than the early years. This is not reasonable unless the later flows are in fact riskier. If probabilistic information is not available, it is hard to see how the firm picks the size of the discount. Indeed the payback rule is probably most useful in just such cases where uncertainty is so overwhelming; the reciprocal of the payback may be thought of as the required rate of return or cost of capital hurdle for such thoroughly unpredictable projects.

Furthermore it would be well to reserve increases in the rate at which the flows are discounted to cases of increased *financial* risk (or actual cost) rather than *business* risk. For example, both expected risk and returns to owners will rise, even though no change in investments projects is made, if bonds are substituted for stock in the finance plan of a company. The increased dispersion of probable returns which results from inserting leverage into the financial plan will be considered later as a factor raising the cost of equity capital. It could be considered here as a factor lowering the utility of the probable returns.

Finally it should be noted that even when exact quantitative data cannot be obtained, merely roughing in the problem may be clarifying and suggest other ways to improve investment decision making. For example, one may generate probabilistic data for replacement and modernization investment projects from past experience; and although investment for expansion and especially for new products may not yield risk estimates, their risk is surely greater than that for cost-cutting types of investment.

The treatment of uncertainty via probability techniques has necessarily been brief and simplified, and you may have the impression that for investment decisions in practice its application would be too difficult or costly. But remember that the probability patterns can be determined from business experience with past variance or by rough but quantified business judgment; of course, this is simply a method of guessing, but reasoned guesses are presumably better than plain hunches or vague intuition. However, it still may be questioned whether the value derived from better guessing is worth the extra cost entailed in the process of improving one's information about the future. This, too—the expected value or the additional profits of perfect information—can be computed by methods growing out of the procedures above. But such matters are beyond the scope of this text.[11] In any case, we do have a *theory* of rational behavior under conditions of uncertainty, and we can in principle apply it to actual budgeting decisions. At the very least, it is a fruitful way of considering capital-budgeting decisions even if a strictly quanti-fied application is not possible.

A NOTE ON THE COST OF FUNDS AND CAPITAL BUDGETING

This reminds us that we have only come about half way in our efforts to understand capital budgeting. Even after we know that the net internal returns from the projected investment are estimated to be 16 percent, based on "certain" *present value*, we cannot be sure that this is a profitable investment to undertake unless we know that the cost of raising the funds to finance the purchase of the investment goods is *less than 16 percent*.

Alternatively, the potential investment could be handicapped for un-certainty by adding a "risk premium" on the cost of capital rather than taking it away from the net returns side. We would say that for the investment to pay, the cost of capital plus the premium for uncertainty of X percent must be less than the 19.5 percent rate of returns based on uncertain present values.

The latter approach is most useful if one thinks that it is only when the investment is financed by bonds that risk aversion becomes marked. For then, one can add an unusual risk premium only to the interest rate on bonds to find the cost of capital to compare with the present value rate of

---

11 On these and other aspects of probability and statistics as applied to capital budget-ing and other business decisions, see the masterly volume by R. Schlaifer, *Probability and Statistics for Business Decisions* (New York: McGraw-Hill Book Co., Inc., 1959), es-pecially chap. vii and xxxiii–xl. See also the following articles which comment on the impact of this book on developments in business decision theory: H. V. Roberts, "The New Business Statistics," *Journal of Business*, January, 1960, pp. 21–30; and J. Hirshleifer, "The Bayesian Approach to Statistical Decision: An Exposition," *ibid.*, October, 1961, pp. 471–89.

net returns promised. For costs of capital that involve raising the funds by selling stock or retaining earnings, the unusual risk premium need not be added to the cost of capital.

If it is believed that management has an aversion to risk no matter how the project is financed (that is, that its fears are not just fears of bankruptcy), then it is more logical to apply the business discount for risk and uncertainty on the net returns side. This is the procedure we shall follow. It has the advantage of allowing us to concentrate largely on the tax aspects of the different methods and financial costs of raising capital without getting involved again with the difficult problems of uncertainty. If there prove to be special additional risks involved when bonds in particular are considered as the method of finance, we shall find it clearer to account for this either as a factor that raises the cost of debt or as a factor that raises the cost of equity, i.e., reduces the price/earnings ratio or the market value of the common stock.

We prefer to think of the risks of a rising debt/equity ratio as involving higher costs of equity capital rather than decreased probabilities of net returns. In either approach, investment will be hindered by unduly heavy reliance on bond finance; but in the approach we propose to follow, uncertainty and risk concerned with the dispersion around the most profitable net returns are kept analytically distinct from the *additional* risk injected into the problem by resorting to fixed-charge finance. The latter risk only arises when capital structure proportions are to be altered in the process of financing the projected investment. To see this clearly, we must turn to the financial cost or supply side of our problem. Given our discounted returns, if we know the cost of finance, we can finally decide rationally whether or not to accept the proposed investment plan.

QUESTIONS AND PROBLEMS

1. What is meant when it is assumed that management has an "aversion to risk"?

2. However, risk aversion is not absolute but relative. Relative to what?

3. Outline the steps of the "trade-off" method of quantifying the discount for risk.

4. Suppose that project X requires an outlay of $20,000, promises the following probable cash flows for 15 years, and that the firm's utility index is as tabulated. Calculate the doubly discounted internal rate of return for that project.

Conditional Cash Flow	Probability of Event	Utility Index
1,000	0.20	1.0
3,000	0.50	0.9
5,000	0.30	0.7

If we had not allowed for risk aversion, what would the internal rate of return have been?

5. What business information is needed if risk is to be quantified? Which of these data are most difficult to obtain? Can an allowance for risk be made in the absence of full information? Explain.

SUGGESTED READINGS

BIERMAN, H.; BONINI, C.; FOURAKER, L.; and JAEDICKE, R. *Quantitative Analysis for Business Decision*, chaps. ii, iii, xiv, xxi. Rev. ed. Homewood, Ill,; Richard D. Irwin, Inc., 1965.

FARRAR, D. E. *The Investment Decision under Uncertainty*, Englewood Cliffs, N.J.: Prentice-Hall, Inc., 1962.

HERTZ, D. B. "Risk Analysis in Capital Investment," *Harvard Business Review*, January–February, 1964, pp. 95–106.

HILLIER, F. S. "The Derivation of Probabilistic Information for the Evaluation of Risky Investments," *Management Science*, April, 1963, pp. 443–57.

MARKOWITZ, H. "Portfolio Selection," *Journal of Finance*, March, 1952, pp. 77–91.

SCHLAIFER, R. *Statistics for Business Decisions*, chaps, i, ii, xiv. New York: McGraw-Hill Book Co., Inc., 1961.

Chapter 15

PLANT AND EQUIPMENT BEHAVIOR: SOME THEORIES AND SOME FIGURES

Before leaving capital budgeting and taking up the cost of capital, we should take a quick look at the economics literature on business investment in fixed assets. This literature is too vast to be surveyed in a few pages. Nonetheless, a student of business finance should at least be aware of several major ideas that pervade that large body of thinking.

The theories offered by economists to explain business capital outlays are, in the main, business cycle theories, and they run very nearly the full gamut in the role they assign to finance. At one end can be found a considerable group who give it no influence at all. At the other, a somewhat more sparse gathering insists that the cost of money is the prime mover in all business decisions and is thus the fundamental determinant of changes in business spending for fixed assets. In between lie many shades of opinion on the relative sensitivity of capital spending to the cost of finance.

DIFFERENT VIEWS OF THE MARGINAL EFFICIENCY OF INVESTMENT

One way to examine these differences is to state them in the form of the marginal efficiency of investment curve (MEI). In particular, questions can be asked about (a) the shape of the curve and (b) its stability. In addition, the same questions may be raised about the marginal cost of funds curve (MCF).

For example, if business investment is seen as completely insensitive to the cost of finance, the MEI curve should be perfectly vertical. With an MEI curve of this type, neither the shape nor the level of the MCF curve will make any difference. Whether the MCF is sharply rising or perfectly flat, its intersection with the *MEI* will indicate exactly the same volume of investment. Moreover, for a given shape of the *MCF* curve, the level of that curve will also have no direct influence on investment. For tight capital markets or easy ones, the investment outcome will be the same. As may be seen in Figure 15–1, neither shape nor level of *MCF* will budge investment from the quantity *A*.

Theories of this sort must offer some explanation, however, for changes in the volume of business capital spending. For changes that occur over the relatively short run, as in a business cycle, one major candidate has been the pure acceleration principle. As we have seen earlier in the chapters on inventories, this theory in its pristine form is a completely nonfinancial explanation. Other essentially nonfinancial theories have suggested that monetary or financial changes elsewhere in the economy get transmuted into price or demand phenomena by the time they have their impact on business decision making. There are business cycle theories, for example, that ascribe a major role to shifting relationships between input prices and output prices.

For our purposes, it is sufficient to note the existence of these theories. It might be added, however, that the acceleration principle raises more difficulties when applied to plant and equipment spending than when applied to inventory behavior. For one thing, the acceleration principle in its purest form would require the stock of plant and equipment to be *reduced* when the flow of demand declined. This reaction is possible for inventories, since business firms must decide at frequent intervals whether

FIGURE 15–1

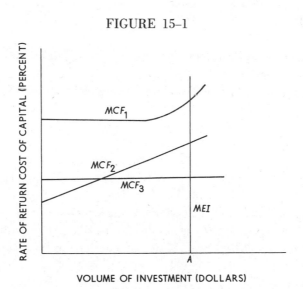

VOLUME OF INVESTMENT (DOLLARS)

or not to replenish their inventory stocks. Cutting back the stock of capital equipment on short notice is more difficult. A decline in demand is likely to result simply in idleness for some of the existing equipment. A further consequence is that when demand picks up again, it will put the idle capacity back to work, with no increase in capital spending until a still further expansion of demand calls forth the need for new capacity.

Once these objections are raised, the acceleration principle must become more complex if it is to explain the forces behind plant and equipment spending. And once the theory becomes more complex, the possibilities for ascribing a role to financial costs are heightened. For example, broadening the principle to make the accelerator flexible will open the door to the cost of capital as a possible influence. This we saw earlier in the inventory case, and perhaps it is an even greater likelihood here. The reason is that fixed assets involve more money, a longer commitment of that money, and a more fundamental commitment of the firm to the mode of living that the new plant and equipment will impose.

In any event, once the model departs from complete denial of financial cost as a determinant, then both the *MEI* and the *MCF* must be examined. Looking first at the shapes of these two curves, we may concentrate on four major combinations. If the cost of money has any influence at all, the *MEI* must have some tilt to it, but its shape can range from nearly vertical to horizontal (i.e., highly inelastic to highly elastic). Similarly, the *MCF* can be flat or steep. Our particular interest focuses (because we assume this is the way the world is) on an *MCF* that is relatively horizontal over some range and rising thereafter. The relevant shape of this curve will then depend on where the *MEI* crosses it. The four combinations are shown in Figure 15-2.

But shape is not all. Stability is important, too, and one strong body of opinion holds that the pattern of capital spending is dominated by shifts in the curves, leaving their shapes as a relatively minor influence. The possibilities are infinite, but four illustrations are sketched out in Figure 15-3, which shows some combined shifts in the same curves as given in Figure 15-2.

For example, in the upper left, the movement of the *MEI* to the right would increase investment to a point to the right of the quantity *B* if there were no accompanying change in the *MCF* curve. But if one firm is experiencing a rightward shift in *MEI*, the economy at large may very well be in an expansion phase generally. Thus, the cost of capital will tend to be pushed up, and the Federal Reserve authorities may act to push it

FIGURE 15–2

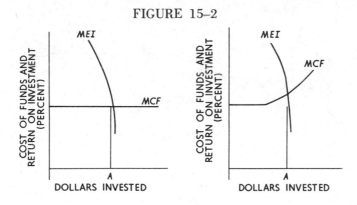

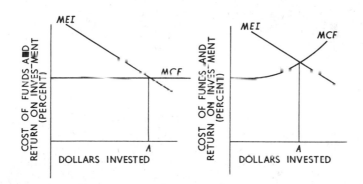

up further. This takes the form in Figure 15–3 of a rise in the *MCF* curve. And it will have the effect of restraining at *B* the quantity of investment that otherwise would have moved further out.

In each of the other three panels of Figure 15–3, the upward shift of the cost of funds curve has a similar dampening effect. The restraint is particularly effective when the *MEI* is highly elastic, as in the lower half of the diagram. In principle, the shift in *MCF* could be large enough to more than offset the potential expansion in investment, actually pressing it back to a lower volume than before the two curves had shifted. In practice, this seems relatively unlikely, and Figure 15–3 gives no illustration of this possibility.

Speaking very broadly, the weight of econometric studies in recent years has moved more and more toward according financial influences a major role in business capital outlays. For a long time, interest rates and

FIGURE 15–3

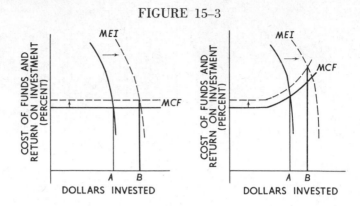

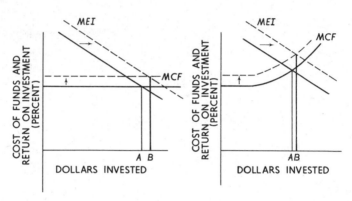

other evidences of the cost of finance came off very poorly in empirical studies. But more recently there has been a reassessment of the quality of the data used in some of these studies, particularly those derived from opinion surveys. In addition a change in the concept of capital costs to include more than interest rates alone has helped change the findings. The influence of liquidity has been given new importance, both in the gross sense of cash on hand or readily available and in the net sense expressed by the restraining effect of existing indebtedness.

There is much that a student of business finance can learn from these econometric studies. We shall content ourselves here with listing some of the more significant ones at the end of the chapter. The student can also profit, however, from a quick glance at data sketching out general trends in plant and equipment spending, and the next few pages present a few of these materials.

GENERAL PATTERNS IN PLANT AND EQUIPMENT SPENDING

A certain amount of capital spending goes on routinely, perhaps too routinely for the good of the firm. Replacement of parts and standard equipment cannot always be justified as the optimal use of funds. For large lumps of spending, however, the decision is much less automatic. Proposals must work their way up to a high echelon before any spending will be authorized. After that, contracts must be let or orders placed, and installation and construction may add still more months to the process.

The first point at which we can observe this process is the decision to appropriate funds. As may be seen in the bottom half of Figure 15–4, new capital appropriations in the manufacturing segment of business have pronounced swings over the cycle. As the chart also makes clear, the flow of these decisions turns up very early in the general recovery of the economy, or even before the recovery gets under way. The dollar volume of new appropriations then rises rapidly. Sometime during the general expansion, however, the flow of appropriation decisions begins to fall—well in advance of the peak in the economy at large.

The appropriation of funds is not, of course, the same as the spending of them. If the general fortunes of the firm take a surprise turn for the worse, or if equipment suppliers or building contractors fall behind in delivery schedules, the appropriations may be a long time turning into actual outlays. They may even be canceled. The figures on *anticipated* capital outlays (compiled by the Department of Commerce and the Securities and Exchange Commission, and by several private organizations) give us forecasts on the timing of expenditures, and recently figures have begun to be collected on plant and equipment *starts*. But the flow of spending must still be measured independently of appropriations, expectations, or the beginnings of the work.

The pattern of outlays made by the entire business sector is seen in the upper half of Figure 15–4. Although these data refer to all businesses and the figures on the bottom half of the chart measure appropriations in the manufacturing sector alone, the cyclical peaks and troughs of the two series may be compared directly. The reason is that manufacturing spending for fixed assets has virtually identical upper and lower turning points as total business spending does, although the swings between these points are much wider than for business as a whole. Making the compari-

FIGURE 15-4

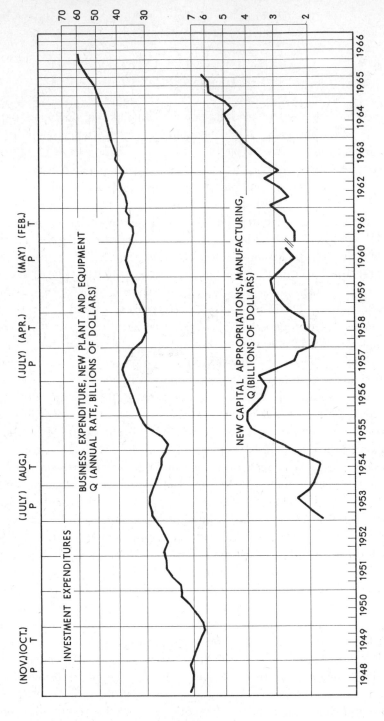

SOURCE: U.S. Department of Labor, *Business Cycle Developments.*

son, we can see the lag between appropriations and spending. Actual expenditures do not begin to move up until the economy is well into its recovery from recession. And the downturn in capital outlays is roughly coincident with the beginning of the general decline, in contrast to the much earlier cutback in capital appropriations.

When the cyclical changes occur, what form do they take? Business investment in fixed assets springs from a variety of motivations, but it is possible to draw a crude line between outlays made to expand capacity and those aimed simply at replacing or modernizing existing capacity. For the postwar years, a rough estimate of these two types of investment spending in the manufacturing sector is shown in Figure 15–5. A certain amount of cyclical behavior may be seen in the outlays for replacement and modernization, but much the largest source of fluctuation is the spending for expansion.

Because of this great volatility in spending for new capacity, the cyclical fluctuations in business investment are much wider than the rise and fall of gross national product. Taking the two kinds of investment together, and looking at the business sector as a whole, this contrast with GNP is clear in Figure 15–6. It is particularly striking for investment in equipment. In part this reflects the shorter life of equipment relative to buildings, which increases the flow of decisions to be made and increases

FIGURE 15–5

COMPUTED MANUFACTURING EXPENDITURES FOR EXPANSION
AND FOR REPLACEMENT AND MODERNIZATION

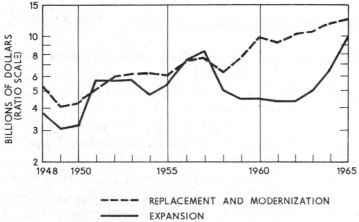

------ REPLACEMENT AND MODERNIZATION
——— EXPANSION

SOURCE: Machinery and Allied Products Institute, *Capital Goods Preview*, No. 65 (Washington, D.C., March, 1966).

FIGURE 15–6

BUSINESS INVESTMENT AND GROSS NATIONAL PRODUCT

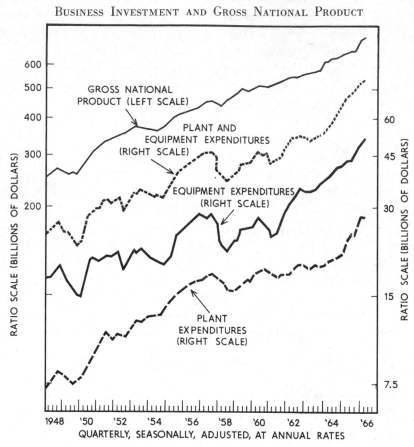

SOURCE: Office of Business Economics, Department of Commerce.

the opportunities to put off expenditures or to speed them up. The chart also points up the larger dollar volume of equipment spending. This again relates in part to the shorter lives and more rapid turnover of such assets, but it is rooted more deeply in technological considerations.

Given the lag in the decision to install new machinery or erect new buildings, and the further lag in getting equipment delivered and construction finished, an important part of the new capacity comes into action after the general economic demand has slacked off. That is illustrated in Figure 15–7, which reports an effort to measure, for manufacturing, the cyclical timing of "functional completions" of projects—i.e., the stages in the general business cycle at which new

FIGURE 15–7

FUNCTIONAL COMPLETIONS OF MANUFACTURING CONSTRUCTION AND
EQUIPMENT PROJECTS IN RELATION TO "FAVORABLE" AND
"UNFAVORABLE" PERIODS

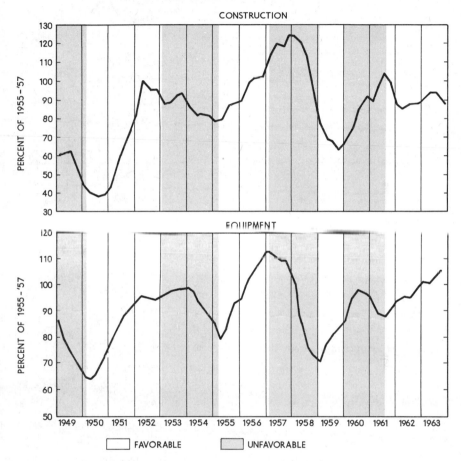

SOURCE: Machinery and Allied Products Institute, *Capital Goods Preview*, No. 55 (Washington, D.C., September, 1963).

capacity becomes operational. This pattern is then compared with the
level of demand for manufacturing output. "Favorable" periods begin
when production first rises above the previous peak and moves into new
higher levels of demand. Favorable conditions are assumed to wane and
turn unfavorable in the last six months before recession began. As Figure
15–7 shows, the manufacturing industries get to their peak of readiness in

FIGURE 15–8

GROSS STOCK OF BUSINESS PLANT AND EQUIPMENT

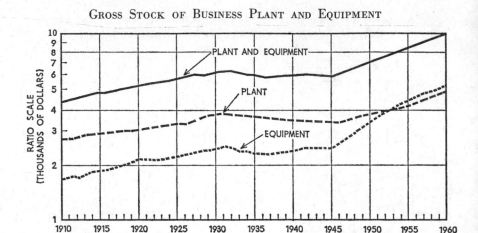

* Midyear estimates.

SOURCE: George Terborgh, *Sixty Years of Business Capital Formation* (Washington, D.C.: Machinery and Allied Products Institute and Council for Technological Advancement, 1960), p. 8.

equipment just as the favorable atmosphere is disappearing, and get to their peak in plant well after the unfavorable times have set in.

In the longer view, these cyclical mishaps diminish in significance, and business capital outlays emerge as a major engine of growth in the American economy—both stimulating demand through the creation of income and feeding that demand through the creation of productive capacity. The enormous growth in the stock of capital goods over 50 years is traced out in Figure 15–8. The strong upward climb was flattened out in the 1930's, but after a barely perceptible dip in the worst year of the Great Depression there was no further decline. That is, through the lean years new plant and equipment continued to replace the fixed assets that were wearing out. There was little or no net expansion, but neither was there net disinvestment. With the end of World War II, the stock began to move up sharply. By 1960 it had climbed all the way to the level that would have been attained if the pre-Depression rate had continued without the interruption of the 1930's.

Some part of this sizable advance represents the overall growth in the American economy—the population, the work force, the national product. But the capital stock has grown much faster than the number of men at work. One measure of this relative expansion is the change in business plant and equipment per worker, which is shown in Figure 15–9. As one

FIGURE 15–9

Average Annual Growth of the Gross Stock of Business Plant
and Equipment per Worker in the Business Labor Force

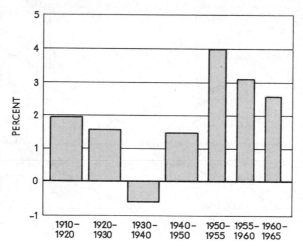

SOURCE: Machinery and Allied Products Institute, *Capital Goods Preview*, No. 61 (Washington, D.C., March, 1965).

would expect, the Depression decade brought a decline in fixed assets per worker, as the work force grew and the capital stock held steady. The 1940's brought a sharp turnaround, however, and the 1950's and 1960's have seen a dramatic surge in capital stock per worker. The years since World War II have also seen a striking shift toward equipment, so that by the 1960's the stock of machinery per worker had come to exceed the stock of buildings per worker.

But there is more to the process than simply giving each worker additional tools to work with. There is the extremely important matter of the quality of those tools. The march of technology has worked wonders in the last 50 years, as indeed it has in any 50-year period for at least the last couple of centuries. Some scholars have gone so far as to say that nine tenths of the growth in output per worker has stemmed from technological progress—i.e., improvements in the quality of the capital stock—and only one tenth of it from the increased quantity of that stock. One is entitled to be skeptical of such figures, but no one seems inclined to doubt the profound importance of invention and innovation and the resulting advances in productivity of capital. The general contours of these advances, as estimated in one careful study, are shown in Figure 15–10.

FIGURE 15–10

INDEXES OF PRODUCTIVITY IN THE UNITED STATES, 1889–1957
Estimates for the Private Domestic Economy

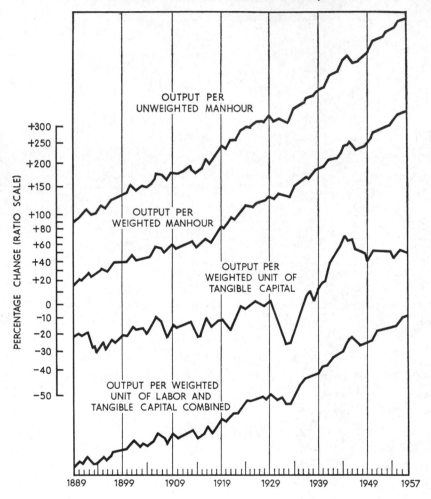

SOURCE: Solomon Fabricant, *Basic Facts on Productivity Change* (New York: National Bureau of Economic Research, 1959), p. 13.

In the end, the pattern of spending for plant and equipment may come down to a question of history. The burst of populations, the sweep of migrations across oceans and continents, the surge of inventive vigor in different peoples at different times—all these forces and others make history a narrative, and keep it from being a catalogue of predictable cause and result. Business investment is central to the subject of business finance; but for ultimate understanding of its ebb and flow, we may have to turn to economic historians.

SUGGESTED READINGS

ANDERSON, W. H. LOCKE.   *Corporate Finance and Fixed Investment.* Boston: Harvard Business School, Division of Research, 1964.

BENNETT, J. P.   "Cyclical Determinants of Capital Expenditures: A Regression Study of the United States Steel Industry," *Southern Economic Journal,* January, 1966, pp. 330–40.

DE LEEUW, FRANK.   "The Demand for Capital Goods by Manufacturers: A Quarterly Time Series," *Econometrica,* July 1962, pp. 407–23.

EISNER, ROBERT, and STROTZ, ROBERT.   "The Determinants of Business Investment," in the Commission on Money and Credit Research Monographs, *Impacts of Monetary Policy.* Englewood Cliffs, N.J.: Prentice-Hall, Inc., 1963.

GRILICHES, ZVI, and WALLACE, N   "The Determinants of Investment Revisited," *International Economic Review,* September, 1965.

HAMMER, FREDERICK S.   *The Demand for Physical Capital. Application of a Wealth Model.* Englewood Cliffs, N.J. Prentice-Hall, Inc., 1964.

HICKMAN, BERT G.   *Investment Demand and U.S. Economic Growth.* Washington: The Brookings Institution, 1965.

KUH, EDWIN.   *Capital Stock Growth: A Micro-Econometric Approach.* Amsterdam: North Holland Publishing Co., 1963.

MEYER, JOHN, and GLAUBER, ROBERT.   *Investment Decisions, Economic Forecasting, and Public Policy.* Boston: Harvard Business School, Division of Research, 1964.

TARSHIS, LORIE.   "The Elasticity of the Marginal Efficiency Function," *American Economic Review,* December 1961, pp. 958–85.

TERBORGH, GEORGE.   *Sixty Years of Business Capital Formation.* Washington, D.C.: Machinery and Allied Products Institute and Council for Technological Advancement, 1960.

Part IV

THE COST OF CAPITAL OR OPTIMIZATION OF SOURCES—PROFIT MAXIMIZATION JOINED WITH FINANCIAL UNCERTAINTY

Chapter 16

THE COST OF EXTERNAL EQUITY
CAPITAL—SALE OF NEW COMMON STOCK

What is the cost of capital? Why do we need to know? The *why* is easier than the *what*, so let us start there.

Financial management, facing its largest job—capital budgeting—has to know the cost of the funds used for a project to compare with the expected rate of returns from that project, if the project's profitability is to be determined. Whether using the Internal Rate of Return or Net Present Value method, the rate of financial cost is needed as a "hurdle" or "cutoff" signal. In other words, the cost of capital is the minimal required rate that the project must yield if it is to be adopted. Recalling that projects should only be accepted if they will increase stock price, we can say that the cost of capital is the additional earnings on the new investment required to keep stock price from falling.

It is when we try to get more precise about the *variety* of costs of capital that difficulties arise, for funds can be raised by increasing ownership shares or by trading on the equity, i.e., borrowing. And there are a variety of ways to increase ownership: sale of stock or earnings retention; or to increase debt through bonds, bank loans, etc. Nevertheless in general it is true and useful to know that whatever the method of fund raising selected, funds should *not* be raised unless they add less to cost than they promise to add to returns if employed.

But one needs to know more than the overall cutoff point if one is to compute the profitability of investment programs or, more precisely, the amount by which the addition of supramarginal investment projects will increase stockholders' wealth or stock price plus dividends. In other words, one needs to know the relative costs of alternative sources of funds in order to *minimize* those costs—in order, that is, to choose the optimum capital structure for the company.

Only in the case of a riskless economic system with perfect capital markets is it sufficient to know only the *general* cutoff point—the interest rate. If expected returns are certain to be received, then a firm can raise all its funds, no matter how much or how, at one cost—the risk-free rate of interest—say, the rate on federal government debt. Stockholders could get no better return than bondholders for they would be undertaking no risk. But neither would the creditor's priority claim on income carry any benefit. All providers of funds would be paid the premium on current dollars over certain future dollars, but that is all. But of course, when risk enters, one expects that owners will require a greater return for their supply of funds than creditors because of their assumption of much of that risk. And one expects that in the real financial world, flotation costs will make it cheaper to raise ownership funds internally than externally, i.e., by selling new shares.

In the pure theory of the investment of the firm then, it is assumed that the relevant rate of cost is some given interest rate on borrowed money. But this is too simple an assumption for two reasons: (1) There are other ways of raising funds besides borrowing them, and (2) the rate of interest on borrowed money to the firm is not a constant but is likely to be an increasing function of the amount borrowed. This means that we must expect the cost of funds to rise with the amount of investment and that we must determine the cost of funds raised by retaining profits and selling shares of stock as well as by borrowing.

Precisely what is meant by the *cost* of raising money in these various ways in a world of uncertainty? It might appear that at least the cost of raising money by borrowing is clear; is it not the contractual annual rate of interest that must be paid? But this is *not* correct, for there are usually additional costs of borrowing that must be imputed. For example, if the debt increase is sizable, it will increase the riskiness of the whole enterprise, raise the rate at which earnings per share of stock are capitalized, and thus perhaps lower the price of the stock in the market. This imputed effect must also be considered part of the cost of debt finance. Much more difficult at first glance is the question: What is the cost of raising money by selling additional shares of common stock? But in fact, although there is no quick or obvious (but wrong) answer like "interest rate," to the bond finance question, this is really the easier cost to determine though it is largely an opportunity cost rather than an out-of-pocket cost.

It will be helpful to remember throughout this discussion of the particular costs of capital that out-of-pocket or cash cost is not the whole issue or even the major part of it. Just as we have seen that rate of return analysis must include non-out-of-pocket costs such as depreciation, so, too, must rate of cost analysis include non-out-of-pocket costs such as added risk or alternative investment opportunities foregone. However, the cost of capital in general is best thought of as a measure that is developed to demarcate the cutoff point in capital budgeting. The percentage cost of capital is the minimum *required* rate of return that the investment project must yield if it is to be "profitable" and hence to be adopted. Since profitability is defined in terms of its effect on the stockholder, this required rate is one that will at least not affect the price of the stock or stockholder wealth adversely. That is, if an investment project is to be adopted, it must not depress the net expected returns per share with a constant price/returns ratio; or if the multiplier is adversely affected by the financing, the increased returns per share must be more than offsetting. In short, the cost of capital in general is an opportunity cost concept that sets the minimum rate that the investment must promise to return; at rates of return greater than the cost of capital, the price of the stock or stockholder wealth can be expected to rise.

But let us take these difficulties one at a time. Let us begin our consideration of costs of capital by taking the case of a corporation that has no debt and that pays out all its earnings in the form of dividends. In other words let us first consider a company that raises its funds exclusively by selling stock. In this simple case we will determine the cost of financing by external equity. This is a simple case because when we consider the cost of *internal funds* we have to allow for *growth* or increasing quantity of earnings *per share;* and when we consider the cost of *debt* (or preferred stock) we have to allow for *risk* or falling *quality* of earnings per share as well.

THE COST OF COMMON STOCK

Management's guide in this case, where neither debt nor plowback are considered as possible sources of funds, is essentially that new stock issues will be in the owner's interest so long as the projects in which the equity funds will be used will yield at least enough to maintain earnings per share (*EPS*). Of course, the object is to *increase EPS*, but we are looking for the cutoff point; all projects yielding more than this marginal one will add to *EPS*. Since the degree of risk on investment is unchanged in this case by the financing path chosen, the price/earnings multiple or the rate at which earnings are capitalized by the stock market is also unchanged. Therefore the price per share will rise as new *EPS* rises. In other words, the general cost rule here is that if new projects financed through the sale of common stock promise to yield at least what would have been earned per share if the flotation had not been made, the flotation will benefit the old stockholders. Roughly speaking then, the cost of external equity capital is

$$\frac{\text{Current Earnings after Taxes}}{\text{Stock Price in the Market}} \text{ or } \frac{Ec}{P},$$

when future earnings per share are presumed to be the same as earnings today if no new net investment were undertaken. Remember that this assumes no growth and no change in risk.

For example, take a company with one million shares outstanding, earning $2.50 per share and selling at $25 per share in the market. Assume that the company has a project that will cost $5 million and will yield $550,000 annually. Should the company sell stock to finance the project? Assuming that the $2.50 is future EPS (or Ea) if the investment is not adopted, the answer would seem to be yes. While 200,000 new shares (at $25 per share) will provide the required $5 million, new earnings of $550,000 will also be added. The result will be that total shares rise to 1,200,000, total earnings rise to $3,050,000, and EPS *after* the investment is made will be $2.54. Given the P/E ratio of 10, the stock will rise in price to $25.40 and it would seem in the interest of the old stockholders to float the new stock. The project promises to yield more than the Ea/P without expansion. Old Ea/P was $2.50/$25.00, or 10 percent, but the project promises to yield 550,000/5,000,000, or 11 percent.

However, the answer would not be so obvious if we had added a flotation cost to the new stock to be sold. Assume that the new stock will bring in proceeds of only $20 per share, with $5 going to the investment bankers, lawyers, the SEC, etc. Then to raise $5,000,000 for itself, the company has to sell 250,000 new shares, not 200,000. Now does it pay to go ahead with the project?

If the firm does go ahead, it will raise the total number of shares outstanding to 1,250,000. Thus to maintain EPS of $2.50 (the minimum requirement) will require earnings of 1,250,000 shares $\times$ $2.50, or $3,125,000. But the expected earnings without the project are $2,500,000, and when the new earnings of $550,000 are added they will bring the total to $3,050,000, or *less* than the required $3,125,000. In other words, the *required return* from the project when flotation costs are included is $625,000 on $5M. This is a rate of 12.5 percent. Since the project promises only 11 percent, it should not be adopted. If it were, EPS

would fall to $2.44 (i.e., $3,050,000 ÷ 1,250,000 shares) and price to $24.40. When flotation costs were not considered, the Ea/P was 250/25, or 10 percent, which was less than the 11 percent return promised by the project. A flotation cost as large as 20 percent ($5 on $25) is not unusual for small or little-known companies. For the large corporation whose stock is listed, however, a more typical charge would be say $1 or 4 percent on stock selling at $25. In this case

$$\frac{Ea}{P - FC} = \frac{\$2.50}{\$25 - 1} = 10.4 \text{ percent.}$$

This example is summarized for your review in Table 16–1.

TABLE 16–1
I. EFFECTS OF STOCK ISSUE ON STOCK PRICE

		If Project Adopted	
		A. Flotation Cost	B. With Flotation Cost
If Project Not Adopted		Neglected	of $5 per share
No. shares	1,000,000	1,200,000	1,250,000
Total earnings	$2,500,000	$3,050,000	$3,050,000
EPS	$2.50	$2.54	$2.44
P/E ratio	10	10	10
Market price of stock	$25.00	$25.40	$24.40

II. REQUIRED RATES OF RETURN ON INVESTMENT TO PREVENT STOCK PRICE DECLINE

Stock Price Decline

Required *EPS*	$2.50	$2.50
No. shares	1,200,000	1,250,000
Total required earnings	$3,000,000	$3,125,000
Total earnings without the new investment	2,500,000	2,500,000
Increase in earnings required	$ 500,000	$ 625,000
New investment	5,000,000	5,000,000
Required rate of return	10%	12.5%
Actual rate of return on new investment ($550,000/$5,000,000)	11%	11%

Thus, to take Ec/P as the cost of fresh sales of common stock would be an oversimplification on two scores:

1. The earnings that are relevant to the computations are *expected* earnings (Ea), not current earnings (Ec); and
2. The price that is relevant is not the current market price (P) but that price *less* the costs of flotation of the stock and the price discount that is usually given to sell stock when a large fresh supply surges into the market, ($P - FC$).

Only if the future earnings are expected to be in line with current and past earnings, that is, if the company's stock is not priced as a *growth* issue, and if the fresh stock is sold to old stockholders at a trivial market price cut, will Ec/P serve as a good measure of the cost of raising funds via sale of new common stock.

In any case it is clear that the project must promise to return *more* than the Ea/P to allow for the costs of flotation, i.e., for that part of the proceeds *not* received by the issuing corporation. In other words the basic minimum required return—the hurdle—is *always* higher when equity funds are provided from external rather than internal sources. This does not mean that corporations should never float stock, for, after all, internal funds are limited in amount even if payout policy is such as to cut cash dividends to zero. Moreover, flotation cost can be cut to the bone by selling the new stock—via so-called privileged subscriptions—to the old stockholders. Presumably the marketing costs including risks are minimized by offering the stock to a pre-sold group. But the issuing costs cannot be nil, and as a consequence, financing through increasing the equity is cheaper when done internally rather than externally. As will become apparent later, there is also a tax advantage for internal equity that favors it over external equity finance. (See below pp. 264 ff.)

Some readers may be wondering why dividends/price is not a good measure of the cost of common stock finance. For those accustomed to think of cost as a cash outlay, this is a natural approach. In fact, if cash dividends are assumed to be a constant percentage of earnings, say 50 percent, it would be easy to reword our formulation so that expected *dividends* hold the center of the stage. But we prefer not to stress cash dividends paid out, not only to avoid emphasis on cost as a cash outlay but because it is earnings, *whether paid out or not,* that are the fundamental determinants of market prices of common stock. In the next chapter and in Chapter 26, we consider this matter in depth.

The cost of common stock finance then has both an out-of-pocket flotation cost and an opportunity cost. To say that the company should not adopt a project which promises to yield less than $Ea/P - FC$ is to say that individual stockholders would be better off buying the *outstanding* stock than the new stock, and of course the opportunity to buy more stock in the open market is an option stockholders always have. Obviously they also have the opportunity to sell this company's stock and buy the stock of a similar company which does not plan to sell new stock, when the cost of equity capital (Ke) exceeds the expected rate of return (IRR).

Dilution

It is a customary caution in the financial world that in issuing new stock, management should be careful to avoid "dilution." Although precise definitions of dilution are as hard to come by as the warnings are common, if management follows the rule that

$$IRR \geq \frac{Ea}{P - FC},$$

dilution by any sensible definition will be avoided.

In general, dilution refers to a loss in a stockholder's relative share of earnings and a consequent markdown of the stock's price in the market.[1] Since risk is unaffected (or reduced) by recourse to equity finance, the multiplier can be assumed constant; if then the stock price falls, it must have been caused by a fall in *EPS*. What then is there in issuing new stock that is likely to cause *EPS* to fall—and hence to cause stock "dilution"?

1. If flotation costs are neglected and the new project yields just Ea/P, then the stock price will indeed fall. We define flotation costs to include not merely the investment bankers' fees but all factors that reduce the proceeds from stock sale below the pre-issue market price.
2. If the new project is expected to yield *Ea* but there is a lag between the time when the stock is sold or the proceeds are sunk into investment and the time when the new additional earnings flow back to the company, in the interim the stock will have been diluted. That is, *EPS* will fall because more stockholders have been added but not more earnings.

But both of these possible causes of dilution are obviated by the use of the hurdle: $Ea/P - FC$. Because *Ea* is the present value of the future stream of earnings, the time lag is allowed for in the process of finding the project's "true" *Ea*. Because flotation costs are in the denominator, the required rate of return or hurdle for the project is raised, thus obviating "dilution" of *EPS*.

Indeed, dilution cannot occur no matter what the method of finance if the appropriate capital budgeting rules are followed. For example, dilution—in the sense that the adoption of a project diminishes stockholder

---

[1] Of course relative *voting* power may be diluted by new issues but voting power is seldom of concern to the stockholder, and in any case, old shares are available at market price. We do not consider dilution of control.

wealth—can occur when the project is financed by *internal* equity, if the general capital budgeting test of E/P is not met.

For example, assume as before one million shares outstanding; annual earnings of $2.5 million, or $2.50 per share; and market price of the stock, $25. Then the E/P is 1/10, or 10 percent. An investment project of $2.5 million with an expected return of 8 percent is being considered.

If the project is adopted, the $2.5 million in current earnings are used to finance the project (plowback); if the project is not adopted, the $2.5 million in current earnings is paid out as a cash dividend (payout). See Table 16–2.

TABLE 16–2

If Project Adopted		*If Project Not Adopted*	
Earnings	$2.5 million		
Plus 8% of $2.5 million ..	0.2 million		
	$2.7 million		
Earnings per share	$ 2.70	Earnings per share	$ 2.50
Price per share (10 times earnings)	$27.00	Price per share	$25.00
Plus dividends per share .	0	Plus dividends per share	2.50
Total per share value of stock and cash received	$27.00	Total per share value of and cash received	$27.50

Note that although $2.50 per share was retained, the price of stock rises by only $2.00.

If the shareholder had 100 shares, he would lose $50 if the project were adopted. He could always buy ten more shares of stock with the extra $250 in cash dividends received, ending up with 100 shares at $25 each, or $2,750 worth of stock, versus 100 shares at $27, or $2,700, if the project were adopted.

Thus adoption of the project in this case "dilutes" the stockholder's position in that his wealth is less than if the project had not been adopted. Note that dilution occurs because the cost of capital rate hurdle has been violated; dilution has no essential connection to selling new stock or *any* particular method of finance. In this case dilution occurred even though finance was internal.

The Tax Penalty on External Equity

If one considers the stockholder's position *after* personal income taxes, the relative cost advantage of internal over external equity as alternative means of finance is augmented beyond the flotation costs saved because the opportunity costs are really not identical. For example, if the average stockholder's personal income tax bracket is 37.5 percent, then the opportunities open to the stockholder to take his earnings out of the company to invest in another company are handicapped by having to pay taxes on those funds prior to reinvestment. Reinvestment in one's own company via retention is not penalized so heavily for it is subject only to capital gains taxes or at most half the tax bite, i.e., $t/2$. Thus the cost of external equity finance as an alternative to internal finance is not only penalized for flotation cost, it suffers from a tax penalty as well.

$$\text{The cost of external equity or } Kex = \frac{Ea}{1 - \dfrac{t}{2}} = \frac{\$2.50}{1 - \dfrac{0.375}{2}}$$

$$= \frac{\$2.50}{1 - 0.1875}$$

$$= \frac{\$3.08}{\$24}$$

$$= 12.8 \text{ percent.}$$

That is, the comparative cost of selling stock is not 10.4 percent, for that neglects the tax "cost"; nor is it just 10 percent for that neglects flotation costs as well as tax cost. In short, the required rate of return on funds raised by selling common stock is higher on two scores than funds that are raised internally.[2]

But this only tells us that a firm which does not incur debt should never sell common stock so long as internal funds are available. This is *not* to say that common stock should not be issued but only that it should not be issued in order to increase payout of earnings. If, however, all earnings have been plowed back, and there still remain investment opportunities that promise to yield more than *Kex*, then it would be profitable to issue common stock.

In other words, if there were under consideration a single investment project by a nondebt firm, then surely one would expect it to be financed completely by internal means, if funds of sufficient size were available.

---

[2] See the appendix to this chapter for a more detailed example of how the tax structure increases the relative cost of finance by selling new stock.

However, this decision would insure only minimum costs of finance; it would not insure maximum profits through investment unless *all* projects that yield net returns over cost of finance were adopted. In terms of continuous schedules, the cost of finance will rise when internal sources are exhausted, but this is not the cutoff point unless the schedule of expected returns from investment falls below the next scheduled means of finance—say, selling stock. To maximize profit requires that the difference *between* total net returns and total financial costs be maximized. Minimizing costs is only part of the job.

Common stock may still be an appropriate means of finance provided the *IRR* > *Ke*, when internal funds are exhausted or when debt is a more expensive means of finance. But we have not yet examined the cost of internal funds directly nor the cost of debt. Thus in the next chapter we turn to a closer examination of the first of these two alternatives—the cost of internal funds.

QUESTIONS AND PROBLEMS

1. The cost-of-capital concept involves opportunity costs, imputed costs, and out-of-pocket costs. Define each of these costs and give an example of each within the field of corporate finance.

2. In a world of certainty, the average cost of capital would be a constant and equal to the interest rate. Explain. How would you generalize about the average cost of capital in the real, uncertain world?

3. What is the cost of capital to a firm that raises all of its funds by selling new shares of common stock?

4. The stockholders position cannot be "diluted" if the proper cost-of-capital cutoff rule is used. Discuss critically.

5. Given the following information, compute the cost of external equity capital:

Market price of the stock	$12.00
Expected earnings per share on existing investment	$1.50
Flotation costs per share	$1.00
Marginal tax brackets of average stockholder	40%
Dividends	$1.50
Debt	None

6. "A firm which does not incur debt should never sell common stock as long as internal funds are available." Discuss.

SUGGESTED READINGS

BINGHAM, E. F. "Cost of Equity Capital to Electric Utilities," *Public Utilities Fortnightly*, September 24, 1964.

LINTNER, J. V. "Dividends, Earnings, Leverage, Stock Prices and the Supply of Capital to Corporations," *Review of Economics and Statistics*, August, 1962, pp. 243–69.

MILLER, D. C. "Corporate Taxation and Methods of Corporate Financing," *American Economic Review*, December, 1952, pp. 839–54.

SOLOMON, E. *The Theory of Financial Management*, chaps. iii and iv. New York: Columbia University Press, 1963.

APPENDIX TO CHAPTER 16
CALCULATING THE COST OF EXTERNAL
EQUITY—AN EXAMPLE

Once again, assume stock selling in the market at $25, no other securities or debt outstanding. The corporation has been earning $2.50 per share (one million shares; $2.5 million earnings) after corporate income taxes. The stock is selling at ten times earnings, or at a price to yield 10 percent. Thus, to maintain the selling price or earning power of the stock, any new shares needed to finance new investment must promise to yield at least $2.50 per share after tax if the investment is to be in the stockholders' interests.

Now, assume that this $25 million corporation (as measured in market value of equity) has a $1 million investment project to consider. The question is: What rate of return must the project promise to yield to make it profitable to finance by selling new common stock?

Flotation Costs

To raise $1 million by selling stock will require that *more* than 40,000 shares of stock be sold because new stock cannot be sold to *net* $25 to the corporation. New stock may be sold to the *public* at $25, but the investment banker will require a commission ("spread") to cover the costs of designing, underwriting, and distributing the issue to the public. Let us assume that the commission per share is $5 (exaggerating to ease the arithmetic); then, to raise $1 million, the corporation must sell 50,000 shares which will yield it $20 for each of the shares. This will increase the number of shares by 5 percent from 1,000,000 to 1,050,000; therefore, the *total* earnings, if earnings per share are to be maintained, must increase as a result of the investment by 5 percent, or $125,000, if the investment is to be worth undertaking. This means that earnings after corporate income taxes must rise from the current $2.5 million to $2.625 million. The new investment of $1 million *must promise a yield of $125,000 annually*, or *12.5 percent*, to make the new investment worth undertaking.

Note that *on old investments or on new investments financed internally a 10 percent rate of return is satisfactory;* but the rate on the new investment must be higher—25 percent higher, in fact—because the new issue's flotation costs require that new stock be sold at a net price to the corporation of $20 rather than $25, a 25 percent excess of money raised over money received by the firm.

After the investment is made, the return that *all* stockholders taken together will be earning per share will still be only 10 percent, or $2.50 per share of the $25 market price per share.

Old earnings after taxes	$2,500,000
Plus new earnings	125,000
Total earnings after investment	$2,625,000
Number shares outstanding after investment	1,050,000
Earnings per share after investment	$2.50

Thus, to keep earnings per share at least as high as before investment requires that new issues *not* be issued unless the funds so obtained can be used to earn 12.5 percent, even though the old shares and the old investment earn but 10 percent. Therefore, stock should *not* be issued so long as there are *flotation costs*, when new investments merely promise to maintain the old earnings rate. The required rate is higher, and thus the cost of finance is higher.

Taxes as a Cost of Selling New Stock

Now, in fact, because of the *personal income tax*, the cost of financing by new issues in our example is even higher than 12.5 percent. This corporation has been earning $2.5 million per year, or $2.50 per share on one million shares. Assume that it pays out $2.00 per share in the form of dividends and that stockholders receiving the dividends are in the marginal personal income tax bracket of 37.5 percent. In order to show how this tax increases the cost of financing by new issues still further above the cost of financing by retained earnings, assume also that the new stock is all bought by the old stockholders. The old stockholders receive $2 million in dividends, of which $750,000 is taxed away at the 37.5 percent rate, leaving them $1.25 million after taxes. This sum will be just enough to allow them to buy the new 50,000 shares at the market price of $25 per share. But this is the equivalent of paying $40, pretax, for stock which will yield their corporation only $20 in usable funds. The firm will have disbursed $2 million in dividends to its stockholders and got back only $1 million as proceeds from selling them new stock. The tax collector and the underwriters will have taken the rest.

Thus, the cost of selling new shares under these conditions is *twice* what it would have been if the corporation had financed itself by retained earnings. By using retained earnings, the corporation saves $250,000 in flotation costs ($5.00 per share times 50,000 shares), and the stockholders save $750,000 in taxes. The cost of retained earnings is but 10 percent, that is, the investment must yield 10 percent, just as the old investments yield 10 percent, to keep stockholders' per share return from slipping below the rate which prevailed before the investment program was instituted. But if stock is sold, it must promise to yield 20 percent rather than 10 percent; an additional 2.5 percent to cover flotation costs plus 7.5 percent to cover the loss of dividend income taxed away. In other words, the corporation must expect to earn $200,000 on the projected $1 million investment (not $100,000) to make it worth while if the $1 million is raised by selling stock.

If we consider (1) that the stockholders are, in effect, paying $40 per share for the stock; and (2) that they therefore must receive a 10 percent return on their investment, or $4 per share, if the investment is to pay them as well as their current holdings; then (3) the corporation must earn $4 times 50,000 new shares, or $200,000, to justify the investment. Since the corporation is in fact receiving only $20 per share sold times 50,000 shares, or $1 million, it must earn 20 percent on the stockholders' fresh contribution to justify selling stock to them.

Let us compare these two forms of equity finance. When selling shares under our assumed conditions, the Ea/P-type formulation will be:

$$\frac{Ea + Tax\ cost}{P - Flotation\ cost} = \frac{\$\ 2.50 + \$1.50}{\$25.00 - \$5.00} = \frac{\$\ 4.00}{\$20.00} = 20\%\ \text{Cost of common stock finance}$$

The retained earnings formula was simply:

$$\frac{Ea}{P} = \frac{\$\ 2.50}{\$25.00} = 10\%\ \text{Cost of retained finance}$$

Qualifying the Disadvantages of New Common Stock Issues: Retained Earnings Not Available

It is important to note that this demonstration does *not* show that equity shares are too expensive to use as a method of financing investment. It does show that *as long as retained earnings are available*, they will be a *cheaper* method of finance than new shares. But obviously, when retained earnings are exhausted, profitable investment projects may remain. If they promise to earn a sufficiently high rate of return, it will, of course, pay to issue new stock or to borrow. This example does show, however, that higher rates of return on investment are required for stock issue finance than for retained earnings finance. This means that equity finance is usually resorted to only after retained earnings are exhausted, and then only for projects that yield relatively higher rates of return. Of course, new shares will be issued in many instances before all retained earnings are exhausted, for example, when corporations have a long-established dividend policy which is in part responsible for the established price of the stock. And occasionally, when the stock market booms, the price of the corporation's stock may be reevaluated at a higher price/earnings ratio, and flotation costs may be quite low in so buoyant a market. Under these circumstances, resort to stock issues is more likely because the new investment need not promise so large a return at the new capitalization rate to avoid hurting *old* stockholders.

Reducing the Tax Disadvantage: Capital Gains Taxes

Another complicating factor that reduces the advantage of retained earnings finance over new-issue finance is the fact that our tax structure includes a capital gains tax as well as a personal income tax. Only in the case where stock is held until death is the capital gains tax avoided. Thus only in this case does the full income tax disadvantage of new issues apply. If, at the other extreme, the stockholder is in the 25 percent income bracket and realizes a short-term capital gain which is taxable at 25 percent, there is no tax advantage to him of the corporation's having relied on retained earnings for finance rather than paying out dividends and recapturing them by sales of stock. (The flotation saving remains, however.) The fact that *retained earnings raise the market value of the stock* is the key to understanding this point; capital gains taxation, of course, is applied to the increase in the market value of the stock when the stock is sold. This is to be thought of as an alternative to receiving dividends and being taxed on them at the personal income tax rates.

If our stock remains at a price of $25.00 when $2.50 is paid out in dividends, then the price of this stock would rise by $2.50 to $27.50 if the dividends were retained in the corporation and were expected to earn at the same rate of 10 percent as in the previous years. Now, assume that the typical stockholder is in the 37.5 percent personal income tax bracket, and compare this rate with the long-term capital gains rate of 18.75 percent. The stockholder's net tax advantage through retention of earnings and later sale of stock over that of dividend payments is halved. Net, only 18.75 cents more of each $1.00 will be taxed away if dividends are paid out instead of being retained—not 37.5 cents more, as our prior illustration implied.[3] It was this full 37.5 cents loss plus the loss of 20 percent of the proceeds of new stock sales as cost of flotation that led us to observe that the cost of new issues was 20 percent, rather than the 10 percent cost of using retained earnings. Now, if we use our new tax calculation which allows for capital gain, the cost of new issues is only 16.25 percent, not 20. And if we use a more typical lower cost of flotation, $2.50 of the $25.00 sales price rather than $5.00, the cost of new shares becomes 15 percent as against 10 percent for retained earnings finance. There is still quite a significant cost advantage to retained earnings finance, but it is not twice as expensive to resort to sales of new stock; rather, the established corporation on the average will find new issues about 50 percent more expensive.

Reducing the Flotation Cost Disadvantage: Privileged Subscriptions

This disadvantage of new issues is still further reduced if the corporation uses the *privileged subscription* technique, that is, sells the new stock to the old stockholders. The costs should be less than would be necessary to sell to outsiders—i.e., for investment bankers to buy and resell the stock. Moreover, there will be savings in other services of investment bankers that are not needed here. Suppose we cut the costs of flotation in half again when sales of new stocks are made to old stockholders. Then, the costs of flotation will be $1.25 per $25.00 share, which will require that

---

[3] Of a $2.00 dividend, the stockholder will be able to keep $1.25 plus his old share worth $25.00 = $26.25. If the $2.00 profits are instead retained in the corporation, his stock will be worth $27.00, but he will be subject to capital gains taxes of 18.75 percent of $2.00, or 37.5 cents. Thus, in this alternative, selling his stocks would yield him net $26.625. This is only 37.5 cents more, not 75 cents more, than the dividend alternative.

the new rate of return be 0.625 percent greater than if retained earnings are used, plus the 3.75 percent greater yield that is needed to offset the net disadvantage of personal income taxation (at the 37.5 percent rate) over capital gains taxation (at the 18.8 percent rate). Thus, new shares issued by privileged subscription cost (or must promise to yield) 14.375 percent, whereas retained earnings cost only 10 percent. Here, new issues of stock cost less than one half more than retained earnings finance.

This is less prohibitive than is popularly believed to be the case. There must be other reasons why management hesitates to sell new stock. We shall examine these reasons in the chapters on common stock which follow. Here, it suffices to point out that it may prove cheaper to go outside for debt finance rather than equity finance. When this is the case, equity finance, though not greatly more expensive, is last to be resorted to because it is the most expensive. And only when corporations have heavy investment projects that cannot be profitably postponed will they be driven to move so far up the cost of finance curve as to reach the point where new-issue finance is the only source of finance that remains.

Chapter 17

THE COST OF INTERNAL EQUITY
CAPITAL—RETAINED EARNINGS

If we are to determine the cost of retained earnings or internal equity as a form of finance, we must lift our restriction that 100 percent of earnings are paid out as cash dividends. This means that we must drop the assumption that our firm is *not* growing, for retention necessarily implies that: (1) the firm's net assets or net worth and the earnings per share (EPS) are growing, and (2) given the earnings multiplier, the price of the stock will be rising: capital gains will be made in lieu of cash dividends. But if the expected rate of return on projects is stable, abstracting from taxes, the larger flow of earnings will be capitalized at the same rate as the dividends would have been so that stockholder wealth will be unaffected by the retention: the stockholder's wealth consists either of stable stock value plus a cash dividend or of a higher stock value. So long as the expected return from investment projects is a constant, aside from the savings in flotation costs and taxes, what the stockholder gains via internal expansion he loses through dividends foregone that might have been reinvested elsewhere. In other words, when retention simply finances more expansion at the same rate of return, the Ea/P formulation of the cost of equity capital is still useful. The hurdle rate is the same for the stable rate firm whether or not it retains earnings.

Retention of earnings, then, always implies that the firm is *larger* in net assets or net worth than it would be if the earnings had been paid out in cash dividends. But the *rate* of return on the larger assets need not be greater, though it should not be less. When assets are growing but the rate of return is not, we have mere *expansion* of the firm: assets continue to earn Ea/p or Ke, the same rate earned on the firm's assets before expansion. But, if the firm's assets are growing *and* the rate of return on the new addition to assets (r) is greater than the rate of return on the outstanding assets (Ke), then we have *growth*.[1]

THE COST OF RETENTION IN GROWTH FIRMS

Thus the internally expanding firm is also a growth firm if its new investment projects promise rates of return *above* the average of past investments. In the case of growth firms, the cost of internal equity capital is *not* given by a simple Ea/P formula—this would provide too low a minimum required rate of return; we must allow for the fact that the retained earnings are reinvested at a rate of return, say r, *greater than Ke*. However, the simple Ea/P formula will always determine the cost of *external* equity because the rising payout will match the rising price at which the stock will be sold to finance expansion. In short, to be a growth firm requires that a company retain earnings and employ them at above past average rates of return.[2]

To illustrate, let b represent the percent of earnings retained.

Let m represent the multiple that r, or future investment return, is of Ke, the current investment return—that is: $m = r/Ke$.

Then in a growth firm b is < 1 but > 0, and m is greater than 1.

Keg—the cost of internal equity funds to a growth firm—equals E/P plus the growth in future EPS.

EPS growth equals funds retained per share, or bE/P.

Times the additional rate of profit earned or m

Minus the cost of EPS growth or bE/P

(the dividends foregone to make the investment to obtain the growth).

$$\text{Thus } Keg = \frac{E}{P} + \frac{bEm}{P} - \frac{bE}{P}$$

$$= \frac{E}{P} + \frac{bE(m-1)}{P}$$

$$= \text{current } EPS + \text{growth in } EPS \text{ via the new investment.}$$

For example, if E is \$15 and P is \$500, Keg is unlikely to be E/P or \$15/500, i.e., 3 percent. In such a case it is likely that the market pays

---

[1] Expansion or growth can also be determined in the same fashion when the source of funds is debt. But we continue to assume throughout this chapter that our firm is debt-free.

[2] See Ezra Solomon, *The Theory of Financial Management* (New York: Columbia University Press, 1963), especially Chapter 5, a valuable part of a useful book. Much of this section's approach follows Solomon.

33 × *current* earnings because great earnings growth is anticipated. But earnings growth is not possible if r—the rate at which new investments are being made—is 3 percent! Rather, assume that r is 27 percent and m consequently is then 9.

$$\left(m = \frac{r}{Ke} = \frac{0.27}{0.03} \right)$$

Assume further that b is 0.6 or that 60 percent of current earnings are retained (to be reinvested at r rate of return).

Then substituting in our equation—$E/P + \dfrac{b(En-1)}{P}$ —we get:

$$Keg = \frac{\$15}{500} + \frac{0.6(15)\ (8)}{500} = \frac{15}{500} + \frac{72}{500} = \frac{87}{500}$$

$$Keg = 17.4 \text{ percent.}$$

That is, the cutoff rate for projects in this growth firm is not 3 percent— the Ea/P, but 17.4 percent; that is, still further investment will have to yield in excess of 17 percent to be acceptable because without further investment this is the rate the stockholders expect to earn.

To review this argument and to introduce you to the dividend discussion, let us restate the basic Keg formula in terms of payout rather than retention.

Recall that $$Keg = \frac{E}{P} + \frac{bEm}{P} - \frac{bE}{P}.$$

Clearly if b is 0 or earnings are all paid out, $Ke = E/P$ and there is no growth. Similarly, if $m = 1$, that is, if $r = Ke$, or future rates of return are expected to be the same as today's, the last two terms cancel.

$$Kc = \frac{E}{P} \text{ and there is no growth.}$$

Next, add the first and last terms of the equation so that:

$$Keg = \frac{E\ (1-b)}{P} + \frac{bEm}{P} = \frac{D}{P} + \frac{bEm}{P}$$

Now $E(1-b)$ is dividends, and bEm is the fruits of plowback or capital gains.

Thus the cost of equity capital in a growth firm can be expressed in either of two ways: (*a*) in terms of the value of current dividends *plus* expected capital gains or, (*b*) as we did before, in terms of current earnings plus net expected additional earnings on reinvestment. In the specific example this may be seen as:

$$\frac{\$15(1-0.6)}{500} + \frac{0.6(15)(9)}{500} - \frac{6}{500} + \frac{81}{500} = \frac{87}{500} = 17.4 \text{ percent.}$$

Hence, further retention beyond 60 percent would benefit stockholders only if new projects were available which would yield 17.4 percent or more. To put it another way, if management retained more earnings and invested them in projects that promised to earn even as much as 15 percent, this would not be in the stockholder's interests for the price of the stock would fall. Tax considerations aside, the stockholder would be better off to receive the dividend and buy more of the outstanding stock, for it "yields" 17.4 percent. Such is the meaning and utility of the Keg—the required rate of return to justify investing additional stockholder funds in a growth company.

RETENTION POLICY IN PRINCIPLE

For a firm that does not use debt finance but does incur substantial flotation and tax costs when selling new equity shares, it would seem that dividend policy ought to be passive. In other words, under the conditions assumed, cash dividends should be a residual, to be paid out only when the company cannot use the funds profitably. Retention policy would seem to be the active decision variable: if new investment opportunities promise a (doubly discounted) rate of return that is greater than the cost of internal equity—$\dfrac{E}{P} + \dfrac{bE(m-1)}{P}$—the funds should be retained.

If the cost of external equity—selling new common stock—did *not* entail flotation and tax costs, retention policy would be a matter of indifference. In effect the equivalence of our formulation of the generalized cost of equity in a growing firm—$\dfrac{D}{P} + \dfrac{bEm}{P} = \dfrac{E}{P} + \dfrac{bE(m-1)}{P}$—showed that payout policy was a "mere detail." In other words, when a firm faces investment opportunities that would benefit the stockholders, when in short $r > ke$, it would not matter whether the firm exploited those opportunities by obtaining the funds by withholding dividends and using the earnings thus retained or by paying the earnings out in dividends and selling new stock. Under these conditions, dividend policy is irrelevant.

That is, dividend policy is "irrelevant" if retention policy is correct or if new stock is sold to correct wrong dividend policy.

Now if we allow for the extra costs of equity when obtained externally rather than internally, it would seem that retention ought to be 100 percent or that no cash dividends should be paid so long as above average new investment opportunities are available, i.e., $r > Ke$. On the other hand payout should be 100 percent when $Ke > r$. Under these slightly more realistic conditions, dividend policy is not a matter of indifference but rather is a passive function of investment opportunities. This is a "capital budgeting" theory of dividends which requires payout, the dependent variable, to fluctuate continuously in response to investment opportunities, the independent variable. In this case payout will always be either 100 percent or 0.

But this result too is unsatisfactory for it does not explain the fact that payout policy in practice is rather rigid and is seldom set at either extreme. The average corporation in the United States pays out about half its earnings and is very slow to alter that ratio. Could such a payout policy possibly be an optimum policy? The answer is yes. Let us preview the arguments which we will develop in some detail after we review actual payout policies of United States corporations.

First allow for the fact that investment opportunities yielding above-average rates of return are limited. Then note that, as the marginal efficiency of investment (MEI) curve of Chapter 12 demonstrated, these opportunities are exploited in order of merit. It then becomes clear that as funds are retained (and invested), the excess of r over Ke is progressively reduced. It is quite possible to exhaust the above-average investment opportunities before internal funds give out. At that point, Ke would begin to exceed r, and earnings should be paid out to stockholders. Optimal payout policy thus need not be 0 or 100 percent; it may well be, say, 40 percent.

Similarly we must allow for the possibility that new investment opportunities can be financed by debt and that, within limits, the cost of debt may be less than the cost of internal funds. As a consequence, a combination of some retention and some cash dividends plus some borrowing can provide optimal or least-cost finance. Obviously if the cost of debt (Ki) is less than the cost of retained earnings (and a fortiori of selling stock), then the firm should finance new investment by borrowing the funds and paying out rather than using its own funds ($r > Ke$ but $Ke > Ki$). But it is unlikely that payout will be 100 percent because the cost of debt (as we shall see) rises as additional debt is incurred. As investment expands then, not only does r fall but Ki, the cost of debt, rises. When Ki rises above the cost of internal funds, Ke, but Ke remains below r, the firm should finance further investment by internal funds rather than debt ($r >$ Ke and $Ki > Ke$). Thus just as falling r precludes the necessity of 100 percent retention in a no-debt firm, so rising Ki precludes the necessity of 100 percent payout in a leveraged firm.[3] Again, optimal finance may specify a fractional payout ratio.

Finally, not only is partial payout policy possibly optimal, but the relative rigidity of payout ratios may also be a rational response to stockholder's desires. Suppose that a 50 percent payout has been arrived at by capital budgeting principles; that is, given a schedule of investment opportunities, expected profit flows and the cost of debt, the least-cost combination of finance requires retention of half of the profits. If, for some years, the principal variables alter little, the payout ratio of 50 percent will be taken as a constant by the stockholders who will formulate personal plans based on receipt of certain dividends. Similarly new stockholders will buy the stock because, among other things, it offers a particular dividend policy. If after some years, the investment opportunities for this firm improve—the *MEI* curve shifts to the right—and r begins to exceed Ke, capital budgeting principles would seem to call for increased retention and reduced payout. On the basis of the new opportunities, the stockholders would appear to be better off if more of the earnings were retained and invested than paid out in the form of dividends; that is, the stockholders' extra capital gains would exceed the amount of the cash dividend foregone. But this conclusion would *not* necessarily benefit this particular set of stockholders if a dollar increase in capital gains was felt to add less value than would be lost by a dollar decrease in dividends. Under these conditions even more dollars of capital gains might not compensate the stockholder for the loss of disposable (dividend) income.

Although one cannot generalize about stockholders' relative preferences for cash dividends versus capital gains, it is true that specific companies tend to attract particular clienteles for their stock based among other things on the apparently established payout policy. A change in that policy, even when induced by so pleasant an event as a rise in the profitability of new investment, may be so unfavorably viewed as to more than

---

[3] So long as internal funds are available, recourse to sale of stock for funds is precluded by their extra cost. Of course, if remaining investment opportunities still promise a $r > Ke$ although $Ki > Ke$, and internal funds are exhausted, then new stock issues may be the solution unless tax and flotation costs are sufficiently large to close the $r > Kex$ gap.

offset the worth of the absolutely increased profitability of the firm. In short, if at the margin stockholders capitalize capital gains at a less favorable rate than cash dividends, as they are likely to do when payout policy has been stable for some time, the result is likely to be continued stability or rigidity of payout ratios. The more this is so, the more retained earnings are considered a residual and dividends a decision variable, although capital budgeting theory calls in general for dividends to be the residual.

To sum up, the factors influencing retention policy include the expected rate of return on new investment opportunities, the degree to which leverage is advantageous, and the extent to which stockholders capitalize dividends more or less favorably than the alternative capital gains. In general, these factors tend to cause a payout ratio to be positive but less than 100 percent, and once chosen, to tend towards rigidity.

PAYOUT POLICY IN PRACTICE

Most firms appear to follow a pair of standards in setting dividends.[4] (1) Firms behave as if they had a specific ideal or *target payout ratio* of dividends to earnings, most frequently between 40 and 60 percent of earnings. (2) When earnings change, the speed of adjustment of dividends to the new level of earnings is *lagged* or spread over a given period of years with only partial adaptation to the new level of earnings in any one year. For example, take a firm with an established payout ratio of 50 percent and an adjustment rate of one third (Table 17–1).

TABLE 17–1

STABLE BUT LAGGED PAYOUT POLICY

Year	Earnings per Share	Dividends per Share
1	$6.00	$3.00
2	6.00	3.00
3	9.00	3.50
4	9.00	4.00
5	9.00	4.50

With the *EPS* rising from $6.00 to $9.00 in the third year, the payout target moves up from $3.00 to $4.50. But only a third of this adjustment is made in the same year. It thus takes three years to close the gap

---

[4] The classic article in which these standards were first set forth systematically is John Lintner's "Distribution of Income of Corporations among Dividends, Retained Earnings and Taxes," *American Economic Review*, May, 1956, pp. 97–113.

between actual and target level payout. (In passing, note the close similarity to the accelerator models discussed in Chapter 5 on inventories and Chapter 15 on plant and equipment.)

On the basis of such evidence it has been alleged that dividends rather than retained earnings are the decision variable or that the capital budgeting theory of dividends (as a mere residual) is false. But this is not at all obviously so, for the choice of target ratio and adjustment pace in the first instance depends primarily on the firm's estimated growth potential and need for funds. Growth firms may have stable payout ratios and adjustment rates, but the ratio may be set quite low and the rate quite slow. In such a case the relative stabilities are intended not to make dividends the decision variable but to assure that any dividend increase need not be rescinded. Even though the emphasis in such a company is on plowback and capital gain, the clientele would be upset by a cut in the cash payout. Moreover the lagged adjustment makes possible substantial, even if temporary, sources of additional internal finance. Furthermore, in most studies the payout ratio is not found to be stable for a minority of one third of the firms, and these again are predominantly the growth firms. It is only for such firms that a variable retained earnings program is pertinent; non-growth firms—the majority of firms—have no call to alter payout ratios, etc., and their stability indicates indifference or inertia rather than that dividends are the decision variable. Growth firms can easily step up retention and step down the payout ratio while still allowing cash dividends to drift up a bit absolutely. To illustrate let us alter the prior stable payout example of Table 17–1 to the figures in Table 17–2.

TABLE 17–2

ALTERING PAYOUT POLICY

Year	Earnings per Share	Dividends per Share
1	$ 6.00	$3.00
2	9.00	3.00
3	12.00	4.00
4	15.00	5.00
5	18.00	6.00

Here the payout ratio has been dropped to one third from one half while dividends have not only been absolutely maintained but even increased.

It is also significant that in most studies of actual dividend policies, there is always a large minority of firms, usually about one third of the total sample of firms which do *not* follow any regular dividend policy.

These maverick firms, all of which have skipped paying dividends on occasion, generally treat *dividends* as a residual. The typical firm in this group is marked by smaller size, faster growth, and lower payout than the firms in the majority group.[5] And breaking the majority group into sub-groups reveals that the faster growing firms not only have lower payout ratios but also change dividends more frequently. Even firms whose growth rate is slow tend to alter standard dividend policy by frequent use of "extra" dividends.

Thus even if standardized target payout ratios and lagged rates of adjustments of dividends are typical of United States corporations as a whole, this does not mean that the capital budgeting theory of dividends is disproven, nor that retained earnings are the passive residual of a positive dividend decision. Since most firms are not growth firms (with $r \gtrless Ke$) but are stationary or simply expanding, one should expect that "average" or "national" dividend policy would stress payout rather than retention, but for growth industries alone, retention outweighs dividends in management's decisions. The capital budgeting theory of dividends calls for heavy payout when the firm has no above-average investment opportunities to exploit.

It may well be that lack of change in a firm's payout ratio merely confirms management's long-run expectations of needs for funds. It has been shown, for example, that a firm whose assets earns a 10 percent profit and whose life is 25 years can grow at an annual rate in excess of 7 percent without any external financing if it picks a payout policy of 50 percent. And with a payout of only 30 percent, it could finance a 10 percent rate of growth with no external funds.[6] Thus if a firm properly predicts its investment requirements, it can select a payout ratio which will over time meets its capital budgeting needs without recourse to external finance and without altering the payout ratio. In other words, stability of the payout policy does not necessarily imply that dividends rather than retained earnings are the basic decision variable of the firm.

This secular argument is further underscored by the automatic generation of additional retained earnings during cyclical expansions. At such times the current payout ratio lags behind its target precisely when investment requirements are cyclically large. During the expansion the

---

[5] J. B. Michaelsen, "The Determinants of Corporate Dividend Policy," 1965, unpublished paper.

[6] E. Kuh, *Capital Stock Growth: A Micro-Econometric Approach* (Amsterdam: North-Holland Publishing Co., 1963), pp. 42–43. Strictly speaking this argument holds only for a no-debt firm.

lagged adjustment process generates additional retention relatively as well as absolutely without alteration of the payout target.

Thus even where stable target payout ratios are the rule, retained earnings and not dividends may be the decision variable. For rapidly growing firms the ratios are not stable and internal funds requirements clearly dominate payout policy. The one thing that is clear about dividend policy for all firms regardless of the stability of the target payout ratio is the great reluctance to *cut* a cash dividend once it has been established. Presumably such an act would have an unfavorable effect on the price of the company's stock. But, despite a great deal of general misinformation on the matter, it is not evident that, given a firm's investment policy, an increase in cash dividends *causes* the price of the stock to rise.

PAYOUT POLICY OR DIVIDENDS AND STOCK PRICES

In developing the concept of the cost of internal funds we have seen that the price of the stock of a growing firm (assuming no debt) is the same whether computed as the net present value of the current earnings plus the net expected growth in earnings or as the present worth of the current dividend plus the expected capital gains. In short, logic dictates that given a firm's investment policy or specified growth, stockholders' wealth ought to be unaffected by dividend policy or payout. If borrowing is not considered as a source of funds, every dollar paid out must be replaced by a dollar raised by new stock issues; the higher the cash payout the less the capital gain to the stockholder. If anything, high payout under these circumstances would be less favorable to stockholder wealth because of the flotation and tax cost penalty when the external rather than the internal equity path is chosen. But we can ignore these "frictional" costs for the moment to concentrate on the logic that the stockholder ought to be indifferent to payout or dividend policy, for statistical studies seem to show that he generally *prefers* payout to retention, rather than the reverse. This would seem to imply, contrary to Chapter 16 and this chapter, that the cost of internal funds was not a relatively cheap source of funds.

Statistical Findings

Typically, stock market price is found to be responsive both to current earnings and to current dividends with dividends carrying the heavier weight. In other words higher payout is associated with higher P/E ratios or earnings multipliers.[7] The market seems to be telling us that stock price responds more to dividends than to earnings or that a dollar of dividends is more highly valued than a dollar of capital gains.

However, stock prices, as we know, are a function of *expected* earnings not current earnings. In fact, given a stable payout ratio, there is considerable evidence that current dividends are a better indicator of *future* earnings than are current earnings. For example, knowing that firms do not increase dividends unless they are sure they can sustain them and do so in programmed (lagged) stages, a dividend increase is a good predictor of future earnings. Thus the correlation of dividends with stock prices is likely to be the consequence of the information dividends provide about expected earnings. That is, when stable payout ratios are the rule, current dividends are weighty in determining stock prices because dividends are better proxies for expected earnings than are current earnings.

The apparent dominance of dividends in market valuation is also attributable to other statistical biases[8] such as:

1. A high-risk firm with a low price/earnings ratio may also have a low payout ratio to hedge against the risks of reducing dividends. The low P/E ratio is not caused by the low payout ratio but by the high risk.

2. High price/earnings ratios may lead management to sell stock at what they consider to be an advantageous price and in such a situation to set a high payout ratio. In other words high payout ratios are the result rather than the cause of high P/E ratios.

Thus allowing for the information effects of dividends and for statistical biases removes much of the *apparent* premium that stockholders are presumed to pay for dividend-paying over retaining firms; still some such preference may still remain, though it would seem to be small.

Possible Causes of Stockholder Preference for Dividends

Since nongrowth firms are predominant in the economy, if management has a bias towards bigness and would retain earnings even when its investment opportunities do not merit it, knowledgeable stockholders in such companies would surely place a premium on dividends. Although the opposite would be true of stockholders of growth companies, the net effect

---

7 M. J. Gordon, *The Investment, Financing, and Valuation of the Corporation* (Homewood, Ill.: Richard D. Irwin, Inc., 1962), especially chap. 11.

8 For exemplary exposition of these biases see Friend and Puckett, *American Economic Review*, September, 1964, pp. 659–65.

for the economy as a whole may be an understandable bias towards dividends. But this is not saying much more than that payout depends upon investment opportunities (r) and should be, for example, 100 percent if $r < Ke$, etc. Dividends are not preferred in general but only in lieu of *disadvantageous* retention.

Stockholders might also value a dollar of dividends more highly than a dollar of capital gains, or \$1 now more than the net present value of the extra expected earnings. But why might stockholders *rationally* capitalize dividends at a more favorable rate (K) than earnings? Recall that if the Ke are not the same

$$\frac{D}{Ke} + \frac{bEm}{Ke} + \frac{E}{Ke} \neq \frac{bE(m-1)}{Ke} .$$

Risk

There is more risk to the stockholder in future capital gains over current dividends because stock prices fluctuate around intrinsic value and it is likely that the stock may be below true value at a time when sale is necessary or for protracted periods. The added risk is simply the added variance in the possible outcomes. Given risk aversion, even though capital gains may be more than expected as well as less than expected those equal chances are not equally valued.

Note that it is *not* the futurity of capital gains versus the current dividend that is rationally penalized; the waiting for the fruits of investment (as well as its riskiness) is presumably allowed for in determining the expected net rate of return (r) used in deciding whether the project was in the stockholder's interest. We cannot penalize retention (versus dividends) on the assumption that capital budgeting procedures are faulty.

Lack of Information

If the investor does not know what management knows about the expected profitability of investment, then retention may be undervalued and dividends correspondingly overvalued. It is hard to see how management can convey to stockholders the exact value (e.g., the degree to which $r > Ke$ after discounting for risk) of retention as compared with the clear present value of dollars in current cash dividends. But here again, no bias towards dividends can be assumed; investors, lacking information, may overrestimate as well as underestimate the present value of retained earnings.

Inconvenience and Transaction Costs

Inconvenience and transaction costs may be incurred by any *change* in payout policy. If payout is less than expected, then the expense and risk of selling some of the stock or borrowing on it is incurred. But if payout is more than expected, there are the costs of reinvesting the funds. This cost cuts either way and is not a special penalty on lower payout. It is indeed true that *any* change in the dividends expected by the established clientele for a stock will lead to some fall in the price of that stock. But again there is no reason to expect that, quite apart from what it predicts for future earnings, a cut in dividends is more upsetting than a rise in dividends. The implication for earnings might be good or bad but the inconvenience to the clientele is clear. A cut in dividends may mark the sudden discovery of marvelous investment opportunities and a rise in dividends might mark the end of years of extraordinary investment opportunities. What would be the effect on the price of IBM stock, do you imagine, if its payout were rationally raised to 80 percent?

Since in practice the majority of firms follow a stable payout policy, an increase in dividends is viewed favorably and a decrease unfavorably, because it is a simple reflection of a shift in the earning power of the firm and one's investment. And for growth firms that do not follow a stable payout policy, an increase in dividends is also viewed favorably if it is accompanied by an even larger rise in earnings so that in fact though dividends are absolutely rising, the payout proportion is falling. Growth firms should never find it necessary to cut absolute dividends for while it would inconvenience the "clientele" for the stock, it could not provide much in the way of funds as compared with a stable proportion of a rising earnings stream and a rising capacity to borrow.

As we will next see, it is possible for the cost of debt (though not the cost of stock) to be less than that of retained earnings. When such is the case, a firm should use borrowed funds while raising the payout ratio, unless the firm has opportunities to invest at greater than the cost of retained earnings as well. The only generalization about payout policy that seems quite safe to make is that a cut in absolute dividends is likely to depress the price of the stock for it usually signals either a decline of earning power or the inability to borrow.

QUESTIONS AND PROBLEMS

1. Distinguish between expansion and growth of the firm. Why is the cost of internal funds greater for the growth firm?
2. Under what conditions is dividend policy a mere detail?
3. The capital budgeting theory of dividend determination would seem to call for either 0 or 100 percent payout. How do you reconcile this model with dividend policy in practice, i.e., with stable, partial payout?
4. Assume that a corporation's target payout ratio is 60 percent, its adjustment rate is one fourth, and that its earning per share for 1960–66 are $3, $4, $4, $4, $5, $6, $7.

    a) What dividends per share will have been paid 1960–66?

    b) Does this result demonstrate that dividends are the basic corporate decision variable? Discuss critically.

    c) If in 1964 the firm's investment opportunities soared, and it felt it had become a strong growth firm, how might its dividend policy be altered to generate more funds internally without *cutting* dividends?
5. "Given a debt-free firm's investment policy, an increase in cash dividends does not affect stockholder wealth." How then do you reconcile this analysis with the demonstrated fact that stock prices better correlate with current dividends than with current earnings?
6. Under what circumstances might the stockholder be expected to value a dollar of dividends more highly than a dollar of capital gains?

SUGGESTED READINGS

BRITTAIN, J. A. *Corporate Dividend Policy*, especially chaps. i, v, and ix. Washington, D.C.: Brookings Institution, 1966.

DHRYMES, P. J., and KURZ, M. "On the Dividend Policy of Electric Utilities," *Review of Economics and Statistics*, February, 1964, pp. 76–82.

FRIEND, I., and PUCKETT, M. "Dividends and Stock Prices," *American Economic Review*, September, 1964, pp. 656–82.

GORDON, M. J. *The Investment, Financing, and Valuation of the Corporation*, especially chap. xi. Homewood, Ill.: Richard D. Irwin, Inc., 1962.

LINTNER, J. V. "Distribution of Income of Corporations among Dividends, Retained Earnings and Taxes," *American Economic Review*, May, 1956, pp. 97–113.

MILLER, M. H., and MODIGLIANI, F. "Dividend Policy, Growth and the Valuation of Shares," *Journal of Business*, October, 1961, pp. 411–33.

ROBICHEK, A. A., and MEYERS, S. C. *Optimal Financial Decisions*, chap. iv. Englewood Cliffs, N. J.: Prentice-Hall, Inc., 1965.

SOLOMON, E. *The Theory of Financial Management*, chap. v. New York: Columbia University Press, 1963.

WALTER, J. E. "Dividend Policy: Its Influence on the Value of the Enterprise," *Journal of Finance*, May, 1963, pp. 280–91.

Chapter 18

THE COST OF BORROWED CAPITAL—
THE CONTRACTUAL AND IMPUTED
COSTS OF DEBT

Just as optimum dividend or retention policy was a function of the company's investment opportunities and the stockholder's attitudes towards risk, so optimum debt policy is similarly dependent on expected rates of return and the rates at which these expected revenue streams will be capitalized. Moreover, just as we saw that optimum retention in the end also depends on the cost of debt (or alternative means of finance), optimum debt depends on the cost of retention. Indeed total finance and its component parts are interacting and can only be exactly determined simultaneously. However, in order to uncover the essentials of debt finance —the cost of debt and the optimum role of debt in a firm's financial plan—let us proceed under simplified conditions that expose plainly the essentials we are concerned with.

As before we can define the cost of debt finance in terms of the required rate of return that the debt-financed investment must yield to prevent damage to the stockholders' position. Clearly then the investment must return *at least* the rate of interest—the out-of-pocket cost of debt.

In the case of *certain* income streams there is no cost of debt nor any finance problem: all returns would be equal to the riskless rate of interest based on pure time preference. Owners and creditors would be not distinguishable—all would be rewarded equally not for risk taking but just for foregoing the present use of their funds. But so long as the expected returns from investment are to some degree uncertain, the project must yield more than the interest cost to allow for the additional uncertainty that has been injected into the residual earnings stream belonging to the stockholders. Note that this is *not* double-counting the danger that the most likely returns will not be received; this uncertainty we have already allowed for in our probability approach in estimating net returns over cost *not* including costs of finance. Rather, the additional risk here is purely a function of the *method* of finance; it would not occur if equity finance were used.

BORROWER'S RISKS AND REWARDS—LEVERAGE

The expected rate of return to the owners (say, E/P) must promise to exceed that offered to the creditors (say, i) to make up for the extra burden of risk carried by the stockholders. Stockholders are willing to give bondholders a priority of claim to earnings (along with the right to force the firm into bankruptcy to satisfy their claims to unpaid interest or principal) because the owners expect to earn E/P ($> i$) with the funds. But the expected return from investment is uncertain, that is, it may turn out to be more or less than E/P while the i is fixed or certain. In a very restricted sense the interest rate is the certainty equivalent of the E/P rate of return.

Thus when a firm borrows funds, it necessarily increases stockholder's risk at the same time that it increases stockholders expected returns. Presumably stockholders become stockholders rather than bondholders because they prefer a combination of higher probable returns and higher risks to lower fixed returns and lower risk. The essence of trading on the equity—obtaining funds with a fixed annual cost—is that expected earnings on equity are enlarged at the cost of injecting financial risk. The bondholders, on the other hand, are quite willing to accept an i return that is less than the promised E/P return to equity because of the greater stability or lesser risk of the i return. Bondholders in effect have "traded-off" some return in exchange for less risk.

Consider a firm with an all equity capital structure that is planning to expand. To avoid growth stock complications, let us assume that all earnings are paid out in dividends and that expansion can only occur by sale of new stock or bonds. Let us also assume that flotation costs are identical for stocks and bonds and therefore irrelevant to the decision, and let us postpone tax aspects to a later stage. If, as is roughly average for all corporations, E/P is 0.10 and the firm can sell bonds with an interest rate of 0.05, should the firm sell bonds or stock? The answer is *not* obvious for the cost of debt is not simply equal to the interest rate but must also include the "inputed cost" of debt to the stockholder: the cost of the additional uncertainty or variability that is injected into the residual earnings stream. If the total cost of debt were just the interest rate then of course the firm should incur debt; indeed this firm should continue to sell bonds and use the proceeds to buy back stock so long as $E/P > i$ and conceivably would end up with 99 percent debt in its capital structure. This is silly not so much because interest rates would rise as a firm increased its debt/equity ratio—that would simply reflect the risk to the *lender*—but because it neglects the risk to the stockholder of increased indebtedness.

But how is such risk measured? Fortunately we have previously developed a method of quantifying risk that is quite applicable here. Recall that in Chapter 14 we considered a firm's choice among alternative projects in terms of the mean (or most probable) expected return and the expected variance around that mean. Choice was easy when two projects promised the same mean value but different variance: one always picked the project with less variance because stockholders are presumed to have an aversion to risk or to taking even-money gambles. When neither mean nor variance is the same, choice is usually more difficult, requiring the measurement of variance and its weighting by a utility index, because higher most probable return is usually not available except at the cost of more variance or risk. We discussed the trade-off of such measured risk against return and adopted the riskier project so long as more was added to expected returns than was deducted to allow for the added risk.

In that process we were measuring *business* risk: comparing projects with different probability distributions. Now we are measuring *financial* risk: comparing the *same* project financed in two different ways; the different probability distributions of expected returns that result are not due to differences in returns on assets but in returns to stockholders. But the fundamental technique of measurement of risk is the same. And one is engaged in the process of trading off the *increased average return* on equity obtained by trading on the equity or borrowing against the *increased variance of returns* around the average which is also the inevitable fruit of trading on the equity rather than increasing the equity.

Trading on the Equity—An Example

Interest on debt *must* be paid, and it is a *fixed* amount. The result is the leverage effect on common stock earnings after interest. When a corporation has no debt outstanding, then earnings per share simply vary as total earnings vary. But when there is debt in the capital structure, earnings per share are bound to fluctuate more from year to year unless by chance the rate of earnings is precisely equal to the effective rate of interest paid on the debt. When the rate of earnings before interest payment exceeds the interest rate, the profits per share after interest will be greater than they would be if the finance had been by fresh equity issues rather than fresh debt issues, for fresh equity issues would share *equally* in earnings. Per share earnings, of course, have the potential of greater fluctuations downward when debt is used because interest must be paid even when earnings before interest are at a lower rate than the interest rate; clearly, what is left for stockholders is less than they would receive if the capital structure were all equity shares.

Let us consider the effect on earnings per share with debt financing versus pure equity finance under varying degrees of corporate success in profit making for a given year.

For example, assume that our corporation has assets and net worth of $1,000 and is considering whether to finance another $1,000 of assets by borrowing versus selling stock. If the funds are borrowed the interest costs will be $50. If the money is raised by stock sales the number of shares outstanding will be doubled. Assume further that the project before us promises 12 percent as the most probable return on $1,000 investment but that the full distribution of probable returns is as follows:

| | | Change in Return to Old Stockholders | |
Probability	Return on $1,000	If Debt Financed	If Equity Financed
0.25	$ 60	$ 10	$30
0.50	120	70	60
0.25	180	130	90
	Average Expected	$ 70	$60

If the return is $120—
  a) If bonds are sold, $70 is added to old stockholders earnings ($120 − i of $50).
  b) If stock is sold, $60 is added to old stockholders earnings, as the $120 in new earnings is split evenly between new and old stockholders.
If the return is $60—
  a) If bonds are sold, $10 is added to old stockholders earnings.
  b) If stock is sold, $60/2, or $30, is added to old stockholders earnings.
If the return is $180—
  a) If bonds are sold, $130 is added to old stockholders earnings.
  b) If stock is sold, $180/2, or $90, is added to old stockholders earnings.

The effect of financing by debt rather than by equity is clearly twofold. (1) the *average* expected return is greater ($70 over $60) but (2) the *range* of probable returns is greater ($10 to $130 versus $30 to $90). In other words, both the most probable value and the dispersion around that value are increased when financing is via trading on the equity rather than increasing the equity. Or, most briefly, both expected *return* and *risk* are increased when debt financing is used. Note that the *business* risk—the probability distribution of expected returns—is unchanged; it is financing risk superimposed on the given business risk that generates both the additional risk and returns.

We can see the same results per share of stock by assuming there were ten shares outstanding as the problem begins. Thus the ranges of earnings per share are $1 to $13 when 50 percent of funds are raised by debt; and $3 to $9, precisely half the variability, when finance is all via equity. This is what is meant when it is said that debt finance adds *leverage* to earnings per share. For example, when corporation earnings on total assets rise 50 percent above "average" (i.e., 12 percent to 18 percent), earnings per share rise 50 percent (from $6 to $9) with pure equity finance but almost 100 percent (from $7 to $13) with 50 percent debt finance. This magnified effect of increased total earnings on earnings per share is leverage.

But note that the heightened effect can work against the stockholder when total earnings slide below average. When total earnings slip from 12 percent to 6 percent, the comparative drops are $6 to $3 and $7 to $1. Recall the argument in Chapter 14 that increased variability of earnings is not looked on favorably by stockholders and management when the odds of gain and losses are even. Here, the odds are not even, so that *some* trading on the equity, i.e., borrowing money, is likely to be favored. The odds favor some debt because the most probable total earnings are 12 percent, while the cash cost of debt is but 5 percent, with the result that a 50–50 chance of a swing in earnings down to 6 percent or up to 18 percent is matched by a swing in earnings per share of $1 to $13 if debt is undertaken, and $3 to $9 if debt is not undertaken. Within this range of variability (plus or minus 6 percent of total earnings), debt allows a gain of $4 per share if above-average earnings are made, and $2 loss of earnings per share if below-average earnings are made. So far, so good; but note that if earnings should fall *below* 5 percent on total assets, the drop in earnings per share will be magnified because interest must be paid at a rate of 5 percent whether earned or not and there will be less left for stockholders than if the finance had been purely equity.

Trading on the equity thus gives better than even chances of improving earnings per share, as long as the most probable earnings on total assets exceed the interest rate, but this is offset at some level of debt/ equity finance by the owners' and managers' positive aversion to increased variability of earnings.

The fact that $Ke > i$, that stockholders can borrow at a cost less than they expect to get in average return, is the factor that raises average expected returns. But we must not forget that the leverage effect applies to returns above and below the most probable value as well and thus increases the range or risk of extreme results. Stockholders discount dispersion both because of distaste for variability of expected returns (even at even odds) and in extreme cases because of the risk of ruin which in this case may be called bankruptcy, should earnings be so low or negative as to cause default on interest or principal at maturity.

Thus the basic business risk and return—the basic expected returns distribution—is altered by the combination of two factors: the gap between E/P and i, and the debt/equity ratio. The greater the probable gain per dollar of "cheap" debt and the greater the relative amount of debt financing used, the greater the opportunities from leveraging earnings and the greater the risks of doing so. For all increases in borrowing, right up to 99.9 percent of the capital structure, the average expected or most probable returns to stockholders increase proportionately but of course so too does risk or dispersion around that higher average return.

In other words, the most probable EPS rises as the D/E ratio rises but the confidence in that expected EPS falls; the higher average stream of probable returns is capitalized at a higher rate of discount. In more familiar market terminology: a rising D/E ratio raises EPS but depresses the earnings multiple people are willing to pay; the quantity of EPS is up but the quality is down.

OPTIMAL BORROWING OR IDEAL D/E RATIOS

This dual effect of corporate borrowing is undisputed but there is considerable debate as to whether the rise in EPS is offset exactly by the fall in the multiplier at each level of the possible debt/equity range. Traditional financial thought has always claimed that below some D/E ratio, the increase in EPS outweighs the discount for risk implicit in the decline of the earnings multiple, and that beyond some D/E level the reverse was true; the upshot of course being that there is in the traditionalist view some optimal level of debt to equity. This means that up to some point, the cost of debt while always greater than i by a risk component is less than the cost of equity. Beyond some point presumably this is no longer true and the cost of debt (i + inputed risk) rises above the cost of equity because risk rises nonlinearly while *EPS* rises linearly with the D/E ratio. Risk is often presumed to rise exponentially because of the special weight of a risk of ruin which increases at a faster rate than does the increase in the debt burden; this has the result of causing a disproportionate fall in the multiplier beyond some point as a measure of stockholder risk and/or a rise in interest rates as a measure of bondholder risk. Before the optimum D/E ratio is struck, the cost of debt is less than the cost of equity, and debt is chosen as the method of finance. At the optimum level the cost of debt and equity are equal.

Now, it is clear that fluctuations in earnings per share will be greater the higher the interest rate on debt and the larger the proportion of capital structure that consists of debt. The larger the D/E ratio, given the interest rate, the larger is the absolute size of the lump of interest payments that must be made. It is not so much that the chance of bankruptcy is increased but rather that, in general, earnings per share of stock, though higher on the average over the years, will be more unstable.[1] When stockholders feel that the chance of *unusual* profits or losses is no longer offset by the higher *average* return they can receive, they will view further debt issues unfavorably; that is, they will capitalize the probable average earnings at a higher rate to account for the increased risks of incurring additional fixed charges, and the accompanying increased variability of net earnings per share of stock. This will prevent the probable increased average earnings from increasing the value of the stock in the marketplace. Once again, we see that the ultimate sanction of methods of finance is the effect of such finance on the price of the common stock. In this case, further debt would only pay if the project being considered offered a sufficiently higher *average* expected return to offset the rising imputed risk cost of debt. The required rate of return that will sanction debt finance has risen; or simply, *the cost of financing by debt has risen.* Projects that at a lower D/E ratio of the company would have been adopted are now rejected. In this way, it is possible not only to determine the cost of debt but also to see the limits of debt finance.

In *addition,* not only does the borrower (that is, the corporation or the stockholders) view an increased D/E ratio as increasing risk beyond that calculated on the net returns side, but so too does the *lender* see an in-

---

[1] One could also measure the risk incurred by borrowing by considering the degree to which expected earnings cover the fixed charges on the debt. Obviously, the greater the debt, the greater the fixed burden; and the more variable the earnings in the downward direction, the greater the danger of inability to meet obligations as they come due, i.e., the greater the danger of bankruptcy or at least a serious problem of liquidity.

creased risk. The lender will insist upon a higher contractual rate of interest for additional loans made when the amount of outstanding loans is heavy relative to the owner's stake or the trader's equity. Here, the fear is more clearly a fear of bankruptcy and default of interest or principal.

Thus, the cost of debt finance, given the equity, rises above the actual initial rate of interest charged as more debt finance is used, (1) because the actual rate of interest will rise and (2) because the total debt cost should include not only the interest paid but also an additional hidden cost of borrowing that can be imputed from the rise in the rate at which earnings on common stock are capitalized.

Another way to view the cost of debt vis-à-vis the cost of equity is to consider that the risk introduced by borrowing funds is added to the cost of equity funds rather than to the cost of debt; the cost of debt is then considered as measured only by the out-of-pocket interest cost. With this approach it is necessary to consider *total* costs of finance per dollar of investment or average cost of finance. The optimal combination of debt and equity will be at the point of minimal total costs per unit or minimal average cost (Ka). In other words, when debt is incurred it can be said to drive up the cost of equity. The fact that the cost of debt (in terms of interest rate) is less than the cost of equity does not imply that the "cheaper" debt is the appropriate means of finance; rather one needs to find the least-cost *combination* of debt and equity. For example, in this approach, one would add debt so long as the average cost of finance were lowered in the process. Of course this would only occur so long as the rise in EPS (the leverage introduced by the excess of E/P over i) were greater than the fall in the multiplier (the rise in the rate at which the riskier earnings flow is discounted—Ke).

Finding the Optimal D/E Ratio—An Example

Consider a company—totally financed via equity—with an earnings stream of $1,000 which the stock market capitalizes at 10 percent; thus stockholders' wealth is $10,000. (Assuming 100 shares outstanding, the market price per share is $100). Now assume that this company is faced with a $10,000 investment opportunity that promises another $1,000 annual returns stream of exactly the same business risk as the firm's going investment. If the interest rate at which the firm could borrow the needed $10,000 were 5 percent, is it advantageous to borrow the funds or to raise them by selling additional shares of stock?

We cannot answer this question without some information about the way the stock market will evaluate the additional risk injected into the stream of earnings on equity by the act of borrowing or raising the D/E ratio. It seems unlikely that the $1,500 most probable returns to the old and the new equity combined ($2,000 — $500 in interest) will be capitalized by the market at 10 percent. If it were, the borrowing would raise the net worth of the firm to $15,000 or the price per share to $150 from $100. But we know that the additional financial risk injected into the earnings stream by borrowing the funds will be discounted for by the market. This can be described either as lowering the multiplier or raising the rate at which earnings are capitalized. In an uncertain environment, E/P or Ke is always greater than i, the interest rate, because one presumes that priority of claim entails less risk and thus requires a price of less return. But since $E/P > i$, there would be no limit to debt if it were not for the fact that the *added* financial risk of borrowing in effect drives up the cost of borrowing above i or by driving up the cost of equity, raises the combined cost of debt plus equity.

Assume then in our example, that the equity capitalization rate would rise in the marketplace from 0.10 to 0.12; that is, assume that the borrowing will lower the multiplier from 10 to $8\frac{1}{3}$ (Table 18–1). Does it pay to borrow the needed $10,000 or should the funds be raised by increasing the equity rather than trading on it?

TABLE 18–1

FINDING THE OPTIMAL D/E RATIO—AN EXAMPLE

	Increasing the Equity Column 1	Trading on the Equity		
		Column 2	Column 3	Column 4
Expected earnings after tax	$ 2,000	$ 2,000		$ 4,000
Debt			$10,000	$30,000
Interest (i)			0.05	0.05
Interest cost			$500	$ 1,500
Earnings on equity (E)	$ 2,000	$ 1,500		$ 2,500
Capitalization rate (Ke)	0.10 (10X)	0.12 $(8\frac{1}{3}X)$	0.15 $(6\frac{2}{3}X)$	0.20 (5X)
Capitalized (market) value of equity	$20,000	$12,500	$10,000	$12,500
No. shares	200	100	100	100
Price per share	$100	$125	$100	$125

The answer is that the company should borrow the funds because it increases stockholder's wealth—price per share (see Column 2). It does so because the borrowing increases earnings per share by 50 percent (the leverage) while raising the capitalization rate by only 20 percent. It will always pay to borrow so long as the percentage increase in *EPS* exceeds the percentage rise in the capitalization rate; or so long as the quantity improvement exceeds the quality deterioration. This relationship is also evident in Column 3, where the same rate of increase in Ke as in EPS— 50 percent—gives the same price per share as in the equity case.

It is the excess of E/P over i that accounts for the quantity gain; it is the rise in Ke as D/E rises that accounts for the quality decline. *Both* components are essential to an analysis of the benefits and costs or net gain from borrowing; the former insures that firms will want to borrow; the latter insures that there are limits to their doing so. The traditionalist notion is that although the $E/P.i$ ratio is constant and thus provides the same proportional gain from borrowing within wide ranges of debt/equity ratios, the risk element increases more than proportionally with rises in the debt/equity ratio. For example (see Column 4), if in our case we added still another $20,000 in debt on top of the prior $10,000 debt, the market might feel that the additional risk of the larger stream ($2,500) ought to be discounted at 20 percent rather than 12 percent. The additional borrowing in this case would not be advantageous because although it would raise the earning stream to equity by two thirds ($1,500 to $2,500) it would also push the capitalization rate up from 12 to 20 percent, having the net result that the total or per share value of the equity is unchanged.

The Cost of Debt—The Example Extended

If the capitalization rate will rise to 12 percent from 10 percent when the debt/equity ratio rises from 0 to 50 percent, to keep the stock selling at $100 per share requires that earnings be at least $12 per share. Before incurring the debt, $10 per share was sufficient to keep the stock selling at $100 because the unlevered stock was more favorably capitalized at 10 percent:

Earnings required for 100 shares ...	$1,200
Minus earnings available before the new debt and investment	1,000
Additional net earnings required of new investment	$ 200
Plus interest charges	500
Total pre-interest earnings required .	$ 700
Required rate of return $\left(\dfrac{\$\ 700}{10,000}\right)$	7%

In other words, the cost of debt is 7 percent; so long as the $10,000 project returns net better than 7 percent, it will pay to finance it by a debt issue. The project must yield better than 5 percent, or $500, to return the out-of-pocket interest charges; plus another 2 percent, or $200, to offset the fall of the multiplier from $10X$ to $8\frac{1}{3}X$. In other words then, the cost of debt—the required rate of return when financing by borrowing—in this case is 7 percent, consisting of 5 percent in interest plus 2 percent in imputed cost.

If the new investment had only promised 6 percent, it would not have paid to borrow even though the interest rate at 5 percent was lower:

Earnings before the new investment and borrowing	$1,000
Plus earnings on new investment ..	600
	$1,600
Minus interest charges (0.05 × $10,000)	500
Earnings available for stockholders	$1,100
Per share earnings	$ 11
Times new multiplier	×8.33
New market price of the stock	$91.63

Thus the price of the stock would be lowered by borrowing funds at 5 percent to use to earn 6 percent because while *EPS* rose one tenth, the earnings multiple fell by one sixth. What must the project promise to earn to keep the stock from falling below $100 in the market? The answer is 7 percent, and that required rate of return is the cost of debt.

The two projects taken together must promise to yield 8½ percent. In other words when capital is earning 10 percent and we double the size of the company by borrowing, the combined return will be at least 8½ percent if the new investment (half the total investment) earns 7 percent for

$$\frac{0.10 + 0.07}{2} = 0.085.$$

The Cost of Debt and Optimal Debt Finance

Note then that so long as the rise in *EPS* (the quantity gain) more than offsets the decline in the multiplier or $1/Ke$ (the quality loss), it pays to borrow. When this is the case we can say either that:

1. The cost of additional debt is less than the additional returns to be obtained from using the funds:
$$Ke > [i + \triangle Ke].$$
   In our example, $0.10 > 0.05 + 0.02$.
   The marginal cost of debt then was 7 percent, of which 2 percentage points was the inputed risk.

or

2. The cost of debt is such as to lower the weighted *average* cost of finance (Ka). (Increasing debt pulls down the average cost more than the rise in equity cost raises it).

a) $Ka = Ke = 0.10$ with no debt.

b) With 50 percent of the structure in debt:

The expected rate of return > The coupon cost of debt + the rise in the rate of capitalization or fall in the multiplier

$$Ka = \frac{1}{2}(i) + \frac{1}{2} \text{ (new } Ke)^2$$
$$= \frac{1}{2}(0.05) + \frac{1}{2}(0.12)$$
$$= 0.085$$

(Note that the average cost of capital is 0.085 in 1 above too—

$$\frac{0.07}{2} + \frac{0.10}{2} = 0.85.$$

In the earlier case, the approach taken was to raise the cost of debt above the coupon cost to allow for the risk of borrowing rather than to raise the rate of capitalization of the equity stream.

One may say either that given $r > Ke$, it pays to borrow so long as (1) the *marginal* cost of debt is less than the cost of equity or (2) so long as it will lower the *average* cost of capital. One uses the former approach when one wants to stress the true cost of debt—the imputed risk as well as the out-of-pocket costs—and the latter when one wants to stress the optimal mix of the sources of funds.

Ordinarily it would be said that when the marginal cost of debt and equity are equal, it is a matter of indifference to stockholders *how* one raises the funds; and if $r = Ke$, it is also a matter of indifference *whether* one raises the funds. In either case stock price will not be affected one way or the other. This would be the case in our example if the multiplier had deteriorated from $10X$ to $6\frac{2}{3}$ (see column 3 of Table 18–1) rather than to $8\frac{1}{3}X$ (as in column 2). Stockholders do not gain because the 50 percent increase in *EPS* is exactly offset by a 50 percent increase in the rate of capitalization. $r = Ke = Kd$—$0.05i + 0.05$ imputed risk— or the cost of equity has risen to 0.15 from 0.10 as half the capital structure is raised by 0.05 debt money, leaving the average cost of funds unchanged at 0.10. It may be said that the use of debt is optimal or that finance costs are minimized when additional borrowing will cost more than equity or will cause the average total cost of finance to rise. Optimal debt finance implies minimum average costs of finance.

---

[2] To generalize, the weighted average cost of capital is equal to the coupon cost of debt $\left(\dfrac{\text{Debt}}{\text{Debt + Equity}}\right)$ plus the new higher cost of equity $\left(\dfrac{\text{Equity}}{\text{Debt + Equity}}\right)$. In brief:

$$Ka = \frac{D}{D + E}(i) + \frac{E}{D + E}\text{ (new } Ke).$$

QUESTIONS AND PROBLEMS

1. Distinguish between business risk and financial risk. Is the method of quantifying business risk (Chapter 15) applicable to the quantification of financial risk? Explain.

2. Define the cost of debt verbally, graphically, and in terms of a formula. How is lender's risk incorporated in this definition? Borrowers' risk?

3. Company A, an all equity capitalized firm, is considering borrowing money to undertake an investment which would double its total size and earning capacity. At present, A's earnings, divided up among 10,000 shareholders, are $150,000 which the stock market capitalizes at 12 percent. If A borrows $1,250,000 it will add $150,000 in estimated earnings of the same business risk as its current earnings; the funds will be available at 6 percent interest cost, and it is estimated that the market will increase the earnings capitalization rate to 16 percent.

   Does it pay for this firm to borrow the funds? Explain. What is the total cost of debt in this case? (Show your computations.)

   How low a rate of return can the new investment offer and still be worthwhile financing by debt? What has happened to the average cost of total funds after the borrowing? (Show your computations.)

4. "It pays to borrow (a) so long as the marginal cost of debt is less than the cost of equity or (b) so long as it lowers the *average* cost of capital." Demonstrate that these two statements are identical in setting debt limits. Also indicate when you would prefer one approach to the other.

SUGGESTED READINGS

Donaldson, G. *Corporate Debt Capacity*. Boston: Harvard Business School, 1961.

Fisher, L. "Determinants of Risk Premiums on Corporate Bonds," *Journal of Political Economy*, June, 1959, pp. 217–37.

Gordon, M. J. "Security and Investment: Theory and Evidence," *Journal of Finance*, December, 1964, pp. 607–18.

Hunt, P. "A Proposal for Precise Definitions of 'Trading on the Equity' and 'Leverage,'" *Journal of Finance*, September, 1961, pp. 377–86.

Solomon, E. *The Theory of Financial Management*, chap. vi–viii. New York: Columbia University Press, 1963.

Walter, J. E. "The Use of Borrowed Funds," *Journal of Business*, April, 1955, pp. 138–57.

Chapter 19

OPTIMUM DEBT POLICY
AND CAPITAL STRUCTURE

If we make quite restrictive assumptions, we can prove that capital structure (like payout) is always a matter of indifference. Under these special circumstances, a firm can never lower the average cost of capital no matter how much it shifts toward debt, the "cheaper" form of finance. As we have seen, however, these special circumstances require that the cost of equity rise by precisely the amount necessary to offset the "lower" cost of borrowing. Such a precise offset will occur if the rise in the equity capitalization rate matches the rise in the *EPS*.

Another way to look at this new, higher capitalization rate for the residual earnings is to break it into its two components: the original equity capitalization rate (Ke) before the addition of more debt, plus a premium to offset the decline in the quality of the residual earnings stream when borrowing is injected. The old rate for equity is Ke, and the additional premium can be stated as $D/E \; (Ke - Ki)$.

TABLE 19–1

FINDING THE OPTIMAL D/E RATIO—AN EXAMPLE

	Increasing the Equity Column 1	Trading on the Equity		
		Column 2	Column 3	Column 4
Expected earnings after tax	$ 2.000	$ 2,000		$ 4.000
Debt		$10,000		$30,000
Interest (i)		0.05		0.05
Interest cost		$500		$ 1,500
Earnings on equity (E)	$ 2,000	$ 1,500		$ 2,500
Capitalization rate (Ke)	0.10 (10X)	0.12 ($8\frac{1}{3}X$)	0.15 ($6\frac{2}{3}X$)	0.20 (5X)
Capitalized (market) value of equity	$20,000	$12,500	$10,000	$12,500
No. shares	200	100	100	100
Price per share	$100	$125	$100	$125

301

For example, using column 3 of Table 19–1, the post-borrowing capitalization rate

$$Kcb = Ke + D/E \ (Ke - Ki)$$
$$= 0.10 + 1/1 \ (0.10 - 0.05)$$
$$= 0.10 + 0.05$$
$$= 0.15 \ .$$

That is, if trading on the equity—borrowing at 5 percent when the cost of unlevered equity (Ke) is 10 percent—is not to reduce unit costs of capital, the equity capitalization rate (Ke) must rise, in this case by exactly 5 percent. Precisely such a rise is needed to prevent a fall in the average cost of funds when funds are raised by a mix of one-half debt and one-half equity. Before borrowing, the cost of capital (Ke) was 10 percent; after borrowing half ($\frac{1}{2}$) the total capital, the cost of capital is

$$\frac{Keb}{2} + \frac{Ki}{2} \ \text{or} \ \frac{0.15}{2} + \frac{0.05}{2} = 0.10.$$

The average cost of capital is 0.10 whether the corporation borrows or not, *so long as* the cost of equity rises as borrowing proceeds according to the formula $D/E \ (Ke - Ki)$. The average cost of capital is constant under these conditions, and capital structure variation neither helps nor hurts the stockholder. Of course, the funds should not be raised by *any* method unless $r > Ke$; but the point here is that the cutoff point is always the same regardless of the means used to obtain the funds—it is always equal to the unlevered return on equity.

THE MODIGLIANI-MILLER HYPOTHESIS: CAPITAL STRUCTURE DOESN'T MATTER

But what is the force that makes the equity cost rise (or, in other terms, the multiplier fall) just exactly the amount required to keep the average cost unchanged? The answer is arbitrage or swapping of securities in perfect securities markets. No one doubts that the cost of equity varies directly (or the multiplier inversely) with the D/E ratio—compare columns 1 and 2 of Table 19–1. But what makes the cost of equity rise to 0.15 or the multiplier necessarily fall to exactly $6\frac{2}{3}$ in our example? Professors F. Modigliani and M. H. Miller in a justly celebrated article demonstrate that in perfect markets no other price per share but $100 can be sustained regardless of leverage.[1] They argue as follows, treating

[1] "The Cost of Capital, Corporate Finance, and the Theory of Investment," *The American Economic Review*, June, 1958.

the columns of Table 19–1 as representative of companies of varied leverage but otherwise identical:

Column 2 in which *EPS* rises to $15 from $10 and the multiplier falls from 10 to $8\frac{1}{3}$ as 50 percent debt versus 100 percent equity finance is chosen is said to result in an overvaluation of the stock of the debt-incurring firm. A stockholder with one share in this levered firm could gain by selling his share for $125 in the market, borrowing $100, and buying $225 worth of the stock of the column 1—the unlevered—type of company. The new investment has a yield of $22.50 (10 percent of $225), leaving a net income of $17.50 after allowing for $5 interest on the $100 debt. When he owned the levered stock, the yield was $15—12 percent on $125. Thus stockholders of the levered stock find it overvalued in the sense that they can improve their income by selling the levered stock and buying the unlevered stock while injecting their own personal leverage into the new portfolio.

Note that the required personal leverage is in the same ratio as the corporate leverage in the company whose share the stockholder initially held. Hence his risk under the new arrangement presumably is the same although he has improved his return by the shift. In the levered case, the *D/E* is $10,000/12,500 and the old stockholder's 1/100 share of this is 100/125; in the unlevered case with personal debt, the stockholder's *D/E* is 100/125 or the same ratio. Thus with no increase in risk, the investor's return is increased 20 percent (from $15 to $17.50) by selling his overvalued stock and reinvesting in the unlevered company. Of course, the significance of this shift is that it will press the price of the levered stock down toward $100 a share at which point no profit can be made by further shifting. And at the price of $100, the multiplier is precisely $6\frac{2}{3}$ (see column 3). The leveraged company's increase in *EPS* of 50 percent ($10 to $15) is precisely offset by the 50 percent rise in the capitalization rate from 0.10 to 0.15.

M & M's conclusion from this demonstration of the effects of rational trading in perfect security markets is that corporate debt or leverage can not be used to improve the stockholders' wealth. For two firms of the same business risk class, there cannot be any lasting advantage to leverage, for the arbitrage process will drive the cost of capital to constancy and equality with the cost of equity for the unlevered firm. Capital structure is thus a "mere detail."

There is no arguing with this conclusion; it follows logically from the assumptions made. But its applicability to the real world of capital markets is another matter. Let us examine the principal assumptions made; as we alter those assumptions to make them more realistic, we will uncover the real reasons why capital structure does indeed matter. Then we can return to the question of the *optimum* capital structure.

Allowing for Corporate Income Taxes

Income of large corporations is taxed by the federal government at a rate of almost 50 percent. Interest payments, unlike payments to owners, such as dividends, are tax deductible as normal business expenses. Thus, in effect, the government subsidizes corporate debt finance; even under the perfect market assumptions of M & M, the average cost of finance can be reduced by choosing debt in preference to equity finance.

Let us reconsider columns 1 and 3 of our leverage example in which arbitrage or security swapping resulted in lowering the price of the stock of the leveraged company or raising the capitalization rate sufficiently to offset exactly the increased *EPS* of trading on the equity with explicit allowance in column 3 for the 50 percent corporate income taxation:

	Increasing the Equity Column 1	Trading on the Equity Column 3
Expected earnings before tax	$ 4,000	$ 4,000
Debt		$10,000
Interest rate		0.05
Interest cost		$ 500
Earnings subject to 50% tax	$ 4,000	$ 3,500
Earnings on equity after 50% tax	$ 2,000	$ 1,750
Capitalization rate	0.10	0.15
Capitalized value of equity	$20,000	$11,667
No. shares	200	100
Price per share	$ 100	$116.67

If we allow for corporate taxes, earnings on equity after borrowing are not $1,500 but $1,750 while in the pure equity case the stockholders' earnings are $2,000. Since the latter figure must be divided among 200 stockholders while the levered earnings on equity are shared by only 100, the comparisons to be made are $17.50 *EPS* (not $15.00 *EPS*) for the levered company and $10.00 *EPS* for the unlevered company. Even if arbitrage drives the multiple of levered earnings on equity down to 6⅔ from 10, as is required by the M & M formula, the price of the levered stock will sell at a higher price than the unlevered stock:

$$6\tfrac{2}{3} \times \$17.50 = \$116.67$$
$$10 \quad \times \$10 \quad = \quad 100.00$$

After allowing for the tax subsidy, it is clear that debt finance does lower the average cost of finance and does raise the price of the stock. The capitalized value of the tax subsidy is $250/0.15, or $1,667, exactly the amount by which the value of the firm is increased by trading on the equity.[2] While allowing for taxes does show that capital structure matters, it does not tell us the *optimum* debt/equity ratio. Indeed if we follow the logic of the M & M model with taxes, it seems to say that the more debt, the better, for the process illustrated by our example holds for a debt/equity ratio of 100:1 as well as 1:1. As we will see shortly, this extreme conclusion is just as unrealistic as is the concept that the capital structure does not matter at all.

Allowing for the Greater Total Cost of Personal Leverage over Corporate Leverage

It is the perfect substitutability of personal for corporate debt that keeps the market price of the levered stock from rising above that of the unlevered stock. Whenever the stock market offers a premium to the levered stock presumably the owners sell that stock to buy unlevered stock in a corporation (of the same risk class) with the proceeds of the sale plus the requisite amount of personal borrowing. In short, personal leverage is assumed to be no more costly nor more risky than the equivalent amount of corporate leverage. This is an unrealistic assumption.

1. Corporations have limited liability while individuals are liable to the full extent of their personal fortunes for personal debt incurred. In other words, it is less risky for individuals to have their corporation do their borrowing for them rather than to do it directly.

2. Institutionalized debt is also likely to be cheaper. The lender's rate is likely to be lower to the corporation (say, G.E.) than it is to an individual margined account (secured by G.E. stock). Moreover, the transactions costs of the single large corporate borrowing are likely to be less

---

[2] The capitalization factor is not changed because presumably the discount for risk is unchanged:

$$Keb = Ke + (Ke - Ki) \ D/E$$
$$= 0.10 + (0.10 - 0.05) \ 1/1$$
$$= 0.15$$

than such costs for numerous smaller stockholder loans. Furthermore there are extra transaction costs of the stock swaps which are essential in the process of substituting personal for corporate leverage.

Thus both the imputed (risk) cost and the out-of-pocket (interest + transaction) costs of personal leverage are likely to exceed those of corporate leverage. As a result, just as in the tax amended case, it seems clear that adding debt to the formal capital structure of a corporation will lower the average cost of funds. But thus far it would seem that we have proved too much: if small additions to debt reduce the average cost of funds (or raise the price of stock), why shouldn't larger and larger amounts of debt be added? These tax and debt cost advantages of corporate over individual borrowing hold for any amount of debt. It is perhaps even more unrealistic to conclude that a 100 percent debt structure is optimum than to conclude that any debt/equity structure is ideal. The solution is that while it is to the stockholder's advantage to use corporate rather than personal debt up to 100 percent of capital structure, it is not to the *lender's* advantage to make funds available to the corporation at the same rate regardless of the proportion of debt to equity in the capital structure.

Allowing for Lender's Risk

While borrower's risk which rises with the D/E ratio may be thought of as being offset by the proportional increase in average expected EPS that also follows from increasing leverage, the latter offsetting factor is not compensatory to the lender as it is to the borrower. In order to increase his return (as risk rises) the lender can be expected to raise the rate of interest charged to highly leveraged firms. Or the lender may seek to reduce his risk by imposing restrictions on managerial choice of investment opportunities, working capital position, etc. In either case the cost of borrowing will be higher for higher D/E than lower D/E ratios. Thus beyond some point the falling *average* cost of finance will be arrested and then raised as the rising marginal costs of debt offset and then exceed the marginal benefits of the tax subsidy to corporate debt.

As pointed out previously, it is also likely that borrower's (i.e., stockholder's) risk will rise more than proportionally beyond some D/E ratio since the risk of ruin, although not earnings variability, increases *exponentially* with D/E although EPS rises proportionately. That is, beyond some point the quality deterioration exceeds the quantity improvement. In this case the formula for the rise in the equity capitalization rate ($Keb = Ke + (Ke - Ki) \, D/E$) is no longer applicable.

FIGURE 19–1

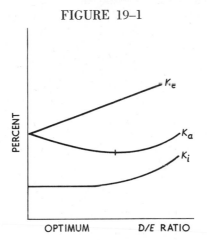

This final, realistic case may be graphed as shown in Figure 19–1.[3]

And to review, the earlier cases where borrowers' risk or the rise in the equity capitalization rate exactly offsets the effect of the rise in *EPS* via leverage are:

   a) The M & M case with no allowance for taxes or lenders' risk is illustrated in Figure 19–2.

FIGURE 19–2

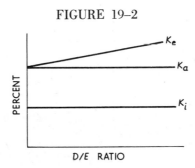

---

   [3] Allowing for the increase in borrower's as well as lender's risk could be graphed as follows:

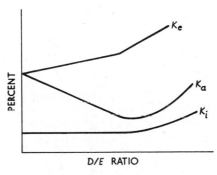

b) The M & M case after allowing for the tax subsidy is illustrated in Figure 19–3.

FIGURE 19–3

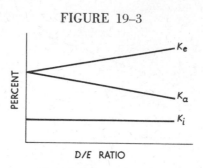

EMPIRICAL STUDIES OF CAPITAL STRUCTURE

It has proven to be very difficult to test the M & M thesis that the capital structure does not matter. One needs to compare the average cost of capital for corporations with the same business risk and growth rates but with different capital structures. Perhaps the best case for comparison of firms belonging to the same equivalent risk class is to be found in the electric utility industry. But even there, one must allow for differences in expected growth rates among the companies because higher earnings multipliers may be the consequence of faster growth as well as lower D/E ratios, and probably faster growing firms have higher D/E ratios. Moreover, even if one were to find that in the utility industry the cost of capital is relatively constant for a fairly narrow range of D/E ratios, this may not demonstrate that capital structure does not matter. Rather it may merely demonstrate that regulatory commissions not only specify "balanced" capital structures but also set rates so as to provide relatively stable net rates of return on equity. Or it may simply mean that corporate management of the various companies has found the least-cost capital structure and the similarity of businesses assures that the optimum lies say between 40 percent and 60 percent of debt/debt plus equity for each of the companies. If capital structure does not matter, one would expect D/E ratios at all levels for an industry rather than a clustering around a given level. The failure of companies to alter a given capital structure may mean not that the ratio is irrelevant but that the optimum has been found and is being retained.

In other industries the test is almost impossible to make because of our inability to allow for differences in risk for reasons other than D/E

differences. Moreover, differences in growth rates compound the difficulties. For example, a company with a very high D/E ratio may have a
low equity capitalization rate if its expected returns are subject to little
business risk and are expected to grow rapidly. In any case our analysis
tells us that allowing for corporate taxes and lender's risk will cause the
average cost of capital to fall with increasing leverage down to a trough
and then to rise gradually and later to rise at an increasing pace.[4] Even if
one found that for most industry groupings the average cost of capital was
steady at slightly different rates of cost, it might only prove that the firms
had found the trough or least-cost capital structure (Figure 19–4).

FIGURE 19–4

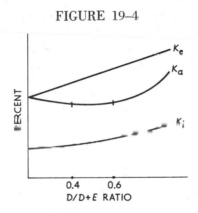

OPTIMAL CAPITAL STRUCTURE AND AVERAGE COSTING

The optimal or equilibrium average cost of funds is simply the lowest
cost package of funds. In equilibrium the cost of raising additional funds
will be the same whether debt or equity sources are used. That is, the
marginal cost of debt or the marginal cost of retained earnings are equal
to the average cost of funds which in turn presumably is equal to the
expected returns from the new marginal project being financed. In our
example the marginal cost of internal equity was 0.10 and the marginal
cost of debt was 0.05 interest plus 0.05 imputed risk, and the weighted
average cost was also 0.10 for a capital structure of ½ debt and ½ equity;
the minimal required expected rate of return on investment was, of course,

---

[4] There is nothing in the M & M thesis that would argue that secular or cyclical
changes in lender's attitudes towards risk or changes in interest rates and taxes would
not affect capital structures. M & M's essential point is not that capital structure is unchanging, but that, under given circumstances, there is no cost advantage to altering the
debt/equity composition of capital structure.

also 0.10. Notice that in equilibrium, the average cost is essentially equal to the pre-debt rate of return on equity, just as it would be in a nonlevered firm; but this condition is true only for the equilibrium capital structure, not as M & M would have it, for any and all capital structures.

Note too the minimum average cost (Ka) is a weighted average.

$$Ka = Ke \ (\tfrac{1}{2}) \ + \ Ki \ (\tfrac{1}{2})$$
$$= \frac{0.15}{2} + \frac{0.05}{2}$$
$$= 0.10 \ .$$

Then *at a point in time* any additional projects or funds can only be handled at increasing financial cost or at a higher required rate of return. Assuming that payout policy cannot be quickly or easily altered, the additional funds will be raised by additional debt or sale of new common shares. The choice will depend on whether the flotation cost plus personal tax costs—the extra costs of external over internal equity—are greater or less than the extra costs of adding debt beyond the ideal D/E ratio. (The alternative of financing via preferred stock need not be considered since its cost will always be greater than that of debt. See Appendix to this chapter).

In other words, in *the short run*, unforeseen investment opportunities, say, in a cyclical expansion, will drive a firm up the given average cost curve (Ka) in its eagerness to exploit them. A firm will finance projects at greater than minimum average cost as long as the profitability of the project justifies it.

But, given time or, as it is usually put, in *the long(er) run*, management will alter the whole capital structure so as to provide the additional funds at least average cost.

Short-Run Equilibrium Capital Structure

The point of most profitable volume of investment, where the marginal efficiency of investment (MEI) curve intersects the marginal cost of funds (MCF) curve, is also the trough or minimum point on the average cost of funds (Ka) curve (Figure 19–5).

Short-Run Disequilibrium Capital Structure

When unexpected opportunities arise—shift the MEI curve to the right to MEI'—and the firm is unable to alter the capital structure in optimal

FIGURE 19–5

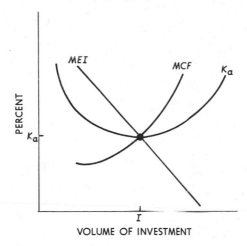

VOLUME OF INVESTMENT

proportions, finance costs per unit will rise above the *Ka* level to *Ka′*
(Figure 19–6). Note that the new higher volume of investment is *I′* as is
determined by the intersection of the new *MEI′* at a higher level of the
given *MCF* curve.

Long-Run Equilibrium Capital Structure

Given sufficient time, management will normalize the capital structure
vis-à-vis the new investment opportunities by restoring the least-cost

FIGURE 19–6

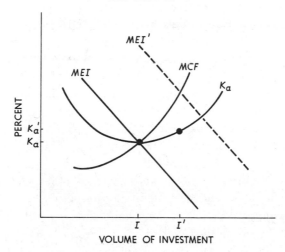

VOLUME OF INVESTMENT

FIGURE 19-7

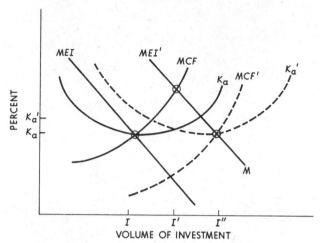

VOLUME OF INVESTMENT

package of sources of finance for a new larger volume of funds. Ka' is the new, larger financial "plant," and MCF' represents the new incremental costs associated with it (Figure 19-7). Over time, presumably, this firm will readjust its capital structure back toward minimum average cost. This may involve future retention or it may involve new equity issues if the debt path has been chosen for the short-run financing; on the other hand, if the new higher level of investment is to be sustained, it may involve new borrowing, if new *stock* issues are the short-run path chosen.

The path of external equity is unlikely to be the short-run disequilibrium technique unless the investment requirements are expected to be permanently greater *and* additional retention is judged incapable of providing the additional equity funds over time. Temporary bank loans or other short-term debt would seem to be the more usual disequilibrium source of funds—a source that can be funded or otherwise replaced by a desired permanent source, if long-term needs require it.

As we will soon observe, except for peak boom demands, corporations raise almost all their funds via debt and retention while keeping the debt/equity ratio rather stable except for very short periods. It would seem that firms, after estimating their average needs for funds, set their *long-term* financial plans to generate that quantity of funds by a least-cost combination of retained earnings and debt. In other words firms set "normal" payout ratios and debt/equity ratios in such a fashion as to minimize the average cost for the long haul. This explains why corporations which take the weighted cost of capital from their current balance sheet data and market rates of return may well arrive at a reasonably correct required rate of return or cost hurdle against which to gauge the expected rate of returns of new projects. In effect the firm's long-term financial plan is determined by a simultaneous consideration of expected investment opportunities (r or the marginal efficiency of investment) and the costs of internal finance (b or target payout policy) and external finance (L or target debt/equity policy).

Of course, as we have seen, over the cycle or within the short run, the marginal efficiency of investment (MEI) for example will shift. In a boom for example, it may intersect the marginal cost of funds (MCF) above and beyond the minimum average cost of funds; but given time if, the investment opportunity schedule is sustained, a balanced expansion of the "normal" capital structure will provide funds in such a fashion as to equate the MEI with the minimum average cost as well as marginal cost of funds. Alternatively, the onset of recession will shift the MEI back to the left. Then, just as during the boom extra debt and external equity may be used for expansion, so in contraction, excess retention may be used to pay off debt. This is likely to happen if the firm's investment plans are heavily curtailed relative to the decline in its sales revenues.

QUESTIONS AND PROBLEMS

1. Under what circumstances is capital structure a matter of indifference?
2. "If personal leverage is a perfect substitute for corporate leverage, M & M are quite right and capital structure is irrelevant." Explain.
   But why is perfect substitutability an unrealistic assumption?
3. M & M's equalizing capitalization rate is defined as $Ke + D/E(Ke - Ki)$. Explain. If Ke were 15 percent with a capital structure of $2,000 of pure equity, while $1,000 of initial borrowing at 5 percent were being considered, what would be the pure M & M effect on the equity multiplier?
   What is the post-borrowing average cost of capital? Show that it is the weighted average of the cost of equity and the cost of debt.
4. Demonstrate that the average cost of capital in the real world is likely to be U shaped. (Be sure to explain both the descending as well as the ascending portion of the curve.)
5. Why is it so difficult to test empirically M & M's thesis that changes in capital structure do not matter?
   Why is the utility industry in particular such a popular testing ground for the thesis?
6. Distinguish between short-run and long-run equilibrium capital structure.
   Why is it that the common weighted average cost of capital concept tends to approximate the long-run equilibrium solution?

SUGGESTED READINGS

BARGES, A. *The Effect of Capital Structure on the Cost of Capital.* Englewood Cliffs, N.J.: Prentice-Hall, Inc., 1963.

DURAND, D. "The Cost of Capital, Corporation Finance and the Theory of Investment: Comment," *American Economic Review*, September, 1959, pp. 639–54.

————. "Costs of Debt and Equity Funds for Business: Trends and Problems of Measurement," pp. 215–47 in *Conference on Research in Business Finance.* Princeton, N.J.: Princeton University Press, 1952.

MODIGLIANI, F., and MILLER, M. H. "The Cost of Capital, Corporate Finance and the Theory of Investment," *American Economic Review*, June, 1958, pp. 261–97; "A Reply," *Ibid.*, September, 1959, pp. 655–69; "A Correction," *Ibid.*, June, 1963, pp. 433–42.

ROBICHEK, A. A., and MEYERS, S. C. *Optimal Financial Decisions,* chap. iii. Englewood Cliffs, N.J.: Prentice-Hall, Inc., 1965.

SOLOMON, E. "Measuring a Company's Cost of Capital," *Journal of Business,* October, 1955, pp. 240–52.

————. *The Theory of Financial Management,* chap. ix. New York: Columbia University Press, 1963.

WESTON, J. F. "A Test of Cost of Capital Propositions," *Southern Economic Journal,* October, 1963, pp. 105–12.

APPENDIX TO CHAPTER 19
THE COST OF PREFERRED STOCK FINANCE:
THE SEVERE TAX DISADVANTAGE

Preferred stock lies quite outside the discussion of optimum capital structure; except for very special circumstances, preferred stock is never the appropriate instrument for raising funds: since debt is always a cheaper alternative means of finance to preferred stock, when common stock is cheaper than debt, it is even more advantageous as compared to preferred stock. There would seem never to be an occasion when preferred stock is a least-cost source of funds. Convertible preferreds might seem to be an exception. But they are best understood as lagged common stocks.[5] And even in the case of convertible issues, bonds are preferable in terms of short-run out-of-pocket cost.

---

[5] See below Chapter 24.

The fundamental disadvantage of preferred stock is the treatment it gets in the tax laws. Consider the penalty on preferred stock financing as compared with debt financing. For the moment, assume that these two methods of finance are available at the same contractual cost of $6 per $100, or 6 percent per year, and that this is the total cost of such finance; that is, there is no additional imputed cost. Then the addition to pretax earnings that is required to justify such investment when preferred stock is used will be 12 percent if the corporation is to be able to pay the 6 percent dividend on the preferred. To have something left over for the common stockholders, the earnings rate will have to exceed 12 percent. This is because the new preferred must earn enough to cover the dividend after the tax on the additional income yielded by the new investment. On the other hand, when the investment is financed by debt, we can ignore the corporation income tax in calculating the required returns because no tax is imposed on that part of the additional earnings which is used to pay the interest charges.[6] Note that to break even, the company must earn at least at the rate of 6 percent if it is to cover interest expenses. The tax deductibility of interest does not reduce the required returns on investment when financed by debt; it increases the required returns on investment when financed by preferred stock.

This fact alone has practically stopped the use of straight (nonconvertible) preferred stock in modern corporate finance.[7] It might be thought that stockholders would view the additional cost of preferred stock over debt as worthwhile, since the risk of bankruptcy due to failure to pay the preferred dividend is not involved. But the aversion to debt does not arise primarily out of fear of bankruptcy but out of the increased leverage imposed on the common stock earnings. Increased variability in returns available to common stockholders is precisely the same whether the prior claim to earnings is due preferred stockholders or bondholders. Therefore, in the most important sense the *imputed cost* of preferred stock to be added to the contractual dividend rate to find the full cost of such finance is *almost* as great as the imputed cost of debt which is required to be added to the cash interest rate. We say *almost* as great in order to allow for that part of the imputed cost of debt that is attributable to the fear of legal bankruptcy. But even this relatively small additional imputed cost of debt versus preferred stock is offset by the additional coupon cost of

---

[6] See D. T. Smith, *Effects of Taxation: Corporate Financial Policy* (Cambridge: Harvard University, 1952), pp. 118–27, for further discussion of this matter.

[7] Except in the public utilities, where financial cost-plus practices prevail. (See Chapter 23 on preferred stock.)

preferred dividends over bond interest.[8] The workings of the corporate income tax then are left as almost a pure advantage to bond finance over preferred stock finance.

When a corporation *fails* to earn additional income equal to charges— say, $60,000 on $1 million of debt—the corporate income tax absorbs half this "loss," and income available to common stockholders after interest is paid is reduced by only $30,000. On the other hand, if 6 percent preferred stock is used, and no additional income results from the investment, after the dividend is paid, income available to common stockholders is reduced by the full $60,000 paid out in preferred dividends. "Thus, if debt financing is used, taxation subsidizes losses or inadequate returns, in the sense that the cost of the financial charges will be reduced by the tax savings, while success must pay its way in full. If preferred stock is used, there is no comparable subsidy for failure or inadequate returns, while success must carry the load of additional taxes as well as the full measure of the new preferred dividends." [9]

If, therefore, there is little difference in the imputed cost of debt and preferred stock, the doubled pretax earnings requirement or contractual cost of preferred should effectively preclude the use of preferred stock. When fixed-charge finance is used, it will almost invariably take the form of debt finance. The few exceptions to this general rule we shall consider in later chapters where specific types of capital structure are examined (e.g., electric utilities); there are special situations (e.g., mergers) and special types of preferred that sometimes crop up. But in the last decade the total amount of outstanding preferred stock has *declined* although, of course, total corporate capitalization has grown enormously. One brief example of the current trend is the increased use of subordinated debentures in lieu of preferred stock; the former, although having a priority just above preferred stock, is not subject to the tax penalty.[10] For practical purposes, preferred stock is not one of the alternative methods of finance that needs to be evaluated seriously by financial management today.

---

[8] Perhaps, too, the cost of flotation of preferred stocks is on the average higher than that of bonds. But this is likely to be an insignificant matter. (See below, pp. 446–47.) In fact, both prior-claim securities are frequently privately placed at nominal cost.

[9] Smith, *op. cit.*, pp. 20–21.

[10] See below pp. 377–78 where income bonds are discussed.

Part V

CAPITAL STRUCTURE

Chapter 20

CAPITAL STRUCTURE: ANALYSIS

Capital Budgeting and Capital Structure

We have seen that at a given point in time—say, at a meeting of top management—the decision to undertake particular investment projects is largely dependent on the relationship between the expected returns from that investment and the costs of financing it. Taking the projects one at a time, each is accepted as long as the addition to returns exceeds the additional costs of finance involved. Now, it is important to stress another aspect of this managerial decision making. *Every time management makes its decision to undertake a new investment project, it is at the same time making a decision as to the appropriate capital structure the firm should have.* That is, every decision to build a specific new plant or to buy particular new equipment implies a specific way of financing that investment.

There are really only two broad ways to finance investment or the acquisition of any business asset: to increase the claims of the owners or to increase the claims of the creditors. The sum of the various means of raising funds comprises the financial structure of the business. Thus, the financial structure of any business is revealed by the right-hand side (liabilities plus net worth) of the balance sheet.

It is customary to omit short-term borrowing, i.e., debt maturing in under one year, from this list and to call the remaining assorted claims the *capital structure* of the business. The expression *capital structure* is preferred presumably because it implies a degree of permanence in the financing techniques selected. However, given the great importance of bank credit and trade credit, it seems artificial to omit short-term or informal debt from capital structure problems especially for small firms where current liabilities comprise a large part of the sources of funds. For the first part of this discussion of capital structure, we too shall concern ourselves only with the long-term bonded debt. At a later point, we shall consider the role of the shorter term and less formal debt in capital structure problems.

The effect of new investments on capital structure depends, of course, on the location of the point of intersection between the returns curve and the cost curve; this will indicate the mix of financing methods called for. Adding these additional financial claims to those already in being—the capital structure before the new investment is undertaken—is almost certain, barring incredible chance, to alter that preinvestment capital structure. Let us see why this is so.

Simple and Complex Capital Structures.   Every going concern has a capital structure that includes, as a minimum, the claims of the common stockholders—or the proprietors if we were considering unincorporated firms. A capital structure that is restricted to such claims is usually called a "simple" capital structure. Such a capital structure consists of a common capital stock account and surplus accounts. Even in the case where such a corporation's new investment decision does not call for sales of preferred stock or bonds—which would, it is customary to say, make the capital structure "complex"—the nature of its simple capital structure is likely to change. That is, the proportion of capital stock to surplus will alter unless the new investment happens to be financed equally by retained earnings and sales of new common stock.

We have seen that there is good reason to expect that retained earnings will be given priority by management. And even in the cases where retained earnings sufficient to finance the whole investment are not available, there is no reason to assume that they are just *half* of what is needed. Even in the case of a capital structure that remains simple after adoption of new investment plans, the composition of that simple structure will alter as a result of the decision to invest. Similarly, given a complex capital structure, there is even less reason to expect that a piece of new investment will be financed by expanding each of the outstanding claims in such a way as to make the new larger capital structure identical proportionally to the old capital structure. At any given moment a firm's capital structure is the sum of all its previous capital-budgeting decisions. Capital structure is an *effect* of decisions to invest, and these decisions we have studied in earlier chapters.

It is often *assumed* that any change in capital structure that occurs follows the precise mix of the outstanding sources of funds or capital

structure. In other words, it is assumed that the cost of additional funds—
the marginal cost of capital—is the same as the average cost of outstanding capital, and that that given capital structure is a least-cost mix of
financial methods. This "average costing" procedure, which is considered
in more detail in the appendix to this chapter, is not very helpful in
analyzing *optimum* capital structure for it assumes the problem away. It
is true that marginal capital costs will approximate average capital costs
for some limited amount of additional funds or in some capital rationing
circumstances, but we are dealing with *schedules* covering wide ranges of
returns and costs. Rather than assume that whatever average capital structure is, is right now and forever, we *seek* a constantly changing ideal overall capital structure by assuming that any change in structure will result
from following finance paths of least cost. It must not be thought that
such a "marginal" approach to financial costing ignores the past or
starting average cost of capital. As we know the debt/equity ratio of the
outstanding structure affects the marginal cost of debt, etc. In other
words although marginal and average cost curves are interdependent,
they are not identical.

***Influence of the Shape and Position of the Marginal Cost of
Funds and Returns Curves.*** To the extent that the marginal cost of
funds curve depends in part on the preinvestment capital structure, or the
net sum of previous finance of investment, the old capital structure influences the change in capital structure that results from new investment.
The marginal expected *returns* curve, however, is quite independent of
alternative methods of finance, past or present. *Where the returns curve
cuts the cost of funds curve, we find not only the volume of investment
that is profitable to undertake but also the optimum means of financing.*
All we need do is "read" the portion of the cost curve that lies to the left
of the point of intersection with the returns curve. This will yield the
optimum means of financing the investment or the ideal *change* in capital
structure which the investment calls for.

It is misleading to view the total resulting capital structure—old plus
new—as a fixed ideal or optimum structure, for this seems to imply some
index of excellence in the structure's proportions that ought to be maintained over the years. Rather, the firm's capital structure today is the sum
total of the changes in its initial capital structure that were implicit in the
series of varied discrete investment decisions it made at various points of
time in the past. At each of those times of investment decision the shape
and position of our two critical curves determined the point of intersection, and the points of intersection determined the capital structure effect.

To understand the forces determining the capital structures of firms, we must find out what influences the shape and position of those curves at any point in time, and what causes them to shift in position or change in shape over time.

Comparative Costs of Funds in a Given Period of Time: Illustrated by Graphs. Perhaps some crude graphs will help to clarify these comparative incremental or marginal costs of finance.

Where Only Retained Earnings Are Used. For a corporation that incurs no debt and restricts itself to internal expansion through retained earnings or net cash flow after dividends the graph in Figure 20–1 applies. That part of retained earnings that arises through depreciation accounting provides funds whose cost is average current returns/market price of the stock. In other words, it pays to carry out replacement investment as long as expected earnings per share can be maintained.

However, in practice, depreciation as a source for funds may be used by management even if a *lower* rate of return than Eu is probable, say in the case of a declining company. The alternative to investing in its own company should be to put the funds into the securities of other companies or to buy back its own shares. This amounts to a slow liquidation of its own company as a producing unit. In time, all the assets will have been depreciated, and the company's assets will consist of securities of other companies. If one cannot get the requisite Ea/P rate in one's own com-

FIGURE 20–1

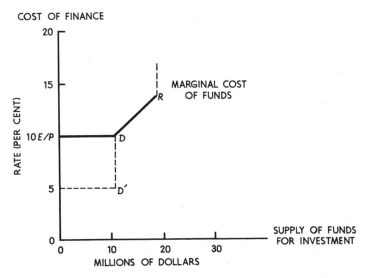

pany, the producing company should turn itself gradually into an investment company. But in practice, firms do not do this unless they think that the long-run Ea/P of their company will continue to remain below the required level.[1] Such companies may go on with replacement for a time *as if* the old E/P were going to be earned. Therefore, it is possible that the depreciation part of earnings available for investment will be supplied for a short time as long as the expected rate of return exceeds that obtainable on bonds, say 5 percent, rather than only being supplied if at least the E/P rate, say 10 percent, is expected. Thus, we insert a lower dotted line to indicate this short-term opportunity cost. But doing so involves a leap or discontinuity—or kink—between the use of the depreciation funds retained and the use of those earnings that are retained when a conscious decision not to pay dividends is made.

When these net retained earnings or net cash flows after depreciation are invested, they must yield at least the same earnings per share as is currently expected to be earned, or the stockholder would be better off to receive dividends and use the funds to buy additional shares of stock which are available at a price to yield 10 percent. And note that the supply of funds available from such retained earnings is described by a curve that rises gently from the minimum E/P level as investment proceeds. Further investment must yield slightly higher and higher returns to justify keeping those funds in the corporation. Recall that this is because the rate of returns on successive investments will exceed the old E/P to some degree and therefore will pull up the new average E/P that becomes the new required rate.

When a given *set* of projects is adopted, it is only the marginal project that earns Ea/P; but the supramarginal projects all will yield returns greater than Ea/P. Therefore, when the cost of funds curve is reconstituted as a hurdle for the next set of projects, the Ea/P barrier will be higher. This point raises complexities we cannot deal with adequately in this text: e.g., the interdependency of the marginal efficiency of investment (MEI) curve and the marginal cost of funds (MCF) curve. The nature of the investment opportunities or the shape of the MEI curve in part determine the shape of the MCF curve. Or, one may think of the

---

[1] Management might resist even more liquidating the company over time by paying out the funds in cash dividends. The tax laws, merger possibilities, etc., as well as turning the company into an investment trust, would all be considered first. Management would likely try all methods prior to abolishing its job. Moreover, production-minded business is reluctant to play the stock market. Before management does this, it is likely to consider selling the assets as a whole to another corporation, or even piecemeal liquidation.

marginal returns on stockholders' alternative investment opportunities as rising as his funds are plowed back rather than paid out to him for investment outside this particular firm. For our purposes, a rising cost of equity curve represents the higher rates of return required as management estimates what average future earnings would be if each of the *series* of proposed capital expenditures were not made. In other words, as projects are adopted (from the top down) *Ea* changes and with that change come changes in the *Ea/P* that must at least be met if additional funds are to be raised.

Note that when retained earnings are exhausted, the investment program is cut short regardless of the rate of returns promised unless the company considers selling additional shares of equity or borrowing—say, selling bonds.

Where Retained Profits and New Equity Shares Are Used as Sources of Investment Funds.   It is to be expected that firms will not resort to new equity shares until they have exhausted retained earnings. While both sources must meet the same basic rule—that the investment will yield as much as or more than the expected earnings per share—the selling of equity shares involves costs of flotation that are nil when retained earnings are used. Thus, it does not pay to issue new shares until retained earnings have been used up in internal investment. That is why we have drawn a short vertical line *R* to *F* to mark the costs of flotation (see Figure 20–2). And, as we have just seen, the cost of equity shares *F* to *E* is rising as more and more investment is made.

When Retained Profits, Equity Shares, and Debt Are All Considered as Sources of Funds for Investment.   To introduce debt into this picture is difficult because the cost of debt varies for two quite separate reasons:

1. The effective contractual cash payment rises as the volume of debt outstanding rises simply because lenders' risk rises with the increasing size of the lump of interest charges that the corporation must pay if it is to avoid bankruptcy.
2. The additional imputed cost of debt rises as the debt/equity ratio rises with successive lumps of additional borrowing, given the ownership interest.

In order to show these two factors on our graph, we assume that debt is incurred in discrete lumps at a cost equal only to contractual cost in interest as long as some chosen debt/equity ratio is not disturbed. Let us

FIGURE 20–2

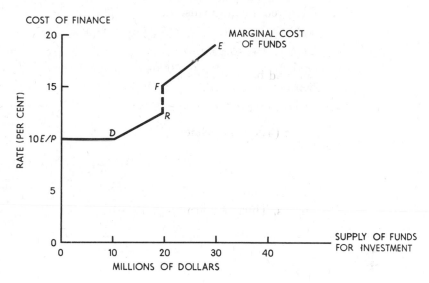

say that a sale ratio in our example is $1 equity to $1 debt. Then, if we began our corporation with $4 in original stock issues, we could borrow $1 at a cost equal to the going bond interest rate. We also assume that it is not convenient to incur debt in lumps of less than $1. Then we could not borrow again at this cost until equity had increased by four times as much as the proposed debt we wish to incur. Let us look at our graph extended to include the possibility of borrowing (see Figure 20–3).

FIGURE 20–3

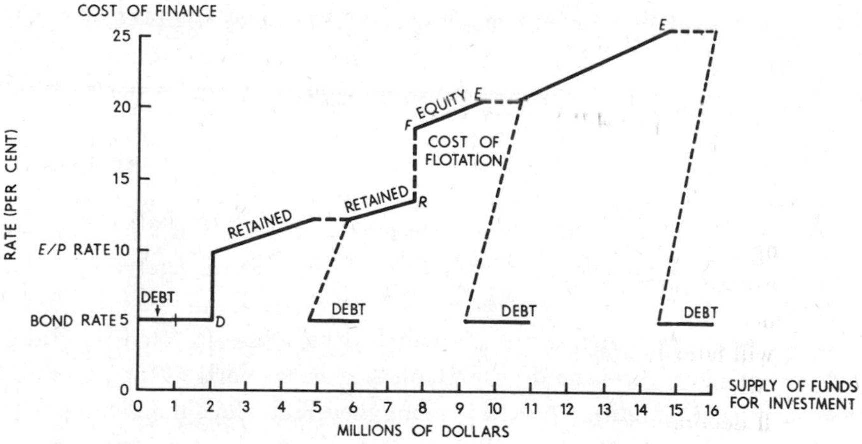

Of course, in principle the cost of debt varies as the debt/equity ratio varies, and in our example this would be in finely graded steps. We have used the widest possible steps for ease in illustration and also because debt in practice is incurred in large discrete lumps. Alternatively the cost of debt part of the graph (see the dotted line) can be thought of as providing the first $1 of debt at coupon cost and then rising until the last dollar is borrowed at the same cost as the equity finance technique for which the lump of debt had been (to this point) the cheaper alternative.

We began the problem with $4 in equity shares sold. Then we can incur the small debt of $1 at the countractual interest charge of 5 percent. We assume no additional imputed cost because this is presumably a "safe" debt/equity ratio (4:1) and lenders do not require a penalty rate nor do stockholders fear the debt will affect their residual earnings unfavorably. But further debt issues cannot be incurred in this period except at higher costs because both the coupon rate and the imputed cost of added riskiness of the debt will put the cost above other alternative ways of raising the funds. Thus, the firm shifts to the retained earnings sources, if the *MEI* justifies it.

But *as the company's equity* grows with its assets, when the equity has grown by $4, additional debt of $1 can be incurred without pushing the debt/equity ratio above 1:4 ($2/$8). The firm cannot afford to borrow more than $1 at this stage because the additional imputed cost—the riskiness—of debt will push the cost of debt above the cost of resorting anew to retained earnings. Similarly, if retained profits are exhausted, it is cheaper in our diagram to resort to selling fresh shares of equity until the total equity retention plus proceeds of sales of stock has increased by $4. Then it will pay to add more debt in the amount of $1. Further finance will be more cheaply raised by selling stock, for the cost of debt rises above it as the imputed element of riskiness becomes heavier and heavier when the established debt/equity ratio is increased.

Just as the debt quota is not fixed during a given short decision period independently of the nature of the other sources being used, it is not fixed for all time. Remember that the reason for the increased cost of debt was the rising debt/equity ratio; *but this ratio will decline as retained earnings are used to finance investment.* In other words, the rise in assets (equipment, etc.) which at first is matched by a rise in fixed liabilities (debt) will later be reflected by a rise in the surplus parts of the net worth account when no additional debt is being incurred. Thus, the debt/equity ratio will decline due to the rise in the denominator, and some point will be reached after which debt will once more be available at a cost that makes it pay to finance further investment by new debt issues. Indeed, because the cost of new shares is so much higher than the cost of using retained earnings (due to the tax effect), it is a likely pattern for corporations to finance themselves over time by alternating between retained earnings and debt with little opportunity to use new common stock finance. This is especially likely because the cost of using retained earnings will rise too because of the very success of previous finance by retained earnings. But before they become exhausted the cost of debt may fall back due to the improved debt/equity (D/E) ratio. The long-run cost of funds curve, which covers a series of periods, is probably flatter than the short period decision curve of Figure 20–3 in the absence of plans to float stock.

A Summary (Smoothed) Graph.   Although the graph in Figure 20–3 is based upon a number of oversimplifications, it provides a realistic overview of the sequence that is followed by corporations in seeking out sources of funds for investment. We can generalize further from the graph in Figure 20–3 to show a smoothed-out marginal cost of funds curve as shown in Figure 20–4.

What this shows is a gradually rising cost of funds except (in the middle) where the shift to stock issues takes place. This requires a jump in the cost of additional finance. But both the early retained sources and the later equity sources are flattened out (the cost rises slowly if further finance is sought) because, in addition to factors already built into the diagram, of the possibility of reopening the borrowing source which is

FIGURE 20–4

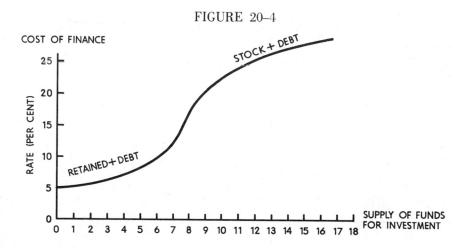

available for a given D/E at a constant interest cost. The smoothed-out curve in Figure 20–4 is the result of recognizing the following additional factors:

1. The vertical discontinuity (between retained earnings and sales of new stock issues) is elongated by the fact that taxes increase the relative cost of new shares.
2. Recourse to recurrent debt issues is even more likely than our diagram shows, owing to the fact that interest is tax deductible.

Difficult though it is to add the cost of debt to our overall marginal cost of funds, it should be clear that lumps of debt are injected as persistent use of equity finance has the effect both of raising the cost of equity and lowering that of debt. In other words the addition of debt to internal equity sources flattens out the initial segment of the cost curve just as introduction of debt (after internal funds are exhausted) between bouts of stock sales flattens out the final segments of the cost curve.

Simplified as this diagram is, it explains important aspects of current capital structure practices. It shows in sum that as investment is financed by retained earnings, the cost of such financing will rise slowly; and simultaneously, the cost of finance by debt will fall. And if the cost of new stock issues is significantly higher than the cost of retained earnings, finance of new investment will be carried out largely by the alternating means of debt and retained earnings.

It thus explains that some corporations that resort to equity issues have been driven by huge and profitable investment projects. Their vast needs for finance outstrip their retained earnings and require them to dip so quickly and so heavily into debt that the D/E ratio becomes sufficiently unfavorable to push the cost of debt above the cost of external equity.

It also explains the absolute declining role of straight preferred stock in (nonutility) capital structures.

Preferred stock is the one case where tax considerations play the dominant role in the choice of the method of finance. Although common stock and retained earnings as alternative methods of finance also suffer from the corporate tax penalty, both have the offsetting advantage that the mounting risk aversion element is absent. Of course, common stock is penalized relative to retained earnings by the net *personal* income tax effect (after allowing for capital gains taxation). But retained earnings are not an unlimited source of funds at a given point of time. Thus, although tax considerations virtually rule out preferred stock finance,[2] they do not rule out use of new common stock finance, although they do restrict it to periods of heavy investment when the demand for funds is very great. Thus, the validity of complex corporate capital structures, i.e., those that make use of *all* methods of finance, is the result on the cost side of two principal factors: the complex tax structure of the nation and the aversion to sizable debt owing to the riskiness of leveraged capital structures.

Comparative Returns in a Given Period of Time: Illustrated by Graphs. Not only does the cost of finance rise as the volume of funds needed in a given period rises, thus confronting additional investment with increasingly higher obstacles to surmount, but *additional units of investment also have increasingly less to offer.* The volume of investment projects adopted is then limited both by the increasing cost of additional finance and by the declining rate of return on additional investment projects. But the marginal returns curves for various firms may begin to fall from a relatively high or low initial level and may decline from that level at varying rates of speed. For example, some firms (*A*, Figure 20–5) are faced with investment opportunities that promise high rates of return for great amounts of investment; that is, the *MEI* curve starts at a high level and falls slowly as opportunities are taken up. Other firms face a "weak" *MEI* that offers low rates even for the best opportunities and even those are rapidly exhausted (see *B*). Other firms perhaps have *MEI's* that afford high rates for initial investment volume but fall off rapidly (see *C* in Figure 20–5). The lines describing firms *B* and *C* can also be thought of as representing the same firm's investment opportunities in a period of contraction (recession) and how they shift outward in a period of expansion (boom). If the projects became more numerous as well as more profitable, one could think of the change from *B* to *A* as descriptive of a single firm's fortunes over the business cycle.

The Transition from Capital Budgeting to Capital Structure Analysis. Although it is still quite correct to say that any firm's marginal cost curve is a rising curve, we must find out what makes one firm's cost curves rise sharply while others rise only slowly and in long, easy

---

[2] It is as if the cost of preferred stock is a curve lying above the cost of debt finance at all points where debt finance is a potential sources of funds for investment. When debt funds become too expensive to use profitably, preferred stock finance is even more expensive. On the other hand, common stock finance is an alternative means of finance that may come into use late—only after the cost of debt has soared. But when the cost of debt has soared, so too has the cost of preferred finance. When common stock finance is cheaper than debt finance, it is, of course, even cheaper than preferred stock finance.

FIGURE 20–5

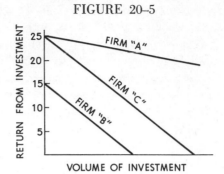

stages. In other words, we must examine in detail the forces that determine the *length* and the *slope* of the segments of the cost curve, including the debt interludes, and the *height of the kinks* between the segments.

Similarly, although we shall find no reason to question the generalization that the expected net returns curve is a falling curve, the *height* from which it begins to fall and the *rate* of fall will vary widely both between and within industries. Clearly, the shape of the returns curve depends on the number and profitability of the investment opportunities open to the firm at a given time or, in short, on the firm's rate of growth.

In addition to explaining why cost and returns curves vary in shape, we must also examine the forces that will cause them to *shift their position over time*. Investment decisions or capital budgets are made at points in time and could be so analyzed. But the capital structure which results from these decisions is an evolving or continuous process.

And such shifts, which will of course shift the intersection point of the two curves, will consequently affect the nature of the resultant capital structure. To explain these shifts of the curves over time, we must look, for example, to changes in the state of the nation: We must now begin to consider such matters as the way general boom conditions will push up and flatten out the returns curves of most firms; or the way the same boom will raise interest rates and stock prices and thus shift the position of cost of funds curve of all firms. Thus, the state of the financial markets and the state of the economy as a whole will influence the capital structures of firms by affecting the volume and kind of business financing that is undertaken.

We already know that *all* firms prefer to finance investment internally because it is often the cheapest and always the "safest" source of funds. But we have not specified what factors determine their *ability* to do so.

1. What characteristics of the individual *firm*, the particular *industry* of which it is a part, and the *financial and economic* conditions applicable to all firms and industries in the economy as a whole, promote or inhibit the capacity of firms to finance themselves internally?

2. Under what circumstances is the firm likely to go outside itself to raise funds by the sale of stocks and bonds?

3. And when the firm does undertake external financing, what factors determine the specific choice of particular kinds of stock and bond instruments that are chosen?

Answers to these questions will provide the answer to the broad question: What determines the capital structure of a firm?

Ideal or Optimum Capital Structure

When we find a firm that finances all of its expansion out of retained earnings, we can be sure that such a so-called "simple" capital structure is the result of the great profitability of past expansion or investment and/or the small profitability expected of future expansion or investment. In other words, for a firm to restrict itself to expansion from within, the marginal efficiency of investment must persistently intersect the marginal cost of capital funds in the "low-cost" retained earnings stretch of the latter curve. This occurs either because the marginal efficiency curve is weak begins to turn down sharply at low levels of capital investment (see unbroken line in firm I, Figure 20–6)—or because the cost of funds curve (see unbroken line in firm II) has a long, slowly rising retained profits portion.

FIGURE 20–6

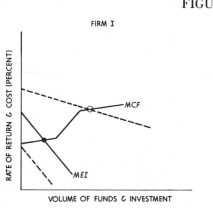
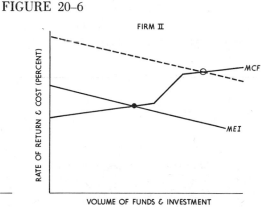

That a firm is able to finance itself entirely from its own profits is, therefore, not necessarily a sign of strength. It may well be that the firm is stagnating in the sense that further investment is simply not sufficiently promising to warrant going outside the firm to obtain funds and that it can make do with the small stream of retained profits its past investment is generating. Indeed, if the firm's marginal efficiency curve lies below the cost even of retained earnings, the firm, if it acts for the benefit of stock-holders, should not retain earnings at all, and perhaps should not even replace depreciating fixed assets. (See dashed line in I.) Even the case of the profitable firm that generates huge sums of retained earnings and then can finance substantial quantities of profitable investment is not to be thought of as ideal. Would it not be still better if the firm had so many and such profitable investment opportunities that it was *forced* to resort to external finance, i.e., stocks and bonds, to raise the needed funds? (See dashed line in II.)

But on the other hand, it must not be thought that evidence of resort to sales of stocks and bonds—a complex capital structure—is necessarily evidence that such a firm is overwhelmed with profitable investment projects. It may well be that its retained profits are so small as to provide little in the way of funds for expansion. (See dotted line in I.) Note that retained earnings may be low even in successful firms if the dividend payout proportion is high, e.g., department stores, or if the firm is in a regulated industry, e.g., electric utilities. But plowback may also be small because earnings are so poor, as, for example, some railroad companies with their immensely complex capital structures.

Thus, except with respect to straight preferred stock—it is always too expensive—we cannot make any specific statements about ideal capital structure that will apply to all firms. The optimum capital structure for each firm will depend upon the characteristics of the industry in which the firm operates, the particular attributes of the firm itself, and the state of the capital and money markets.

But we do assume that all firms should aim to pick that capital structure which will maximize that market price of the outstanding common stock. And this allows us to say that in general, the optimum capital structure can be determined from the time series of points where the marginal efficiency of capital curves have intersected the marginal cost of funds curves. Whether these points of intersection have been far to the right on the marginal cost curve—implying a complex capital structure—or close to the vertical axis—implying a simple capital structure—will have depended upon the slopes and positions of the two curves over time.

The Many Faces of Simple Capital Structures

There is one element that is important in both schedules or curves: profits. A firm that has many highly profitable investment projects and thus a strong elastic *demand* for funds may also anticipate that a good part of the *supply* of funds will be generated internally from the very profitability of implementing those investment projects. But obviously, there is a question of timing or lags. And more important, one must also consider the *stability* as well as the *absolute amount* of anticipated *profits*.

In principle, it would also seem that a growth firm that can see a long and steady *need* for large amounts of investments is also likely to be able to anticipate a large steady stream of retained earnings. And a firm whose future promises a stable demand for small amounts of funds for investment is likely to be a firm with a small but steady flow of retained earnings sufficient to finance the low-powered investment program. In both cases a simple capital structure—one with little or no recourse to outside funds by sales of stocks or bonds—seems implicit. However, a little thought soon reveals that the assumed characteristics of the two firms are unrealistic.

The first firm is almost certainly a strongly entrenched monopoly. High and regular profits year after year are certain in our economy to lead either to entry by competing firms or to government regulation of the monopoly. In either case the profit rate will be lowered; in the case of regulation the rate will remain steady, but it will be relatively low; in the case of competition the future rate of profit will become less stable as well as lower. Thus, it is unrealistic to postulate high and stable profits over a long period. Therefore, it is also unrealistic to assume that retained profits will automatically be the *sole* source of finance. For example, public utility finance tends to tap many sources rather than just one. Although, say, electric utilities are steadily growing firms, their profits are restricted to a given steady low level by regulatory commissions, thus necessitating recourse to issues of bonds and stocks to obtain the required funds. A similar need to consider external funds will also be forced upon a monopolistic industrial firm as its regular high profits are affected by new entrants. Here, the capital structure effect is more difficult to predict because the effect on profits may be to make them more irregular and unpredictable, as well as lower on the average. If expected profits are merely lowered, the effect will be to drive the firm, assuming numerous investment projects present themselves, to seek funds from outside itself.

The second firm is also not likely to have a simple capital structure just because of its small needs and correspondingly small retentions. The steady though *low* profit possibilities will make the sale of bonds both a safe and an attractive method—safe, because of the steadiness of earnings to meet interest charges; attractive, because the borrowing should, by trading on the equity, raise the residual return to stockholders. Sales of common stock, however, will for some time prove to be too expensive or simply unnecessary.

The need to resort to new common stock issues is likely if a rapidly growing firm does its growing or its profit making in irregular spurts. This third type of firm may need to raise so large a sum in so short a time as to outstrip the sums available currently from retained earnings as well as from borrowing at conventional interest rates.

Common stock is also likely to be issued when the firm's growth is marked by great *irregularity* in year-to-year *profits*. The average profit over a decade may have been and promises to be a healthy 15 percent; but if it ranges from years of heavy deficit to years of 50 percent profit rates, neither retained profits nor bonds are likely to provide a sufficient source of funds, especially if the investment projects are implemented in irregular bursts. Bonds would have to carry a high interest rate as well as a high imputed cost for the risk involved; and it would be difficult to establish a regular payout policy in such a way as to generate from retained profits the spasmodically large amounts required for investment.

Thus, it would seem that dynamic firms, whether growing at a slow or fast rate, regularly or irregularly, will prove to be either unable or unwilling to finance that growth entirely from retained earnings. Recourse to debt from time to time will complicate the capital structure. Flotation of new common stock will also be used whenever the growth needs become headlong.

The only case, a fourth type of firm, where retained profits or a simple capital structure is likely to be the right capital structure is when a firm has had and can expect small and steady need for investment funds and a moderate and steady rate of profits and therefore retained earnings. In this case, it has *no need* to go outside the firm for funds; it is not that it has a prejudice or fear of doing so. Such a combination of characteristics is likely to be found in industries that are in a monopolistic situation but are not taking full advantage of it. If the rate of profits were much higher, it would encourage entry by competitors or the government; if profit rates were lower, stockholders would want management to trade on the equity. There are examples of such industries and firms, but they should not be thought to be either typical or stable. An innovation, requiring sudden large investment, or a shift in demand, altering the moderate profit level, frequently upsets the scheduled demand for and supply of investment funds and thus destroys the simplicity of their capital structures.

The Principal Determinants of Capital Structure

The principal determinants, then, of the nature of capital structure are (1) the level and the stability of earnings and (2) the level and the stability of investment opportunities. These determinants derive largely from the *nature of the industry* in which the firm operates.

For example, the stability of the firm's sales or total revenues and the importance of fixed costs of production are the principal determinants of the stability of profits. But this industrially determined variability of profits (per share) can be influenced by the amount of leverage introduced into the capital structure. If variability of profits due to variability of sales and heavy fixed/total costs of production is quite large, small increases in financial leverage will push the cost of funds up sharply. Then it is likely that variability in investment opportunities will produce a low-leveraged capital structure. Aside from possible variations in dividend and debt policy, there is little that management can do to alter these conditions. These are the "givens" or the industrial framework within which management makes its capital structure decisions.

However, these industrial characteristics do not predetermine the precise arrangement of capital structure for any firm within a specific industry. Two further sets of factors will affect the choice of capital structure: (1) the state of the financial markets at the times when financing is needed; and (2) the attitudes or objectives of the particular firm's management and stockholder owners. For example, capital structure at a particular point in time will be influenced by some or all of the following conditions set by the *financial markets:* the going rate of interest; the kinds and amounts of debt instruments that the suppliers—individuals and financial institutions—prefer; the state of the stock market; and the prevailing tastes of potential purchasers of ownership shares. In addition, capital structures of specific firms will be influenced by *management's judgments and feelings* with respect to aversion to debt, possible loss of control, publicity, and growth itself. Moreover, management will take into account its particular stockholders as well as its own attitudes toward retention rather than payout of profits, trading on the equity, sales of additional shares in the equity, and the like.

There are factors other than money cost that sometimes induce management to *prefer* retained earnings finance to issuing new securities. For example, management may not, as we have been assuming all along, act at all times in the interests of the common stockholders. Management may prefer a simple capital structure—one that relies on retained earnings and perhaps on an occasional privileged subscription—because such a capital structure involves the least possible challenge to managerial control, while fresh equity issues might introduce strong dissident voting elements, and fresh debt issues might require in the bond indenture specific restrictions on managerial freedom of action.

Another example where management does not develop as complex a capital structure as available profitable investment projects would seem to call for is when management, faced with the necessity of resorting to expensive new issues to finance a highly profitable investment, decides against it because from *its* point of view the risk of gain is not worth it. This can happen because foregone profits are not reported in financial statements or anywhere else, while even the small probable losses that may occur if the project is adopted will show up on the profit and loss statement. Such a project may well have been profitable to undertake from the stockholders' point of view. Management's feelings of aversion to risk and fear of loss of control may be stronger than stockholders' feelings in these matters. And the upshot would be simpler capital structures than our analysis would seem to predict.

In addition, there are a host of other factors that affect management's financial decisions and hence the company's resultant capital structure. For example, although the corporation is prospering, its stock may be unduly depressed for a time because it has been pulled down in a mass downward sweep of the stock market. At such a time, new shares of common stock will not be issued. In other words, we must allow for the tastes of the purchasers of securities—the demand side—as well as the supply.

But although we must take into account these market and personal influences in capital structures, the industrial influences are predominant. If we can determine the kind of capital structure that the nature of the industry seems to call for, then all firms within that industry are likely to reveal a rough similarity in capital structure. There will be variations from this basic structure, depending on the individual firm's particular management and owners, and depending upon the financial market conditions at the time of capital structure changes. But an underlying similarity of capital structure for all firms within an industry will be apparent.

Let us, then, in the next chapter, explore the interindustry differences in capital structure and point up the factors that account for these industrial distinctions. Advanced discussions would also consider groups of firms *within* industries to see the departures from the industrial norm and the probable causes of those variations. These are the principal capital structure questons; and they can best be answered, given an understanding of the capital-budgeting background of financial decisions, by surveying the past and current trends and cycles in actual capital structures of various industrial groupings.

QUESTIONS AND PROBLEMS

1. Distinguish between:
   a) Capital structure and capital budgeting.
   b) Simple and complex capital structure.
   c) Marginal and average cost of capital.
2. Why does the marginal cost of capital curve tend to be a rising curve in S-shaped form (as in Figure 20–4)?
3. How does the shape and position of a firm's *MEI* curve affect that firm's capital structure?
4. What are the principal forces determining the capital structure of firms? (Organize your answer in terms of the firm's particular attributes, the characteristics of the industry of which it is a part, and the state of the money and capital markets.)
5. The fact that a firm finances itself 100 percent internally is not necessarily a sign of business success nor even that it has a least-cost capital structure. Discuss.
6. The nature of capital structure is primarily dependent on—
   a) The level and stability of earnings, and
   b) The level and stability of investment opportunities. Explain. Translate your discussion into graphs utilizing *MCF* and *MEI* curves.

SUGGESTED READINGS

ANDERSON, W. H. LOCKE. *Corporate Finance and Fixed Investment*, chaps. i, iv, and viii. Boston: Harvard Business School, 1964.

KUH, E. *Capital Stock Growth: A Micro-Econometric Approach*, chaps. i-vii, x-xii. Amsterdam: North-Holland Publishing Co., 1963.

LERNER, E., and CARLETON, W. T. "The Integration of Capital Budgeting and Stock Valuation," *American Economic Review*, September, 1964, pp. 683–702.

MEYER, J. R., and KUH, E. *The Investment Decision.* Cambridge, Mass.: Harvard University Press, 1957.

MILLER, M. H., and MODIGLIANI, F. "Some Estimates of Cost of Capital to the Electric Utility Industry, 1954–57," *American Economic Review*, June, 1966, pp. 333–91.

ROBICHEK, A. A., and MEYERS, S. C. *Optimal Financial Decisions*, chap. viii. Englewood Cliffs, N.J.: Prentice-Hall, Inc., 1965.

SCHWARTZ, E. "Theory of the Capital Structure of the Firm," *Journal of Finance*, March, 1959, pp. 18–39.

SOLOMON, E. *The Theory of Financial Management*, chap. x. New York: Columbia University Press, 1963.

WESTON, J. F. "The Management of Corporate Capital: A Review Article," *Journal of Business*, April, 1961, pp. 134–37.

APPENDIX TO CHAPTER 20
NON-MARGINAL APPROACHES TOWARD OPTIMUM CAPITAL STRUCTURE: THE WEIGHTED AVERAGE COST CONCEPT

The Weighted Average Cost Concept

It is a fairly widespread practice to consider the cost of capital as a weighted *average* of the cost of all the methods of financing that the firm has used.[3] For example, take the right-hand side of the corporation's balance sheet, as shown in Table A20–1. Convert the forms of finance to proportions, as in column 2. Determine the coupon cost or, better, the market yield for the fixed-charge securities after tax, and insert the

TABLE A20–1

WEIGHTED AVERAGE COST: AN EXAMPLE

Type of Security	Market Value (1)	Proportions (2)	After-Tax Cost of Funds (Yield) (3)	Weighted Cost (4)
Bonds	$ 3 million	30%	0.03	0.9%
Preferred stock ...	1	10	0.06	0.6
Common stock ...	6	60	0.10	6.0
	$10 million	100%		7.5%

---

[3] Some financial analysts using this method take balance sheet values at original or historical costs. This procedure makes the process even less useful. Current values and costs are the only figures relevant for current finance decisions, and we have used them in order to present average costing at its best.

current E/P for the cost of the common stock (see column 3). Multiply columns 2 and 3 to get the *weighted* cost for each method of finance (see column 4). Then, add this column to find the weighted average cost of capital.[4]

Note that this method assumes, in effect, that each project will be financed with additional bits of debt, preferred stock, etc. Of course, this is *not* how funds are in fact raised. But much more important, this method *assumes* that the past methods of raising funds were and are ideal. That is, it assumes that the firm already has the optimum capital structure—the least-cost method of finance—and all it needs do is repeat its past pattern of finance forever. This, of course, *assumes away* the *whole problem* that engaged us in this chapter, viz., to *find* the least-cost method of finance. Moreover, the actual costs—say, interest rates or the E/P—are constantly in flux. These very changes in market costs may call for changes in the proportional weighting of various forms of finance. The ideal capital structure is in constant flux because the average cost of capital is constantly being altered by shifts in the marginal cost of funds raised in various ways.[5] The real issue of how to determine the least cost of funds or the ideal capital structure is not even explored by assuming that it is already known and is constant.

In this latter respect, the average weighted cost of capital notion is akin to the Modigliani-Miller theorem. They both arrive at a simple single permanent formulation of what an ideal pattern of financing methods is. For the weighted average cost adherents, it is whatever has been done in the past, though one aches to know how the original determiners arrived at their weights. For Modigliani and Miller the whole subject is dismissed because the cost of capital in equilibrium is always equal to Ke. In the one case, marginalism is disregarded as the key to costing, and in the other the whole process of costing is dismissed.

In sum, average costing follows a rule of thumb—indeed, an *ancestor's* rule of thumb—the received capital structure;[6] the Modigliani-Miller

---

[4] Alternatively, one could find the average weighted cost of capital by taking:

$3 million × 0.03 = $ 90,000
1 million × 0.06 = $ 60,000
6 million × 0.10 = $600,000

$750,000 ÷ 10 million = 7.5%

[5] We prefer to say that capital structure is the *result* of optimum finance decisions, not that finance decisions are determined by the given optimum capital structure.

[6] If the debt/equity structure used is the historical or actual structure of the corporation, then, whatever is, is right forever; if the structure used is an "ideal" structure, then the cost of finance problem has been solved somehow, but we have not been told how.

theorem requires no rule or indeed any decision at all—whatever is done is a matter of indifference, for no matter what financing technique is used, the cost of capital is the same. Is there really any doubt that the best mix of methods of finance is constantly subject to change, never achieved but sometimes approached closely, then lost as financial conditions in the market shift, and sought again by altered patterns and sequences of finance? Does not financing take place in discrete surges by a sequence of methods?

It is true that when relatively small amounts of new funds are raised, there will be little change in the average cost of capital and hence little change in marginal finance costs. Under these circumstances the weighted average costs (AC) may serve as an acceptable substitute for marginal costs (MC) or as the obstacle with which to confront the MEI curve. But this is *not* to say that we may assume away for all financial matters the problem of determining the ideal weights or mix of the alternative sources of funds. Nor does this concession apply to substantial lumps of financing which in themselves will cause changes in such given market costs as interest rates (Ki) and equity capitalization rates (Ke) and hence in average total costs of capital (Ko). In all but trivial cases it is significant in practice as well as analytically sound to compute the *marginal* cost of the new financing. Of course one might say alternatively that one is *seeking* the least-cost package of funds or trying to minimize the average cost of capital.

The only serious objection that has been raised to the kind of *sequential* marginal costing which we have presented in this chapter is that this approach allows the mere *order* in which investment projects are adopted to determine the profitability of those projects. It is said that if the cutoff point comes when debt is used, the cash cost of debt is a bad measure of the cost of capital because the next project, this year or next, will be tested by a more stringent cutoff point—say, the cost of equity—which is higher.

This criticism is misleading.

1. In our method the projects are arranged in order of decreasing profitability; the cost of finance determines merely the cutoff point, not the *order* of adoption of projects.
2. We did not use the cash cost of debt as the total cost of debt; we allowed for the imputed cost of debt as well. That is, we allowed for the fact that when debt is increased, some of the equity base is used up.
3. Investment decisions are made at a given time, and the expected returns and costs of finance are before the finance committee; what is wrong with cutting off some projects when financing them is too ex-

pensive in this period? The projects are lower in their expected returns than the ones adopted. The cutoff project, if it stays at the top of the list of projects for the next round of investment decisions, will be adopted as soon as the passage of time makes its financing possible. During the passage of time, there may occur a build-up of retained earnings, for example, or a fall in interest rates, or a rise in the price of the stock. If other projects are discovered that pass above it in order of profitability, so be it—these other projects are more profitable to adopt.

4. There is nothing in the marginal costing method that attaches particular projects to particular methods of financing them; it is simply a matter of continuous anonymous ordering of projects and continuous sequences of financing.

It might be thought that caution is needed when, for example, the marginal cost of financing provides a cutoff rate which is *lower* than the weighted average cost of capital. But usually, this will happen at a time when investment opportunities are weak, and the failure to adopt projects at that time is owing to the weakness of the profit prospects, not the schedule of marginal costs of finance. There is no real need to fear that in one year, projects of low expected profitability will be adopted because, say, cheap debt finance is available that year, and that next year, with a higher D/E ratio, only projects of higher profitability can be accepted. If one thinks of *schedules* of expected marginal returns and costs *continuously adjusted over time*, the marginal procedure assures that projects will be adopted in order of profitability at the least cost of finance. If one remains unconvinced by this—and there is certainly still much to be learned about the appropriate cost of funds to use as the cutoff point—then use the marginal costing approach while keeping the average weighted cost of capital under continuous surveillance.

In any case, it is clear that averaging costing alone, whether of the Modigliani-Miller variety or the weighted variety, is not correct. Capital structure should fundamentally be viewed as determined by a series of financing decisions, and not vice versa. And certainly, it is no solution to assume that the average cost of capital is constant. For Weston the average cost is a constant and is determined by the average weighted cost of the existing corporate structure within the range of leverage that is customary to the firm.[7] For Modigliani and Miller, it is constant and, re-

7 J. F. Weston, "The Management of Corporate Capital: A Review Article," *Journal of Business*, April, 1961, pp. 134–37; and *Managerial Finance* (2d ed.; New York: Holt, Rinehart & Winston, Inc., 1966), pp. 285–91.

gardless of the degree of leverage, equal to Ke. Rather, the average cost of capital may or may not be constant, depending on financial market conditions, profitability of projects considered, payout policy, etc. And in any case the average cost of outstanding capital is not directly relevant to decisions as to methods of financing new investment.

Chapter 21

CAPITAL STRUCTURE: TRENDS AND
RECENT DEVELOPMENTS

CAPITAL STRUCTURE IN PRACTICE, 1900–1950:
THE TRENDS AND THEIR CAUSES

The Trends, 1900 1950[1]

All Nonfinancial Corporations. There have been unmistakable broad shifts in the methods of financing corporations since 1900. Comparing the beginning of the period—the pre-World War I decade—with the end of the period—the post-World War II decade—we find that:

1. The proportion of gross *investment financed internally* rose from 71 percent to 78 percent. This rise was fairly equally divided between depreciation and net retention.
   a) Depreciation financed 36 percent of gross investment in the early 1900's and 39 percent in recent years.

---

[1] Sources of data:

Three volumes, listed below, of the National Bureau of Economic Research and published by Princeton University Press:

Simon Kuznets, *Capital in the American Economy: Its Formation and Financing,* chap. v, especially Tables 38 and 39; and chap. vi, especially Tables 48–50. This chapter summarizes the findings of the two volumes below in addition to providing data for all corporations.

M. J. Ulmer, *Capital in Transportation, Communications and Public Utilities: Its Formation and Financing,* chap. vii, especially Tables 46–48.

D. Creamer, S. Dobrovolsky, and I. Borenstein, *Capital in Manufacturing and Mining: Its Formation and Financing,* chaps. vi and vii, especially Tables 39–41 and 50.

In most cases the data from these works have been freely adapted and arranged for our purposes. Many conclusions have been drawn from the data that the Bureau authors have not drawn and might well dispute. By and large, these volumes have been treated as sources of raw data, largely uninterpreted.

    b) Net retentions provided 35 percent gross investment funds in the early period and 39 percent recently.

2. Obviously, then, the proportion of gross investment financed by *external* methods has *fallen* from 29 percent to 22 percent in this half century. But this fall was not at all equally divided among stocks, bonds (notes and mortgages), and short-term debt.

    a) *New stock financing* as a proportion of total external financing *fell* from 31 percent to 15 percent.

    b) Thus, *debt rose* to 85 percent of all external finance from 69 percent.

        (1) Bonds, etc., fell from 51 percent to 35 percent.

        (2) Short-term borrowing rose from 18 percent to 50 percent of total external finance.

Thus, while total external financing's proportion fell off by one fourth, equity finance in particular fell by over half. The proportion of *long-term* borrowing also fell but by a lesser amount—about three tenths. Hence, in long-term or permanent external finance, the role of stocks clearly declined; stock issues were 60 percent of bond issues in the 1900's and only 43 percent of bond issues in the 1946–56 period.

Of course, the stock/total debt proportion fell even more sharply, owing to the large increase in "short-term" debt. But a good part of bank debt consists of "term" loans, which should not be considered as short-term debt. If we shifted term loans from the short-term category to the "bond-note-mortgage" category, it is likely that long-term debt would show little decline over the half century. *The principal shift in external finance has been the relative fall in stock finance, not in long-term debt finance.*

It is interesting to note that *the debt/equity ratio has not fallen over the period despite the relative decline in stock financing.* Of course, this is due to the rise in retained earnings.

For example, in the early period, 71 cents of every $1 in gross investment was financed internally; and of the 29 cents per dollar raised externally, 31 percent, or 9 cents, was raised by sales of stock. This 80 cents of every dollar of gross investment was financed by means of equity. In the recent period, 78 cents of every dollar of gross investment was financed internally; and of the 22 cents raised externally, 15 percent, or 3+ cents, was raised by sales of stock. Thus, 81 cents of every dollar of gross investment was financed through the owners. Hence, although corporation finance has seen a substantial rise in debt finance relative to stock finance, this rise has *not* entailed an increase in debt/equity ratios, owing to an offsetting rise in earnings retained.[2]

It must not be thought that the trends toward internal finance and away from stocks when external finance is required have proceeded smoothly over the last 60 years. These trends were slight during the early years, and were even reversed for a time in the 1920's, when stocks were easy to sell at good prices. But the trends have been quite strong over the last 30 years and, as we shall see, show little indication of changing direction in recent years.

It must also be noted that we have been discussing aggregate trends—applicable to all nonfinancial corporations taken in one great lump. If we break this great aggregate down into the traditional tripartite grouping—industrials, public utilities, and railroads—do the trends noted for the aggregate hold for each of the parts? Let us take "manufacturing and mining" to represent the industrials and "electric utilities" to represent the regulated industries.

Unfortunately, we have no breakdown of current asset statistics by industry for the years prior to 1922. Consequently, we must ask how gross investment, excluding inventories, was financed. This does not much affect the comparative results for the regulated industries because inventories are of little significance there; but for "industrials," inventories are important, and their absence from our figuring does leave the trends in finance of industrials incomplete.

The Regulated Industries: Electric Light and Power.   Once again, comparing the pre-World War I decade with the most recent decade available (1938–50), we find a shift toward internal financing and within external financing toward bonds. However, *the shift toward internal financing is stronger than for all corporations taken together;* consequently, the shift toward internal financing by industrials is less strong than for all corporations and especially less strong than for the regulated industries. *But the shift toward bond financing is much less strong* for the electric utilities than for all corporations or for the industrials alone.

---

[2] The *net* debt/equity ratio is also stable over the period. Net investment was 64 percent of gross investment in the early period and 61 percent in the recent period. This net investment was financed by 35 cents of net retentions plus 9 cents of stock in the first period; in other words, 44 cents of 64 cents net investment, or 69 percent, was financed by the owners. In the recent period, net retentions (39 cents) plus stock sales (3 cents) were 42 cents when net investment was 61 cents; here, too, equity sources financed 69 percent of net investment. The debt/equity ratio of financing investment has not changed over time despite the sharp shifts away from stock sales.

1. The proportion of gross investment (excluding inventories) financed internally rose from 8 percent to 51 percent for the electric utilities. But *eight tenths of the rise was due to depreciation* rather than net retained earnings.

    a) Depreciation financed 3 percent of gross plant and equipment in the early period and 38 percent in recent years.

    b) Net retentions provided 5 percent of investment funds at the turn of the century and 13 percent recently.

2. Clearly, *external financing* or investment fell from 92 percent to 49 percent—*a far sharper drop than shown for "all corporations."* But the shift within external financing from stocks to bonds was slight.

    a) Stock financing fell from 51 percent of all external finance to 37 percent.

    b) Thus, debt rose to 63 percent of external finance from 49 percent.

       (1) Most of this increase was in bond finance, which rose from 40 percent to 51 percent of external finance.

       (2) Hence, the rise in short-term debt's part of external finance was slight—from 9 percent to 12 percent.

The most striking change is the rise of financing through depreciation. *The shift from stocks to bonds is present but not so striking as for all corporations taken together.*

As a consequence, the overall debt/equity picture is stronger. In the earlier period, 8 cents of every dollar of gross investment was raised internally; and of the 92 cents raised externally, 51 percent, or 47 cents, was raised by selling stock. Thus, 55 cents of every gross investment dollar was raised by equity techniques. In the more recent period, 51 cents of the gross investment dollar was raised internally. And of the 49 cents raised externally, 37 percent, or 18 cents, was raised by selling stock; hence, 69 cents of each dollar of gross investment was financed by the owners of the corporation and 31 cents by lenders; lenders provided 45 cents of each gross investment dollar at the turn of the century. Thus, again, despite the rise in utility bond sales relative to stock sales over the half century, the rise in *gross* retained earnings was so great as to swamp this effect and to lead to a fall in the debt/equity ratio of financing gross investment. Even if we net out the huge depreciation shift, which is the greatest element involved, the debt/equity ratio does not rise but is quite constant over this long period.[3] Thus, once again, *as for all corporations,*

---

[3] Removing depreciation from both sides so as to compare the proportion of *net* investment financed by *net* retained earnings plus stock sales reveals that *52 percent of net investment was owner-financed in both periods.* (In the period 1881–1912, net retentions were 5 cents plus 46 cents in stock, or a total of 51 cents; 51 cents of 97 cents net invest-

the shift away from stock sales has not had the effect of raising the debt/equity ratio.

The electric utility trends in *external* finance as a whole are representative of the entire regulated industry, but the trends among the *components* of external finance (stocks and bonds) have differed sharply. Both steam railroads and telephone have experienced a sharper trend toward bonds from stock than was true of the electric utilities. While the electric utilities show that stocks as a proportion of stocks plus bonds (total securities) fell over the half century from 56 percent to 42 percent, they fell from 62 percent to 16 percent in telephone and from 41 percent to 18 percent in steam railroads. Thus, the drift away from stock issues in the regulated industries as a whole was even sharper than indicated by the electric utility data, although the shift away from external financing was no sharper for regulated industry as a whole than it was for the representative electric utility industry alone.

But the principal conclusion is that internal financing for the regulated industries increased at a far faster rate over the 50-year period than did that of all corporations. This, we shall see, is largely due to the surge in depreciation allowances in the regulated industries. As a consequence, the mining and manufacturing group, the other great subsector of "all corporations," must show a lesser rate of increase in gross internal financing, though not necessarily in *net* retained earnings, as a method of financing investment.

Mining and Manufacturing Corporations. Comparing the period 1900–1914 with that of 1946–53, we find that internal financing provided the equivalent of 88 percent of total expenditures on plant and equipment in the early period and 112 percent of those expenditures in the later period.[4] This *increase in internal financing by over one fourth is much smaller than the increase noted for the electric utilities,* but it must be noted that the principal reason for this is that internal finance has

---

ment is 52 percent. In 1938–50, net retentions were 13 cents plus 19 cents in stock, or a total of 32 cents; 32 cents of 62 cents net investment is also 52 percent.) On this *net* basis the debt/equity ratio was unchanged, despite the shift to bonds from stock. This is the same result we reached for all corporations on a gross or net basis.

[4] The unavailability of early inventory investment data leaves a major gap here. Obviously, if there were no inventories to finance (as is roughly true for the utilities), there would seem to be no need at all for external finance in the later period, when internal finance provided the equivalent of over 100 percent of financing for industrials. But of course, industrial inventories are sizable; and *when joined* to plant and equipment needs, the financing requirements are greater than can be provided internally. Moreover, many individual companies had low retained earnings and had to sell securities, while others with large retained earnings made small investment expenditures.

always been of major importance in financing industrials. The reasons why this has been so we shall consider shortly.

1. *The increase in gross internal financing* was far more equally at-tributable to net retained earnings as to depreciation than was the case for the electric utilities, where only one tenth of the increase in gross internal financing was due to extra net retained earnings.
   a) In mining and manufacturing, depreciation increased from 43 per-cent to 57 percent of gross plant and equipment, while net retained earnings rose from 45 percent to 55 percent of gross plant and equipment.
   b) The increase in net retentions between the two periods was by almost one fourth, while the increase in depreciation was by one third. The combined increase, as we have seen, was over one fourth.
2. *External finance fell, then by 27 percent.* This is just about the same decline registered for all corporations. But the fall in the proportion of external finance provided through new stock issues, bond issues, and short-term credit was different.
   a) *Stock financing* fell from 50 percent of total external finance to 15 percent—a much more *severe decline* than that which occurred in all corporations or especially that of the electric utilities.
   b) Thus, *debt rose sharply* from 50 percent of all external finance to 85 percent. This increase was even sharper than the increase in the debt proportion shown for electric utilities. But unlike the latter, in-dustrial bond issues *declined* proportionately! Clearly, the increase in short-term debt must have been huge. (1) Actually, the bond fi-nance proportion of total external finance fell from 42 percent to 25 percent. (2) But short-term debt rose from 8 percent to 60 per-cent of total external finance by industrials.

Thus, the most striking features of the financing trends in mining and manufacturing, aside from the rising internal financing similar to that which we noted for all corporations, is the sharp turning away from finance through stock issues and the sharp rise in short-term financing tech-niques. Bond finance is far more important today to industrials than is stock finance. Stocks as a percentage of total stocks plus bonds is only one third today; after the turn of the century, it was well over one half. (See Figure 21–1.)

But once again, it is clear that the relative increase in retentions of earnings outweighed the relative fall in new stock issues so that the debt/equity ratio for industrials has not deteriorated.

FIGURE 21–1

NEW BOND AND NEW STOCK ISSUES, ALL MANUFACTURING
AND MINING CORPORATIONS, 1900–1953
(Averages during Positive Business Cycles)

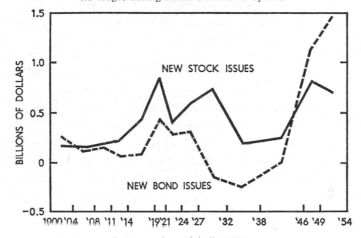

Source: D. Creamer, S. Dobrovolsky, and I. Borenstein, *Capital in Manufacturing and Mining: Its Formation and Financing* ("Studies in Capital Formation and Financing," Vol. III [National Bureau of Economic Research]; Princeton. Princeton University Press, 1960), Chart 19, p. 165.

The Causes of the Trends Observed in Corporate Finance as a Whole and in Particular Sectors

Three major trends have been observed in varying degrees for all corporations taken together and for each major type of corporate industry:

1. The increase in the proportion of *internal* corporate finance.
2. The decline in new stock issues and the rise in debt as a proportion of total external finance and, a fortiori, of total finance.
3. The rise in short-term debt as a proportion of total external *debt* finance.

Now, we must ask *why* these trends have occurred.

The Rise in Internal Financing. The rising trends in retentions of earnings for replacement of and expansion of plant and equipment are the two ingredients of the rising trend in internal finance. But what lies behind corporations' ability and willingness to retain increasingly larger proportions of earnings for depreciation and net expansion of fixed assets?

Depreciation. Since at least 1900, depreciation or replacement of plant and equipment has *been a rising proportion of gross investment.* In 1902, depreciation was 48 percent of gross investment of all corporations; by 1950, its proportion had risen to 74 percent. In other words, other things being equal, gross retentions have been a growing percentage of gross funds for investment. The reasons for depreciation, as a percentage of gross investment, to grow are:

1. Year by year since 1880, *net investment has been growing at a decreasing rate,* while, of course, depreciation on past investment continues and becomes an increasing proportion of gross investment.

Between 1880 and 1950, net investment as a proportion of national income has declined by over half—from 14.6 percent to 7 percent. Over this 70-year period, net investment did grow to over fourfold the starting level, but capital consumption or depreciation rose much more rapidly—by thirteenfold the initial level. Net investment was 60 percent of gross investment in the 1870's but only 35 percent of gross investment in the 1950's.

Note that net investment is still growing, but the *rate* of advance has been tapering off for over half a century! In the early part of the period, some of the regulated industries reached and passed their investment peak. Railways reached their peak rate of increase of net investment before 1890, and electric light and power by 1920; net investment in the telephone industry is still increasing. While net investment today is actually negative in railroads, it is positive, though increasing by decreasing amounts, in electric utilities, and positive and still increasing by increasing amounts in telephone. The upshot is that for the regulated industries *as a whole* the rate of *net* investment has been falling since World War I.

For the whole mining and manufacturing sector, the current rate of advance in net investment is greater than that of the regulated industries, but not of telephone alone. The rate of advance slowed down between 1880 and 1950. It averaged a 90 percent increase per decade between 1880 and 1900, 60 percent from 1900 to 1929, and 20 percent from 1930 to 1950. No doubt, the rate of advance is over 20 percent for the last decade; but surely, it is not as high as the 90 percent rate. Note that net investment in manufacturing is still expanding rapidly (unlike, say, steam railroads)—perhaps expanding currently at a rate of over 50 percent per decade—but there is nevertheless a decline in the rate of advance as compared with 1900.[5] This means that even in this sector, net investment as a proportion of gross investment is less than it was at the turn of the century; consequently, the weight of capital consumption in gross sources of investment funds must have risen. This major fact derived from the growth process explains a good part of the rising trend of gross internal finance since 1900.

2. Depreciation as a proportion of gross investment also grew as a result of the trend toward the *shortening of the average economic life of investment goods*. Since 1900, equipment's share of total investment has grown at the expense of plant or construction and inventories.[6] A piece of

Years	Construction	Equipment	Inventories	Total Investment
1897–1904	53%	33%	14%	100%
1945–54	31	61	8	100

equipment is typically a much faster depreciating item than a building not only because of the physical durability element but also because the equipment in a factory becomes economically obsolescent more readily than the factory building itself.

This development is part of the broader argument that when industry's early tremendous rate of net investment tapers off, depreciation rises. When an industry is beginning (and growing rapidly), it is building plant; but once built, the job is done for a long time. Net investment in plant falls off, but depreciation goes on.

3. The argument thus far has stressed the "real" or nonfinancial factors stimulating depreciation's share of gross internal financing, but there is also a monetary stimulant that became important during and after World Wars I and II. The *tax-saving aspects of accounting for depreciation expense* did not become important until World War I, at which time business not only began to account more fully for depreciation but also had a lot of catching-up to do. This surge of accounting for depreciation coincided with a period of strong net investment and thus offset a possible

---

[5] Note that *as compared with the regulated industries*, the mining and manufacturing sector is still expanding rapidly, though it is not expanding as fast as it did in its earlier history. In 1880, only 11 percent of the stock of net durable investment goods was in mining and manufacturing, as compared with 57 percent in the utilities. In 1948 the figures were 38 percent and 44 percent. Manufacturing's share more than tripled, while utilities' share fell 25 percent. But mining and manufacturing's rate of growth relative to its past has fallen off.

[6] Kuznets, *op. cit.*, chap. viii, Table 1.

rise in the net investment: gross investment ratio. The same thing happened in the 1940's and early 1950's; corporate taxes and net investment soared, but so too did depreciation expense. It is interesting that since the very periods when net investment surges are likely to be periods of high profits and high taxes, the urge, and often the ability, to step up depreciation are also very strong. It is likely that this factor accounts for the continuous proportionate rise in depreciation to gross investment even during periods when net investment grows at increasing rates.

Note that the first two factors above would apply more strongly to the regulated sector as a whole than to all other corporations or to the manufacturing and mining sector because the utility sector grew old earlier. But the financial incentive to "beef up" depreciation allowances is stronger for the nonregulated sector because its profits are not limited by regulatory commissions. This indeed, is one of the principal factors that explains the relatively greater importance of *net* retained earnings as a factor in the rise of gross internal financing in the nonregulated industries. In the regulated industries, 90 percent of the rise in gross internal financing is due to the rise in depreciation alone; in the mining and manufacturing sector, 40 percent of the rise in gross internal financing was due to the rise in *net* retained earnings.

Net Retained Earnings.   What has happened over the last century to increase the proportion of corporate investment that is provided internally by *net* retention of earnings? Obviously, it must be, on the one side, either that the rate of earnings has increased or the percentage of earnings retained has increased, or, on the other side, that the volume of net investment required for each sales dollar (and hence for net profits) has fallen. In fact, it seems that the rising ratio of net retained profits to gross investment owes something to each of these factors.

1. Apparently, the extra amount of net investment required per extra dollar of output—the marginal capital/output ratio—has been falling since before 1900 in the regulated industries,[7] and since the late 1920's in mining and manufacturing.[8] It seems that technological trends, which tend to increase the capital/output ratio, get overwhelmed by financial

---

[7] While the fall in the marginal capital/output ratio in utilities began over 60 years ago, its further fall has been very slight since the 1920's. Heavy capital expenditures per dollar of output in electric utilities and telephone account for the recent steadiness.

[8] Cf. Simon Kuznets' introduction to Creamer *et al.*, *op. cit.*, pp. 20 ff. The growth of the mining-manufacturing sector was most rapid between 1870 and 1920, when its share in national income rose from 16 percent to 25 percent. Today, it is 33 percent.

trends, which tend to reduce the sunk capital per unit of output, when the *rate* of advance of technology slows. When an industry's great period of rapid growth falters, the managers turn their attention from headlong expansion of capital investment to concentrate on economizing in the use of capital. In any case, a fall in the marginal capital/output ratio, even if the rate of profits earned and retained remains constant, will increase the *proportion* of investment financed by net retentions. That is, if output, sales, and profits earned and retained all remain constant, while the investment required per unit of output falls, then the total volume of net investment required will fall. But the absolute amount of earnings retained has remained steady. Therefore, the *same amount* of retained earnings can[9] finance a *larger proportion* of the firm's smaller absolute amount of investment. Thus, net internal financing will be increasing, even though profits and retention are unchanging!

2. Whether the net *rate of profit* has risen *secularly* is difficult to determine. It seems that it has remained rather constant in the utilities, which one would expect, considering the regulatory commissions. But the evidence for the mining and manufacturing sector is harder to come by. One may reason, however, that the secular rise in price levels would seem to favor some secular rise in profit rates, as would the absence of deep depressions or protracted recessions over the last twenty years. But the prices of capital goods tend to rise fastest when prices in general are rising, so that the rising profit trend may not result in much increased capacity to finance investment out of earnings. In any case, this stimulant to net internal financing of all corporations has probably been moderate in recent years (and nil before 1940) and always inapplicable to the regulated industry sector.

3. While there is considerable doubt that the *rate* of profit has risen over time, there is little doubt that the *percentage of profits retained in the corporation has risen,* especially in recent decades. Corporations, especially the nonregulated ones, have been strongly motivated since 1940 to step up the proportion of earnings retained or to reduce the dividend/ earnings or payout ratio. Management, of course, prefers to raise investment funds without subjecting itself to the vagaries and restrictions and costs of the open securities markets; and considering the high and highly progressive personal income tax of recent decades, the stockholder

---

[9] Given the general preference of management for internal over external financing, this word *can* should be read as *will.*

is much more amenable now to registering his gains in terms of rising market values of his stock than in terms of cash dividends received.

Thus, we see *why* gross internal finance of gross investment has risen secularly. In all corporations the role of depreciation has been of increasing importance; and in the nonregulated sectors, net retained earnings have grown in importance relative to finance of investment.[10]

The Decline in External Finance. Of course, as a corollary, the proportion of gross investment financed by external finance has relatively declined. And this is explained by the same factors already discussed above. But why is it that external finance by means of new issues of stock has declined so much faster than external debt finance? And why has short-term debt grown in importance relative to long-term debt?

The Falling Ratio of New Stock to New Bond Issues.   There are both real and financial explanations for the relative decline in stock financing. Large corporations, which have been the principal issuers of stock, have less *need* to finance themselves by sales of fresh stock because, having grown large already, their rate of growth of investment is past its peak, while their retention of earnings continues to be large and fairly stable. Moreover, as we have seen, the *cost* of raising money by selling stock is higher than the cost of retaining earnings. If possible, the corporation would prefer to step up the proportion of earnings retained rather than issue fresh stock. And many stockholders, even if they had direct control over corporate financial policy, would approve such reduced dividend payments for tax reasons.

But stock financing has suffered relative to bond financing as well as relative to internal financing. And once again, there are both real and financial causes.

1. In real terms, we have observed that although debt financing has grown faster than stock financing, the debt/equity ratio has not been impaired, because the retained earnings component of net worth or equity has risen sufficiently as an offset. Thus, corporations have been *able to*

---

[10] Throughout this discussion, it must be understood that we are ignoring business fluctuations in our pursuit of the smoothed long-run trend. Quite different and even paradoxical results flow from analysis, say, of investment finance during a boom. For example, it might be thought that with soaring profits a booming corporation might be able to step up its proportionate internal financing. But frequently, the pace of investment needs is stepped up even faster in the boom, with the result that external finance instead becomes relatively more important. Of course, these cyclical surges are more typical of the industrials than the regulated industries. But *even when external finance has a cyclical surge, the swing to debt and away from stock is notable.* Of course, during recessed or stable phases of the cycle, internal finance resumes its relative dominant position, and because these phases outweigh the short periods of investment boom, the trend reveals the generally rising role of internal financing.

increase their borrowing with safety—that is, without raising the traditional debt/equity ratio. Moreover, the *economic stability* of the last twenty years, i.e., the absence of a serious depression, has led some corporations to *step up their safe debt/equity ratio*, or to reduce the discount on returns for risk. It is not merely that the borrowing corporation feels more confident in borrowing because its earnings records show comforting stability; lenders, too, under these beneficent cyclical conditions find corporations more creditworthy than was the case in earlier, more volatile decades.

2. In addition, the *interest burden* relative to earnings (before taxes and interest) is far *lower today*, even after the great increases in bond flotations, then it was in 1929 or 1939, although it is higher than it was in 1949. For example, in 1929 or 1939, for all corporations, interest payments were 30 percent of earnings before taxes and interest; in 1949 the low ratio of 7 percent was hit; in 1956, they were about 12 percent of earnings.[11] Even in 1959, after interest rates had risen close to the 1929 levels, only 13 percent of all net corporate income was being absorbed by interest payments. The difference, of course, is the result of low coupon bonds issued over the last few decades and the higher corporate tax deduction today as compared with 1929—52 percent versus 10 percent!

3. But equally important has been the *falling cost of bond finance relative to the cost of stock issues*. There are three strands to this relative cost argument:

a) Bond *rates of interest* were far lower in the 1930–59 period than they were in the 1900–1929 period, while the stock yield rate was little changed.[12] (In the current decade these trends have been reversed.)

b) The *deductibility of interest*, but not dividends, as a cost in computing corporate income tax liability became important only after 1940, when the high tax rate made the tax savings worth having.

c) The *secular rise in the price level*, pronounced since 1946, favors debtors and thus stimulates the issuance of corporate bonds.

Thus, corporate management, when looking around for means of external finance, observed that interest costs were not only low in coupon cost but were especially so in after-tax terms; and further, the fact that the later interest and principal repayments would very likely be paid in depreciated dollars made bond finance seem even cheaper. Large corpora-

---

[11] For the mining and manufacturing sector the interest burden was 13 percent of earnings in 1929 but 5 percent in 1956; for the utilities the comparison is 39 percent and 18 percent.

[12] Cf. Kuznets, *op. cit.* chap. vi, Table 5.

tions, the only ones able to issue readily marketable bond issues, were also most likely to have built up their equity position through retained earnings, thus favorably impressing lenders and stockholders with their creditworthiness. Under these circumstances, it is no surprise that stock issues declined sharply relative to bond issues.

The Rising Ratio of Short-Term to Long-Term Debt. We have observed that in external finance the trend toward bonds from stocks raised the debt/stock ratio; but this ratio has been pushed even further by the sharp rise in short-term debt financing, especially in the manufacturing and mining sector. What accounts for this rising ratio of short-term debt to long-term debt? The arguments of the previous section also can serve to explain why the *short-term* debt/stock ratio has risen, but they do not explain the relatively even faster growth of this ratio when short-term debt rather than long-term debt is the numerator. As usual, we can find the explanation by seeking the financial and real advantages of short-term debt over long-term debt.

1. Short-term interest rates were three times as high in 1901–12 as compared with 1946–55, falling from 5.5 percent to 1.7 percent, while bond rates were not even half again as high, falling from 3.9 percent to 2.8 percent. However, this contractual cost advantage of short-term debt over long-term debt is reduced when we consider the comparative posttax costs, and it might be completely whittled away by the "inflation" argument. That is, the postwar II posttax costs of debt would be 0.85 percent (short) and 1.4 percent (long), assuming a 50 percent corporate income tax in 1946–55 and none in 1901–12. Then, for short-term debt the cost comparison is 5.5 percent to 0.85 percent—a sixfold difference; and for long-term debt, 3.9 percent to 1.4 percent—almost a threefold difference. The posttax advantage of short-term debt is reduced to twofold. And even this relatively greater saving in short-term over long-term interest costs between the periods would be further reduced if management expected continuously rising prices and some rise in future interest rates, because the short-term debt would have to be renewed at higher rates of interest while the long-term debt would continue in force at the lower rates for the term of the bonds. Probably *some net cost advantage* remains to explain the surge in proportion of short- to long-term debt, but additional support is needed to explain the strength of that surge.

2. It is on the "real" side that further support can be found. Short-term assets of corporations increased over the half century by about tenfold, while total assets increased only 7.5 times. In other words, the ratio of

CA/TA rose from 0.28 in 1901–12 to 0.37 in 1946–55,[13] while the ratio of short-term debt to all sources of finance ($CL/[TL + NW]$) was rising from 0.08 to 1.4 percent. Thus, *about one third of the rise in short-term debt may be attributed to the rise in short-term assets.* Current assets increased over the period by 33 percent while current liabilities were increasing by 75 percent. Although there is no rigid relationship between short-term uses and short-term sources, it is likely that the two rise and fall together simply because it is easy or *automatic to finance some short-term assets by incurring short-term liabilities.* (And some short-term debts arise merely as a consequence of accrual accounting and the like. For example, accrued tax liabilities on corporate balance sheets in recent years found their counterpart in the increased amounts of short-term governments carried as current assets by corporations.)

3. The third and final part of the explanation of the rise in short-term debt is that in fact a *good part of the rise is spurious.* All bank loans are included in the statistics as short-term debt; but since 1933 the proportion of bank loans that are term loans has increased sharply. And it is over the last 25 years that short-term debt statistics show the unusual rise. Term loans, which were only 8 percent of all bank loans to business in 1933, have been as much as 36 percent (1948) and currently run about 40–50 percent. But term loans, while not short term (less than one-year maturity), are not as long term as bonds. The average maturity is about five years. Corporations that are reluctant or unable to float bonds are getting longish term credit through their bankers. Such firms might well in the past have issued stock rather than resorted to continuous short-term borrowing. Hence, the *rise of the term loan,* while *reducing the apparent rise of the ratio of short-term debt to total debt,* helps to explain the rise of the total debt to total external finance ratio or the relative falling-off of stocks as an instrument of external finance.

Thus, we come to the end of a broad survey of the shifts in the means of corporate financing of investment 1900–1950 and the factors explaining those shifts. Next, we turn to a closer look at the last 20 years for which a new series of statistics have been developed. We shall see what the current trends seem to be and what explains them. We shall be particularly interested to see whether the trends noted for the period between 1900 and 1950 have continued and whether the underlying

---

[13] Kuznets, *op. cit.*, Table 7 in chap. vi. Even more striking is the similarity of the movement of the ratio short-term assets/external finance between 1901–12 and 1946–55. The ratios rise and fall in good correspondence to one another.

determining factors remain the same. Then, with a good understanding of current and past trends in the flow of corporate financing of investment, we shall be ready to study the capital structures of various types of corporate business.

CAPITAL STRUCTURE IN PRACTICE, 1947–66:
RECENT DEVELOPMENTS AND
THEIR CAUSES

For the years since the end of World War II, we have quite complete data on corporate finance. When we compared 1900 with 1950, the data for the years after 1946 were very scanty for all industries except manufacturing and mining. With these new statistical series, we can get a more complete picture of the current state of the methods of corporate finance. From this information, not only can we see whether the trends noted for 1900–1950 have continued over the last decade and a half but we can note the shorter trends and cyclical variations in finance methods since 1946, and forecast corporate finance for the 1970's from the observed drift of the 1950's and 1960's.

Between 1900 and 1947, we observed the relative increase in internal financing, especially in depreciation, and the relative decline in external financing. Within the external finance category, we noted the decline in stock relative to debt; and within the debt subcategory, the rise in short-term debt relative to long-term debt. Have these trends continued in whole or in part during the years 1947–66?

It is quite clear that the trends noted for the period 1900–1947 have been continuing in recent years; indeed they have been reinforced. (See Table 21–1.)

1. *Internal financing* as a percentage of total financing continues to grow at almost the same pace, reaching 68 percent for all corporations between 1957 and 1966. However, this pace has been maintained by the increasing importance of depreciation allowances; retained earnings in recent years have been weakening as a source of funds for expansion. This change is traceable to the manufacturing sector. Net retentions were never important in the utilities and in any case have been growing recently, and the railroads show little change of importance; but in manufacturing, they were of outstanding importance. In recent years, net retentions in mining and manufacturing have provided about one quarter of total finance, whereas from 1947 to 1951, they provided four tenths.

TABLE 21-1

Percentage Distribution of Corporate Sources of Funds,
1947–51, 1952–56, 1957–61, and 1962–63

Source of Funds	Manufacturing and Mining	Railroads	Public Utilities and Communications	All Corporations
Internal financing:				
1947–51	61%	69%	25%	56.0%
1952–56	72	91	32	62.0
1957–61	80	134	45	70.0
1962–63	75	106	61	69.0
Retained profits:				
1947–51	41	31	3	34.0
1952–56	32	43	3	24.0
1957–61	29	−26	5	23.0
1963–63	24	−27	10	21.0
Depreciation:				
1947–51	20	38	22	22.0
1952–56	40	48	29	38.0
1957–61	51	160	40	47.0
1962–63	51	133	51	48.0
External financing:				
1947–51	39	31	75	44.0
1952–56	28	9	68	38.0
1957–61	20	−34	55	30.0
1962–63	25	− 6	39	31.0
Stocks:				
1947–51	2	0	21	5.5
1952–56	1	− 4	27	7.0
1957–61	2	− 4	19	4.0
1962–63	− 3	0	10	1.0
Bonds:				
1947–51	6	8	36	13.0
1952–56	10	3	27	16.5
1957–61	6	−19	31	10.0
1962–63	6	− 7	21	7.0
Short term, etc.				
1947–51	31	23	18	25.5
1952–56	17	10	14	14.5
1957–61	12	−11	5	16.0
1962–63	22	1	8	23.0

Source: Department of Commerce, *Survey of Current Business*, September, 1957, Table 6, p. 12; *ibid.*, October, 1959, Table 2, p. 15; *ibid.*, November, 1961, Table 1, p. 18, and Table 2, p. 21; *ibid.*, November, 1964, Table 2, p. 9.

Note that these percentages are not comparable to those used in the first half of this chapter because here the percentages are taken of *total* sources or uses of funds by corporations. That is, uses include not merely plant and equipment expenditures, but increases in inventories and in short-term assets, such as receivables. Thus, the absolute percentages will be smaller.

And this has reduced the share of net retentions finance for "all corporations" from one third to about one fifth.

Of course, absolute amounts of net retentions have been increasing steadily, but the needs of finance have increased even faster in this postwar period. As is usual in such a period of relatively high investment, retained earnings weakened as a proportion of total finance. But the rise in depreciation allowances has been sufficiently strong—rising from less than one fourth of all financing to one half in the 1960's—to overcome the slip in relative net retentions so as to maintain the rate of increase of the share of gross internal finance to total finance. And this has been especially true in the very sector—manufacturing—where the net retentions slippage was greatest. Even there, internal finance comprised three fifths to four fifths of total finance between 1947 and 1966.

2. *External financing*, as a whole, continues to slip relatively as a source of finance; from providing 44 percent of total finance in 1947–51, it fell steadily to 31 percent for 1957–66. However, long-term debt which seemed to have halted and even turned up slightly between 1947 and 1956 has resumed its decline in the last decade.

No doubt, a good part of the shift from debt to stock of the 1950's, and within debt from the short-term to the long-term form, was due to the persistent rise in interest rates since 1951, i.e., the cost of debt,[14] while the cost of new stock issues fell as stock prices rose faster than dividend yields. But the relative cost argument is, as we have seen, not thoroughly persuasive, owing to tax and institutional demand considerations.[15] However, the relative decline in the role of retained earnings, when added to the "cost" argument, probably does explain the short-lived *renaissance of stock as a source of corporation finance*. After all, the ratio of debt (short term and long term) to equity (retained earnings plus new stock issues) provides a critical financial rule of thumb.

However the slight renewal of stock issues has collapsed in the most recent period. From 1962–66 new stock issues provided barely 1 percent of total sources. But note that during this period, retained earnings revived.

Thus we find that the long-trend shift from external financing continues

---

[14] During periods of rising interest rates short-term interest rates rise faster than long-term rates, thus causing a shift from all debt and within debt from short to long term.

[15] This, however, is also shifting as more and more financial institutions are introducing equities into their portfolios.

and that the *composition* of external finance which shifted back to stock a bit from debt has recently resumed its prior pattern.[16] In parallel fashion, the shift in the composition of internal finance toward depreciation and away from net retained earnings also seems to have halted; while internal equity finance continues to rise relative to external equity finance which continues its secular decline.

The broad differences in the sources of finance between types of industries are also apparent in these statistics. Currently, the mining and manufacturing sector raises about three quarters of its funds internally, while the utilities raise only about two fifths–three fifths internally. Although the railroads raise *all* their funds internally, they are expanding so little that the percentage does not mean much. The principal factor accounting for the difference between the utilities and manufacturing is the slimness of retained earnings in the regulated industries, although the recent protracted expansion has made retained profits the source of as much as 10 percent of utility finance. On the external finance side the importance of security issues to the utilities is obvious. Not only do they rely greatly on stock issues, unlike the industrials, but they also rely more heavily on bonded debt than short-term debt. Of course, the mining and manufacturing sector relies far more heavily on debt than stock for external finance; and in the debt area, its short-term debt far exceeds its long-term debt. These external differences can be explained in part in general financial terms; manufacturing maintains its debt/equity ratio by heavy retentions which the regulated utilities are not permitted to make; and the tax disadvantage of issuing stock is not so effective against utilities which are granted, so to speak, cost-plus privileges in setting their take-it-or-leave-it prices.

It remains to draw some conclusions about how and why capital structures differ between industries. For this purpose, we are not interested in changes and differences over time, but rather want to concentrate on differences between types of industry at a point in time. We shall use the two decades beginning in 1947, for which the data are available in final form.

---

[16] Note that throughout this chapter, we have not referred to preferred stock; use of the word *stock* implies common stock. Preferred stock financing has been relatively insignificant for some years, or ever since the tax advantage of *bonds* (from the issuers' point of view) became substantial. *For all practical purposes, preferred stock can be ignored in current capital structure discussions.* Of course, a great number of preferred issues from prewar years are still outstanding. It is *new* preferred issues as an alternative method of finance today that we are disregarding as unimportant.

RECENT METHODS OF CORPORATE FINANCE IN THE SEVERAL INDUSTRIAL SECTORS: A STUDY OF COMPARATIVE CAPITAL STRUCTURES

Table 21–2 contains a vast amount of information about recent techniques of corporate finance, not only for all corporations but for each of the major sectors of industry.[17] We cover in this four-part division all but about 20 percent of all corporate finance. As we draw out and analyze the data of Table 21–2, we can get a good view of recent corporate financial structure both in general and for the different sectors. If, as we do this, we can see *why* as well as *how* the sectors differ, we can go a long way toward understanding the determinants of capital structure. For clarity and ease of comparison, percentage figures are used extensively, but sufficient dollar figures are given at the edges of the table to permit the translation of any particular percentage figure to a dollar figure.

TABLE 21–2

PERCENTAGE DISTRIBUTION OF SOURCES OF CORPORATE FUNDS BY INDUSTRY, CUMULATIVE TOTALS, 1947–63*

Sources	Manu- facturing and Mining	Rail- roads	Transpor- tation Other than Railroads	Public Utilities and Communi- cations	All Corpo- rations	Total Sources† (in Billions of Dollars)
Total sources	100%	100%	100%	100%	100%	$713
Internal:						
Retained profit	30	19	8	5	23	164
Depreciation ...	40	69	62	36	42	299
External:						
Stock issues ...	2	−6	0	20	5	36
Long-term debt	13	6	15	31	14	100
Short-term debt	13	6	12	7	16	114
Other	2	6	3	1		
Total sources† (in bil- lions of dollars)	$336	$16	$26	$112	$713	

*Department of Commerce, *Survey of Current Business*, September, 1957, Tables 2 and 3, pp. 10 and 11; November, 1964, Table 2, p. 9; November, 1965, Table 1, p. 10.

†Given these two rows of absolute figures, and applying the appropriate percentages, you can derive the absolute amounts of the various sources for any one of the classified types of corporations.

[17] For further study in these fields, see H. I. Liebling, "Financing the Expansion of Business," *Survey of Current Business*, September, 1957, pp. 6–14; D. Meiselman and E. Shapiro, *The Measurement of Corporate Sources and Uses of Funds* (New York: Columbia University Press, 1964); R. W. Goldsmith, *The Flow of Capital Funds in the Post-War Economy* (New York: Columbia University Press, 1965).

Internal Financing.   It is quite clear that gross internal financing is very important for all sectors as well as for corporations as a whole. Except for the public utilities, all sectors individually (and all corporations) raise at least seven tenths of all funds internally. Even the utilities get two fifths of their funds in this way. The degree of variation among the sectors is for the most part due to intersectoral differences in net retentions rather than depreciation allowances. Depreciation alone provides between one third (trade and public utilities) and two thirds (transportation) of all funds; for all corporations (and industrials in particular), the proportion is 42 percent.

This great and rising importance of depreciation allowances in the years since 1947 is a consequence of the great postwar investment boom itself and the tax laws' encouragement of increased depreciation allowances, whether by more rapid amortization of defense-related facilities, investment credit techniques, or by use of the sum-of-the-years' digits or double declining balance methods of depreciation instead of the straight-line method.

But net retained earnings provide as much as three tenths of all funds in industrials, and as little as five one hundredths in the utilities, with the average for all corporations being under one fourth. Of course, this low retained profits element in utility finance is due not merely to the regulators' restraints on absolute utility profits but also to the high payout ratio. In the utilities, 80–90 percent is the typical dividend/earnings ratio; whereas in manufacturing, it averages around 45 percent of after-tax profits.

External Financing.   Although over the last 17 years only the utilities have sought the bulk—three fifths—of their funds externally, manufacturing and mining corporations are also important in the stock and bond markets. Here, we must turn to the dollar figures for elucidation. Although manufacturing and mining go outside of the corporation for only three tenths of their funds, they spend three times as many dollars as the utilities. Thus, utilities required external finance for three fifths of their $112 billion needs, or $66 billion, while industrials required external finance for three tenths of their $336 billion needs, or about $101 billion. Thus, despite the utilities' overwhelming proportionate need for external finance, the very size of the manufacturing sector gave it even more importance in overall external finance, despite the slim proportional weight.

But we must go further. The utilities may not dominate overall external finance, but they are the most important of the sectors in issuing new stock. Of the $36 billion of new stock sold by all corporations, 60 percent were utility stocks; the rest, some $14 billion, were issued by manufacturing and mining corporations, etc.

The dominance by the utilities of the long-term debt market was ended in this decade by the incredible increases registered in the manufacturing-mining sector. Although manufacturing and mining corporations raised but 13 percent of their funds through long-term debt, this amounts to $44 billion, while the heavy (31 percent) reliance of utilities on long-term debt adds up to but $35 billion. These two sectors together undertake almost 80 percent of total corporate long-term debt finance.[18] When we consider all long-term external finance—long-term debt plus stock issues —these two sectors are about equally important and together use almost 80 percent of all corporate long-term external finance—38 percent for utilities plus 42 percent for manufacturing and mining.

The only important short-term debt user is the industrial sector; it meets only one seventh of its needs this way, but this amounts to almost $60 billion, or about half of all corporate short-term debt. Clearly, the "other" corporation group—small businesses, etc.—used some $60 billion, or half of the total; this finance met almost half their total needs.

In this discussion, little attention has been paid to the transportation industries because together, over the 17-year period, they used but $4.2 billion, or 6 percent of total corporate external finance. Other than the fact that transportation issued net no new stock issues at all, there is little of importance to note here.

Cyclical Variations in the Sources of Funds

Typically during the course of the business cycle, internal funds supply an above-average proportion of funds needed during the recession and early period of recovery but a lower than average share during the later

---

[18] Between 1946 and 1955, industrial bonds outstanding rose from $3 billion to over $17.5 billion, while utilities' outstanding bonds rose from $10.5 billion to $27 billion. True, utility bonds rose over the decade by $17.5 billion to the industrials' $14.5 billion; but in 1946, utilities had three and a half times as many bonds outstanding as industrials; by 1955, this excess had fallen to about one and a half times. This was an extraordinary decade for issuance of industrial bonds. In 1955, total corporate bonds outstanding totaled $54 billion, so that industrial bonds comprised almost one third of all outstanding bonds; they were one eighth of outstandings in 1946. Utility bonds were about one half of all those outstanding both in 1946 and 1955. Apparently, industrial bonds outstanding have gained at the expense of railroad bonds and others.

stages of expansion—i.e., the boom phase and after the boom has broken. During recession, the need for funds is slim so that even the reduced profits and their retention suffices to meet a great part of needs and during the early stages of expansion although needs for funds grow rapidly, profits grow faster still. In the late stages of the expansion—the boom—the rise in profits slows, while the need for investment funds continues to rise, and when the boom is broken, profits fall off relatively faster than investment needs.

The accompanying chart, which compares the course of fixed investment and internal funds over the last three business expansions shows that in the late stages of the expansion, internal financing gives out relatively and external finance becomes more important. And this is true, even though in an absolute sense internal funds rise strongly. During the most recent expansion, external funds become important only late in the expansion; but this is just another way of saying that the upswing beginning in 1962 was a very powerful one, generating very heavy profits for an above-average number of years. Still internal funds began to give out here too. By late 1965 sale of bonds and use of bank loans began to soar, and external finance began to rise relatively as well. The degree to which stock has diminished as a source of funds is underscored by this last expansion. Even when in 1965–66, recourse to external funds became heavy, little or no stock was being floated (see Figure 21–2). The secular decline in the role of common stock was reinforced by the failure of even a brief boom-time revival in new issues.

During the most recent expansion internal funds provided as much as 73 percent of total corporate needs for funds and as little as 62 percent in the later stages of the expansion (see Table 21–3). Still the *average* share of total funds provided internally was higher in the 1960's than in the 1950's; that is, the *trend* toward internal funds continues unabated. The cyclical rise in external finance is predominantly via short-term borrowing with "permanent" bond-type debt following as the new greater needs are seen to be other than temporary. During the great investment boom of 1965, total uses of funds rose by 30 percent, or $20 billion in one year. Of this $20 billion increase, three fourths was raised externally: $6.5 billion via bank loans, $8 billion via other short-term finance such as trade credit. Bonds rose by $1.5 billion, and stocks as a source of funds actually *fell* net by $1 billion (see Table 21–4). New stock issues as a source of funds hit a low point in its long decline; if during so great a

FIGURE 21–2

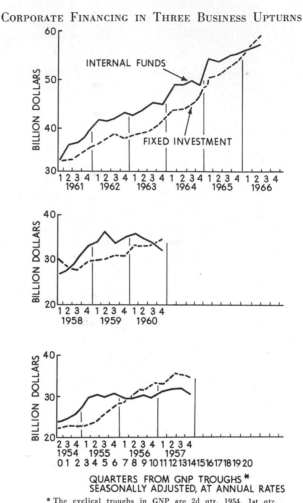

CORPORATE FINANCING IN THREE BUSINESS UPTURNS

QUARTERS FROM GNP TROUGHS *
SEASONALLY ADJUSTED, AT ANNUAL RATES

* The cyclical troughs in GNP are 2d qtr. 1954, 1st qtr.
1958, and 1st qtr. 1961.

SOURCE: *Survey of Current Business*, May, 1966, Chart 6,
p. 10.

boom stock is not sold to raise funds, when will it ever be sold again?
Recall our "cyclical" explanation of new issues of stock.

In the later 1950's as compared with the 1920's, although the trend
away from financing via preferred or common stock issues toward debt
and retention can be explained largely in terms of the lesser post-tax costs
of the latter forms of finance the *occasional* surge in new issues of
common stock is probably attributable more to forces on the demand

TABLE 21-3

Percentage Distribution of Corporate Sources of Funds during the Current Business Cycle, 1962–66

	Expansion		Boom
	1962–66	1964	1965–66
Internal sources	67	73	62
Retained profits	23	24	24
Depreciation	44	49	38
External sources	33	27	38
Stocks	1	2	1
Bonds and mortgages	11	11	11
Short-term	21	14	26

Sources: Department of Commerce, *Survey of Current Business*, November, 1965, Table 1, p. 10; and May, 1966, Table 1, p. 10.

TABLE 21-4

Changes in Sources of Funds in 1965 as Compared to 1964 (Billions of Dollars)

Total sources	$20 billion (from $69B to $89B)
Internal sources	+$ 5
External sources	+$15
Long-term	
Stock	− 1.0
Bonds	+ 1.5
Short-term	
Bank loans	+ 6.5
Trade credit, etc. ...	+ 8.0

Sources: Department of Commerce, *Survey of Current Business*, November, 1965, Table 1, p. 10; and May, 1966, Table 1, p. 10.

side—that is, to the demand for funds for boom-type profitable projects at a time when other sources are exhausted. Of course, the fact that during such booms soaring stock prices reduce costs of financing via stock is helpful to corporate decisions to float stock. But since internal equity finance is always cheaper than external equity finance, even when the latter is at bargain rates, it is the lack of internal funds that fundamentally explains the surge of new common stock issues; that stock prices tend to be high at such times would seem to be an accompanying feature of the boom conditions. In short, if stock prices rise but investment plans do not, there will *not* be a surge of stock financing.

Ordinarily, cost conditions favor the alternation of retention and debt as sources of finance. In the rare boom year the cost conditions become less relevant because of the absolute lack of funds from the least-cost sources.

During such rare years, common stock, though still high in cost, is at its cyclically low-cost point; but the necessary condition for its issuance is the lack of alternative sources, not its cost advantage.

In the 1960's the prime prerequisite for common stock issues was not met: profits soared so high that net retention was sustained for longer than the usual period. Then in the mid-60's when external funds were finally needed in greater proportions, the debt/equity ratio had been so strengthened that external *debt* rather than equity was the chosen financial path even at the peak of the boom.

Thus, as we theorized, a firm with an established debt/equity ratio is essentially a firm which acts as if the cost of debt, including the charge for risk, is equal to the cost of *internal* equity. The firm raises funds by steady plowback and sequential debt issues, keeping the debt/equity balance stable. In the ordinary course of events it never considers preferred stock or common stock flotations, because the former is always more costly than debt and the latter is always more costly than internal funds. If the firm's anticipated rate of growth, profitability, and needs for funds unexpectedly accelerate, and neither the debt/equity ratio nor the payout ratio is considered alterable, a common stock issue will be forthcoming. It will not be in place of a debt issue but in tandem with it.[19]

Common stock's role in corporate finance which had been 12–14 percent of total sources 1900–1929 fell to 5 percent in the first decade after World War II. In the period since 1958 stock's role has declined even further and comprises perhaps 3 percent of total corporate sources of finance. Should its rise even in strong cyclical expansions be curtailed, it will not seem strange to dismiss common stock as a source of new funds for it may well provide but 1 percent of total corporate funds in the future as it did 1962–65.[20]

Note that among the sources of funds to all corporations the greatest year-to-year variation is found in short-term debt (external) and retained earnings. The most stable source by far was depreciation allowances.

Finally, what we have said about cyclical sources of funds for all corporations holds for the industrials in particular but not for the utilities. The utilities not only experience little year-to-year change in funds retained but also relatively little variation in fixed investment, which is fairly constantly 90 percent of their total needs for funds. As a conse-

---

[19] However, there will never be an occasion on grounds of either cost or availability for preferred stock to be used in lieu of bonds or any other source of funds.

[20] See A. W. Sametz, "Trends in the Volume and Composition of Equity Finance," *Journal of Finance*, September 1964, esp. pp. 459–62.

quence, although the utilities have persistent recourse to external sources —for retention, though steady, is small—their needs for external finance are quite unvarying. Contrast this with the industrials, which one year need little external finance and another year make heavy demands on the security markets and the banks.

EXTERNAL SOURCES AND SECURITY ISSUES

Now that we have surveyed all corporate as well as interindustry sources and uses, one final large job remains to be done: to examine corporate implementation of external finance via issuance of securities. We have surveyed uses (plant and equipment, inventories, receivables, and cash), internal sources (depreciation and net retained profits), and external short-term sources analytically in earlier chapters and statistically in this chapter. Now, we have only to explore corporate sale of bonds, preferred stock, and common stock as a means of external finance. We know the role they play as a proportion of total sources of funds, but it remains to answer such questions as: What are the differences among these means of external security finance? What industries issue what kinds of securities? How important are such issues to financing various types of corporations? Are there any significant trends in corporate security issuance? Thus, Chapters 22–26 deal with stocks and bonds.

There is also a series of questions to answer as to how such new securities are sold and who buys them. Hence, in our final chapters (27–28), we study investment bankers as marketers, and financial institutions as purchasers of corporate securities. Then, we shall have completed our analysis of corporate finance from the uses-sources point of view.

Let us proceed then to consider in the remainder of this text the differences in the *particular kinds of securities* commonly used in various sectors of business, why those particular securities are so used, and how they are sold or placed by the capital-raising corporation. That is, we shall conclude the book by considering the *sources* or *providers* of external corporate finance and how the corporation goes about tapping those sources.

QUESTIONS AND PROBLEMS

1. Outline briefly the principal trends or broad shifts in the methods of financing corporations since 1900.

   Despite these shifts, the aggregate debt/equity ratio for all corporations has remained quite steady. How do you explain this?

2. What have been the principal causes of the secular rise in the role of—
    a) Internal finance vis-à-vis external finance.
    b) Stocks vis-à-vis bonds.
    c) Short-term debt vis-à-vis long-term debt.
3. What are the principal differences between the capital structure of the average industrial and the average electric utility? To what factors do you attribute these differences.
4. Considering cyclical rather than secular forces, external finance in general has not, although common stock has, lost its boom-time importance. Discuss, making use of external financial data for the extended expansion and boom of the mid-1960's.

SUGGESTED READINGS

GOLDSMITH, R. W. *Flow of Capital Funds in the Post War Economy*, chaps. iv, v, viii, and ix. New York: Columbia University Press, 1965.

KUZNETS, S. *Capital in the American Economy: Its Formation and Financing*, chaps. v, vi, ix, and x. Princeton, N.J.: Princeton University Press, 1951.

LINTNER, J. V. "The Financing of Corporations," *The Corporation in Modern Society* (ed. E. S. MASON), pp. 166–201. Cambridge, Mass.: Harvard University Press, 1959.

MILLER, M. H. "The Corporation Income Tax and Corporate Financial Policies," pp. 381–470 in The Commission on Money and Credit, *Stabilization Policies*. Englewood Cliffs, N.J.: Prentice-Hall, Inc., 1963.

SAMETZ, A. W. "Trends in the Volume and Composition of Equity Finance," *Journal of Finance*, September, 1964, pp. 450–69.

Part VI

LONG-TERM EXTERNAL SOURCES

Chapter 22

THE ISSUANCE OF CORPORATE BONDS

We have seen that corporate finance has changed substantially in recent years. Not only has there been the trend toward internal versus external finance; but within the sphere of external finance, there has been a trend toward the use of bonds rather than stock. We shall now see further that there have been marked changes in the *types* of new bonds and stocks issued as well as in the methods of *marketing* those securities and in the identity of the *principal purchasers of corporate securities*.

SOME BASIC CHARACTERISTICS

All bonds are essentially long-term, formal, interest-bearing IOU's (debt) of the issuer. No matter how fancy the various clauses or names of corporate bonds may be, the fundamental characteristics are firm:

1. Scheduled repayment of the principal sum borrowed: maturity.
2. In the interim, a fixed rate of return to be paid on the outstanding debt: interest.
3. As creditors, the bondholders have claims prior to those of stockholders with respect both to earnings (toward interest payment) and to assets (toward repayment of principal).

The specific details of these essential terms, and other minor characteristics of the corporate bonds, are expressed in full in the formal legalistic contract drawn up between borrower and lender. Except in the case of bonds sold in blocks directly to large financial institutions such as life insurance companies—called direct placements of bonds—the formal contract (or indenture) between debtor and creditor involves a third party, the trustee. This third party is needed to represent the interests of the thousands of scattered bondholders who have neither the time, the competence, nor the organization to see to it that the debtor corporation lives up to the detailed provisions of the indenture.[1] In the case of a simple loan involving a single or a few creditors such as a bank, or an insurance company, or a wealthy individual, such a trustee arrangement is unnecessary.

Note that it is the widespread ownership of bonds—the massive tapping of the public's savings—that has made necessary the formality of the bond indenture and the need of a trustee arrangement. Before the middle of the last century, business was financed largely by a relatively few wealthy individuals, often foreigners, and by government. Not only was there little use of formal bonds—simple notes or IOU's sufficed—but the use of the corporate form itself was not so pressing; for the principal advantage of this business form, as contrasted with the general partnership, is its usefulness in raising large quantities of money, composed of small contributions from numerous individuals, in exchange for various kinds of securities.

WHY THE VARIETY IN TYPES OF BONDS?

To the basic complexity of tapping thousands of sources of funds for which the trustee arrangement was a solution,[2] a much greater complexity was added as corporations, experiencing varied degrees of success and growth, and vying with other corporations for the public's funds, developed variations in the types of securities offered.

Most of the complex variations of the basically simple bond form were developed in the last half of the nineteenth century in the struggle to finance the great railroad network. This vast development of transportation required constant financial innovations to attract the public's interest not only because of the vast sums required but also because of the indifferent success of some of the undertakings. More new wrinkles in bond varieties, and stock varieties, too, arose in the early years of this century as the great power system (electric utilities) was being developed. And in recent years the third area of vast growth—the industrials—has led in the development of new species of bonds. However, as we shall soon see, since

---

[1] The trustee also serves to represent the bondholders' interests in case of financial distress, bankruptcy, and legal reorganization.

[2] In the case of common stock, the numerous unorganized owners are represented by the board of directors. Once again, one must concede realistically that the great bulk of owners (stockholders) have neither the time nor the competence to manage or to control the business corporation.

the 1940's a simplification of the forms of bonds has been in process—indeed, a simplification of the total capital structure of corporations as a whole is well under way. In general, the broad current trend toward simplification is due to the fact that the need to cater to masses of individual security purchasers is less intense today because:

1. Institutional purchasers of new issues predominate.
2. The rate of growth of corporate enterprise, and hence the need for funds, is less rapid than it was in our earlier history.
3. Further, corporate needs for outside funds have been reduced by the lessened severity of business fluctuations and the absence of financial panics, the consequent greater stability of profits, and the resultant trends toward internal finance.
4. The general public is both more willing (sophisticated) and able (richer) to buy securities without varied sweeteners.

But first, we must consider the reverse of these conditions which prevailed for, say, the hundred years from 1830–1930, when corporations, constantly in need of outside funds, sought them by developing a mass market among the public for corporate securities.

THE VARIETY OF BONDS: PRIORITY OF CLAIM

If a corporation had but one mass creditor—the holders of a single bond issue—there would be no point in specifying priority of claim for payment of principal or interest; the bondholders as creditors would come first, ahead of the owners, whether represented by preferred or common stock. But of course, from the very beginning, corporations tended to have outstanding bank debt and short-term trade credit; and as time passed and additional bonds were sold, a variety of long-term debt and different clases of creditors developed.

Mortgage Bonds

In order to sell additional bonds, especially under uncertain financial prospects, it became the custom to attach to each new issue a specific set of fixed assets to which that particular issue would have first claim in the event of financial difficulties. Such bonds, of course, were called *mortgage bonds*—specific assets were pledged as security or as a lien to the bondholders. In the event of failure to pay interest or principal when due, the bondholders, through their trustee, could look to the ultimate liquidation value of those particular assets for the funds necessary to pay their claims, or at least could use their exclusive claim to strengthen their bargaining power with other creditors and with the ownership interests in determining the future of the business. The variety of mortgage bonds that developed in the nineteenth century can easily be imagined when one realizes that not only could the different bonds have claims to different sets of assets, but different orders of priority to the same set of assets became common by the name of second or third mortgage. Moreover, the claim to specific fixed assets did not exhaust the mortgage bondholders' priority as creditors. If the proceeds from sale of the specifically pledged assets were inadequate to meet their contractual claims, they joined the "unsecured" creditors in their claims against all assets for full satisfaction ahead of the owners.[3]

Collateral Trust Bonds and Equipment Trust Certificates

Other less important types of bonds with specific pledges of assets were developed in nineteenth-century railroad finance. As the railroads expanded, they acquired not only the roadbeds and other real estate which were suitable to the mortgage form, but they also acquired securities in other railroads during the waves of consolidation and merger; and of course, they were constantly acquiring additional rolling stock even after the basic system had been completed. Bonds secured by marketable securities (stocks and bonds) of other corporations are called *collateral trust bonds;* debt secured by specific and exclusive pledge (indeed, title) to pieces of equipment, such as freight cars, are called *equipment trust certificates.* The complexity of railroad bonded indebtedness should now be evident. Under the pressure of surging growth and lack of internally generated funds owing to spotty financial success, ever new and fancier securities had to be invented to coax forth the public's money. When a railroad wanted to buy control of another road, in essence it pledged the controlling common stock in a bond which it then sold to raise the money to pay for the stock. When a railroad was already heavily mortgaged and did not show strong earning power, it developed a new device to allow it to finance the rolling stock it needed to continue operations. This was the

---

[3] Of course, if the proceeds from sale of the pledged assets were *more* than adequate to pay off the interest and principal sum due the mortgage bondholders, the residual proceeds went to meet the claims of the other classes of creditors.

equipment trust certificate. In order to sell these "bonds," it was necessary to give them sole claim to the most readily salable assets—the rolling stock itself. These brand-new standardized and mobile assets (unlike the trackage, buildings, or land) were subject to instant repossession in the event of default and, being usable on any railroad, had instant salability.[4]

Receiver's Certificates and Income Bonds

Two further aspects of railroad development complicated the structure of outstanding bonds: merger and recapitalization. Imagine the complications when two railroads merged their individually complex capital structures! Add to this the perennial financial embarrassment that railroads have long experienced, with occasional trips to court for reorganization of the financial structure. Since, in practice, it has seldom been feasible to sell off the fixed railroad assets to satisfy the bondholders' claims which have been defaulted, the only possible solution has been to try to keep the concern going by reducing the fixed charges and raising additional funds.[5] In this process, two additional types of corporate indebtedness developed: trustees' certificates and income bonds.

Trustees' certificates were given a special priority both as to assets and as to interest over all outstanding bonds. Why, it may be asked, would the holders of the outstanding bonds agree to their own demotion? In effect, they had no choice; liquidation was either not permissible, owing to the public interest, or liquidation would have provided but a small proportion of the total dollars needed to pay off outstanding debt. Their best bet was to get the concern going again and hope that future earnings would improve. To this end, immediate additional cash was needed, and only a superpriority "bond" could be sold. On what other basis could the locked-

---

[4] In addition, the marketability of such "bonds" was improved (even in the case of quite financially sick railroads) by their short maturity—usually fifteen years, much shorter than the actual life of the asset—and by provisions setting up sinking funds to retire portions of the debt serially prior to maturity. In effect, the equipment was being sold on the instalment plan with a substantial down payment. In strict law, these were not bonds but certificates or notes—a legal fiction to allow these special provisions and priorities to stand up against prior mortgage bond issues that had been issued with sweeping claims to assets acquired in the future. This so-called "after-acquired property" clause, which many railroads were compelled to put in mortgage bonds to make them salable, often forced the railroads to seek out varied alternative bond forms in future finance. For example, only new *second mortgages* could be issued against newly acquired property, and such inferior claims were less salable, unless high interest rates were included in the indenture. In effect, equipment trust certificates have liens prior to such mortgage bonds in the event of default.

[5] Of course, in this process, stockholders were forced to make even greater sacrifices.

in bondholders expect new lenders to be attracted? Moreover, the old bondholders usually had to make more sacrifices, and this further complicated the structure of bonded indebtedness.

In the process of scaling down the railroads' fixed charges and principal sums due, bondholders were often compelled to accept a new bond, or even stock, in exchange for their old one. Customarily, this involved not merely a proportionate scaling-down of principal but a brand-new instrument of lesser quality in either terms of priority as to assets or earnings, or both. The classic new bond type developed in this process was the *income bond*. This bond is unique in the fact that it moves to the bottom of the list of bonds in its priority as to claim on earnings. (Recall that the other strange "bond"—the trustees' certificate—was unique in that it moved to the top of claimants as to assets as well as earnings.)

Interest on an income bond is a *contingent* rather than, as on all other bonds, a *fixed charge*. The interest must be paid *if* earned; but if not earned and not paid, the interest is ordinarily accumulated, and the corporation is not considered in default. Note that in all other respects, it is a bond; for example, default in principal repayment is just as serious as with any other bond, and the income bond may have a mortgage lien, etc. Note, too, that although its claim to earnings is just superior to that of preferred stocks, the fixed return on the latter need not be paid even if earned, and cannot be paid unless interest on the income bonds has been fully paid, including charges in arrears.

Debentures

We have been able to present the classic catalogue of bond types, categorized by priority of claims to assets and earnings, while at the same time reviewing the record of railroad finance, because this was the first major industry in the United States to develop by mass sale of securities to the public.[6] We shall find the same procedure suitable for the briefer discussion of types of preferred stock. Only one bond type of current importance has not been mentioned thus far—the debenture. The *debenture* is a bond which carries no claim to specified fixed assets. It is misleading to say that this bond is "unsecured," although this is common business and academic parlance. The bond is secured by all the assets of the corporation, for it is a creditor instrument, although, of course, if other bonds have specific prior claims (say, via a mortgage or collateral trust indenture), it has in effect only a secondary claim on those assets. But note that if de-

---

[6] Seventy-five percent of all bonds outstanding in 1900 were railroad issues.

bentures are the only outstanding bonds of a particular company, they have in effect a first mortgage on *all* assets.

The notion that debentures are "unsecured" bonds stems from too much dwelling on railroad finance and on nineteenth-century corporate finance in general. It is true that debentures played a small role in railroad finance. By the time their extensive use was considered, the bond structure of the railroads was so complex with mortgages, etc., that debentures in effect would have had to be considered as weak third mortgages on real property, second mortgages on marketable securities, and first mortgages only on assets that had somehow been overlooked. Thus it was that debentures were issued by the railroads only during those brief periods (1904–15 and 1925–31) when the roads' earnings and confidence in the industry were high. In practice, the debenture, of constantly increasing importance in corporate finance, was and is important in the public utility field and is the predominant form of bond issued by industrials—that group which includes all types of businesses aside from the two great regulated ones. Owing to the relative decline of railroad finance, it is easy to see why the debenture is of increasing importance in corporate finance as a whole.

While it remains true that the most common classification of bonds is the one that follows the lines of claim to assets, it is well understood that the fundamental security of a bond is the *earning power* rather than the liquidation value of the assets. Knowledge of this fact made it possible to make increasing use of debentures in the electric utility industry as soon as its stable earning power could be demonstrated.[7] Of course, first mortgages were of first and continuing importance in the public utilities, and collateral trust bonds were used extensively during the period (1910–30) when holding companies were being established in the electric utilities. The use of debentures in industrials was always of importance owing to the feeling that industrial fixed assets were either too insignificant—current assets predominated—or too specialized to serve as suitable security for a mortgage. From the very beginning of bond financing of industrials, the emphasis was placed on the size and stability of earnings as the primary source of creditor protection. In addition, bond finance was thought mostly unsuitable to industrials in any case; but when bonds were sold, the debenture form was frequently used. It is only in relatively recent years,

---

[7] Moreover, increased public knowledge about securities reduced the intensity of the demand for "security" or specific liens; and the more predictable needs for finance, combined with the absence of periodic financial distress, allowed the utilities, unlike the railroads, to develop more reasoned plans for raising external funds.

that is, since the late 1940's, that massive bond flotation by industrials has become common. This is attributable largely to the relative stability of the economy and of industrial corporations' earnings in the postwar period.

THE VARIETY OF BONDS: TYPES OF PROTECTIVE CLAUSES

Indentures are long and complex documents not merely because of the detailed description of the liens involved but also because of additional protective clauses. Such clauses seek to protect bondholders' priority of claims to assets and earnings against undermining by new future issues of bonds, and sometimes of stock, too. The classic examples are the "after-acquired property" clause and the "times charges earned" restriction.

Mortgage bonds frequently prescribe that all property acquired after the bond is sold will be added to the lien of that bond. Of course, as long as new units of the old bond issue can be sold as new property is acquired, that is, as long as the mortgage is "open end," future finance is not hobbled by the after-acquired clause.[8] Of the same nature is the common restriction of new bond issues to a given percentage—say, 50 percent to 60 percent—of the value of new property. In general, these restrictions on future finance are intended to prevent corporate management from adding claims to assets in such a way as to dilute the earlier bondholders' claims. In the case of debentures, such clauses are especially important, for, lacking any specific claim to assets, their position would otherwise be quite vulnerable. In the case of these increasingly important bonds, it is usual to include as well an "equal coverage" covenant which provides that the old bond will have equal claim with any future bond issue that is granted a specific lien on assets.

The other major type of protective clause is concerned with preventing the dilution of the safety margin of earnings over fixed charges. If, when a bond is issued, there is a healthy excess of expected earnings over the

---

[8] It is easy to see that if the bond is closed end—no additional bonds of the same class may be issued—additional property could only be financed by extensive second mortgages. But such a crippling financing technique would obviously not be voluntarily undertaken by management unless it expected little need for future finance via bonds. However, railroads, under pressure of financial difficulties, issued such bonds in order to make them salable. The story of their efforts to "get around" the after-acquired clause in future finance is long and complicated and, although of considerable historical interest, is of little current importance. Railroads are not important bond issuers today, and other expanding industries have avoided the financial strait jacket that harassed railroad management designed for itself.

certain future interest costs, it is important to these bondholders to prevent future bond issues from impairing that margin of safety. The simplest method is to devise a protective clause which specifies that future bonds can only be issued if the new fixed charges entailed will be covered by average earnings by, say, a multiplier of two or three.[9] Clearly, such a clause is of particular importance in the case of debentures, which look primarily to the earning power of the going concern, rather than to its liquidation value, for their safety.

There are a host of protective provisions other than those specifying the new debt/new fixed asset ratio or the new fixed charges/earnings ratio. Often, the outstanding bonds will be further protected by asset-claim clauses specifying the maximum permissible percentage of total debt/net worth, and by earnings-claim clauses requiring the maintenance of specific working capital ratios or limiting the total amount of current liabilities or cash dividends. Regardless of the specific nature of the protective clauses, they are intended to set forth appropriate asset and earnings requirements for new debt and to prevent the undermining of protection specified for prior bond issues.

THE VARIETY OF BONDS: REPAYMENT OF PRINCIPAL

Quite simply, the distinctions here are (1) whether it is planned to wait for the maturity date to retire the debt; and (2) at maturity, whether to refund the debt or to pay it off.

In either or both cases, the further question is whether to set aside (earmark) cash on a regularly scheduled basis—i.e., whether to set up a sinking fund. Bond indentures may provide for retirement of bonds before maturity either at the option of the corporation—"call" provision—or as a fixed obligation to retire a certain proportion of the total issue annually—"serial" retirement.

The call provision protects the corporation against declines in prevailing interest rates. While corporations can always retire debt by buying up

---

[9] In practice, the "times charges earned" ratio has tended to be two in utilities and 3.5 in industrials. (See W. B. Hickman, *Corporate Bond Quality and Investor Experience* [Princeton: Princeton University Press, 1958], Table 81, pp. 399–401.) For railroads the ratio has ranged from one to two on the average, but this was low not by design but because of poor earnings. It would have prevented further bond issues in any case; but railroads, in fact, have actually reduced their bonds outstanding since the 1920's and have only used equipment trust certificates to raise new money.

their issues in the open market, the premium paid might be very great if interest rates have fallen sharply since the issue was sold. Call provisions usually involve a premium or penalty payment over par of a few dollars, but this is to compensate the bondholder for the trouble and expense of seeking out another investment; it may not cover the full amount by which the bond has appreciated in the marketplace. Most bonds issued today are callable. Only railroads—our oldest issues—have many outstanding noncallable bonds; but even there, about 60 percent of the aggregate par value of outstanding rail bonds are callable. Of all *new* bonds issued (1900–1943), less than 10 percent of the par amount were noncallable, and these were largely railroad issues; 5 percent of new utility issues have been noncallable, and less than 3 percent of the industrial issues.[10] Recently, during a period of relatively high interest rates, corporations have compromised by issuing bonds that are noncallable for typically five years.

It is also interesting to note that the average number of years from offering to scheduled maturity of all bonds issued in 1900–1939 was 25.5 years, with railroad bonds averaging 34 years, public utilities 26 years, and industrials only 15 years. The growing acceptance of industrial bonds is indicated by the fact that their average scheduled maturity has lengthened to 21 years by the end of the 1950's.[11] In other words, another way to ease concern about repayments of principal is not to set the maturity date too far off into the unknown future; thus, industrials' scheduled maturity average is only 60 percent of that for all corporate bonds. Also, note that the actual number of years from offering to extinguishment averaged 14 years for all corporations and only eight years for industrials (25 for railroads and 13 for utilities). This measures the extent to which calls and sinking funds were utilized to "retire debt" before the final maturity date.[12]

Serial retirement of bonds prior to maturity is a bondholder's protective provision, especially when combined with a sinking fund provision, because presumably there is a double fear being allayed: (1) that the corporation should not have that much debt outstanding in the first place,

10 W. B. Hickman, *Statistical Measures of Corporate Bond Financing since 1900* (Princeton: Princeton University Press, 1960), Table 109, pp. 192–95. Recently, however, the practice of making bonds noncallable for the first three to five years after issuance has become common.

11 R. W. Goldsmith, *The Flow of Capital Funds in the Postwar Economy* (New York: Columbia University Press, 1965), p. 210.

12 W. B. Hickman, *The Volume of Corporate Bond Financing* (Princeton: Princeton University Press, 1953), Table 6, p. 76.

and (2) that it cannot be trusted to provide for the massive redemption or refunding that will be required at a single future maturity date.

For the most part, corporations borrow on a permanent basis; that is, they do not borrow with the intention of reducing the scale of debt in the future; The debt is less likely to be paid off than to be turned over. "Only 41 percent of the total volume of bonds extinguished [1900–1943] was actually repaid without refunding."[13] Certainly, this is true of growing firms where bonded indebtedness is an accepted means of finance. Hence, electric utility bonds seldom have serial retirement or sinking-fund provisions. Indeed, for such companies, consols—bonds with no maturity date at all—would seem quite suitable. Such bonds are bought for their yield, and repayment for most investors is a nuisance, for they then have to go out and purchase other bonds. On the other hand, industrial bonds—always suspect owing to the unstandardized or slim proportion of fixed assets and their historically unstable rate of earnings—frequently carry prematurity provisions. It is as if the purchasers of such bonds think that large bond issues are really not suited for industrials. In fact, these protective provisions would seem most applicable to the financial condition of the railroads; but of course, in the past the roads simply were not able to afford them. New railroad issues—almost exclusively restricted to equipment trust certificates—all do provide for serial retirement and sinking funds. And at maturity, there is here no question of refunding.

Serial retirement is quite rare in bond issues aside from equipment trust certificates. Only 3.2 percent of the par value of all outstanding corporate bonds in 1944 were serials, most of these being industrials, and another 2.6 percent were equipment securities.[14] Certainly, today the joint amount of serials is less than 10 percent of the par value of all outstanding bonds. Even industrials have resorted less to rigid serials in recent years; today, when the market questions the company's ability to repay principal at maturity, industrials are more likely to use flexible and partial sinking-fund provisions with their optional time of repayment and reduced danger of default proceedings if a fund payment is missed.[15]

But *substantial sinking-fund* provisions are also relatively rare, except for industrial bonds. While almost half of the par value of all new issues in 1900–1943 had provisions for sinking funds, only about 12 percent provided for retirement of more than half the issue prior to maturity.

---

13 *Ibid.*, p. 13.

14 *Ibid.*, Table 1, p. 32, and Table A4, pp. 266–69.

15 Industrials use a serial technique today not in bond finance but when they make term loans which are repayable on a strict instalment loan basis.

Most of these substantial sinking funds were prescribed for industrials; about three quarters of all new issues of industrials had sinking funds, with almost half of them providing for retirement of over 50 percent of par value by maturity. Less than 8 percent of new utility bonds and 3 percent of railroad bonds, excluding equipment trust certificates, had provisions for *substantial* sinking funds.[16]

CLASSIFICATION OF BONDS ACCORDING TO TYPE OF ISSUER: AN INDUSTRY CLASSIFICATION

Corporate bonds are usually classified as to whether they are industrials, utilities, or railroads, as well as to whether they are mortgages or debentures, etc., callable or serials. Of course, "callable open-ended first mortgages with after-acquired clauses, etc.," for example, have been issued by all types of business, so that this method of classification cuts across the previous ones. Nevertheless, it is true that particular types of bonds and protective and retirement provisions tend to be associated with particular types of issuers. Therefore, although this classification is not an *alternative* method of classifying bonds, it is illuminating supplementary material. Moreover, within this classification, it is possible to shift to consideration of current bond issues, as well as the accumulated outstanding issues, typically issued by various industries. This discussion parallels that on capital structure, where we noted the differences between industries in their methods of finance. Here, we focus on the kinds of bonds issued rather than the overall view of the extent to which bonds as a whole are a source of funds to particular industries.

The dominance of railroad bonds and, in particular, secured (largely mortgage) bonds at the turn of the century is clear from Table 22–1. In 1900, 75 percent of all outstanding bonds were railroad bonds, and less than 4 percent of all outstanding bonds were unsecured. By 1940, railroad bonds were somewhat over 40 percent of all outstanding bonds, while utilities were a slightly larger percent, and industrial bonds were some 14 percent of the total. By 1951 the utilities' share of outstanding debt increased to over 50 percent, with the remainder almost equally divided between railroads and industrials. From the leading position of 75 percent of outstandings, railroads slipped to a trailing position of 10 percent by 1965. The utilities had about 45 percent and industrials the

---

[16] Hickman, *Statistical Measures of Corporate Bond Financing since 1900*, Table 106, pp. 180–188.

TABLE 22–1

OUTSTANDING ISSUES OF ALL BONDS AND UNSECURED BONDS
FOR SELECTED YEARS, 1920–65
(Billions of Dollars)

Year	All Industries	Railroads	Public Utilities	Industrials
Par Amount of Outstanding Issues for Selected Years*				
1900	$ 5.9	$ 4.6	$ 0.9	$ 0.3
1920	18.1	9.6	6.1	2.4
1940	25.4	10.8	11.1	3.5
1951	31.7	8.9	16.4	6.4
1960	69.0	10.0	34.0	25.0
1965	98.0	10.0	44.0	44.0
Par Amount of Outstanding "Unsecured" Issues for Selected Years†				
1900	$ 0.2	$ 0.1	$ 0.1	$ 0.1
1920	1.9	0.8	0.6	0.4
1940	4.8	0.8	2.3	1.8
1960	20.0	1.0	8.0	11.0
1965	33.0	1.0	10.0	22.0

* W. B. Hickman, *Statistical Measures of Corporate Bond Financing since* 1900 (Princeton: Princeton University Press, 1960), Table 17, pp. 29–32. Data for 1951 from W. B. Hickman, *The Volume of Corporate Bond Financing* (Princeton: Princeton University Press, 1953), Table A2, pp. 256–61. The 1960 and 1965 totals are *very* rough estimates deduced from Securities and Exchange Commission data.

remaining 45 percent of the outstandings. Although these recent figures are but educated guesses, it is clear that there has been a postwar surge of bond finance, most marked in industrials but also very substantial in utilities. Corporate bonds outstanding have tripled since 1950, and *industrial* bonds outstanding have increased over sevenfold.

The Growing Importance of Debentures

With the shift in expansion to the utilities and industrials came a shift to the use of debentures; in 1940, almost 20 percent of all outstanding bonds were unsecured. Over half of all industrial bonds were unsecured, and about one fifth of utility bonds; only about 7 percent of all railroad bonds were debentures.[17] Today, perhaps as much as one third of all outstanding bonds and half of industrial debentures are unsecured.

The shift toward debentures is even more striking if one looks at new issues in the two years 1900 and 1940 (Table 22–2). Less than 2 percent

---

[17] "Since World War II, equipment obligations have become the chief, almost the exclusive, source of external capital funds for the railroads. The I.C.C. reported new issues . . . exceeding $5,400 million from 1946 through 1957, as compared with less than $500 million of rail bond financing, and almost no stock financing except for refinancing purposes" (D. M. Street, "The Role of Equipment Obligations in Postwar Railroad Financing," *Journal of Finance*, September, 1960, p. 333).

TABLE 22-2

NEW ISSUES OF ALL BONDS AND UNSECURED BONDS
FOR SELECTED YEARS, 1920–63*
(Billions of Dollars)

Year	All Industries	Railroads	Public Utilities	Industrials
Par Amount of New Issues for Selected Years				
1900	$0.7	$0.3	$0.3	$0.1
1920	1.4	0.3	0.5	0.7
1940	2.4	0.5	1.3	0.7
1958†	9.5	0.1	4.7	4.7
1963†	9.6	0.3	3.7	5.6
Par Amount of New Unsecured Issues for Selected Years				
1900	$0.01	$0.01	$0.0	$0.0
1920	0.6	0.04	0.05	0.5
1940	0.6	0.0	0.2	0.4
1960	4.5	0.0	1.0	3.5

* Sources of data same as for Table 22–1, except for 1958 and 1963.
† Data for 1958 from A. B. Cohan, *Private Placements and Public Offerings: Market Shares since 1935* (Technical Paper No. 1; Chapel Hill: School of Business Administration, University of North Carolina, 1961), Tables 1–3, pp. 6–8.
Data for 1963 based on I. Friend, *Investment Banking and the New Issues Market* (Philadelphia: University of Pennsylvania Press, 1965), p. 110.

of new issues in 1900 were debentures; in 1940, they were over 25 percent (and had been almost half in the year 1920). Of all new industrial bonds issued in 1940, about 60 percent were unsecured; one in six utility bonds issued in 1940 were debentures. Today over half of all new bond issues are debentures, and three of every four industrial bonds are debentures.

TYPES OF BONDS IN RECENT CORPORATE FINANCE

Thus with the end of railroad expansion in the early twentieth century, corporate debt finance took on a wholly different complexion. Experience with railroad mortgages demonstrated the greater importance of earning power rather than liens for determining bond quality. It was true that mortgage bonds did provide greater relative protection than debentures in reorganization bargaining procedures *after* trouble ensued, but the presence of the specific pledge of assets in the bond had little to do with the primary fact: the danger of default.[18]

Although as early as 1904, unsecured new issues comprised over 20 percent of total new issues, the weight of unsecured bonds in *total bonds outstanding* remained small, owing to the large volume of old railroad

[18] Hickman, *Corporate Bond Quality and Investor Experience*, chap. vii.

bonds outstanding. Between 1920 and 1965, while outstanding bonds increased about 5.5 times, corporate debentures increased 20 times. If one is concerned with going concerns and current corporate financing techniques, it is clear that railroad finance in general and mortgage bonds in particular must not be permitted to dominate the discussion. Most of the varied detail of corporate securities owes its origin to railroad expansion and decline; it must not be thought that such detail is of importance in current corporate finance. Since World War II, railroads have done little new financing, and what they have done has been by means of equipment trust certificates.[19] New bonds have been originating in the utilities and industrials. The utilities—always heavy bond issuers—have been shifting steadily to the use of debentures, and industrials—always heavy debenture issuers—have been the fastest growing business sector and have been relying more heavily on debt financing.

Simplification of Bond Finance

As a consequence, recent bond finance has been simplified in the sense that debentures have been the principal mode of finance. Indeed, new wrinkles in debenture finance are developing just as, in the past, varieties of mortgage bond finance developed. And in the utilities, where mortgages remain of first importance, a simple form of mortgage predominates —a single, open-end first mortgage with no fancy retirement provisions.

Electric utilities, with their steady predictable growth and earnings, tend to borrow money simply by adding new series of the same mortgage bond to finance additional plant and equipment. Later mortgage issues have equal claim to assets with the earlier issues, although the contractual interest rate is likely to be different. The new fixed assets serve as security; and protective clauses specify that, say, only 60 or 70 cents of additional bonds may be sold for each $1 of new fixed assets pledged. And there is always a clause to provide adequate earnings coverage of the new contractual interest cost—say, that earnings in the preceding year must have equaled two to three times the interest requirement. It should be clear that no great change is involved for a utility to choose to issue debentures in a series instead of first mortgages in a series, provided that the assets and earnings coverage protective clauses are equally rigorous.

---

[19] The use of this device has also spread to other sectors of the transport industry, e.g., the airline industry, where it is used to finance the acquisition of expensive new commercial aircraft.

After all, when a corporation has nothing but debentures outstanding (with equal coverage covenants), in effect they share first claim on all assets just as do the various series of the one big open-end first mortgage.

Because of the varied separate mortgage issues typical of the railroad industry, rail debentures have a second-rate status; this factor must not be generalized to debentures as a whole. Would you say that a first mortgage on the New York, New Haven and Hartford Railroad was safer than an American Telephone & Telegraph debenture? Are X utility first mortgages safer than Y utility debentures? Given no unreasoned fear of debentures, utilities can avoid much expensive red tape by avoiding the mortgage arrangement; for example, it is necessary to file legal papers to "record the property" in all states where property is located, etc., when using the mortgage form; and the indenture will be complex and large— literally book size. Since, as we shall see in detail in Chapter 28, financial institutions are the principal purchasers of new corporate bonds, corporations can depend upon rational and informed buyers not having silly prejudices against debentures. However, some financial institutions are required by state law—legal lists—to give preference to mortgages. But even these statutory restrictions are slowly being removed; the drift to utility debentures would be even stronger if it were not for these restrictions which are traditionally difficult to erase quickly.

In industrials the predominant use of debentures in bond finance is not new. What is new is the surge in bond finance, and hence the *volume* of debentures and the variety of debenture forms developed in the last twenty years. As compared to utilities, industrials need to be very concerned about the burden of debt in terms of both interest charges and principal repayment. Lacking both the assured long life and stable earning power of utilities, industrial corporations must provide for the contingencies of cyclical loss of earning power and secular loss of demand for their product. Having learned that "cheap" bond finance is possible, industrials have not been deluded into thinking that they are utilities.

Varieties of Debenture Forms

For fear of possible default on interest, industrials have made considerable use of the income bond device, that is, industrial issues of *income debentures* are quite common. In earlier years, such bonds were exclusively the *outcome* of financial stress in railroads, where they were given in exchange for defaulted bonds; now, they are becoming common as devices used by industrials to avoid the legal consequences of possible *future* financial stress.[20] Of course, such income debentures must carry a higher interest rate than plain debentures, but the corporate tax savings through their use—as compared with the next alternative, preferred stock—is more than compensating.

To provide for retirement rather than automatic refunding of debt, industrial bonds almost always provide for sinking funds unless the issue is a *convertible debenture*. In short, industrial debentures are seldom issued without planning for repayment of principal at or before maturity. Convertible bonds in many cases may be thought of as term "loans" to be liquidated by the "proceeds" from "sale" of common stock in those cases where the corporations' expectations of growth and rising stock prices are realized. For the most part, then, convertibles should be analyzed as indirect common stock finance.[21] But in those cases where the stock price does not rise to the point where conversion becomes profitable for the bondholder, the bond will remain outstanding, and that possible continued burden must be anticipated. Note that convertible debentures have been issued in large quantities in recent years, and this exaggerates the true extent to which industrials have swung over to bond finance from equity finance.

Between 1900 and 1943, over $9 billion par amount of all bond offerings were convertibles; this was about 12 percent of the total value of all bond issues. Industrial convertibles were $3.3 billion, or almost 20 percent of all bonds issued by them over the period 1900–1943.[22] That proportion has been growing in recent years as industrials have resorted to income debentures, most of which are convertible. Probably one third to two fifths of all industrial bonds issued in recent years have been convertibles. An average of 15 percent of all corporate bonds, in dollar amount, issued between 1955 and 1965 were convertible; for example, in 1959, 26.6 percent of the number of all listed new issues were convertibles;[23] remembering that most utility issues are not convertible and that railroads issue few new bonds, it is clear that this 26.6 percent of the

---

[20] Income bonds have also been substituted for outstanding preferred stock as well as to raise new money. See S. M. Robbins, "A Bigger Role for Income Bonds," *Harvard Business Review*, November–December, 1955, pp. 100–114.

[21] See below, in Chapter 24.

[22] Hickman, *Statistical Measures of Corporate Bond Financing since 1900*, Table 118, pp. 211–14.

[23] *Forty-first Annual Report of the National Bureau of Economic Research* (New York, May, 1961), Table 11, p. 65.

number of all issues probably represents well over 50 percent of the number of industrial issues and over 25 percent of the dollar amount of all industrial bonds issued.

One other interesting form of industrial debenture that has become important recently is the *subordinated debenture*. This is a bond whose claim to assets comes after (i.e., is subordinated to) all other current or future creditors. In terms of claim to assets, then, it is like a "first" preferred stock. Note that income debentures are analogous to preferred stock in their claim to interest; subordinated debentures are analogous to preferred stocks in their claim to assets. The motivation to issue subordinated debentures is to protect or extend the corporation's future borrowing power by building up what is almost an equity base from the standpoint of senior creditors. This instrument was developed by sales finance companies whose particularly heavy recurrent needs for bank loans required that they be free to give prior creditor status to commercial banks in order to maintain their line of credit for use at times of heavy need. In recent years the instrument has been used by a variety of industrials and banks.[24]

All of these junior debentures have been invented to raise money at cheap debt costs without incurring the usual accessory burden of debt. In effect, a subordinated income debenture—and it is common today to combine these features—is a preferred stock which carries an interest charge that is doubly less than the preferred dividend would be: (1) Even the lowliest bond carries a lower coupon rate than the preferred would; and (2) the interest, unlike the dividend, is tax deductible by the corporation as an expense. Moreover, when a subordinated income debenture is made convertible as well, the maturity burden will also be removed if the price of common stock rises sufficiently in the future. All of these junior bonds, though often so junior as to be hardly distinguishable from preferred stock, are eligible investments for some financial institutions which are still legally restrained from purchasing stocks for their portfolios. It is easy to see why industrials make little use of preferred stocks in current corporate finance.[25] Nevertheless, we must consider preferred stock because it is still a method of finance of some importance to the

---

[24] Dow Chemical and Sinclair Oil, for example. See R. W. Johnson, "Subordinated Debentures: Debt That Serves as Equity," *Journal of Finance*, March, 1955, pp. 1–16.

[25] Of course, there are prudent limits to the use of such junior bonds, but the limits are more akin to preferred stock limits than debt limits. For example, the limits are usually expressed in terms of adequate earnings coverage (interest/earnings) rather than a traditional debt/equity limit.

utilities and because it *was* of considerable importance in the past; and hence there remain outstanding in the marketplace large amounts of old preferred stock. However, of the three principal types of securities issued by corporations to raise money today, it is by far the least important.

Corporate bonds, on the other hand, despite numerous changes in detail, played about the same overall role in financing corporations in the postwar period as in the first third of the century. However, great changes occurred in the "distribution of corporate bonds among issuers, the share of industrials increasing at the expense of railroads; in the distribution among investor groups, financial institutions, particularly insurance organizations, almost entirely supplanting individual holders; and in market techniques, direct placement and competitive bidding acquiring equal importance with negotiated public offerings. Another important change . . . is the increasing flexibility of corporate bonds as instruments of financing. This is evidenced in a wider range of maturity, security, and callability provisions and an increasing ease of modifying original bond indenture provisions, all contributing to adapting corporate bonds to the specific needs of individual borrower and lender groups."[26]

QUESTIONS AND PROBLEMS

1. Distinguish between:
    a) Indenture and debenture.
    b) Collateral trust and equipment trust certificates.
    c) Serial bonds and series bonds.
    d) After-acquired property clause and equal coverage covenant.
    e) Income bonds and preferred stocks.
2. Describe the simplification of the form of bonds over the last 25 years. What have been the causes of this trend towards simplification?
3. Why have "subordinated income debentures often with a convertibility feature" proven to be the most proper industrial type bond of the last decade?

SUGGESTED READINGS

BLOCH, E. "Pricing a Corporate Bond Issue—A Look Behind the Scenes," Federal Bank of New York *Monthly Review*, October, 1961, pp. 172–76.

HICKMAN, W. B. *Corporate Bond Quality and Investor Experience*, Princeton, N.J.: Princeton University Press, 1957.

---

[26] Goldsmith, *op. cit.*, pp. 232–33.

JOHNSON, R. W. "Subordinated Debentures: Debt that Serves as Equity," *Journal of Finance*, March, 1955, pp. 1–16.

ROBBINS, S. M. "A Bigger Role for Income Bonds," *Harvard Business Review*, November–December, 1965, pp. 100–114.

WINN, W. J., and HESS, A. "The Value of the Call Privilege," *Journal of Finance*, May, 1959, pp. 182–95.

Chapter 23

THE ISSUANCE OF PREFERRED STOCK

Preferred stocks are a hybrid security with a checkered history; sometimes, they were issued in lieu of common stocks and sometimes in place of bonds. Currently, they are of little importance for raising money; corporations tend to issue common stocks or bonds. But they were of importance in several past financial eras, and a complex array of outstanding preferred stocks is in existence. At the very least, we must survey their lively past, and the current languor, and explain their current unimportance in new finance.

SOME BASIC CHARACTERISTICS

Preferred stocks are preferred over common stocks as to dividends in the going corporation and as to assets in the case of liquidation or reorganization. Preferred stocks are not superior to common stocks; they are simply different from them. They have *prior but limited* claims to earnings and assets. This is the only flat statement that can be made about preferred stocks as a whole.

Preferred stocks, then, must be paid their full fixed dividends—say, 6 percent of $100 par, or an unchanging annual $6—before the common stockholders can be paid anything. This is not to say that they *must* be paid or, like bonds, default results. No, the dividend may be passed forever by the board of directors, whether or not cash is in fact available, with no necessary legal consequences. Of course, the board is under pressure to pay the dividend, for unless it does, the common can receive nothing. This is especially so if preferred dividends are *cumulative*, for then the arrears have to be paid in full before the common can be paid a penny. When a preferred stock is cumulative, it takes on the major characteristic of bonds—fixed prior charges. Such bondlike preferreds also tend to provide for their extinguishment by sinking funds or call provisions.

However, a preferred stock can also be more like a common stock. For example, it may be noncumulative but *participating;* i.e., it may provide that the preferred stock will get additional dividends, beyond its fixed preferred quota, *after* the common stock has gotten some dividends, too. This feature reduces the "limited" aspect of preferreds' claims. A great variety of participating schemes were dreamed up in gaudier financial days, but perhaps the typical one was "simple" participation. This type granted the preferred stock the right to an equal share with the common stock in further dividends, if declared, after the common stock had received a dividend equal in amount to the preferred's fixed dividend. Such preferreds clearly are like superior common stocks, just as the other broad class of preferreds is like inferior bonds.

EARLY VARIETIES OF PREFERRED STOCK
1830–1920

But why did corporations invent this hybrid form? For the most part, preferreds were issued in surges fostered by unusual developments in a particular industry or in the economy and financial markets of the country as a whole.

Railroad Preferreds: "Superior Common Stocks"

The first use of preferred stock in the United States was by the railroads during their first great building period in the late 1830's.[1] As was to be reflected throughout the growth period of this industry (1830–80), the need for funds was unceasing, and the immediately available earnings were slim. Therefore, the rails were unable to sell common stock, for lack of an enticing dividend record; and they were afraid to sell bonds, for fear of the fixed charges. These preferreds were thought of as a temporary means of finance; they were to become common stock as soon as a decent dividend record could be established. Thus, the preferred stocks of the mid- and late-nineteenth century were sold out of weakness and to cater to a public that had lost faith in the common stocks of the railroads. These were "superior common stock" types of preferred stock.

Later on, as the railroads experienced financial recapitalization, preferreds were also issued in exchange for defaulted bonds. A similar rash

[1] Baltimore & Ohio Railroad, 1836.

of noncash issuance of preferreds by the railroads occurred during the period of combining railroad systems, the consolidation movement of the end of the nineteenth century, when such shares were created to be exchanged for the issues of the company absorbed. (See Table 23–1.)

TABLE 23–1

NEW ISSUES OF PREFERRED STOCK, 1897–1964
(Millions of Dollars)

Years	Total	Industrials	Utilities	Railroads
1897–99	376	260	5	111
1900–1909	603	467	10	126
1910–19	1,851	1,644	192	15
1920–29	7,572	4,009	3,495	68
1930–39	1,535	857	779	−101
1940–49	4,380	3,048	1,417	− 85
1950–59	6,200	2,500	3,700	0
1960–64	1,500	700	1,200	0
(1955–64	4,000	1,500	2,500	0)

SOURCES: 1897–1949, R. W. Goldsmith, *A Study of Saving in the United States* (Princeton: Princeton University Press, 1955), Vol. I, Table V17, p. 493. 1950–1964, SEC *Annual Reports*, Table 8, Part 4, and *Statistical Bulletins*. (The industrial breakdown is a very rough estimate.)

Industrial Preferreds: "Inferior Bonds"

The industrials replaced the railroads as the chief issuer of preferred stocks before the turn of the century. But industrial preferred stocks were not issued under pressure or in lieu of stocks but as a normal means of raising leveraged funds without issuing bonds. In other words, industrial preferreds served as the means of trading on equity in an industry in which bonds were considered to be unsuitable, owing to the dangerously volatile earnings records of these unregulated cyclical business. Preferred stocks continued to be of importance for this reason in industrials until the early 1950's, when a combination of relative stability of earnings and the tax deductibility of interest (but not of dividends) led industrials to issue bonds instead of preferreds. But between 1897 and 1949, industrials issued over $10 billion of preferreds—about two thirds of all preferreds issued during the period.

THE HEYDAY OF PREFERRED STOCK: THE 1920'S

The other principal twentieth-century issuer of preferreds is the utility industry; and it alone, the latest to enter the field, remains today the only important issuer of these securities as a means of permanent finance.

Unlike the railroads, the utilities were under no financial pressure to issue preferreds; and unlike the industrials, they had little fear of issuing bonds. However, during the 1920's the public's fancy turned to stocks. The economy was prosperous and expanding, the railroad bond record gave bonds a bad name, and industrial preferreds were doing well. It was simply easy and cheap to market preferreds, and the utilities proceeded to do so.[2] Not only was it possible for utilities to sell preferreds at rates little higher than bonds, but it also had the effect of improving the quality of their outstanding bonds by expanding their "equity" cushion. Even today, this factor, which improves the legal list quality of the utilities' bonds, plus the prejudice of utility regulatory commissions in favor of "balanced" capital structures (i.e., structures including preferreds), results in more issues of preferreds by utilities than one would expect.

Industrials, too, took advantage of the 1920's mania for stocks, issuing over $4 billion of preferreds during the decade. Indeed, almost half of all preferred stock issued over the 52-year period 1897–1949 were marketed during the 1920's alone. These preferreds tended to be closer to common stocks than to bonds, often being noncumulative, participating, and nonredeemable. And like common stocks, they suffered badly in the 1930's, giving preferreds as bad a repute as common stocks.[3] They were seen as having all the disadvantages of common stocks and none of the advantages of bonds.

TYPICAL PREFERRED STOCKS OF RECENT YEARS

When next preferreds found favor again, it was as bondlike instruments rather than as "superior" common stocks. Between 1945 and the early 1950's—before, that is, the fear of another deep depression and hopes of tax cuts had been firmly dissipated—the last substantial surge of issues of straight (i.e., nonconvertible) preferred stock took place. These modern (straight) preferreds have tended to be far more uniform in character than the great variety of issues of the previous 100 years. They are almost uniformly *cumulative, nonparticipating, callable, nonvoting,* and *preferred as to assets.*[4] In short, they are being used as substitutes for bond issues; the majority of them even have sinking fund provisions.

---

[2] Moreover, preferreds also played a role in the creation of public utility holding companies, for, like bonds, preferreds are almost always nonvoting.

[3] "[The] average price of all domestic preferred stocks on the New York Stock Exchange declined over 70% in the 1929–1932 collapse . . ." (B. Graham and D. L. Dodd, *Security Analysis* [3d ed.; New York: McGraw-Hill Book Co., Inc., 1951], p. 355).

[4] D. A. Fergusson, "Recent Developments in Preferred Stock Financing," *Journal of Finance,* September, 1952, pp. 444–62.

Moreover, a fairly standard set of *protective provisions* are commonly attached to these preferreds, making their resemblance to bonds even more striking. These provisions serve to protect the preferreds' prior claim to assets and earnings. For example, the following provisions are typical:

1. Restriction of size of dividends on common stock to provide liquidity for future preferred dividends.
2. Limitations on further issues of the same preferred or of new issues of securities (such as bonds) that would have prior preferences, by a requirement that the preferred must vote approval by more than a majority, usually two thirds,[5] of such new issues or that certain financial ratios be satisfied.
3. In the event that dividends are passed, usually for two to six quarters, the preferred stockholders acquire voting power sufficient to elect a number of the members, sometimes a majority, of the board of directors of the corporation. This *contingent* voting power, of course, expires when dividends are resumed.
4. A statement about the preferreds' claim to assets, usually specifying that they are entitled to share the proceeds of assets in liquidation ahead of the common stock to the extent of the par or stated value plus dividend arrears.

Clearly, these are bondlike preferred stocks.

THE SMALL AND DECLINING ROLE OF PREFERRED STOCK IN MODERN CORPORATE FINANCE

Poor Substitutes for Bonds and Common Stocks

Although it is clear that recent preferreds have been issued in lieu of bonds, their advantages over bonds have been rapidly diminishing. As a consequence, new preferred issues have become an insignificant source of funds to corporations, with a slight exception in the case of utilities. As compared with bonds, preferreds have always been more costly; but presumably, the added expense was justified by the avoidance of the risky fixed charge and legal default possibilities connected with bonds. But the fear (and actuality) of bankruptcy have declined sharply in recent years, while the cost of preferreds has risen sharply. The fear has declined as the economy has demonstrated convincingly that it is depression-proof, though recession-prone; and the relative cost of preferreds has soared as

---

[5] This is usually called the veto power of preferred stock. Note that they are ordinarily nonvoting shares.

peak corporate tax rates (52 percent) become more and more widely and continuously applicable to growing and profitable corporations. The cost of preferred dividends was always a bit higher (say, 1 percent more) than interest on comparable bonds, owing to the contingency of the dividend; but since World War II the gap has widened, owing to the halving of the interest cost via tax deductibility.[6]

On the other hand, there is little motivation to issue the old speculative type of preferred stock as a substitute for common stock issues. Corporations in the past issued what were essentially "prior" common stocks in order to preserve voting control or because common stocks had a poor market, or in exchange for senior securities impaired by bad times. None of these factors are currently of general importance. With rare (headlined) exceptions, voting control is an academic matter; new common stocks have been in a seller's market for over a decade; and there has been no generalized financial distress for thirty years. Moreover, it used to be argued that in good times, it was wise to issue preferred instead of common stocks in order to avoid sharing lush profits with additional common stockholders. This argument, often alternatively expressed in terms of avoidance of dilution of the common stock interest and trading on the equity or in terms of the high cost of issuing common stock, is also of little current significance. Corporations today use the alternative of retained earnings rather than preferred issues to raise equity funds without resorting to the sale of additional common shares. And, if indirect equity is wanted via conversion, convertible bonds rather than convertible preferreds are the logical instrument.

In short, *today, preferred stocks play a small and declining role in financing corporations, for they are a poor substitute for alternative debt or equity issues.* However, they remain of some importance, owing to the issues still oustanding from earlier periods of heavy issuance, and their consequent place in corporate capitalizations. Furthermore, utilities continue to issue some bondlike preferreds for special reasons. To the limited degree that industrials still issue preferreds, they tend to be substitutes for—indeed, usually convertible into—common stock.

Preferred-Stock Finance Never of Great Importance

From Tables 23–2 to 23–4 it can easily be observed both how limited a role preferred stocks have played in financing corporations in the past

---

[6] If dividends were 6 percent and bond rates 5 percent, with a gap of 1 percent against preferreds, the gap becomes 3.5 percent when the effective cost of interest is cut to 2.5 percent against a 6 percent dividend cost.

fifty years and how sharp the falloff in their use has been since World War II. To the extent, always important and increasingly so in recent decades, that corporations finance through retention of earnings, the capitalization figures of these tables exaggerate the role of preferred stocks, and all security issuance, in corporate finance.[7]

Railroads.   The railroads, which introduced the preferred stock into American corporate finance, made their heaviest proportionate use of this security as long ago as the turn of the century; and even then, only 11 percent of the total, or 19 percent of fixed-charge railroad capitalization, consisted of preferred stocks. The amount of outstanding railroad preferred stock has been *falling* ever since the late 1930's. Since that time the roads have financed their limited investment by sale of equipment trust certificates and via retained earnings. New preferred issues are almost unknown there today; indeed, between 1950 and 1961, outstanding railroad preferreds fell by $800 million, or 40 percent! Today, there are but $1.2 billion worth outstanding, and these comprise but 7 percent of total railroad capitalization, or 11 percent of fixed-charge capitalization. Except for some market interest in a handful of widely varied outstanding issues, railroad preferred stocks are of little concern today.

Utilities: The Last Stronghold.   The situation is quite different in the electric utilities. Here, 12.5 percent of total and 17 percent of fixed-charge capitalization consists of preferred stocks today, but even this is down almost two fifths from the 1946 peaks of 17 percent and 24 percent. Considering that internal finance is of little help in utility finance, preferred issues do supply a significant share of total utility finance. But utilities did not make heavy use of such finance until after World War I, and it now looks as though post–World War II marks the turn toward heavier bond finance in place of preferred stock finance.

Between 1946 and 1961, outstanding bonds increased by three and a half times, from $6.2 to $22 billion, while preferred issues doubled, rising from $2 to $4.5 billion. Of course, this is a substantial increase in preferred stock outstanding, and this alone prevented straight preferred stocks from being written off as a totally antiquarian means of finance. Over the same 15-year period, industrials issued but $1 billion additional

---

[7] To the extent that the common stock figures in these tables do not include the total proceeds received from their sale (only the par value and not the premium over par or the paid-in surplus), the capitalization figures overestimate the significance of preferred and bond issues as against common stock issues. Nevertheless, the capitalization figures do reflect the broad trends in security flotation. A more limited but more accurate view of the trends is provided by considering the relationship of preferred to preferred plus bonds as well as to total capitalization.

TABLE 23–2

CAPITALIZATION OF RAILROADS, SELECTED YEARS, 1890–1957

	(Billions of Dollars)				The Ratio of Preferred to:	
Year	Bonded Debt	Common Stock	Pre- ferred Stock	Total Capital- ization	Total Capital- ization	Fixed- Charge Capital- ization
1890	4.6	3.8	0.6	9.0	0.07	0.12
1900	5.6	4.5	1.3	11.4	0.11	0.19
1910	10.3	6.7	1.4	18.4	0.08	0.12
1920	12.8	7.2	1.9	21.9	0.09	0.13
1930	14.2	8.0	2.1	24.3	0.09	0.13
1940	13.3	8.0	2.1	23.4	0.09	0.14
1950	10.9	7.5	2.0	20.4	0.10	0.15
1957	10.6	6.7	1.4	18.7	0.07	0.11
1961	9.8	5.8	1.2	16.8	0.07	0.11

SOURCE: U.S. Bureau of the Census, *Historical Statistics of the United States: Colonial Times to 1957* (Washington, D.C.: U.S. Government Printing Office, 1960), Series Q 95–105, pp. 432–33; and *Historical Statistics, Continuations to 1962 and Revisions*, p. 62.

preferreds, so that if utilities had not been issuing preferreds, railroad retirements would have depressed total outstanding preferreds. After all, total outstanding preferred stock reached a peak of $19.5 billion in the mid-1930's; today, the total is about $17.7 billion, and it would be down further if it were not for utility finance. Of course, by contrast, totals of outstanding common stock and bonds have been increasing continuously by sizable amounts.

But why do utilities alone continue to issue substantial quantities of preferred stocks? The answer is that the relatively higher cost of pre- ferreds versus bonds is less pressing in their industry because:

1. As a regulated monopolistic industry, its prices are set to cover cost, including finance costs, and demand is unaffected by slight price in- creases. Thus, the competitive pressure to finance as cheaply as pos- sible is not so pressing as it is for industrials.
2. Moreover, many of the regulatory commissions believe preferred stocks belong in every capital structure for "balance." It is not clear why they believe this; but as long as they do, utilities will be encouraged to incur unnecessarily high costs of finance.[8]

---

[8] Perhaps it is thought that the presence of preferreds in the capitalization keeps down the interest charges on bonds by increasing the equity cushion. But this is surely not a significant effect, considering how bondlike utility preferreds are. (If the pre- ferreds are convertible, they should be considered as common stocks in effect.)

TABLE 23-3

CAPITALIZATION OF CLASS A & B ELECTRIC UTILITIES,
SELECTED YEARS, 1902-61

| | (Billions of Dollars) | | | | The Ratio of Preferred to: | |
Year	Bonded Debt	Common Stock	Pre- ferred Stock	Total Capital- ization	Total Capital- ization	Fixed- Charge Capital- ization
1902	0.3	0.3	0.02	0.62	0.03	0.06
1907	0.6	0.7	0.08	1.4	0.06	0.12
1917	1.3	1.3	0.3	2.9	0.10	0.17
1927	5.3	3.7	1.4	10.4	0.14	0.21
1932	6.9	4.8	2.1	13.8	0.15	0.23
1937	6.9	4.3	2.1	13.3	0.16	0.23
1946	6.2	3.8	2.0	12.0	0.17	0.24
1956	15.2	7.2	3.7	26.1	0.14	0.195
1961	22.0	9.3	4.5	35.8	0.125	0.17

SOURCES: 1902–32: Raymond W. Goldsmith, *A Study of Saving in the United States* (Princeton: P.ᵢ ᵗⁱᵒⁿ University Press 1955) Vol I Table V33, p, 515. 1937–56: Federal Power Commis- ᵘⁱᵒⁿ *Statistics of Electric Utilities in the United States* (Washington, D.U., U.b. Government Printing Office, 1937, 1946, 1956, and 1962).

3. The dividend rate that is required to sell preferreds is lower than one would expect, owing to the demand of some investing institutions to purchase them. That is, the margin by which the dividend rate would normally have to exceed the interest rate is obliterated in a seller's market. Certain investing institutions, such as nonlife insurance com- panies, are particularly keen to add preferreds to their portfolios be- cause dividend receipts, unlike interest, are not subject to the full corporate tax treatment—say, 50 percent—but rather are treated as intercorporate transfer payments and taxed at a far lower rate—say, 7.5 percent.[9] Under these conditions, "A 3¾% preferred stock will yield . . . [an investing] corporation . . . about the same net re- turn as a 6% bond, or about twice as large a net return as a 3% bond."[10] Still other institutions, such as life insurance companies, are specially taxed at much lower rates than the corporate income tax; in these cases, almost the whole excess of preferred dividends over com- parable bond interest will become income.

Nevertheless, the utilities too are currently swinging over toward a heavier relative use of bonded fixed charges instead of preferred fixed

---

[9] Only 15 percent of dividend receipts (intercorporate transfers), as against the whole of interest receipts, are subject to the corporate tax. Thus, with a 50 percent cor- porate tax rate, the effective tax on dividends received is only 7.5 pecent.
[10] Graham and Dodd, *op. cit.*, p. 360 n.

TABLE 23–4

CAPITALIZATION OF INDUSTRIALS ("ALL OTHER" INDUSTRIES),*
SELECTED YEARS, 1927–61

| | (Billions of Dollars) | | | | The Ratio of Preferred to: | |
| | | | | | | Fixed-Charge Capitalization |
Year	Bonded Debt	Common Stock	Pre-ferred Stock	Total Capital-ization	Total Capital-ization	Fixed-Charge Capital-ization
1927	18.4	62.7	14.4	95.5	0.15	0.44
1932	25.6	65.5	15.0	106.1	0.14	0.37
1937	28.4	64.9	14.2	107.5	0.13	0.33
1946	28.0	56.8	10.9	95.7	0.11	0.28
1956	72.6	82.3	10.7	165.6	0.06	0.13
1961	133.0	113.6	12.0	259.0	0.045	0.08

* Computed by removing railroad and electric utility stocks and bonds from totals for all industries.

SOURCE: U.S. Bureau of the Census, *Historical Statistics of the United States: Colonial Times to 1957* (Washington, D.C.: U.S. Government Printing Office, 1960), Series V 65–97, pp. 580–81; also *Historical Statistics Continuations to 1962*, p. 80.

charges. But this is the last major source of new nonconvertible preferred stock in America; slight tax and administrative changes would probably close this last avenue as well.

Industrials. The unregulated industries (the "industrials") have been making sharply less use of preferreds, both relatively and absolutely, ever since the stock mania of the late 1920's. In 1927, preferred stock comprised 15 percent of industrials' total and 44 percent of their fixed-charge capitalizations; by 1961 the proportions had fallen to 4.5 percent and 8 percent, respectively. Outstanding preferreds fell from $15 billion in 1932 to $12 billion in 1961.

However, these overall statistics conceal a further significant shift in industrials' use of preferred stocks. During the 1920's, speculative preferreds predominated; but during the early post–World War II period, industrials used bondlike preferreds to raise some of the large amount of funds needed for the postwar expansion. Today, industrials have shifted to bonds from bondlike preferreds, but some industrials in the last five years have begun to experiment importantly with speculative preferreds, especially with convertible common-stock-like preferreds. But these are only short-run issues, likely to be outstanding only a few years. They are essentially common stocks; the high cost of the few years of preferred charges are thought to be a small price to pay for what is essentially an issue of delayed common stock at a higher than current market price.

In any case, in the most recent period for which complete statistics are available (1946–61), industrials expanded their bonded debt by $105 billion, while their total preferreds outstanding increased by $1 billion. Whatever the future of speculative preferreds may be, they cannot much affect this massive shift from the use of preferred stock finance to that of bonds. As recently as 1937, industrial bonds outstanding were but twice the total of preferreds outstanding; in 1961 the multiple was eleven times! Industrials have resorted to the costly sale of common stocks as well as to cheap debt finance, but they have effectively rejected preferred stock finance. Clearly, we are well on our way back to simple industrial capitalizations. The hybrid preferred stock has been found to have all the disadvantages of bonds but not their low cost, and none of the advantages of common stock and almost as high a cost.

The Overall View

An overall view of the extent to which bonds in recent years have been supplanting preferred stocks as *the* fixed-charge technique of corporate finance can be seen in Table 23–5. Here, you will see that while the total of preferreds outstanding is about the same as in 1926, bonded debt has increased more than fivefold. The ratio of preferred stock to bonds has fallen from more than 1:2 in 1926 to about 1:9 in 1961. While preferred stocks remain of some importance to investors (and in courses in investment), they are of little importance in contemporary corporate finance.

TABLE 23–5

OUTSTANDING FIXED-CHARGE SECURITIES, ALL INDUSTRIES COMBINED,
SELECTED YEARS, 1926–61

	(Billions of Dollars)			Ratio	
Year	Preferred Stock	Bonded Debt	Total Liabilities and Net Worth	Preferred $(L + NW)$	Bonds $(L + NW)$
1926	17.1	31.8	262.2	0.07	0.12
1930	19.1	50.3	334.0	0.06	0.15
1935	19.5	49.8	303.2	0.06	0.16
1940	17.1	49.2	320.5	0.05	0.15
1945	14.8	41.0	441.5	0.03	0.09
1950	14.9	65.7	598.4	0.03	0.11
1955	15.8	98.4	888.6	0.02	0.11
1961	17.7	165.0	1,289.0	0.00	0.13

SOURCE: U.S. Bureau of the Census, *Historical Statistics of the United States: Colonial Times to 1957* (Washington, D.C.: U.S. Government Printing Office, 1960), Series V 65–97, pp. 580–81; and *Historical Statistics Continuations to 1962*, p. 80.

Perhaps the rise and fall of preferred stock can most succinctly be described by noting that preferred provided 2.5 percent of all corporate funds at the turn of the century, as much as 5 percent in the 1920's, and but 1 percent in the 1950's with still less than that in the 1960's to date.

The Recent Sharp Decline in Preferred Stock Issues for Cash and Future Prospects

In terms of new issues for cash—the focus of business's interest in securities markets—preferred stocks are obviously unimportant. These figures (see Table 23–6) reveal that in the 1960's, of the average annual $12 billion in *cash raised by sale of securities by corporations*, only $400 million, or *less than 4 percent of the total cash, was raised via sale of preferred stock*. The best percentage year that preferreds can show for the whole period of the Securities and Exchange Commission figures— 1935–64—is about 10 percent, and that was during the immediate post-World War II period; the average for the whole period was but 8 percent, with the trend down steadily from the middle of the span of years. (See Figure 23–1.)

A revival of preferred stock financing is quite unlikely. It might be thought that the vast expansion of bonded indebtedness would soon have

FIGURE 23–1

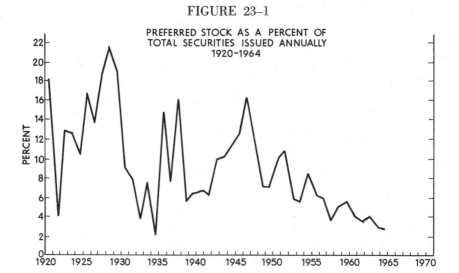

Source: W. C. Freund, *Investment Fundamentals* (New York: American Bankers Association, 1966), p. 116.

to come to a halt and, given that common stock financing is expensive, that preferred stock finance might surge as a pleasant hedging alternative. This is unlikely because the great expansion of bonded debt has been accompanied by a similarly great wave of earnings retention which has

TABLE 23–6

New Securities Offered for Cash Sale in the
United States, 1935–64
(Billions of Dollars)

Years	Pre-ferred Stock	Bonds and Notes	Common Stock	Total All Securities
1935–39	0.9	11.9	0.7	13.5
Average per year	0.2	2.4	0.1	2.7
1940–44	1.0	9.4	0.5	10.9
Average per year	0.2	1.9	0.1	2.2
1945–49	3.6	25.6	3.4	32.6
Average per year	0.7	5.1	0.7	6.5
1950–54	3.4	32.8	5.9	42.1
Average per year	0.7	6.5	1.2	8.4
1955–59	2.8	42.2	10.4	55.4
Average per year	0.6	8.4	2.1	11.1
1960–64	1.9	48.1	10.0	60.0
Average per year	0.4	9.6	2.0	12.0
1935–64	13.6	170.0	30.9	214.5
Average per year	0.4	5.7	1.0	7.1

Source: Securities and Exchange Commission, *Annual Reports*, Table 3, Part 2; and *Statistical Releases*.

kept the debt/equity ratio from deteriorating even though little net preferred stock and relatively small amounts of common stock have been sold for cash in the postwar years. Moreover, a good proportion of the increased debt is convertible and will add to the equity base during future periods of expansion of the economy and of increasing stock prices.

If there is to be a revival of sales of preferred stock, it will most likely be of convertible preferreds. But these would be "superior stock" types rather than the "inferior bond" types. The latter seem doomed to decline further; those corporations which still fear to issue normal bonds will resort increasingly to *income* bonds rather than to preferreds.[11] Thus, those preferred issues that are likely to be of contemporary interest will be convertible issues; and these, in the great majority of cases, are not likely to remain outstanding for long. The bondlike preferred stock is dying;

---

[11] Except in terms of cost to the corporation, what substantial differences are there between subordinated income debentures and bondlike preferred stocks?

and although the stock-type preferred may flourish, it is a temporary security that is often best analyzed as if it were a common stock.

QUESTIONS AND PROBLEMS

1. Describe the typical preferred stock of the post-World War II years.
2. What are the principal factors accounting for the sharp secular decline in the role of preferred stock in financing corporations? Indicate several of the ways in which one can measure the extent of this sharp decline.
3. Why do preferred stocks continue to have some importance as a source of finance for public utilities? Does the instrument used differ from that used by industrials?
4. Consider some possible (and not unreasonable) financial developments that might bring preferred stocks back into favor. What probabilities do you attach to these expected developments?

SUGGESTED READINGS

DONALDSON, G. "In Defense of Preferred Stock," *Harvard Business Review*, July–August, 1962, pp. 123–36.

FERGUSON, D. A. "Recent Developments in Preferred Stock Finance," *Journal of Finance*, September, 1952, pp. 447–62.

————. "Preferred Stock Valuation in Recapitalization," *Journal of Finance*, March, 1958, pp. 48–69.

Chapter 24

THE ISSUANCE OF CONVERTIBLE
PREFERRED STOCKS AND BONDS

THE RATIONALE OF CONVERTIBILITY

We have now seen that two of the three traditional reasons for issuing preferred stocks are of little importance today. These rejected two are: (1) it would be dangerous to control of the corporation to issue common stock, and (2) it would be dangerous to solvency to issue bonds. However, a third traditional argument with more merit is that at certain times the market for common stock is so poor, and the need to build up the equity base so pressing, that *convertible* preferreds might prove a happy *temporary* means of finance.

Whenever the word *convertible* is used in this discussion, it means convertible into common stock. This discussion holds for convertible bonds as well as for convertible preferred stocks. The right to convert is stated in the issue in the form of either a conversion ratio or a conversion price. That is, either each share of preferred is convertible into a given number of common shares—say, one for two—or a $100 par preferred is convertible into common at a price of $50. (If the option were stated as the right to convert at a price of $25 a share of common, then, of course, the implied conversion ratio is one preferred equals four common, when, as is usually the case, the preferred par is $100.) Obviously, the common stock cannot be selling at or above the conversion parity, or it would have paid the corporation to issue common stock in the first place. Rather, the common stock typically will be selling in the market at, say, $35 a share at the time the conversion price of $50 is offered to preferred stock purchasers. The new convertible is sold (and bought) in *anticipation* of a rise in the market price of the common towards and beyond $50.

THE ATTRACTIVENESS OF CONVERTIBLES
TO THE ISSUER

But why does the issuer choose to issue convertibles? Answer: to economize on finance costs. First, the dividend that must be offered when selling a preferred stock is less when the issue is convertible, other things being equal, than when it is not.[1] In other words, the convertibility privilege "sweetens" the security, makes it more attractive, expands the demand for it, and thus lowers the effective rate that must be paid to clear the market. As long as the convertible is outstanding, the corporation will be saving on annual fixed charges. However, this cannot be the main reason, for, as we have seen, it is cheaper to have bond fixed charges outstanding.

The second reason, then, is that it is expected that the preferred and its fixed cost will be extinguished in the near future when the market price of the common stock rises to and beyond the conversion parity. In other words, the *principal purpose of issuing convertible preferreds is to sell common stock at tomorrow's higher price but to receive the proceeds today.* If events proceed as the issuing corporation expects, it will in effect have received $100 for two shares of common stock which, if sold immediately and directly, would only have brought in $70.

Of course, if the common stock does not rise to the conversion price, the preferred will remain outstanding. But the corporation must have good reason for thinking that the common stock will rise in price, for it would prefer to have fixed-charge bonds remain outstanding rather than fixed-charged preferred stock. Some of the reasons why a corporation may consider its common stock to be temporarily undervalued in the market are:

1. A general cyclical stock market decline that sweeps all stock prices down, regardless of individual merit.
2. A few recent years of poor company or industry earnings that are in process of being reversed but meanwhile have caused the common stock to sell at distress prices.
3. The corporation is about to take off into a period of great expansion and earnings growth, and the market is likely to increase the multiple of earnings (or the price/earnings ratio) at which the stock sells.

If the issuer's but not the market's expectations are realized, it will, in effect have sold common stock gradually[2] at low cost (high proceeds).

---

[1] Or the preferred is sold at a straight dividend rate but at a premium over par.

Moreover, this indirect or delayed action sale of common stock saves on flotation costs, for it usually costs more in marketing fees to float common stock than preferred stock.[3] All this is very well from the seller's point of view, but what of the buyer?

THE ATTRACTIVENESS OF CONVERTIBLES
TO THE PURCHASER

Why does the purchaser choose to buy convertible issues? After all, if he thinks the common stock is going to rise, he could buy the common stock directly at today's low price and make even greater capital gains. For example, if he buys two common shares today at $35 each and the stock rises to $50, he makes a capital gain of $30; whereas if he bought the convertible preferred, his capital gains would only begin to accrue if the common stock rises beyond $50. That is, the preferred stock will rise proportionately with the common stock only *after* the conversion parity has been surpassed. Therefore, the purchaser of convertible preferreds must be attracted by the "hedging" aspect of the security, i.e., he must value the fixed rate of return he gets so long as the common stock does *not* rise beyond the conversion parity more than he values the capital gain he foregoes by not buying the common stock directly.

Such hedging is typical of the behavior of some important financial institutions and of individual investors during periods of uncertainty and change. Note that even if the common stock never reaches the conversion parity level, the preferred stock presumably will sell at its intrinsic or investment value, i.e., the value of the capitalized fixed dividends.[4] As long as the dividend is paid, and interest rates have not altered since the time of issuance, the stock will sell at par—the price originally paid for it; there is obviously much more risk involved on the downside if one buys the common stock directly. If one is concerned above all to preserve one's principal and to maintain a steady return on it, common stocks are an

---

[2] "In effect, a corporation in issuing a convertible has agreed to keep its books open for common stock subscriptions for a number of years" (C. J. Pilcher, *Raising Capital with Convertible Securities* ["Michigan Business Studies," Vol. XII, No. 2; Ann Arbor: University of Michigian Press, 1955], p. 80). By contrast, sale of common stock directly usually involves underpricing to allow for the depressing effect of the large influx of supply on market price.

[3] Indeed, it is usual to sell new blocs of common stock at a discount from its market price to old stockholders while, in effect, the common stock is sold at a premium via sale of convertible preferreds.

[4] Of course, the convertible issue will sell at more than its investment value as long as some hope remains that the conversion point will be reached in the future. The value of such preferreds is a combination of their investment value and their conversion value. The floor is set by the investment value.

inappropriate investment. Convertibles are of interest because they provide principal assurance while introducing some speculative interest.

While individual investors are only fitfully attracted to convertibles—there is usually an element of fad or fashion involved—financial institutions such as insurance companies provide a more stable demand. Such institutions, being restricted in the amount of common stocks they can legally buy,[5] are enabled to make the capital gains associated with rising common stock prices without buying common stocks. Of course, they need never convert their preferred into the common to realize the gain; they can simply sell the preferred in the open market, where its price via arbitrage will fully reflect the rise in the price of the common.[6]

Individuals are also attracted to convertibles because of easier margin requirements. For example, in mid-1966, margin requirements were such that one had to put up 70 percent of the purchase price in cash in buying the stock of company A but only 10–20 percent to buy that same company's bonds; the latter easy credit was also available on company A's convertible bonds. A speculator in company A's stock might find it advantageous to carry out his operations via the convertible bonds, offsetting the hedge implicit in the convertibles with augmented personal leverage.

CONVERTIBLES AS DELAYED COMMON STOCK ISSUES

But the issuer can and usually does force conversion once the common stock is selling above the conversion parity price; after all, the principal purpose of the convertible issue was to sell common stock indirectly, not to save money on fixed charges. The issuer makes sure that he will be able to force conversion by including a call provision in the instrument. Typically, a $100 par preferred stock will be callable at a premium of $3 to $6. Thus, if the common stock is selling at $60 and the 1:2 convertible preferred at $120, any holder of the preferred will surely not turn his preferred stock back to the company for $105. Rather, he will sell the preferred in the market to one who will convert to common, or he will convert to common himself.

---

[5] "The life insurance companies at the close of 1953 had committed nearly as many funds in convertible securities as the 1.1% of total assets they invested in residual equities" (Pilcher, *op. cit.*, p. 129).

[6] And if the conversion privilege proves of no value, the institution has merely lost the extra return it would have received annually if it had chosen a nonconvertible issue of equal investment merit.

The option to call and force conversion is necessary, for there will always be holders of the issue (for example, insurance companies) who may want to continue to receive the annual fixed dividend, or individuals who do not want to realize and pay the tax on their capital gains. Since the corporation's aim in issuing convertibles is to sell common stock at an advantageous price, it accomplishes that task as soon as the price rises to conversion parity. Any gain beyond that point swells the individual's, not the corporation's, bank account. Thus, insofar as preferred stocks or bonds are convertibles, they are for the most part really common stocks and just emergency or temporary preferred stocks or bonds.

Recent convertibles have clearly been issued as delayed equities and not merely as cheap debt or preferreds. Convertibility today is not used merely to sweeten the security, i.e., to get a lower fixed charge; rather it is used to obtain *equity* funds cheaply. A recent study of new convertibles shows that the great majority were "interested in raising equity capital when they sold convertibles" and that they could have sold debt or common stock if they had wanted.[7] Conversion was expected (and did occur) within three years of issuance for the price of the common stock was expected in that time to reach the conversion point. After that point, conversion was either forced via call or induced via increasing cash dividends on the common stock.

CURRENT IMPORTANCE OF CONVERTIBLE PREFERRED STOCKS AND BONDS

But how important are convertible securities? If they form a large part of recent preferred issues, then the falloff in true preferred stocks is even greater than our discussion thus far has shown. This is indeed the case.

Further, if convertibles comprise a large part of recent bond issues, as is the case, then the great rise in bond finance outlined in Chapters 21–22 was somewhat overdrawn. It also follows that the importance of common stock finance thus far has been underemphasized insofar as much of what has been counted as preferred or bonds from first issuance statistics becomes in time common stock.

Between 1933 and 1952, one third of the number[8] of all new

---

[7] E. F. Brigham, "An Analysis of Convertible Debentures," *The Journal of Finance*, March, 1966, p. 54. See also K. L. Broman, "The Use of Convertible Subordinated Debentures . . . 1949–1959," *Quarterly Review of Economics and Business*, Spring, 1963, pp. 63–75.

[8] It is likely that the percentages would be similar if the par value rather than the number of new issues had been used, for both large and small companies alike issued the convertibles.

preferred stocks were convertibles. Of course, the percentage varied from year to year—the range was 19 percent to 60 percent—but even the lowest year shows a substantial proportion. As one would expect, industrial issues comprised almost three quarters of the number of all convertible preferreds issued over this 20-year period, with utilities issuing most of the remainder. The very great importance of convertibles to industrials is shown by the fact that almost half of all industrial preferred stocks issued over the 1933–52 span were convertible, while but 10 percent of all utility preferreds were convertibles.[9]

This means that, slim as the issues of industrial preferred have been in recent years, they are even less important than they seemed, for almost half of them are, in effect, common stock issues. Thus, the field for permanent preferred stock finance is largely restricted to utility issues.

There is good reason to believe that in the years since 1952 the issuance of convertible preferreds has become even more important. While statistics for preferred convertibles have not been published, those for convertible bonds are available; and it has been observed that "years of popularity and unpopularity for convertibles of both types of senior issues seem to coincide."[10]

Between 1933 and 1952, about 7 percent of the number of bonds issued were convertible; while since 1953, almost 10 percent have been convertible.[11] Assuming that the trend in preferred issues has been similar, it is likely that since 1953, over half of all preferred stock issued was convertible, and that probably more than three quarters of industrial preferreds were convertible.

There are no available figures on the annual volume of conversion of preferred stock into common stock, but it is possible that such conversions are fully equal in value to new convertibles issued; combining this with calls, etc., of straight preferreds may well mean that outstanding preferred stock is once more declining absolutely as well as relatively as a component of corporate capitalization.

More recent statistics are available for conversions of bonds. These indicate that the value of new issues of convertible bonds is just about offset by the value of old convertible bonds surrendered for conversion. Between 1948 and 1958, corporations sold about $5.8 billion of new convertible

---

9 Pilcher, *op. cit.*, Tables 1, 2, 5, and 6 in chap. ii.

10 *Ibid.*, p. 14.

11 W. B. Hickman, *The Volume of Corporate Bond Financing* (Princeton: Princeton University Press, 1953), Vol. I, Table A7, p. 276; and Vol. III, Table 117, p. 210; National Bureau of Economic Research, *Forty-first Annual Report* (New York, May, 1961), Table 11, p. 65; and Securities and Exchange Commission, *Statistical Releases.*

bonds, while during the same period about $5.5 billion of old bonds were converted into stock.[12]

Obviously, there is something to be said for simply not counting new convertible preferreds or bonds in the totals of new issues of these securities. Applying this idea to trends in recent issues would reduce the current apparent total of new preferreds by more than 50 percent, but the large apparent total of new bonds would be reduced at most by only about 10 percent. This would still leave bonds in a commanding position as the major external fund-raising technique of corporations.

Further, this approach reminds us that the apparently relatively small size of new common stock issues should be supplemented by the annual conversion of bonds and preferred. For example, if, as seems likely for the years 1960–64, conversions to common stock were about $1 billion a year, this must be taken into account, for the annual average of new issues of common stock *sold for cash* over this same recent period was but $2 billion. Note that *the use of common stock as a method of raising corporate funds is increased by 50 percent if conversions as well as cash sales are considered.* Obviously, then, common stock is more important and preferred stock less important than indicated by the most widely used statistics. Look back at Table 23–6 on page 405. There, we saw that the average annual cash issues for the period 1960–64 were $0.4 billion of preferred, $2.0 billion of common, and $9.6 billion of bonds. If we allow for $1 billion of conversions, the totals become $0.2 billion, $3.0 billion, and $6.8 billion, respectively.[13]

---

[12] R. M. Soldofsky, *Lectures in Financial Management* (Ames: Iowa State University, 1960), Tables 1 and 2 on pp. 28 and 29.

[13] If we take the averages per year for the whole span of Table 23–6—1935–64—we have:

Preferred stock	$0.4 billion
Bonds	5.7
Common stock	1.0
Total	$7.1 billion

Assuming that over this 30 year period a modest 25 percent of preferred stocks and 10 percent of bonds issued for cash were convertible and were annually converted at these rates, then the adjusted totals would become:

Preferred stock	$0.3 billion
Bonds	5.1
Common stock	1.7
Total	$7.1 billion

Common stock adjusted would be not 14 percent of total securities but 24 percent, and would be one third the size of bonds instead of but one sixth. Instead of appearing to be almost as negligible a factor as preferred stock, common stock is almost six times as large a factor as preferred.

Bonds remain of great significance, but preferred stocks become even less important, *and* the role of common stocks as a method of external finance takes on a new dimension. Instead of being less than one fourth as important as bonds, they become, in fact, almost half as important. While we may justifiably de-emphasize *bondlike* preferred stocks in contemporary corporate finance, common stocks—currently providing almost 30 percent of finance by security issuance—merit careful consideration.

QUESTIONS AND PROBLEMS

1. What factors account for the recent popularity of convertibles—
   a) From the point of view of the issuer?
   b) From the point of view of the purchaser?
2. What evidence is there that the convertible feature has been used primarily as an indirect way to sell common stock rather than as a way of reducing the fixed charges?
3. a) How important a role do convertible securities play in financing corporations today?
   b) If new convertibles are issued annually on average at just about the the same rate that old issues are being converted, how should statistics on new issues of securities for cash (preferred, common, and bonds) be altered to allow for the fact.

SUGGESTED READINGS

BAUMOL, W. J.; MALKIEL, B. J.; and QUANDT, R. E. "The Valuation of Convertible Securities," *Quarterly Journal of Economics*, February, 1966, pp. 48–59.

BRIGHAM, E. F. "An Analysis of Convertible Debentures—Theory and Some Empirical Evidence," *Journal of Finance*, March, 1966, pp. 35–54.

BROMAN, K. L. "The Use of Convertible Subordinated Debentures by Industrial Firms, 1949–1959," *Quarterly Review of Economics and Business*, Spring, 1963, pp. 63–75.

PILCHER, C. J. *Raising Capital with Convertible Securities.* Ann Arbor, Mich.: University of Michigan, 1955.

POENSGEN, O. H. "The Valuation of Convertible Bonds," *Industrial Management Review*, Fall, 1965, pp. 77–99; and Spring, 1966, pp. 83–98.

Chapter 25

THE ISSUANCE OF COMMON STOCK

THE NATURE AND NECESSITY OF COMMON STOCK FINANCE

Common stock is a much simpler and yet more basic type of security than either preferred stock or bonds. A corporation need not—and, indeed, many industrials do not—sell bonds or preferreds. But in order to exist, a corporation must have common stock outstanding, i.e., it must have owners. Consider the formation of a new corporation. Essentially what happens is that in exchange for money (or property or services or other assets of value), the newly chartered corporation prints up shares of common stock and gives them to the asset contributors; these shares represent the donors' ownership interest in the corporation.

Stockholders' Equity

To illustrate, let us use a simplified set of balance sheets. Assume that the corporation sells 5,000 shares of common stock at a price of $20 a share. The balance sheet will show:

ASSETS		LIABILITIES AND NET WORTH	
Cash	$100,000	Common stock	$100,000

It is clear that the $100,000 entry on the right represents net worth, for there are no liabilities or preferred stock outstanding; the common stockholders have an equity or a claim to the net worth of the corporation, which in this case is the $100,000 they have just contributed. Of course, the corporate management, i.e., the board of directors elected by the common stockholders, will turn the cash into earning assets by buying machines, raw materials, etc., in order to carry out the chartered purpose of the corporation—say, to manufacture shoes. After they have done this, the balance sheet will show:

415

ASSETS		LIABILITIES AND NET WORTH	
Cash	$ 5,000	Common stock	$100,000
Machinery	65,000		
Materials	30,000		
	$100,000		$100,000

Stockholders' Claim to Earnings

The stockholders' equity is unchanged; it is $100,000. But their claims are not merely to assets, but to earnings on assets or net worth. In fact, if the corporation soon sought to liquidate itself—to turn all the assets back into cash and to return the cash to the stockholders—it would be unlikely to realize the full $100,000. But investors buy stock principally on the going concern's prospects of earnings on assets.

Now, let the corporation have a good first year, in which it makes a 10 percent net return on its assets and equity. For simplicity, assume that this good profit shows up wholly in the cash account on the balance sheet. The asset side of the balance sheet will then show:

ASSETS	
Cash	$ 15,000
Machinery	65,000
Materials	30,000
	$110,000

Since the corporation has incurred no debt and sold no new securities, the L + NW side can only rise to balance by an equal rise of $10,000 in stockholders' equity. This is simply a sign that the net worth of the company has risen by $10,000. But by law, it is improper to alter the common or capital stock account except when new shares are issued or the charter is amended. Therefore, a new account, called earned surplus, is created, and the balance sheet will show:

LIABILITIES AND NET WORTH	
Common stock	$100,000
Earned surplus ...	10,000
	$110,000

Book Value, Market Value, and Cash Dividends

The "book" or net worth value of the common stock is now $110,000/ 5,000 shares, or $22 per share; whereas on the first day of business, it was $100,000/5,000 shares, or $20 per share—the price paid or the cash contributed to the corporation. The stock has earned 10 percent per share, $2/$20, just as the corporation has earned $10,000/$100,000 or 10 percent on its total assets in this case. Whatever the corporation as a whole earns is what the individual stockholder earns per share, for there are no other claimants. Whether these earnings will be paid out in the form of cash dividends is a matter of management policy. Whether paid out or not, the fundamental record of the corporation shows earnings on assets of 10 percent. This is the crucial fact. If the earnings are not paid out, the book value of the stock has risen from $20 to $22, and it may be expected that the "market" price of the stock—the price old stockholders will require to sell their stock to newcomers—will rise from $20 to $22.

This assumes that the stock was bought originally—$20 was paid—on the expectation that it would earn 10 percent. After one year the stock is worth $22 in terms of earning power because, on assets of $110,000, 10 percent earnings will be $11,000, which is $2.20 per share. Of course, the market price is subject to many influences that may make it either more or less than $22, for example, perhaps earnings expected for the next few years are greater than 10 percent. But in any case, earnings, whether achieved or expected, are the principal determinant of market prices of common stock.

But let us return to our simple example and next assume that the earnings are all paid out in cash dividends. After the dividend the balance sheet will appear as it did at the beginning of the year, for cash will be down by $10,000, and, correspondingly, the surplus of $10,000 will have been wiped out. Thus, a cash dividend reduces net worth or book value. The book value per share will be $20 at the end of the year after the cash dividend, as it was at the beginning of the year before earnings had been made.

From the stockholder's point of view, it can be said broadly that he is equally well off whether the cash dividend is paid out or not. If the dividend is paid, he has $2 in cash and $20 worth of stock; if the dividend is not paid, he has $22 worth of stock. In the latter case, he can sell 10 percent of his stock and get the equivalent of $2 in cash, if that is what he wants, meanwhile keeping his initial investment intact. Of course, the individual stockholder's personal tax situation—whether he prefers income tax payments to capital gains tax payments, now or later—and other factors will determine his attitude toward cash dividends. In effect, stockholders who prefer current income will buy dividend-paying stocks, and the others will buy those stocks which retain earnings and whose success is reflected in rising book and market value rather than in dividends paid out.

Residual Earnings per Share: The Prime Concern of the Stockholder

In any case, it is earnings per share, whether paid out or not, which fundamentally determine the investment merit of common stocks. And thus, we can say that the stockholder buys a share in corporation earnings when he buys a share of common stock. It is the claim to *earnings* on assets, not the claim to the assets themselves in liquidation, that the stockholder is really interested in.

It is this fact which explains why the common stockholder, via the board of directors, is willing to grant *prior* claim to *assets* to both bondholders and preferred stockholders while giving them but a *limited,* though prior, claim to *income.* By obtaining funds at a fixed rate—say, 5 percent—while earning 10 percent on those funds when invested in the business, the common will increase the rate of return or earnings on its investment. It is the common stockholder's conviction that an increase in his earnings per share will be the result (even after discounting for the increased risks of leverage) that makes him willing to become a *residual* rather than an exclusive *claimant* to corporate income; he hopes to gain by creating prior claimants to income. This hope also explains his willingness to grant complex claims to assets to these other fixed-charge security purchasers.

Looking at this from the other side of the balance sheet, the creditors are willing to lend funds because a cushion of assets has previously been contributed by the common, while first claim to those assets, and the income earned on them, is yielded to the creditors. When funds are raised by nonequity means, the equity claimants become residual or secondary claimants.

Out of this process of trading on the equity the complex set of senior securities develops. But the common stock needs no complex indenture or contract specifying assets pledged, provisions for retirement, and other protective provisions. Quite simply, the common stock has residual claim to all assets and income of the corporation, and this need not even be stated. As owners, by common law, what they own is the net worth of the corporation—assets minus (liabilities plus preferred stocks)—and all earnings not paid out to prior claimants are theirs, whether left in the corporation and added to net worth or paid out in cash dividends. This is the reason why we need not get involved with types of common, as we did with types of bonds and preferreds. Common stock is simply entitled to everything that is not pledged to others. Of course, to figure out what this means, one needs to study the other complex security types that may be outstanding, but the common stock itself is a simple contract between the stockholders and the corporation.

Remember that equity sources are tapped when earnings are retained as well as when new common stock is sold. We know that industrials in recent years have made unusually heavy use of bonds. This need not imply an increase in the degree of trading on the equity to the extent that the proportion of preferred stock used has declined and that of retained earnings has gone up. But let us look at the actual figures of common stock issues to shed light on this and other equity finance questions.

THE RECORD OF COMMON STOCK ISSUES AND TOTAL EQUITY FINANCE

Common Stock Capitalization

Unfortunately, it is not possible to use the capitalization figures for common stock as a measure of the relative and absolute importance of sales of common stock as a source of corporate finance. Why, then, were we able to use these figures to measure the importance of bonds and preferred stock? The answer is that the statistics on capitalization are based upon balance sheet values which in turn are so-called "par" or stated value figures. Par value is the dollar figure that appears on the face of the security. In the case of preferred stock or bonds the selling price of the security on first issuance is so close to par[1] that the balance sheet "bond" or "preferred" account (carried at par) accurately reflects the funds received from the sale of those securities.

The Insignificance of Par Values of Common Stock. But this is not at all the case with common stocks. It is customary to set nominal (low or no par) values on common stocks and to sell them at prices that the market will pay, which price is usually far in excess of par. The need for par to state formally sums actually paid in to the corporation is obviously of importance with fixed-charge securities, where the rate of return is figured as a percentage of par, and where redemption or maturity is important. But in the case of common stocks, whose return is

---

[1] Usually $100 for preferreds and $1,000 for bonds.

residual and determined by board action, and which do not mature and cannot be called, there is no need for a par value as a true norm of value. Indeed, the presence of any other than nominal par value on a common stock might mislead the stockholder into thinking that this value might have some significance; in fact, of course, the true value of common stock is the price it can be sold for in the market.

Corporate Preference for Low Par Value Stocks.   But of course, corporate management has other reasons for wanting to carry common stock on the books at nominal value. Let us look at the accounting for cash sales of new common stocks. If the stock has $100 par and sells for $100 on first issuance, the balance sheet entry is:

Cash .... +$100   Capital stock .... +$100

But if, instead, the same security is given a $1.00 par value and sold for $100, the entry on the books is:

Cash .... +$100   Capital stock .... $ 1.00
                                        Paid-in surplus ..   99.00

There is no difference in cash received, or in the total net worth account (which includes the capital stock account plus all surplus accounts), or in the real value of the stock—if it is worth $100, it is worth it for the earnings potential of the company, and this is uninfluenced by the intricacies of bookkeeping. However, the accounting does influence managerial freedom and certain minor corporate tax burdens.[2] For example, management can manipulate surplus in accordance with the felt needs of the corporation; but it cannot, without amending the corporate charter, tamper with the capital stock account. Thus, managerial discretion is increased by channeling as little as possible into the capital stock account and as much as possible into the surplus accounts.[3]

---

[2] Most states tax new stock issues in accordance with par value. Taxes are lower on $1 par than $100 par. The original movement after 1912 away from full par (i.e., equal to dollars received for the stock) was to no par; but after the states interpreted *no* par to mean $100 par for tax purposes, corporations shifted in the 1930's and since to *low* par, e.g., $1 par, which was better for tax purposes and just as good for accounting purposes.

[3] Management is also free of the difficulties of selling additional capital stock at less than par, or amending the charter, which could occur if the price of the stock had fallen in the market since first issuance. It is easy for the $100 par to fall below $100 in the market; it is very hard to imagine the stock falling below a par value of $1 after initial issuance for $100. The difficulty in selling additional new stock at less than par is that the purchaser is liable for paying up to par in case creditors' payments cannot be met from the corporate treasury. In short, stockholder liability is limited *if*, as first purchaser, he paid par or better for the stock on first issuance.

Capitalization Statistics Therefore Understate the Significance of Common Stock Finance.   In any case, another effect of this shift in accounting is to destroy the analytic usefulness of common stock capitalization statistics. They have been (since the 1920's) mere token figures and cannot be read meaningfully without looking at the corporation's paid-in surplus figures. And in the summary of historical figures available, the surplus accounts are reported in one lump, thus making it impossible to determine which part was paid in on first issuance and which part was later earned and retained in the business.

Thus, the capitalization figures doubly understate the significance of equity finance: (1) they neglect the paid-in surplus figures and (2) they neglect retained earnings or earned surplus figures. Accordingly, we cannot use the capitalization (balance sheet) figures to determine the absolute importance of sales of common stock as a method of raising funds or its relative importance as compared to sales of preferred stock or bonds. For this purpose, we must turn to statistics on sales of common stock which include the total cash payment made for such stock. But we must return to the balance sheet if we want to determine the total contribution of equity to corporate finance; the sum of common stock capitalization plus *all* surpluses will tell us the total contribution made by the common stockholder to the corporation's finance through purchase of stock plus earnings left in the business (rather than drawn out in the form of cash dividends). Only in these intricate ways, can we examine, as we did for preferred stock and bonds, the significance of equity finance as a major component of total corporate finance.

The Place of New Common Stock Issues in Corporate Security Finance

The Relative Importance of Sales of Common Stock in Total Sales of All Corporate Securities.   New common stock issues as a proportion of all corporate securities have been rising since World War II, but not until the 1950's have new issues been issued in the pre-World War I proportions. And of course, common is not yet being issued consistently in the heavy proportions of the 1920's. Between 1932 and 1952 the role of *common* stock in corporate finance was quite small. However, note that the relative decline of common stock was cyclical, not secular, as now seems to be the case with preferred stock (see Table 25–1).

TABLE 25–1

ALL NEW SECURITY ISSUES, BY TYPE, 1900–1964
(Billions of Dollars)

Type of Security	1900–1909	1910–19	1920–29	1930–39	1940–49	1950–59	1960–64
Common stock	2.4	2.8	8.6	1.8	3.9	16.3	10.0
Preferred stock	0.6	1.9	7.5	1.5	4.6	6.2	1.9
Bonds	10.9	11.9	23.8	18.8	35.0	75.0	48.1
Total Security Issues	13.9	16.6	39.9	22.1	43.5	97.5	60.0
Common stock / Total securities	17%	17%	22%	8%	9%	17%	17%
Preferred stock / Total securities	4	11	18	7	11	6	3
Bonds / Total securities	79	72	60	85	80	77	80
Total	100%	100%	100%	100%	100%	100%	100%

SOURCES: Tables 23–1 and 23–6 of Chapter 23, and Table 25–2 below; and W. B. Hickman, *Statistical Measures of Corporate Bond Financing since 1900* (Princeton: Princeton University Press, 1960), Table 115, p. 204.

Common stock issues in 1950–64 returned to the relative levels of 1900–1919, supplying 17 percent of all the funds raised by security sales. Preferred stocks, on the other hand, over this most recent 15 year span supplied but 5 percent of total security funds; in the previous cyclical boom (the 1920's), their proportion was 18 percent. In all other decades the rise and fall in preferred stocks almost precisely offsets the opposite movement in the sales of bonds. With bonds replacing preferred stocks in corporate favor, and with preferred stocks not getting a boom-time rise, preferred stock is suffering a double blow. In fact, the *absolute* amount of preferred stocks issued in the 1960's has been falling. The *absolute* amount of common stock issued in the 1950's was almost twice as great as the amount issued in the 1920's.

The easiest way to see the shifts in corporate security finance is to compare the two modern, prosperous decades:

Decade	Common Stock	Preferred Stock	Bonds
1920's	22%	18%	60%
1950's	17	6	77

And a good guess for the 1960's would be:

Common stock	15%
Preferred stock	3
Bonds	82

Considering that much current preferred stock is convertible, this implies the virtual extinction of preferred stock as a means of corporate finance. The secular rise in bonds is the notable feature. But common stock finance, although it retains a significant place in financing industry,[4] is secularly stagnant and has lost its cyclical (boom-time) surges.

The Comparative Importance of Common Stock Issues by Type of Industry. We may disregard the rails, which in the aggregate have issued no new common stock since the 1920's and really did not take part in the surge of finance of the 1920's. Roughly, it appears that utilities have absorbed 35 percent of all funds raised by sale of common stock over the period, 1897–1959 (see Table 25–2).

TABLE 25–2

COMMON STOCK ISSUES, BY INDUSTRY, 1897–1959
(Millions of Dollars)

Years	Industrials	Utilities	Railroads	Totals
1897–99	176	99	— 81	107
1900–1909	779	453	1,195	2,427
1910–19	1,517	314	941	2,772
1920–29	5,720	2,701	193	8,614
1930–39	1,212	680	— 127	1,765
1940–49	2,519	1,555	— 40	4,034
1897–1949	11,923	5,795	1,081	19,799
1950–59	9,600	6,700	0	16,300
Total 1897–1959	21,500	12,500	1,000	35,000
1960–64				10,000

SOURCES: Raymond W. Goldsmith, *A Study of Saving in the United States* (Princeton: Princeton University Press, 1955), Vol. 1, Table V19, pp. 496–97. Data for 1950–59, Securities and Exchange Commission, *Twenty-sixth Annual Report, June 30, 1960* (Washington, D.C.: U.S. Government Printing Office, 1961), Table 3, Part 2, p. 222. See also R. W. Goldsmith's *The Flow of Capital Funds in the Post-War Economy* (New York: Columbia University Press, 1965), Table 94, p. 267.

Note that this 35 percent figure is a significant figure indeed, although the residual 65 percent for industrials is not.

1. Utilities raised but one sixth of the total funds that industrials do so that the 35 percent of all stock sales provides $1 of every $5 that utilities need but only 25 cents of every $5 that industrials need;

---

4 Note, however, that the role of new common stock issues in financing *large* corporations is, perhaps, twice as important as for *all* corporations taken together. The 300 largest corporations account for three fifths of all new stock issues. (See R. W. Goldsmith, *The Flow of Capital Funds in the Post-War Economy* [New York: Columbia University Press 1965], p. 248.)

2. The utility percentage has been rising seculary from 30 thru 40 percent;

3. Industrials have been expanding in total assets since the 1920's at roughly twice the pace of the utilities. The fact that utilities continued to issue approximately over one third of total common stock in both the 1920's and today indicates that they were tending to rely more heavily over time on common stock finance and the industrials were relying relatively less on common stock finance.

Part of the explanation of the relative but not absolute decline in the use of common stock finance by industrials vis-à-vis utilities is that industrials have relied ever more heavily on retained earnings for finance, while utilities, owing to restraining public regulation, have not been able to do so. Utilities continue to be a major force in the new common stock field, despite the fact that they are no longer the leading growth sector of the economy.

THE IMPORTANCE OF TOTAL EQUITY FINANCE— COMMON STOCK PLUS RETAINED EARNINGS

1. As Measured By Stock Sales and Undistributed Profits

There is no better way to underscore the overwhelming importance of retained earnings as a means of equity finance as compared to sales of common stock than to give the available statistics, which, unfortunately, do not go back before 1929 (see Table 25–3).

TABLE 25–3

THE GROWTH IN EQUITY, 1930–64
(Billions of Dollars)

Years	Cash Sale of Common Stock	Undistributed Profits
1930–34	1.0	−18.4
1935–39	0.7	− 0.6
1940–44	0.5	24.2
1945–49	3.4	44.7
1950–54	5.9	48.5
1955–59	10.4	50.0
1960–64	10.0	76.0
Total, 1930–64	32.0	224.0

SOURCES: Table 23–6 of Chapter 23, and Table 25–2 above; and Joint Economic Committee, *1965 Supplement to Economic Indicators*, p. 20.

Over the whole period 1930–64, retained earnings provided over seven times the flow of funds obtained from sales of new common stock. The absolute and relative volume of retained earnings is most impressive, especially when it is realized that most of it originates in the field of the industrials.

2. As Measured By Balance Sheet Data

Another way to see the importance of total equity finance and its trends is to examine the proportion that common stock outstanding plus surpluses are of liabilities and net worth. In order to point out the *error* involved, we also present the ratio of common stock outstanding to total capitalization. (See Table 25–4.)

TABLE 25–4

THE RELATIVE WEIGHT OF EQUITY FINANCE IN TOTAL CORPORATE FINANCE
FOR ALL INDUSTRIES COMBINED, SELECTED YEARS, 1926–62

Year	Common Stock / Total Capitalization		Common Stock and Surpluses / Capitalization and Surpluses		Common Stock and Surpluses / Total Liabilities and Net Worth	
1926	$ 68 billion / $116 billion	58%	$102 billion / $152 billion	67%	$102 billion / $262 billion	40%
1936	78 / 144	54	115 / 180	64	115 / 303	38
1946	68 / 128	53	150 / 210	71	150 / 455	33
1955	97 / 211	46	290 / 404	72	290 / 889	33
1962	129 / 312	41	417 / 600	70	417 / 1,289	32

SOURCE: U.S. Bureau of the Census. *Historical Statistics of the United States: Colonial Times to 1957* (Washington, D.C.: U.S. Government Printing Office, 1960), Series V 65–97, pp. 580–81; and *Historical Statistics Continuations to 1962*, p. 80.

Equity finance, if measured by par values of common stocks (to total capitalization) shows a persistent decline since 1926, with the decline accelerating in the most recent decades. This is surely a misleading picture, ignoring as it does paid-in surplus and retained earnings as well. On the other hand, when all surpluses are added to both numerator and denominator, there seems to be no trend in equity finance. This, too, is somewhat misleading, for it ignores *short-term* debt such as accounts and notes payable. When this debt as well as formal capitalization and surplus are considered, the trend in equity finance was falling between 1926 and 1946, and has been stable since that time.

In either case, equity finance has provided a *stable* and *not* a declining proportion of total corporate financial needs in the post-World War II years. However, remember that the recent stability of equity finance has been achieved in major part not through sales of new common stock but through retained earnings. For similar reasons the debt/equity ratio has not deteriorated since 1945, despite the fact that sales of bonds provided five times the funds that common stock sales did.

3. As Measured by Sources and Uses Data

Plainly, the stability of the ratio of common stock to all security issues demonstrates little, because comparison in terms of ratios of stock issues to *total* finance or to *total external* finance reveal *sharp* declines in the significance of stock as a source of finance in the most recent decades as compared to the 1920's. In brief, this result is attributable to the increase in the later decades over the 1920's in the proportion of total finance attributable to *internal* finance and to *short-term* external finance. These factors have been considered in previous sections.

It is clear (see Table 25–5) that common stock as a source of corporate finance has declined substantially in the postwar era as compared with the 1920's or even the early 1900's. Note that this is even true of common stock as a ratio of long-term external finance alone. It is *not* true that the decline in equity finance in long-term external finance is attributable to the decline in preferred stock alone. True, the relative decline in preferred stock has been extraordinary; but common stock has declined too. But of course the role of common stock in *total* external finance has declined even more—to half its prior importance—owing to a substitution of short-term debt for long-term external sources; and its role in *total* finance has shrunk further to almost two fifths of its prior

TABLE 25–5

COMMON STOCK'S ROLE IN CORPORATE FINANCE,
1901–12, 1923–29, 1947–63

	1901–12	*1923–29*	*1947–63*
Common stock as a ratio of:			
Long-term external sources	0.32	0.34	0.26
Total external sources	0.26	0.31	0.14
All sources	0.12	0.14	0.05

SOURCE: A. W. Sametz, "Trends in the Volume and Composition of Equity Finance," *Journal of Finance,* September, 1964, p. 461.

importance owing to a substitution of internal for external equity finance.

However, *total* equity finance—external equity or stock issues plus internal equity or retained earnings—shows no secular decline as the upward trend of internal equity has offset the downward trend of external equity.

QUESTIONS AND PROBLEMS

1. Distinguish between:
   a) Par value and book value.
   b) Stock splits and stock dividends.
   c) Stock rights and stock options.
   d) Trading on the equity and increasing the equity.
   e) Capitalization and capital structure.

2. Why are common stock capitalization figures a poor measure of the role of common stockholders as a source of corporate finance? What other figures can be used to develop a good measure?

3. "Common stock finance, although it retains a significant place in financing corporations, is secularly stagnant and has lost its cyclical (boom-time) urge." Discuss using rough magnitudes to support your argument. How would your answer differ if the question had asked about "equity" rather than common stock finance?

4. Contrast the role of common stock finance in the utility industry with that of its use in industrials. What, do you think, are the causes of these differences?

5. The debt/equity ratio for all corporations has not deteriorated over the course of the last 20 years despite the fact that over this period the sale of bonds provided five times the funds that common stock provided. How do you explain this?

SUGGESTED READINGS

BERANEK, W. *Common Stock Financing, Book Values, and Stock Dividends: The Theory and the Evidence.* Ann Arbor, Mich.: University of Michigan, 1961.

ORTNER, R. "The Concept of Yield on Common Stock," *Journal of Finance,* May, 1964, pp. 186–98.

SHAPIRO, E., and WHITE, W. L. "Patterns of Business Financing: Some Comments," *Journal of Finance,* December, 1965, pp. 693–707 ("Reply" by A. W. SAMETZ, *ibid;* pp. 708–18).

STEVENSON, H. *Common Stock Financing.* Ann Arbor, Mich.: University of Michigan, 1957.

APPENDIX TO CHAPTER 25
SOME DEFINITIONAL NOTES

Using the Word "Capital" Meaningfully

From this unfortunately complex discussion, it becomes clear how important it is to define precisely which particular finance concept is being considered. The word *capital* should never be used in such discussions; it has no clear meaning. We have capital *stock, capitalization,* and capital *structure,* all of which might be generally referred to as corporate capital but each of which has a quite specific and different meaning.

Capital stock is the account that carries the total common stock issued at par value. To get the total proceeds from stock sales, one needs to add paid-in surplus to capital stock.

Capitalization is the capital stock account *plus* the preferred stock account and the bond account.

Capital structure is capitalization *plus* surpluses, both paid in and plowed back.

Of all the accounts on the right-hand side on the balance sheet, only short-term liabilities have been ignored. To include these in addition to capital structure would give us the total of all positive *sources of corporate funds.* We can link this to our earlier discussion of sources of funds by noting that allowing for *declines* in assets as sources of funds would give us total sources of corporate funds.

Using the Word "Value" Meaningfully

Similar definitional clarity is needed when speaking of the *value* of stock, total or per share. Like the word *capital,* the word *value* has no precise meaning. Common stocks have par, book, liquidation, and market values. Let us define these in terms of total values; to find the respective per share value, simply divide by the number of shares.

Par value is the capital stock account.

Book value is the whole net worth account (capital stock plus surpluses).

Liquidation value is the same as book value if book value, which is really net assets (assets minus liabilities) can in fact be sold at balance sheet figures. Usually, it is considered that liquidation value will be less than book value unless the assets are sold as a whole or hidden asset worth is great.

Market value is simply the price at which the stock can be sold in the market. It is almost always greater than par but may be more or less than book or liquidation value.

It is this market value that is of fundamental importance to the common stockholder; and as we shall now see, it is toward maintaining and increasing the market value of his stock that fundamental stockholder rights are oriented.

Chapter 26

THE RIGHTS AND INTERESTS OF
COMMON STOCKHOLDERS

THE SO-CALLED "FUNDAMENTAL" RIGHTS

There is no need to examine in detail the numerous formal and legal aspects of stockholder rights.[1] Most of them can be included under the three so-called "fundamental" rights: to vote, to have a residual claim against assets, and to share in dividends declared. Moreover, there is no real need to consider in detail any right but the last one; the rights to vote and to assets in liquidation are of significance only in unusual or emergency situations.

The Right to Vote

The customary use of the proxy which, in effect, transfers the vote to the existing board of directors, is evidence of the usual perfunctory nature of this right. Even cumulative (or proportional) voting, which allows the stockholder to concentrate his votes on one candidate so as to enable minority interests to be represented on the board, is significant only in the case of dissension in the corporate household.[2] Such dissension, rare in

---

[1] For example, the right to have and to transfer freely a stock certificate (evidence of ownership) and to inspect the corporate books. Even the preemptive right—the right to participate proportionally to their existing holdings in additional issues of common stock —should (and will) be considered as a mere technique intended to serve the stockholders' fundamental rights as to control, income, and assets.

[2] Under simple majority voting rules, if one owns as much as 49 percent of the outstanding stock, one may not elect a single director. But under cumulative voting, one could elect 49 one hundredths of the number of directors to the nearest lower whole number. For example, of a nine man board, 49 percent of the votes could elect 4.4 members or, of course, four members. In terms of numbers of votes rather than percentages, if one has 49 votes of a total of 100 votes, the votes needed to elect one director (of nine) are 11.

The formula is:
$$\left[\frac{\text{Number of shares voting}}{\text{Number of directors to be elected} +1} +1 \right]$$

any case, is seldom of grass-roots origin; successful minority representation, like the even rarer majority voting-out of the whole existing management, is usually organized by another corporation or a small group of wealthy, informed, and aggressive individuals. In any case, the ordinary stockholder seldom gives a thought to his right to vote, and when he does, it is because the fundamental right to earnings is at issue.

The Right to Residual Claim against Assets

The common stockholder has little hope of getting his money back in liquidation if there are heavy prior claimants, for in most bankruptcies even the bondholders and preferred stockholders cannot be fully reimbursed. When there are no prior claimants, bankruptcy or involuntary liquidation is not likely; hence, again, the common stockholder's right to assets is an empty right.

The Fundamental Economic Right: The Residual Claim to Earnings, Not Dividends

Even *the* fundamental right to *dividends* should be subordinated to a broader discussion of the common stockholder's residual claim to *all earnings*, whether paid out or not. This is not a legal or stated right, but it is his fundamental economic right; it is the principal reason that common stock is bought. Really, the stockholders have no legal right to force the board of directors to declare dividends, except through an unlikely effort to vote the board out of office. Moreover, in general, stockholders have no *economic* reason to try to force cash dividends; undeclared dividends add to the book and market value of the stock, while declared dividends, instead of adding to their investment, add to their cash holdings.

THE PRIMARY OR FUNDAMENTAL RIGHT ILLUSTRATED: THE CASE OF STOCK DIVIDENDS

The overriding importance of earnings rather than dividends in determining stockholder welfare applies to *stock dividend* declarations as well as to cash dividends. The only effect of a stock dividend per se is to relabel certain component parts of the net worth account: The accountant writes down the surplus account and writes up the capital stock account. The total net worth of the corporation and of each stockholder's share of it is unaffected. The number of shares in the hands of each stockholder goes up, but the book value and the market value of each share go down proportionally. If there has been no change in the *earnings* picture, there is no reason to expect the market value of the total stock or any one stockholder's share of the total to change.

There is a general belief that the declaration of a stock dividend, or a declaration of increased cash dividends, has a favorable effect on market value. When there is such an effect and an apparent causal relationship to the dividend change, it is not the dividend that is stimulating but increased earnings which have made for the change in dividend policy. When stock dividends are instituted and there has been no fundamental change in earning power, the aggregate market value of the stock will not change. When the stock dividends are simply a recognition of increased earnings, total market value will rise but no differently in the long run from the manner in which it would have risen if no stock dividend has been declared.

True, there is often a favorable *announcement* effect,[3] but this wears off within six months if the underlying earnings picture is unchanged. This announcement effect may be explained by the ignorance of the small stockholder of the real significance of stock dividends; but such marginal purchasers can have but a temporary influence on market prices, and they, too, learn in time to watch earnings per share as the price-determining factor.

There is one permanent effect of stock dividends which may occur even though the earnings picture be unchanged before and after. The price of the stock is reduced proportionately to the size of the stock dividend declared. For example, a 1:1 stock dividend tends to halve the price of the stock, as well as to halve the book value, earnings, and presumably dividends per share. This may alter the marketability of the stock insofar as it increases the numbers of purchasers who can now afford to buy 100 share or round lots. Brokers' commission schedules do discriminate against odd lots of shares (less than 100), and the New York Stock Exchange reports that a market price of about $25 is most popular with small stockholders. But it is hard to believe that this thickening of the market has a sufficiently significant effect on the demand for a stock to influence its price more than marginally and temporarily.

Of course, if cash dividends per share are not halved in the case of a 1:1 stock dividend, the effect would be the same whether the stock dividend had been granted or not. What difference does it make to the stockholder whether increased—say, doubled—dividends are distributed by increasing the payment from $1 to $2 on the old share or by leaving

---

[3] This is especially true if the time of stock dividend declaration is also the time when increased cash dividends are announced. (See above Chapter 17.)

the dividend at $1 but doubling the number of shares in stockholders' hands? The rate of dividend payment is precisely doubled in either case. And further, we have already noted that the welfare of stockholders is not substantially affected by the *declaration of cash dividends;* if declared, stockholders are richer in cash; if not declared, they are richer in market value of stock owned.[4] Once again, the crucial factor that affects stockholders' futures is the earnings of the corporation, whether paid out or not. Stock dividends are best thought of as simply formal recognition that earnings have been retained instead of being paid out; the retained surpluses are permanently shifted to capital stock by the granting of a stock dividend. But the earnings record and the surpluses are already in existence, and should have had their effect on the market value of the stock, whether the stock dividend is declared or not. The only really new thing that happens when the stock dividend is "paid" is that the market price of the stock tends to fall in proportion to the size of the dividend.

ANOTHER ILLUSTRATION: THE CASE OF STOCK SPLITS

Stock splits are similar to stock dividends in this last matter. If the stock is split two new to one old, and if nothing else has changed, the only effect is to halve the price of the stock and to double the number of shares outstanding. Presumably, the principal purpose of the split is to bring the price of the stock down to a popular price bracket. Unlike the case of the stock dividend, a surplus is not needed to engineer a split; all that happens is that the par value of the stock is reduced by charter amendment—say, from $1 to 50 cents—and the number of shares are doubled. If, under these circumstances, the market value of the stock settles down at a price above 50 percent of the presplit price, so that there has been an increase in the overall and per stockholder market value of shares, it must be as a result of increased earnings or dividends which became public knowledge at the same time as the split. The split per se added nothing to the aggregate or per stockholder market value of shares. However, it is true that management often uses the announcement of a split to make public a record of growth in earnings per share, and this will improve the price of the stock. But it is the earnings record and prospects, not the split itself, that underlie the favorable performance of the stock in the market.

---

[4] Market price in practice declines by 90 percent of actual cash dividends on ex-dividend day (J. A. Campbell and W. Beranek, "Stock Price Behavior on Ex-Dividend Dates," *Journal of Finance*, December, 1955, pp. 425–29). The same reasoning applies to the sale of stock received as a stock dividend. By selling, the stockholder increases his "investment" in cash but reduces his investment in stock.

RESTATEMENT OF THE ARGUMENT THAT THE ONLY FUNDAMENTAL STOCKHOLDER RIGHT IS TO SHARE IN RESIDUAL EARNINGS

It is clarifying, although a bit oversimplifying, to say, then, that stockholders have essentially one right: the right to share in residual earnings of the corporation. They have no enforceable right to dividends, no real stake in their residual claim to assets, and in most cases little interest in their right to vote. But they are deeply—usually solely—concerned with the earnings record, whether paid out in cash dividends or not and, if not paid out, whether retained earnings are finally locked in by the "payment" of a stock dividend or not.

The earnings record (past, current, and expected) determines how much the stockholder will gain, or lose, through owning a particular stock and is therefore the principal determining factor in the purchase of stock.

The gain to the stockholder from sharing in residual earnings is shown either by an increase in cash received (market value of the stock unchanged), or by an increase in the market value of the stock, or by both. The aggregate gain in the long run is the same no matter what kind and amount of dividends are declared. Thus, although the stockholder has no legal "right" to dividends, he need not be concerned, for he has the de facto right to share in earnings pro rata.

The fundamental lesson of this involved although simplified discussion of stockholder rights, claims, and privileges is that earnings per share play the paramount role in determining common stockholders' fortunes. Although common stock prices seem to respond favorably to dividend declarations, splits, privileged subscriptions, etc., at bottom they must be responding to improved earnings, or the gains will prove to be but temporary. These announcements are attention getters, and if there is something real to be noted, the gains will be lasting.[5] If no real favorable change underlies the financial adjustment, the clamor will die down, the ignorant will be "taken," and the stock will resume its basic course—a course that is determined by the earnings per share and the number of times earnings per share stockholders are willing to pay to own the stock.

But there is a stubborn reluctance on the part of students as well as small stockholders to believe that this hardheaded analysis is true in

---

[5] But so, too, would the gains be lasting if the announcement were simply of the actual or prospective rise in earnings per share.

practice. Perhaps the feeling of the individual is that if this is so difficult for him to see through, it is similarly difficult for all others; and if ignorance prevails, stocks can rise permanently, although really they have no reason to do so. The answer to this is that it neglects (1) the predominant influence of professionally advised stockholders and calculating institutional investors, even in the short run; and (2) the passing of time—the long run as a great dispeller of short-term fantasy. Whatever one may *believe* about the value, say, of a stock split, is, in time, either confirmed or dispelled by the actual earnings record per share, quarter by quarter and year by year.

EVIDENCE TO SUPPORT THE ARGUMENT

In fact, careful studies of the effects of splits and stock dividends on stock prices have been made, and the evidence confirms the above analysis. "Stock dividends *per se* have no measurable market value." And stock splits result in "a relative increase in the number of shareholders, yet no ascertainable real price changes [are] attributable to the stock split itself."[6] Barker reached these conclusions after studying the market price behavior of all listed stocks which split or gave stock dividends in the early 1950's. He based his conclusions on the market price six months after the split. Note that the "long run" needed for fundamentals to predominate is not very long—only six months.

A FINAL ILLUSTRATION: THE PREEMPTIVE
RIGHT—AN EMPTY RIGHT

The preemptive right is best thought of as the right of common stockholders to *maintain*, if they wish, their prorata share of earnings when additional shares of common stock are issued by the corporation. This right is implemented by giving the old stockholders first chance to buy the new stock via a so-called "privileged subscription." True, it also gives them the opportunity to maintain their prorata voting power; but in most cases the stockholder is as little interested in future voting power as he has been in his voting power in the past.

Once again, a stockholder's technical right is reducible to an earnings issue. And once again, the central issue is fogged over with irrelevancies.

---

[6] C. Austin Barker, "An Evaluation of Stock Dividends," *Harvard Business Review,* July–August, 1958, pp. 99–114; "Effective Stock Splits," *ibid.,* January–February, 1956, pp. 101–6; and "Stock Splits in a Bull Market," *ibid.,* May–June, 1957, pp. 72–79.

It is commonly thought that the privileged subscription gives the stockholder something of value; in and of itself, it does nothing of the kind, unless votes are of importance.

If the new stock is sold at market value, the stockholder's claim to prorata residual earnings is unaffected whether he buys some of the new issue or not. Say the stock is selling at $50 a share and earns a steady $5 per share annually. If the stockholder buys his prorata share of the total new issue, he adds to his investment and adds to his claim to earnings proportionally, but the rate of return on his total investment is unchanged. For example, before, he had 10 shares times $50 a share, or a $500 investment, on which the corporation earned $50 annually; afterwards, he has, say, 20 shares (if the corporation doubled the total outstanding shares) times $50 a share, or a $1,000 investment, on which the corporation presumably will earn $100 annually. Of course, if earnings on the new money are expected to be better than 10 percent in the future, the price of the stock will rise; but then, in this first case, so too will the subscription or market price. Thus, in the case where the new stock is sold at *market price,* the old stockholder can be indifferent whether he buys the new stock or not. Anyway, he could always add to his holdings if he wanted to do so by buying old stock in the open market at $50.

Typically, however, the privileged subscription is offered at a "bargain" price, i.e., a price below market, to the old stockholders. Does this alter the conclusion that the preemptive right is of no real value to the old stockholder? Yes. Does this alter the conclusion that the stockholder is just as well off not buying the new shares as he would be if he bought them? No. If the right to buy new stock in the ratio of one new stock for one old one held is offered to old stockholders at a price of $45 when the market value is $50, clearly the right is worth $2.50.[7] But it is worth $2.50 whether exercised or not, for the stockholder can *sell* the right in the open market for $2.50.[8] If he exercises the right, he will have two shares worth $95 and be out $45 in cash, or $50 net.[9] If he does not exercise the right, he will have one share worth $47.50 plus $2.50 cash, or $50 net. The stockholder would lose, however, if he were stupid enough

---

[7] If the corporation earns 10 percent on investment (assets), it earns $5 million on $50 million assets and (if there are one million shares outstanding) each share earns $5.00 and sells at ten times earnings, or $50. If $45 million are added to assets *and the firm continues to earn 10 percent on assets,* it will earn $9.5 million, or $4.75 per share ($9.5 million split among two million shareholders). The market price of the stock will be $47.50 after the new issue is consummated, that is, ten times earnings.

[8] The value of the right is analogous to a cash dividend.

[9] All the stockholder really saves is the underwriting costs.

not to exercise his right or to sell it. The pre-emptive right, when a bargain price is involved, does require the stockholder to act if he is not to lose; but he does not *gain* anything through the exercise of this right.

Once again, if future earnings are expected to be greater than past earnings, the market price of the stock may rise (or fall less than proportionally to the bargain), but this would occur whether or not a privileged subscription or a stock dividend or a split were involved.[10] Earnings, earnings, earnings are the key to common stockholder gains from holding stock.

If the privileged subscription does not really give the stockholder anything, one may ask: Why does the common law make this a fundamental right of stockholders? The answer is that if new stock were sold at the market value of the old, the right would be meaningless; but in the United States, new stock is issued in such a fashion (in huge lumps over as brief a time as possible) as to put great pressure on stock prices to fall. That is, the increase in the supply of stock pressed rapidly onto the market drives the price of the stock down. To reduce such pressure, it is customary in American investment banking to try to place as much of the stock with old stockholders as possible, thus keeping it from hitting the open market. To encourage the old stockholders, a bargain price is offered. *Once the bargain price is set*, the old stockholders must get "first crack" at the stock, or their equity in the corporation will be diluted. For example, if the bargain price of $45 were offered only to new subscribers, they would get an average $47.50 value for $45.00, while the old stockholders would see their $50.00 equity shrink to $47.50. (Market price would settle in the neighborhood of $47.50.)

Note that it is the customary use of discount subscription prices for new securities that makes the preemptive right necessary if justice is to be done to the old stockholders. *They do not gain through its use; they avoid a possible loss.* Note still again that what is lost is earning power per share and hence market values; earning power is again at the heart of the problem. And the possible loss is not an inevitable feature of new-issue finance; it is an outcome of the particular methods of marketing securities that have become institutionalized in American investment banking.[11]

---

[10] J. R. Nelson has recently confirmed the quasi-split effects of stock rights. ". . . stock rights have split effects similar to stock splits and stock dividends." Here is empirical confirmation of the hypothesis of this chapter. See "Price Effects in Rights Offerings," *Journal of Finance*, December, 1965, pp. 647–50.

[11] The significance of stock splits and stock dividends, too, is solely a matter of marketing strategy, and we shall refer to these aspects in the next chapter. All these techniques aim by lowering per share prices to broaden and thicken the market for their

Having examined in turn the nature and significance of bonds, preferred stock, and common stock, we must turn now to the methods of marketing these issues. As with any commodity, so with securities: they serve their purpose only after they are placed in the "consumer's" hands. It is our next job to discover how these commodities are merchandised by the middleman, the investment banker, and something about their customers, the purchasers of new corporate securities.

QUESTIONS AND PROBLEMS

1. Describe the principal rights of stockholders. Which of these rights is *the* fundamental right? Why?

    Are there no "obligations" of stockholders offsetting these rights? Explain.

2. Is the right to dividends a prime stockholder right? Discuss. Would your answer be different if stock dividends rather than cash dividends were the case under consideration? Explain.

3. Distinguish between:
    a) Stock splits and stock dividends.
    b) Cumulative and statutory voting.
    c) Preemptive right and privileged subscription.
    d) Liquidation dividend and stock dividend.
    e) Stock rights and stock splits.

4. "Although common stock prices apparently respond favorably to dividend declarations, splits and rights, at bottom, they must be responding to improved earnings or the market price gains will prove to be only temporary." Defend this statement analytically and empirically.

5. "The privileged subscription, when a bargain price is involved, does require the stockholder to act if he is not to lose; but he does not *gain* anything through this exercise of his preemptive right." Explain.

    What particular conditions might cause a stockholder rationally to gain relatively via rights offerings?

SUGGESTED READINGS

BARKER, C. A. "Are Stock Dividends Effective?" *Harvard Business Review*, July–August, 1958, pp. 99–114.

———. "Effective Stock Splits," *Harvard Business Review*, January–February, 1956, pp. 101–6.

shares. The market is broader, for more stockholders can afford round lot purchases and still diversify their total holdings; and the market is thicker, easier to get in and out, for there will be a greater volume of trading.

DURAND, D., and MAY, A. M. "The Ex-Dividend Behavior of AT & T Stock," *Journal of Finance*, March, 1960, pp. 19–31.

EVANS, G. H., JR. "The Theoretical Value of a Stock Right," *Journal of Finance*, March, 1955, pp. 55–61; and September, 1956, pp. 363–70.

HUBBARD, P. M., JR. "The Many Aspects of Dilution," *Financial Analysts Journal*, May–June, 1963, pp. 33–40.

KIMBALL, P., and PAPERA, D. R. "Effects of Stock Splits on Short Term Market Price," *Financial Analysts Journal*, May–June, 1964.

NELSON, J. R. "Price Effects in Rights Offerings," *Journal of Finance*, December, 1965, pp. 647–50.

SUSSMAN, M. R. *The Stock Dividend*. Ann Arbor, Mich.: University of Michigan, 1962.

Chapter 27

THE MARKETING OF CORPORATE SECURITIES: INVESTMENT BANKING

Thus far, we have considered the factors that lead a corporation to decide to raise new money by issuing new securities. The chapters on capital budgeting, on capital structure, and on the types of securities have stressed the issuing corporation's or the seller's point of view. But of course, every sale implies a purchaser. We must now consider, as does the corporation in its decision as to what and when and how to sell, the problem of marketing the new issues.

THE SECURITIES MARKETING PROBLEM: THE NEED FOR THE SPECIALIZED SERVICES OF THE INVESTMENT BANKER

The selling problem has two essential aspects: (1) tailoring the product, the security in this case, to the tastes or needs of the market; and (2) getting the product into the hands of the purchaser—the mechanics of marketing new securities.

A specialized business—the investment banking business—has developed to assist the corporation in the selling job.

Investment banking, like any other specialized service available at a price, developed to meet a need that could be met more cheaply by hiring an outside agency's services than by setting up a special intracorporation department to do the job. Plainly, it would be uneconomic for a corporation to establish a securities marketing divison and then to use it only occasionally, say every three or four years, when external security finance was being tapped.

As soon as businesses began to solicit funds from a circle wider than their own relatives, friends, and business colleagues, the need for a middleman between seller and buyer of corporate securities arose, and the investment banking business developed. In the early days of its development in the mid-nineteenth century, investment bankers were much more than mere middlemen. Not only did they find buyers for the securities, but they often purchased the securities for their own portfolios. In those days the term *investment banker* more truly reflected their activities: They did *invest* in securities, not merely turn them over as brokers or dealers, and they had *banking* affiliates so that many of the securities they bought ended up in the portfolios of banks.

Today, investment bankers are essentially middlemen—or as we shall see later, department stores of finance—and their traditional name is inappropriate. After 1900, corporations began to issue securities in great quantities, and the supply of funds of wealthy individuals was dwarfed by the demand for funds.[1] The need to develop a mass market for corporate securities—to sell a few of the new securities to each of thousands rather than thousands of securities to the few—caused the investment banking business to become more a matter of merchandising securities than of investment or banking. It is interesting to note that in recent years the job of finder has become important again, owing to the great growth in available funds of financial institutions such as insurance companies. In any case, investment banking today is a matter of merchandising and finding, not of investing or banking.

THE FUNCTION OF THE INVESTMENT BANKER:
THE FULL RANGE OF SERVICES—
PRIVATE NEGOTIATION

The full range of services offered by investment bankers includes origination, underwriting, and distribution of corporate securities. A house such as Morgan, Stanley & Company, or Kuhn, Loeb & Company, is prepared to help a corporation decide what kind of security to issue, to buy those securities from the corporation, and then to arrange to resell them to the public.

When a corporation contracts with an investment banker for this full range of services, it is called *private negotiation*. For most issues handled in this way, the originating house does the whole job only for the originating stage; it, as manager, forms a group of investment bankers (a syndicate) to share in the underwriting or purchasing function; and it gathers together a still larger group of broker-dealers to distribute the securities across the nation.

---

[1] After 1933, investment bankers were forbidden to have banking affiliates, and this further reduced their ability to "invest" in securities; that is, it further increased their need to buy securities only for immediate resale.

For these services the corporation, of course, pays a fee. This fee is called a *spread* because it is measured by the difference between the price the corporation receives per share and the price the selling group hopes to be able to obtain from public sale. This spread is divided among the participants in the marketing effort. The originating house gets a flat fee for its work in counseling the corporation, each underwriter gets a fee scaled to his share of the expenses and risk in underwriting the issue, and each broker-dealer gets a slice of the spread as his commission for finding the ultimate purchaser. For example, a high-grade corporate bond might carry a total spread of 2 percent, that is, the corporation would receive $980 for turning over to the investment bankers a $1,000 bond. The 2 percent spread might be divided with 0.3 percent (or $3 per bond) going to the originating house, 0.9 percent (or $9 per bond) to the under-writers, and 0.8 percent (or $8 per bond) to the sellers. In the case of common stock the spread may be as high as 30 percent. What determines the size of the spread, and what makes the corporation willing to pay such fees?

Origination

Many corporations are weak in the financial aspects of management, however strong they may be in the manufacturing or marketing aspects, and almost all corporations lack *expertise* in the securities aspect of financial management. Absorbed as they are in the manufacture, etc., of shoes or generators, they cannot spare the time to become specialists in finance in general or the securities markets in particular. It is here that investment bankers play an important role. *Consultation* on the financial needs of the corporation and alternative means of meeting those needs, and negotiation on the terms of a precise financial plan, constitute the principal components of this origination stage. In this process the origi-nating banker studies the history of the corporation and its plans and prospects, its financial statements, its management, etc., and presumably comes up with a suggestion that the corporation issue a particular security in a specified manner at a certain time.

In helping the corporation to determine whether to issue a bond (or stock), the particular kind of bond to issue, and when to issue it, the banker presumably supplements whatever more general financial plans the corporation may already have made. The current fashion or fads in the security markets can be taken advantage of on the advice of the originating banker; he can also caution on whatever the current or prospective uncertainties in the securities markets may be. Moreover, all of the preliminary investigation and marshaling of financial data will be necessary to register the securities for public issuance under the Securities Act of 1933; here, too, professional advice and direction are customarily needed.

The originating fee is not only paid for these varied services, but also to attach the name of a nationally known house to the securities of a company which in many cases has a much smaller reputation. Moreover, it is customary to make continuing use of the financial advice of the originating banker in the periods between bouts of security flotation.

To hire a securities market consultant is no different in nature from hiring an advertising consultant or a labor relations consultant. In all these cases the corporation pays fees to outsiders for expert advice, presumably because it is cheaper than to add such experts to their own full-time staff. Clearly, this is more often true of securities advice than either advertising or labor advice, because of the more episodic nature of the former.

Underwriting

The underwriting commitment defines the investment banker. The giant corporations may well have sufficiently competent internal financial advice, but (except perhaps American Telephone & Telegraph on occasion) even the giants require underwriting for their security issues. And we do not need the term *investment banker* to describe the distribution function; there, the term *broker* or *dealer* is quite sufficient. The unique function of the investment banker is to assume the risk of security flotations.

In effect, when investment bankers underwrite an issue, they buy the whole issue at a fixed price from the corporation for resale at a markup. The corporation has shifted the risk of failure to sell or of sales only at marked-down prices to the investment bankers. And a major portion of the spread goes to pay the bankers for the costs and risks of such underwriting. Corporations are most eager to shift this risk to the bankers because they wish to confine their risk taking to the sphere of their special competence—say, the manufacture and sale of shoes; they do not want to gamble on the fluctuations of the stock and bond markets in addition to their more calculated gamble on, say, ladies' demands for shoes, the future price of leather, etc. Moreover, corporations need to be assured of a given total dollar sum if they are to carry out their investment plans. By contracting with the investment bankers to receive a certain sum on a specified day, they can go ahead and order the machines, etc. Otherwise, the sale of securities might well yield a smaller amount than needed if the market declines between the time of decision on what to sell and the time of actual sale of the securities. The whole stock market may suffer a sinking spell; or in the case of bonds, interest rates may rise in the interim, pressing down the price of bonds; or the bankers may have overvalued the quality of the security they have chosen to underwrite relative to what the public will pay for it. By pushing off onto the investment bankers the risks entailed in security sales, the corporation is allowed to concentrate on its own business and not on the securities markets.

Obviously, the investment banking firm must have access to considerable amounts of cash if it is to underwrite securities. Most investment banking houses are partnerships with ownership funds of several millions of dollars.[2] But such funds, though counted in the millions, are petty cash, even when supplemented by their borrowing power at the commercial banks, when measured against the size of the new issues of giant nonfinancial corporations, which sometimes run over $100 million and frequently exceed $10 million.[3] This problem is solved by the customary technique of forming syndicates or groups of investment bankers to underwrite the securities. They pool their cash and share the liability proportionately. Depending upon the size of the issue, the syndicate may range from a few bankers to a dozen or more.

This skimpy capitalization of underwriters makes understandable their customary rush to sell the securities. Rapid turnover or return of capital is essential if the investment banker is to go on to another underwriting job. Hence the development of a somewhat hysterical vocabulary and technique in connection with the sale of new issues: "out the window"—a sold-out issue; "stale"—an issue that has taken more than a few days to sell, etc. Investment bankers are prone to dump new issues that stale by cutting selling prices and taking losses rather than waiting, while their capital funds are tied up, for the market to firm up.

---

[2] In 1956, some $7.2 billion of securities were underwritten. In that year the net worth of the whole investment banking industry (382 firms) totaled $0.9 billion. Over half the number of firms had less than $1 million net worth, and all but 44 had net worth of under $5 million. The average capital of even the largest size group was under $12 million, and probably the largest firm in the industry had a net worth of under $50 million. (M. H. Waterman, *Investment Banking Functions* ["Michigan Business Studies," Vol. XIV, No. 1; Ann Arbor: University of Michigan Press, 1958], pp. 141–42.)

[3] In earlier days, investment banking concerns were not so small relative to the size of the business corporations they served; in addition, the investment bankers had the lending power and the capital funds of their commercial bank affiliates at their command. Under such circumstances, a single investment banker could underwrite all but the largest security issues.

Distribution

To achieve *rapid* distribution is the aim of the underwriters; to achieve *widespread* distribution or ownership of their securities is often the aim of corporate issuers. For these purposes a "selling group" of hundreds of brokers and dealers throughout the country is organized by the manager of the "purchasing group" or the syndicate of underwriters. These distributors often assume no liability for securities; they simply sell on a commission basis which, in effect, allots a part of the spread to them. Of course, the members of the syndicate may have many branch offices throughout the country through which they themselves can sell the securities.

Note that some firms, like Bache and Company, and Merrill Lynch, Pierce, Fenner & Smith, can serve as originator, syndicate member, and retail distributor on a new issue. Such "department stores of finance," which do investment banking and a mass brokerage business, can be contrasted with "wholesale" houses such as Dillon, Read & Company, which do no retailing but rather restrict themselves more strictly to the investment banking business: origination and underwriting.

In any case the flotation of new issues for corporations by financial specialists via private negotiation involves three steps which may be thought of as taking the form of an inverted pyramid in terms of the numbers involved at each stage (see Figure 27–1).

FIGURE 27–1

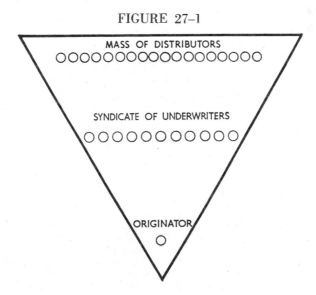

COMPENSATION TO INVESTMENT BANKERS (SPREADS) AND THE TOTAL COST OF FLOTATION

Determinants of the Size of Spreads and Total Flotation Cost

Clearly, the principal determinants of the costs of floating new securities are the extent of the services performed for the corporation and the risk entailed in the underwriting. New or small corporations, requiring extensive financial advice, wanting very wide distribution of the securities, and having a speculative flavor or little established market for their securities are going to have to concede a large spread to get these services. On the other hand, large, well-informed, and well-established stable companies will yield but a small spread. Whatever the character of the issuing corporation, that is, for any given corporation, the fees will be greater for floating stocks than bonds, and greater for preferred stocks than common stocks, owing to the higher risk assumed and the more difficult job of distribution. The stock market obviously fluctuates more than the bond market, and there are relatively few institutional purchasers of bonds to be contacted as contrasted with purchasers of stock. Finally, the spread per security will vary inversely with the size of the issue; given a corporation and a particular security, it is more expensive per unit to float a small issue than a large one. Thus, the spread varies with the nature and size of the issue and with the extent of the services performed and risks assumed.[4]

Some Recent Statistics on Spreads and Total Flotation Costs

The Securities and Exchange Commission (SEC) has made several studies of the cost of flotation of securities, the latest covering the years 1951–55.[5] The median compensation to investment bankers was 0.8 per-

---

[4] In addition to the spread (which is compensation to the investment banker), there are "other expenses" of flotation, including such things as costs of printing, legal advice, state and federal stamp taxes, and the like. These other expenses, too, tend to be smaller per dollar of money raised the larger the size of the issue. *The total cost of flotation, then, is the sum of the spread and other expenses.* And obviously, small issues will be "expensive" on both counts.

[5] *Cost of Flotation of Corporate Securities, 1951–1955* (Washington, D.C.: U.S. Government Printing Office, 1957). 1963 sample data assure that this old but complete study accurately reflects current spreads. See I. Friend, *Investment Banking and The New Issues Market* (Philadelphia: University of Pennsylvania Press, 1965), Table 17, p. 70; and Investment Bankers Association, *Statistical Bulletin*, June, 1964.

cent of gross proceeds for bonds, 3.3 percent for preferred, and 8.8 percent for common; but the range of spreads was far wider, varying with size of issue and issuer, type of business, etc. (see Table 27–1).

TABLE 27–1

INVESTMENT BANKER COMPENSATION
(As a Percentage of Gross Proceeds)

Type of Security	Median	Range
Bonds	0.8%	0.5%– 7.4%
Preferred	3.3%	2.1%–15.0%
Common	8.8%	2.4%–28.8%

The largest spreads, and they are substantial, indeed—almost 29 percent of gross proceeds—were found for small common stock issues of small mining companies. The smallest spreads, under one half of 1 percent, were found in the case of large issues of bonds by large corporations. Except in this latter case the spreads were substantial. It should be clear now why the cost of flotation[6] was considered to be an important aspect of the total cost of raising funds by security issues. Over 85 percent of total flotation costs of common stock are due to investment bankers' spreads; for preferred the average is 75 percent, and for bonds, over 55 percent. Since the other fees, such as stamp taxes, etc., are largely set by law, it is largely about spreads that issuing corporations bargain, and it is largely the size of spreads that discourages security flotation as a method of corporate finance.

Intrastate security issues are not included in the SEC cost data, which cover only issues registered with the SEC. For the most part, such issues are small-scale common stock issues with no established market place—in short, speculative issues. The spreads on some of these stocks no doubt approach 50 percent of the gross proceeds, for presumably the risks assumed in trying to sell them at a given price are very high. This cost may seem so high to the small issuer that he may prefer to seek other sources of finance; or if he thinks the bankers are overestimating the risks entailed, he may try a more economical method of flotation—a so-called best-efforts arrangement.

---

6 *Total flotation* costs include printing and engraving costs, federal stamp taxes, state taxes, trustees' fees, etc., in addition to the compensation paid to investment bankers. The medians of the total cost of flotation range from 1.5 percent for bonds to 4.3 percent for preferred stock to 10.3 percent for common stock; the ranges are 1 percent to 12.1 percent, 2.5 percent to 18.8 percent, and 3.0 percent to 33.4 percent, respectively. For further details, see *Cost of Flotation of Corporate Securities, 1951–1955*, Tables 1–4, pp. 37–40.

CUTTING THE COST OR SPREAD OF
SECURITY FLOTATION

To put it simply, there are only two ways to reduce the cost of a service such as that offered by investment bankers: (1) assuming that the services are being offered at the lowest possible price, reduce the quantity or quality of the service; or (2) assuming that the service price is a monopolistic one, that is, that the price exceeds costs including a normal profit, introduce competition into the industry to force the price down. In recent years, both of these approaches have been used to cut the cost of floating securities.

Best-Efforts Selling

The highest costs of flotation are those for small, little-known common stock issues. Here, the principal cost-reducing technique has been the use of the best-efforts arrangement. In this method the investment banker does not underwrite the issue; instead, he promises to use his best efforts to sell the stock and is reimbursed for his work by a commission on actual sales only. Note that, in effect, the cost is reduced by omitting one of the three principal services of the investment banker; the banker does *not* assume the risk of floating the security, and the corporation is not assured in advance of a certain amount of funds. Rather, the issuer pays only for origination and distribution; there is no purchasing group to compensate, so of course the cost of flotation is lower; that is, the commission rate will be smaller than the spread per share. However, the corporation cannot proceed with its investment plans until *after* the outcome of the flotation is known, and perhaps the issue will not come off at all. (If the selling price of the stock were to be cut to effect sales, this would be the equivalent of increasing the spread or selling to the bankers at cut-rate prices.) In any case, there is no easy way to cut the costs of new small stock issues without increasing the issuer's risks.

And in this sphere, there is little possibility of stimulating competition among the bankers for the issue. Big investment bankers (the 44 largest houses—10 percent of the total number—which have 60 percent of the net worth of the industry) are often not interested in risking their reputation by attaching their names to such a risky flotation. In contacting one of the numerous smaller houses, there is unlikely to be much opportunity to "shop around" or to do comparison shopping because the issue and the company are so little known and so unique that the banker will have to make an intimate study of the issuer before being able to offer a plan and a price. Such a study is costly and lengthy, and it is not easy to get competitive bids on such a small custom order. In most cases the issuer has to depend on the reputation for fairness and competence of the selected banker.

In practice, the small corporation's best protection or cost saving comes from floating his stock in a bull market. In such a market the risk that the issue will not sell is lessened, but it may well be that the issue has been underpriced, and the corporation's proceeds diminished, by more than was necessary to sell the issue; in other words, the corporation pays a high price in proceeds foregone, rather than in spreads to underwriters, to reduce the risk of a selling failure. No matter what the technique used, floating new small stock issues is costly.

Direct Placement

It is not only the small corporation which is concerned with cutting the costs of new issues. The large firms may have rather small percentage spreads, especially on bonds; but since they issue great quantities of bonds, the total absolute money fees paid are sizable. For example, a commission of 0.3 percent on a $100 million issue is $300,000, although it is only $3 per bond. Large corporations have attempted to cut their flotation costs by using the technique of direct or private placement: selling a whole issue of bonds directly to financial institutions—for example, life insurance companies. In such a procedure, there is no underwriting—the corporation receives a check in payment at once from the institution; and there is no distribution, either—the insurance company buys the bonds to hold them to maturity.

The investment banker obviously has but a small role to play in such directly placed flotations; he can serve as originator or finder—the one who brings together the issuer and the investing institution. While he will receive a fee as finder, obviously the investment banker loses out severely in such flotations, for 80–90 percent of the spread in the private negotiation method is paid for underwriting and distribution. Of course, this does not mean that investment bankers lose 80–90 percent of their *profits* as a result of such shifts by issuers from private negotiation to direct placement, because a good part of the spread received in private negotiation goes to cover out-of-pocket or potential costs. But it does reduce the banker to a counseling role.

Neither should it be thought that the corporation saves the total sum of the fees not paid. The institutional purchaser is well aware of the size of the underwriting and distribution costs that the issuer is avoiding and will bargain away some of these savings in the form of a higher rate of return on the bond. In other words, the issuer's savings must be shared with the purchaser, for otherwise the purchaser could just as well buy an issue from an investment banker. Clearly, we are confronted with a bargaining process; and since, in any exchange, we know *both* parties must gain or it will not take place, we can be sure that the issuer effects *some* gain in private placement—some lessened cost of finance as compared with a public offering—or he would not do it that way.

Though both the issuer and the financial institution save by means of private placement as contrasted with underwritten public offerings, the sharing of the spoils need not be 50–50. The proportions arrived at in bargaining will depend on such matters as the following:

1. Is the financial institution flush with funds seeking investment at a time when few bond issues are being floated?
2. Is the issuer uncomfortable about giving up the public relations benefits, etc., of having its bond widely distributed among the population? Or does the issuer prefer a firm commitment to the hazards of selling in the open market?
3. Does the bond need to be tailored to fit the particular needs of the investing institution rather than the issuing corporation?

In all these cases the issuer will obtain a heavy proportion of the savings. But of course, all these conditions might be reversed so that the institution is in the stronger bargaining position. During the 1940's, financial institutions grew so fast as to create a seller's market for bonds; but the issuer tended to want to avoid public marketing, say, because the issuer preferred an unusual indenture that the public would not understand, or because in future difficulties it would be easier to arrange contractual modifications with a single institution than with the trustees representing thousands of bondholders. And both issuers and institutions liked the possibility of tailoring the terms of the bond to their own particular needs.

The cost of debt finance may also be reduced when the offering is privately placed rather than publicly offered if the interest coupon or yield to maturity on the bond is less. There is little evidence of cost differentials, taking the whole period 1935–58. However, it does appear that yields on privately placed bonds were slightly lower than those offered publicly during the first half of the period and slightly higher in the latter half of the period. The principal cause of these differentials seems to have been the relative shifting demand of financial institutions for corporate bonds as compared with the supply of new corporate debt issues. Since 1948 the growth of financial institutions—demand—though still great, has slackened relative to the growth of nonfinancial corporations and especially relative to new corporate debt issues—supply. Moreover, since 1944, public utility debt issues have had another alternative method of floating bond issues—competitive bidding. In other words, in recent years the insurance companies, with relatively less pressing need for private placements, trimmed the price they would pay, and corporations made relatively greater use of public offerings, whether privately negotiated or put up for open bids.[7]

But despite the recent cutback in the proportions of corporate debt privately placed, sharp inroads into the total business of investment bankers have occurred. Between 1930 and 1933, only about 3 percent of corporate debt was privately placed;[8] by 1935 the proportion was 17 percent, in 1940, 32 percent, and a peak in 1950 of 52 percent. Since then, private placement has accounted for about half of all debt issues with a range of 35 to 65 percent.[9] If it had not been for the absolute increase in security flotation during the expanding 1950's, the investment banking business would have been very hard hit. Sixty-two percent of all bonds issued in 1964, were directly placed. With some notable exceptions, it is largely bonds and preferred stock that are privately placed, for financial institutions are severely restricted in their purchases of common stock. This is true of insurance companies, for example, which are the takers of 80 percent of all bonds privately placed. Of course, a few investment banking houses who specialize in finding are busier than ever, but the bond underwriting and bond distribution business has declined as a proportion of total investment banking business. In other words, the traditional private negotiation with its full range of services is more and more confined to common stock flotations.

The final element that tends to encourage direct placement is that such issues, being exempt from the Securities Act of 1933, need not be put through the cost in time and money of registering the issue with the Securities and Exchange Commission. The exemption is granted on the

---

[7] For a detailed treatment of these matters, see A. B. Cohan, *Private Placements and Public Offerings: Market Shares since 1935* (Technical Paper No. 1; Chapel Hill: School of Business Administration, University of North Carolina, 1961), chaps. ii–iii.

[8] *Ibid.*, p. 1.

[9] Securities and Exchange Commission, *Annual Reports.*

basis that the law is intended to protect the nonprofessional public by assuring truth in marketing securities, but direct placements are not publicly marketed. Life insurance companies, for example, presumably are well able to see to their own protection in dealing with the issuer directly.

Considering the advantages of direct placement for both issuer and investing institution, it is surprising that half of the new bonds continue to be issued to the public. In fact, it is government regulation itself that is holding direct placement down: many utility bonds and railroad bonds are required by the Securities and Exchange Commission (and some state commissions) and the Interstate Commerce Commission, respectively, to be sold via a technique called "competitive bidding." In effect, this required technique has encouraged public offerings as against private placement.[10] But investment bankers are not known to cheer about compulsory competitive bidding requirements, which have also tended to cause reduced spreads or compensation for their services.

Competitive Bidding

While best-efforts selling chips away at the underwriting function of investment bankers, and direct placement at both this and the distribution function, competitive bidding diminishes their originating function as well as their distribution function. And just as these other two techniques resulted in reduced spreads, so, too, under compulsory competitive bidding, spreads have been cut. However, with this technique, it was expected that the reduced price of investment bankers' services would be more the result of additional competition than of reduced services. It is not clear that competition itself has been the cause of the reduced spreads that have in fact occurred.

Under the rules of competitive bidding the issuers are required to invite competitive sealed proposals for the underwriting of their securities. Obviously, to entertain bids, the corporation must specify in advance details as to what it wants to issue, when and how it wants it distributed, etc. Thus, the investment bankers are invited to bid *after* the origination

---

[10] Industrial bonds, unsuitable for competitive bidding, comprise an ever-growing proportion of issues privately placed after 1941, when compulsory competitive bidding entered the picture. However, the proportion of all industrial bonds privately placed fell from a high of 91 percent in 1950 to about 75 percent in recent years, owing to the sharply increased supply of such bonds offered in the last decade relative to the increased demand of insurance companies for them. As noted above, these demand/supply conditions reduced the *cost* advantage of placing securities privately.

phase has been completed. Further, the corporation is required to accept the bidder (banker) who offers the best terms; there is no way of knowing in advance which house will win the bid, and it would be unusual indeed for one particular investment banker to win, or at least be sure of winning, the successive issues of a corporation over a period of time.

The objectives of both the SEC and the ICC in the early 1940's[11] in requiring competitive bidding for bonds was not merely to break up allegedly monopolistic practices in price (spread) setting, and thus to lower spreads, but also to end so-called "banker domination" of the issuers. Promulgation of the rule was an attack on the intimate relationship of investment banker and issuer that was, and is, implicit in the practice of private negotiation. The government agencies aimed to alter the nature of the investment banking business as well to lower the cost of security flotation. There is no doubt that they did both, but there is a question whether the spreads have fallen since that time as a result of increased competitiveness or as a result of reduced services.

But first, why did the governmental agencies believe that private negotiation tended to be unfair to the corporate issuer? Briefly, the argument was, and it still goes on, that (1) investment bankers developed long-continuing relationships with particular corporations, in the course of which decisions on new flotations were excessively influenced by what was good for the banker rather than the issuer (the "banker domination" charge); (2) the issuer was tied to his underwriter because the other houses had tacitly agreed not to poach on each other's preserves (and besides, there were only seventeen investment bankers of consequence in the country to choose from; this was the "monopoly" or the concentration charge); and (3) as a consequence, investment bankers charged too much for their services, some of which were not in the best interest of the issuer, anyway (the "excessive" spread charge).

Most investment bankers have denied that the first two charges are of *current* relevance, although the evidence of past malpractices (1920's and early 1930's) are acknowledged by many. Further, and of much greater importance in the debate, is the argument that the issuer is hurt by the absence of the continuing and therefore increasingly knowing counsel of

---

[11] Competitive bidding had long been the practice in issuing municipal securities; but its first application to corporate enterprise was in the middle 1920's, when the ICC required that all railroad equipment trust certificates be bid for competitively. Until the 1940's, however, the practice affected but a small part of corporate finance. Since that time, about three fifths of new utility bonds and all new railroad securities must be bid for competitively.

experts in financial matters; corporations may hire advice for a fee when the occasion arises, but the advice cannot be as competent as under a continuing arrangement.

In the authors' judgment the banker's arguments are weak. Presumably, the issuer can get as good advice as he is willing to pay for in advance before putting up the call for bids; and there is no reason why the issuer cannot retain the same counsel through the years, although it is true that such advising houses cannot bid on that issuer's offerings. Furthermore, if there is the slightest danger of those monopolistic arrangements reviving, and there is surely that from the past record, competitive bidding is a rather simple way to obviate that possibility. If it be retorted once more that the cost of antimonopoly insurance is paid in terms of badly advised and ill-serviced issuers, the rebuttal is that competitive bidding is only required for rather standardized issues, e.g., largely by utilities, issuers which either are well informed as to their needs or can hire advice for a price. Finally, if it is to be said that spreads have only fallen as a result of reduced services, and this is to be doubted, so be it; if that is the choice of the issuer, what other criterion for purchasing services should be used?

In any case, it is clear that compulsory competitive bidding has not only shaken up investment bankers' customary methods of doing business; it has, like direct placement, *reduced* spreads and the volume of business per issue that is done by the bankers. However, there does remain an important part of the new-issues market that is still and will continue to be handled via private negotiation, in which the full range of investment banker services is utilized.

THE CURRENT ROLE OF PRIVATE NEGOTIATION

The issuance of common stocks and some industrial bonds is still handled via private negotiation. Suitability for direct placement can be measured by the issuers' institutional appeal; suitability for competitive bidding can be measured by the issues' degree of standardization.[12] Moreover, even if suitable for competitive bidding, the issuer need not choose competitive bidding unless the law requires it. New issues of common stock is not much bought by institutions, and each issue tends to

---

[12] The investment banker, lacking the intimate knowledge of the corporation and not making a detailed investigation typical of the origination stage in private negotiation, could not volunteer a bid unless the calculation of the risk and distribution problems involved were simple to determine by reference to the issuers' established record and already outstanding securities.

be unique. Similarly, some industrial bonds tend to be riskier and more varied and smaller in size than new utility or railroad bonds; moreover, the law does not require that industrial bonds be bid for competitively. However, most bond issues of established industrials are directly placed. More and more, then, the investment bankers' full range of services is being applied to the stock and some bonds of industrials and to the common stock of utilities; railroads issue few new securities other than equipment trust certificates, and these are subject to competitive bidding.

Issuance of common stocks requires the complete services of the investment banker because there are no obvious answers to such questions as:

1. What price ought to be placed on the stock?
2. Who will buy them, and how difficult will they be to sell?
3. When is the best time to sell them?

High-quality bonds (and preferred stock) are priced largely in accordance with the prevailing interest rate structure and are sold to relatively few and well-known institutions. Neither the pricing nor the marketing of *lesser quality* (or unusual or small issues of) *bonds* is so assured because a credit risk enters into the problem. In other words, assistance is needed:

1. To price the bonds properly or to decide upon the interest premium over relatively risk-free bonds that should be offered. There are no standard answers to this question, for the industrial may well present unique risks of default, etc.
2. To market the bonds, since it cannot be assumed that the large institutions will pick up the bonds; perhaps smaller, scattered institutions will have to be contacted and perhaps individual investors as well.

Plainly, a substantial field remains for private negotiation. However, the average risks of the investment banking business are higher today than they were 10 or, especially, 25 years ago, because a lesser *proportion* of their business consists of quality underwritings. The cream can be skimmed off via direct placements and competitive bids. Perhaps this explains the rise of best-efforts arrangements.

If investment banking houses are to underwrite what is becoming a riskier and riskier residual business, they will have to increase their net worths and rely less on borrowed funds. There has been some tendency for investment bankers to incorporate in recent years since the New York Stock Exchange lifted its ban on the corporate form for member firms. But one hears little of the use of the form to raise permanent funds via sale of common stock to the general public. If the bankers had larger permanent capital funds, they could better afford the risk of underwriting low-quality issues, for in the event of a slow-moving issue, they could simply put the issue on the shelf (invest in it themselves) until the market became more receptive to it. As it is, the bankers are forced to dump such issues at a loss for fear of tying up their limited funds for too long a time. It is to avoid this contingency that best-efforts arrangements were devised. But best-efforts selling reduces the bankers' business and returns as well as their risks. If they would expand their business to offset the inroads of direct placement and competitive bidding, they might do well to incorporate, increase their capital funds, and increase their business by underwriting risky issues. Such a development would also improve the supply of venture (and small business) capital which is allegedly in short supply. More and more, the investment banking business is becoming a venture capital-raising business.

THE CURRENT COMPARATIVE IMPORTANCE OF PRIVATE NEGOTIATION, COMPETITIVE BIDDING, AND DIRECT PLACEMENT AS METHODS OF FLOATING NEW SECURITIES

Direct Placement

Between 1948 and 1964, on the average, about 50 percent of all corporate *bond* issues and 6 percent of all *equity* issues were privately placed, with the result that about 40 percent of *all* types of corporate securities were privately placed. For the latest available year the figures were as shown in Table 27–2.

TABLE 27–2

DIRECT PLACEMENT OF CORPORATE SECURITIES, 1965

	Debt Issues	Equity Issues	All Issues
Totals	$13.7 billion	$2.3 billion	$16.0 billion
Directly placed	8.2 billion	0.3 billion	8.5 billion
Percent directly placed	60%	13%	53%

SOURCE: Securities and Exchange Commission, *Statistical Bulletin*, May, 1966, pp. 11–12.

It is estimated that today, about 70 percent of industrial bonds and 30 percent of utility bonds are being directly placed for a total of 60 percent of all corporate bond issues (see Table 27–3).

TABLE 27–3

NEW DEBT ISSUES DIRECTLY PLACED IN 1965 BY INDUSTRY

	Utilities and Communications	Industrials	Total
All issues	$3.3 billion	$10.4 billion	$13.7 billion
Directly placed	1.0 billion	7.2 billion	8.2 billion
Percent directly placed (estimated)	30%	70%	60%

SOURCES: See Table 27–2 and R. W. Goldsmith, *The Flow of Capital Funds in the Post-War Economy* (New York: Columbia University Press, 1965), p. 217.

Competitive Bidding

Competitive bidding has been dominant in the marketing of public utility bonds for over 20 years. In the 1946–63 period, between 31 percent and 52 percent of utility bonds were issued via competitive bids.[13] If we assume that in 1965, 50 percent of utility bonds, 60 percent of railroad bonds, but only a small amount (say 2 percent) of industrial bonds were competitively bid, we would find that of the $13.7 billion in all new corporate debt issued that year, probably about $2 billion, or say, 15 percent of all debt, was floated via competitive bidding. Previously, we found that $8.2 billion, or 60 percent of the debt, was directly placed.

Private Negotiation

This means that only $3.5 billion of the total $13.7 billion debt issues of 1965, or about one quarter, was handled via private negotiation with a selected investment banker.

Note that private negotiation of debt has revived in the last ten-year period as compared with the low point reached in the 1947–51 span. (See Table 27–4.) But despite this revival of negotiated debt 25–30 percent is less than half of the 74 percent of all debt that was privately negotiated in 1935–40, and less than a third of the 97 percent of the pre-SEC years.

Thus, the investment banker has lost 80 percent of his negotiated utility bond business: to competitive bidding, 50 percent; to direct placement, 30 percent. He has lost over 50 percent of his negotiated industrial bond business, almost all of it to direct placement. He has also lost, although the absolute amounts are small, about two thirds of his

13 P. L. Howell, "Competition in the Capital Markets," *Harvard Business Review*, May–June, 1953, pp. 85–93; Friend, *op. cit.*, p. 59.

TABLE 27–4

METHOD OF SALE OF CORPORATE DEBT BY INDUSTRY, 1935–65
(Direct Placement, Competitive Bids, Private Negotiation)

	Total Debt (Issues in Billions)	Percent Privately Placed	Percent Competitively Bid	Percent Negotiated
Utilities:				
1935–40	$ 7.6	21%	3%	76%
1941–46	7.4	22	53	25
1947–52	16.0	31	51	18
1953–58	22.2	29	50	21
Industrials:				
1935–40	4.9	33	0	67
1941–46	6.0	58	0	42
1947–52	15.4	81	0	19
1953–58	25.2	58	0	42
Railroads:				
1935–40	1.4	6	21	73
1941–46	2.7	8	78	14
1947–52	0.8	9	51	40
1953–58	0.9	8	60	32
All corporations:				
1935–40	13.9	24	2	74
1941–46	16.1	33	37	30
1947–52	32.2	54	27	19
1953–58	48.3	41	24	35
1960–65		54	20–25	25–30

SOURCES: A. B. Cohan, *Private Placements and Public Offerings: Market Shares since 1935* (Technical Paper No. 1; Chapel Hill: School of Business Administration, University of North Carolina, 1961), Tables I–III; *Cost of Flotation of Long-term Corporate Debt since 1935* (Research Paper No. 6; Chapel Hill: School of Business Administration, University of North Carolina, 1961), Tables 1–3; and I. Friend, *Investment Banking and The New Issues Market* (Philadelphia: University of Pennsylvania Press, 1965), p. 57 ff.

negotiated rail bond business, almost all of it to competitive bidding. However, it must be remembered that the bulk of common stock issues are issued via private negotiation. Nevertheless, there is some competitive bidding for and direct placement of common stock of public utilities, say about 10 percent or 5 percent of all common stocks floated. And about 35 percent of utility preferred stocks plus some quality industrial preferred are floated by means other than private negotiation; let us say that 40 percent of preferred stocks are directly placed or bid for competitively.[14] On these assumptions, in 1965, about 33 percent of all corporate securities were handled via private negotiations, as is explained in Table 27–5.

But note that although over 80 percent, or $1.8 billion, of stock

[14] For 1947–49 statistics on utility stocks competitively bid for, see Waterman, *op. cit.*, Table 15, p. 110.

TABLE 27–5

NEW CORPORATE SECURITIES OFFERED FOR CASH SALE
VIA PRIVATE NEGOTIATION IN 1965

Type of Security	Total (in Billions)	Privately Negotiated (in Billions)	Percentage
Common stock	$ 1.5	$1.4	90%
Preferred stock	0.7	0.4	60
Bonds	13.7	3.4	25
All corporate securities	$15.9	$5.2	33%

flotations in 1965 (and other recent years) were originated, underwritten, and distributed by investment bankers, to the extent that the new stock issues are handled as privileged subscriptions, the investment bankers' work and consequently their spreads are diminished. And to the extent that corporations have tended to expand equity finance through internal (earnings retention) rather than external (stock sales) methods, the volume of business which calls for the full range of investment bankers' talents has been constrained more than the percentages show.

The Relative Importance of Each of the Three Methods

These conclusions are confirmed by recent data,[15] which shows that in 1960–63, 40 percent of preferred stock and 4 percent of common stock were directly placed; taking all stock issues together, 7 percent were directly placed. A study of the years 1947–49[16] shows that 31 percent of public utility preferred stock and 15 percent of utility common stock were bid for competitively. Since most new preferred stock is issued by utilities, it can be assumed that some 25 percent of all preferred issues were bid for competitively but that only about 5 percent of all common stock is so handled. On these assumptions the results for methods of issuing new stock are summarized in Table 27–6. Thus, after allowing for the 7 percent of all stock that is privately placed and the 10 percent that is bid for competitively, *83 percent of all stock* (but 91 percent of common stock) *is privately negotiated*. Stock issuance thus remains for the most part a job in which all the talents of investment bankers are used. Recall that less than *one third of all bonds issued are privately negotiated*.

To sum up, let us apply these percentages to the 1965 security flota-

---

[15] Friend, *op. cit.*, Table 14, p. 58 and p. 63.
[16] Waterman, *op. cit.*, Table 15, p. 110.

TABLE 27–6

Comparative Methods of Floating New Stock

	Preferred Stock	Common Stock	Total Stock
Directly placed	40%	4%	7%
Competitively bid	25	5	10
Privately negotiated ...	35	91	83
	100%	100%	100%

tions to estimate the volume of business conducted via private negotiation today (see Table 27–7). Note that about one third of all corporate securities in 1965 were probably handled via private negotiation.

TABLE 27–7

Corporate Securities Issued for Cash Sale in the United States via Private Negotiation in 1965

	Common Stock	Preferred Stock	Total	Bonds	Grand Total
Totals (in billions)	$1.5	$0.7	$2.2	$13.7	$15.9
Percent privately negotiated ...	91%	35%	80%	25%	33%
Amount privately negotiated (in billions)	$1.4	$0.3	$1.7	$3.4	$5.1

Sources: Securities and Exchange Commission, *Statistical Release No. 1822*, April 24, 1962; and Tables 25–2, 25–3, 25–4, 25–5, and 25–6, above.

Privileged Subscriptions and Private Negotiation of New Stock Issues

It would be wrong, however, to assume from the foregoing that investment bankers get the full job to do on almost half of all new corporate issues. To the extent that new issues are not competitively bid for or directly placed, they are counted as private negotiations. But in fact, a good part of these new "negotiated" issues is handled as privileged subscriptions—i.e., offered first to the old security holders—and the job for the bankers to do may be quite small. In short, although a new issue is privately negotiated, it may not bring as much work or spread to the investment banker if it is handled as a privileged subscription.

Except for convertibles, few bonds and preferred stocks are offered to the old security holders, so that the 33 percent of all bonds and preferred stocks privately negotiated reflect full-scale opportunities for the investment bankers. But almost *three fifths of all new common stock issues are offerings to old stockholders via subscription rights.*[17] And the average compensation and work for the investment banker in 1955 was 2.6 percent for privileged subscriptions as compared with 10 percent for stock offered to the general public.[18] The compensation is markedly smaller for privileged subscriptions because:

1. The *origination* is simple for a new issue that is merely more of one that has previously had its initial flotation.
2. The *underwriting* is much less risky because the sale price is usually set sufficiently below market price (a bargain price) to obviate the likelihood that a market decline would push the market price below the subscription price.[19]
3. The *distribution* is simple to the extent that the old stockholders take up the new shares; it is only for the shares not so taken up that new purchasers must be sought out.

Furthermore, about 50 percent of privileged subscriptions are not handled by investment bankers at all.[20] If the corporation is reasonably sure that its shares will be snapped up by the old stockholders, it may well assume the underwriting risks itself, feeling that there is likely to be no distribution problem for which expert handling will be needed. Naturally, in such cases the investment banker earns nothing, though the issue is neither directly placed nor bid for competitively.

As shown in Table 27–8, only *25 percent of common stock issues (not 93 percent) receive the full banker treatment.*[21] Instead of being reduced by the amounts privately placed or competitively bid, they are reduced by privileged and direct subscriptions.

---

[17] Securities and Exchange Commission, *Cost of Flotation of Corporate Securities, 1951–1955*, p. 21. This estimate is confirmed by H. W. Stevenson, who found that from 1947 to 1955, between one half and three quarters of the number and two thirds of the value of new common stock issues were handled via rights. He also found that in 1946 and earlier years, privileged subscriptions accounted for only half of the value and number of all new common stock issues. See H. W. Stevenson, *Common Stock Financing* (Ann Arbor: University of Michigan, 1957), pp. 15 ff. Goldsmith (*The Flow of Capital Funds in the Post-War Economy.* [New York: Columbia University Press, 1965], p. 245) found that in the 1950's over two thirds of marketable common stock issues were offered to stockholders via rights. Further confirmation for the early 1960's is in Friend, *op. cit.*, p. 63.

[18] Stevenson, *op. cit.*, Table 18, p. 60.

[19] This is essentially "stand-by" underwriting. The banker stands ready to buy all stock from the corporation that the old stockholders do not take up. Obviously, stand-by underwriting will be cheaper than the cases where the banker buys up the entire issue for resale.

[20] Friend, *op. cit.*, p. 61.

[21] And even this may be less rewarding than it seems, to the extent that best-efforts rather than full underwriting arrangements are used.

TABLE 27–8

1955 COMMON STOCK ISSUES

How Offered	Amount		Average Spread*
To general public (underwritten) ...	$ 506 million	(¼)	10.0%
To old stockholders (underwritten) ..	931	(½)	2.6
To old stockholders (direct)	490	(¼)	0.0
	$1,927 million		3.8% Weighted average (approximate)

* In percentage of gross proceeds.
SOURCE: H. W. Stevenson, *Common Stock Financing* (Ann Arbor: University of Michigan, 1957), chaps. iv and v.

Comparative Spreads of the Alternative Methods of Flotation

Table 27–9 indicates the slim spreads available for direct placement or competitive bidding as compared with private negotiation. These estimates are very rough and must be taken as indicative rather than definitive.

These estimates of the cost of flotation of *debt* by various methods are confirmed by A. B. Cohan's study, in which the *average* spread for

TABLE 27–9

ESTIMATES OF MEDIAN INVESTMENT BANKER COMPENSATION BY VARIOUS METHODS OF FLOTATION, 1951–55

Method	Bonds		Preferred Stock		Common Stock	
Private negotiation	1.5%		4.3%		10.3%	(public offering)
Competitive bidding ...	0.6		2.1		3.6	(very few issues)
Direct placement	0.5	(finder's fee)	0.8	(*all* stock)	2.6	(privileged subscription)

SOURCES: M. H. Waterman, *Investment Banking Functions* ("Michigan Business Studies." Vol. XIV, No. 1; Ann Arbor: University of Michigan Press, 1950), pp. 116–17; Securities and Exchange Commission, *Cost of Flotation of Corporate Securities, 1951–1955* (Washington, D.C.: U.S. Government Printing Office, 1957), various Appendix tables.

negotiated debt in 1958 was 1.18 percent and for competitively bid issues 0.83 percent. More important, this study, which covers the years 1935–58, shows the degree to which spreads have fallen over this period *and* the reasons for the declines. (See Table 27–10.) Data from spreads in 1963 reinforce the impression that spreads have fallen by half during the (SEC) period—1935 to date.

"The combination of the shift from railroad to public utility and industrial bonds and from scattered individual to relatively concentrated institutional holdings resulted in considerable differences in the methods

TABLE 27–10

ARITHMETIC AVERAGE SPREAD AS A PERCENT OF
BOND OFFERING PRICE, 1935–58

Years	Negotiated		Competitively Bid
1935	2.65%		1.57%
1935–40		2.36%	1.28%
1941–46		2.14	1.03
1947–52		1.49	0.62
1953–58		1.30	0.74
1958	1.18%		0.83%

SOURCE: A. B. Cohan, *Cost of Flotation of Long-Term Corporate Debt since 1935* (Research Paper No. 6; Chapel Hill: School of Business Administration, University of North Carolina, 1961), Table 11, p. 36.

used in offering and marketing corporate bonds. Before 1929, public offering by groups of investment bankers on the basis of direct negotiation with the issuers was predominant. Direct placements were virtually unknown and competitive bidding rare except for railroad equipment trust certificates. This difference was accompanied by considerably higher costs of offerings before the 1930's, reflecting the much smaller average amount per sale and the reliance on retail bond salesmen. Thus publicly offered larger corporate bond issues ($5 million or over) in the postwar period carried an investment banking compensation of less than 1 per cent compared to a spread of 3 to 5 per cent for similar offerings in the 1920's. The predominantly retail market of the first three decades of the century thus contrasts sharply with the wholesale market for corporate bonds of the postwar period."[22]

REGULATION OF NEW ISSUES AND ITS EFFECTS ON THE INVESTMENT BANKING BUSINESS

The revolution in investment banking in the last thirty years is the result of many factors: the great growth of financial institutions and their demand for securities, the secular decline in interest rates (1933–52), the drift of corporations toward internal equity finance, the great increase in issuer size as compared to size of investment banking houses, *and* the extensive regulation of securities issuance, beginning in 1933, by the Securities and Exchange Commission and other governmental agencies. The influence of the new legislation should not be exaggerated—it was only *one* of the forces responsible for the great changes in investment banking. For example, the rise of direct placement would have come

[22] Goldsmith, *op. cit.*, p. 230–31.

about regardless of securities regulation, but there is also no doubt that in the beginning the urge to place securities directly was stimulated by a desire to bypass the frightening new regulations over security issues to the general public.

The Requirements of the Securities Act of 1933

The Securities Act of 1933 is a "truth in securities" act; in essence, it requires that new issues only be sold to the general public after "the truth, the whole truth, and nothing but the truth" about the securities and the issuers have been made available to that public. In other words, all the facts, with no significant omissions or misleading additions, must be revealed by the issuer in a series of publications supervised by the Securities and Exchange Commission. Note carefully that the SEC does not pass on the merits of the new issues but only on the completeness of disclosure. New issues of highly speculative or poor quality can be issued as long as the facts that reveal their speculative or low quality are publicized. The philosophy of the law is that the public should and can be protected against fraud and inadequate information, but not against its own irrationality or the hazards of business and the possible incompetence of management. Obviously, purchasers can suffer losses in buying new securities; all that the SEC is authorized to do is to make sure that those losses are due to the vicissitudes of free enterprise in a fluctuating and unstable economy, and not to inadequate data or misinformation at issuance.[23]

The heart of the Securities Act of 1933 is the requirement that before new issues can be sold:

1. *A registration statement* must be submitted to the SEC.
2. A twenty-day *waiting* or *examination period* must be endured, at the end of which the registration may be made effective.
3. Then a *prospectus* must be presented to every potential purchaser before (or as) an offer to sell to him.[24]

---

23 Many securities acts in the various states (so-called "blue-sky" laws)—and all but Nevada have such laws—do pass on the "quality" of the issue. The state administrators occasionally refuse to register an issue for sale within their jurisdiction if it is deemed too speculative or too risky. They try to protect the average citizen against temptation. This is *not* the purpose of the SEC's activities: If the citizen wants to speculate, he is free to do so; the SEC merely wants to be sure that he knows he is speculating and has the facts to determine the nature of such speculation. In most cases the states accept the SEC's findings and allow such federally registered securities to be issued in their states after mere "notification" of the proper state authorities.

24 For a more detailed review of the work of the SEC than is possible here, see D. Saperstein, "Government Regulation of Investment Banking," pp. 353–89 in *Funda-*

The Registration Statement.   This is, in effect, a book of 50 to 150 pages covering the financial history and prospects of the company. It must include recent financial statements, managerial biographies, purposes and other details of the new issue, arrangements with investment bankers and much more. Presumably, the statement will include all the *facts* necessary to come to a decision on the merits of the issue.

The Waiting Period.   After submission of this statement, *time* must be allowed for the SEC to examine the statement for completeness and accuracy. By law, this period is 20 days; but in fact, the SEC can "accelerate" it or extend it as needed. Acceleration occurs if the issue is already well publicized—say, a privileged subscription of a well-known company; delays are encountered if the SEC feels the statement omits important material or is misleading in what it includes. In this case the SEC ordinarily uses a so-called "letter of comment" itemizing the deficiencies and the amendments required for registration to become effective, and this may all be completed within 20 days if the issuer complies willingly and promptly. (The average waiting period is somewhat over 20 days.) If not, registration may be long delayed or never granted. If the issue is effectively registered and false or misleading statements are found at a later stage, the SEC can use a "stop order" to halt the sale of the issue. If the issuer will not cease selling, the SEC can obtain a court injunction. All of the considerable powers of the SEC are backed up by harsh legal (civil and criminal) liabilities for the parties (management and its advisers) responsible for attempts to mislead the public. But of course, most registrations become effective with little difficulty within the 20-day period. After that time the issue may be sold to the public, but only if a prospectus is first offered to the potential purchaser.

The Prospectus.   This is simply an abbreviated registration statement made more readable for the general public. The prospectus is still a 10–20-page document and far from light reading, but it does provide the essential information on a new issue for those who want to *inform* themselves. This document *must* be given to the potential purchaser whether he plans to read it or not. In most respects, the purpose of the act—full disclosure and punishment of those who violate the requirements—is largely upheld even if the security purchaser never reads the prospectus, for brokers and investment counselors do read them and advise their customers in that light; *and* the law does insure that attempts to misinform will be punished even if the vast majority never read the misleading material. And incidentally, for academic purposes the registration statements and prospectuses provide a vast mine of corporate financial data never available before 1933; it has even led to the issuance of meaty annual corporate reports when in former years a simple four-page brochure with abbreviated financial statements was all that was available to owners and creditors.

Effects of the Securities Act on the Cost and Methods of Security Flotation

The Cost of Flotation.   There can be no doubt that compliance with the law has *increased the cost of flotation*. The expenses of registration, such as printing, legal fees, paying the SEC's fee, etc., may not be a *major* addition to the other costs of flotation (underwriting and distribution, etc.), but they do add to that cost. And they add relatively more to the total cost of bond flotation say 15 percent, than to the total cost of stock flotation, say 5 percent.[25]

Effects on Methods of Flotation.   But even more important to management than the additional cost has been the requirement of full disclosure and the possible liabilities that may be incurred for violation of the law. Certainly, at least in the early days of the law before the Commission demonstrated its reasonableness or lack of vindictiveness, management feared both the legal exposure and the necessity to tell the public, and their competitors, the financial facts of their corporation's life. Here, no doubt, was one of the early motivations toward direct placement.

Since, in a *direct placement*, new issues are not being offered to the general public but to financial institutions, there is no need to register the securities with the SEC.[26] What the issuer gains by not having to register is not so much cost savings or privacy or legal immunity, which are all negative and unimportant elements here. Rather the "primary advantage

---

[25] The SEC's registration fee is one one-hundredth of 1 percent of the security's proposed offering price and amount on the average to 2 percent of all expenses, excluding compensation to investment bankers. For the average bond issue ($15.5 million) the cost of flotation is $235,000, of which $135,000 would be spread and $100,000 other expenses. Of the other expenses, perhaps $35,000 is incurred only because of SEC requirements. This amounts to about 15 percent of total flotation costs. Similar calculations would show for stock issues that only about 5 percent of total flotation costs are due to compliance with the law. This percentage is lower owing to the far greater importance of banker compensation in the case of stock flotations. (See the SEC's *Cost of Flotation of Corporate Securities, 1951–1955*, pp. 11 and 12 and *passim*.)

[26] Also exempt are small issues (under $300,000) and securities of industries, such as railroads, subject to regulation by other federal agencies.

the corporate issuer achieves in direct placement is his ability to obtain from the purchaser at the close of negotiations a firm commitment as to terms. When a company decides to finance through public distribution, it takes the risk that market conditions at the time of flotation may be unfavorable. The time involved in preparing a registration statement and in meeting the SEC's waiting period requirement adds greatly to the attendant uncertainty."[27] Note that this uncertainty was always implicit in public flotation but that the Securities Act of 1933 aggravates the problem and in this respect certainly stimulates direct placement. Of course, if financial institutions had not grown so radically in the postwar years, the issuers' wish for direct placements could not have been fulfilled.

Investment bankers' spreads on bond flotations, regardless of the flotation method used, have just about been cut in half since 1935 (see Table 27–9, p. 462). The securities acts are largely but not solely responsible for this development. The acts stimulated private placement of all bonds and required competitive bidding for most rail and many utility bonds. With the loss of much of their traditional business, investment bankers sought business actively, cut costs, and engaged in much more strenuous price competition on negotiated offerings than was their pre-SEC custom. In other words, the downward pressure on spreads imposed by financial institutions in private placements and by sealed bid in competitive bidding also affected spreads in negotiated underwritings. Issuers with three or even two alternative methods of flotation obviously could and did force investment bankers to compete for the business on a basis of price; prior to 1935, most corporations had no alternative but negotiation, and the bankers did not compete with each other in terms of price. Now, they not only compete with each other for issues, but with other financial institutions as well.

Of course, the legislation is not solely responsible for the halving of spreads since 1935; the decline in interest rates and the growth of financial institutions played important roles. Since 1952, when interest rates began to rise on the average and corporate demand for funds began to grow faster than the supply of funds flowing to financial institutions, the average spread has begun to rise. But the rise is small compared to the fall from 1935. The average spread on all large bond issues was 2.59 percent in 1935, 0.81 percent in 1952, and 0.94 percent in 1958, and 1

---

[27] E. B. Corey, *Direct Placement of Corporate Securities* (Cambridge, Mass.: Harvard University Press, 1951), pp. 141–42.

percent in 1965. Despite the uptrend since 1952, spreads remain under half what they were in 1940.[28]

The recent rise in the average spread is due largely to the increased proportion of industrial bonds being handled via negotiation in recent years and to the increased risks of underwriting when interest rates are rising. Neither of these trends is likely to go much further, and in any case the negotiating investment banker knows his customer is constantly weighing the relative advantages of competitive bidding and private placement as compared with negotiated underwriting. The securities acts are largely responsible for creating these alternative methods of flotation and thus for fostering competition and lower prices[29] in the investment banking business.

THE SEC'S "SYMPATHETIC" ADMINISTRATIVE ADJUSTMENTS

The Securities and Exchange Commission is well aware of the attractiveness of private placement and has in a variety of ways tried to reduce the risks attendant on the time elapsed between perparation of registration statements and the date of first security sales. We have noted efforts to shorten the waiting period. But under the law, this has severe limits, for the SEC must have time to search for omissions, etc., or the law would be meaningless. Rather, the SEC, by administrative rulings, has tried to reduce the time elapsed between preparation of registration statements and the date of *completion* of the sale of the securities. The Commission has done this by a series of administrative rulings which, in effect, enable the investment banker to sell in a rush, and yet smoothly, immediately upon the expiration of the waiting period. The significant rulings at issue here are those that permit the bankers to disseminate information about the issue *during* the waiting period and to engage in stabilization activities *after* the waiting period.

Disseminating Information during the Waiting Period: The "Red Herring" and the "Tombstone"

During the waiting period the investment bankers are now permitted to circulate *red herring prospectuses* to potential customers. These pros-

---

[28] A. B. Cohan, *Cost of Flotation of Long-Term Corporate Debt since 1935* (Research Paper No. 6; Chapel Hill: School of Business Administration, University of North Carolina, 1961), Table 11. p. 36. Friend *op. cit.*, p. 70.

[29] Note that profit margins did not decline so radically; considerable savings in selling costs or concessions paid to nonunderwriting dealers are made when securities are sold

pectuses are in most cases exactly the same as the post-waiting period prospectuses will be, except that they have printed in red ink on their covers the statement that the registration is not yet effective and that this must not be considered an offer to *sell* the securities. In effect, these are "for information and advance study only." The idea is that customers will be prepared in advance, so that on the first day of permissible sales the rush to buy can begin at once.[30] This helps to reduce the risky "exposure" time.

Similarly, the SEC permits the advertising of new issues in newspapers and magazines by means of a so-called *tombstone* advertisement, which merely headlines the issue and the offering price and a list of houses standing ready to sell the issue. Such advertisements must always carry the legend, however, that they are not offers to sell the security and that offers can only be made via the prospectus, which the listed investment bankers or dealers will be glad to present to any potential purchaser.

Stabilizing Activities after the Waiting Period: Price Pegging

There is one other important administrative ruling that permits the investment banker to reduce somewhat the risk that the passage of time will stale the issue and make it difficult to sell at the "list" or offering price. Under strict SEC supervision and limits, and provided that the fact is publicized, the underwriters are permitted to *stabilize the price of the new issue during the period of sale*. That is, they are permitted to buy back, as well as to sell, the new issue. If the issue runs into some temporary heavy weather, the purchasing syndicate can prevent the price from sagging by buying and thus supporting the price. The presumption is that the price will be under pressure owing to the sudden influx of a new supply of stock[31] and that a limited amount of stabilization within a prescribed price range will restore balance to the market situation and allow the distribution to proceed in an orderly manner.

There is no doubt that this is price manipulation, i.e., price would be

---

to a few large buyers rather than to thousands of small buyers, as was usually the case in negotiated underwritings.

[30] Of course, if there are changes in the prospectus between the time of release of the "red herring" and the final official "offer to sell" prospectus, the banking house must make sure that the customers are aware of such changes. This is an impediment to the expediting purpose of the "red herring," but it only applies seriously to a minority of new issues. One amendment occurs in all cases, for the final offering price is not chosen until the last possible moment, i.e., when the issue's registration becomes effective.

[31] The investment bankers, with their long-restrained eagerness, slim capital position, and fear of generally deteriorating market conditions, will try to sell the stock in great volume as quickly as possible.

lower if stabilizing purchases were not permitted; but it is permissible under strict regulation and publicity to a degree necessary to offset the effects of a temporary market glut.[32] The SEC obviously is trying here to assist the investment bankers to reduce risks of reselling which other Securities Act provisions have increased. If, say, six months later, the price of the stock is near its offering price, fundamental conditions having remained the same, it can be assumed that the stabilization was justified for marketing reasons and did not lead to an overpricing of the issue. In any case, SEC supervision assures that the investment bankers will not be able to unload onto the public seriously overpriced issues, issues which will fall sharply in price once the "peg is pulled," i.e., once the bankers stop repurchasing. Stabilization or "permissible manipulation" is intended to aid the investment banker without hurting the security-purchasing public.

The Changing Nature of the Work of the SEC and of the Investment Banker

Most of these direct effects of the Securities Act of 1933 on underwriting procedures apply primarily to common stock flotation. The bond business of investment bankers has been whittled away both directly and indirectly by the Securities and Exchange Commission—directly under the Securities Act via the unexpected encouragement of direct placement, and indirectly via the SEC's and other regulatory agencies' deliberate requirement of competitive bidding for regulated industry bonds.

It is true that *competitively bid bonds*, unlike directly placed bonds, are subject to the Securities Act provisions because they are to be offered to the public. But in practice, the buying public for these high-quality bonds is largely institutional—a well-defined and well-informed market in which little marketing difficulty or risk is faced. Here, the investment banker is largely a money-changer and the SEC a benign overseer; in the case of *direct placement* of bonds the investment banker is but a finder, and the SEC does not even have a "look-in." Thus, the SEC and the investment banker find their only full-scale work with respect to new common stock, industrial bonds, and some low-quality bonds in all fields.

-----

[32] The syndicate cannot push *up* the price of the issue or create the illusion of active investor interest in the issue to induce others to buy. Rather, it is allowed merely to offset or limit a *decline* in price. And the fact that the syndicate may peg must be stated in the prospectus, and the actual volume of pegging must be reported to the SEC at the end of the offering period.

Today, the SEC finds its adventurous and time-consuming work in enforcing the Securities Exchange Act of 1934, which deals with trading in *outstanding* securities rather than the sale of new issues, which is covered by the act of 1933. And the investment banking business, with the decline of private negotiation for bonds and the extensive use of privileged subscriptions for common stock of established companies, has had to extend the range of its services to make up for the loss of the volume of its traditional business of underwriting. Today, investment banking houses are moving over into the business of serving the *individual* investor, rather than just the issuing firm, by offering counseling and brokerage services. In this process, some of them have added trading facilities in noncorporate securities such as municipals, and in commodities, the better to serve the individual investor. And with respect to corporations, some houses are not only stressing the mating of corporate issuers and institutions, but they also are creating new-issue business for themselves by seeking to promote mergers and new businesses (which will issue new securities) and to help private corporations in "going public."

Today, only a small proportion of the investment banking houses' total business consists of private negotiation with its full range of specialized services, and that portion carries a higher risk element on the average than in pre-1930 years. The rest of their business consists of a great variety of services for corporations and investors alike, and for local governments as well. It is no longer possible to use the word *underwriter* as a synonym for investment banker; the investment banking houses are more like department stores of finance. And just as responsible for this development as the Securities Act of 1933 or the trend toward internal corporate finance, or the high tax/low interest complex inducing a shift toward external bond finance rather than stock finance, is the "institutionalizing" of investment. Direct placement is totally dependent and competitive bidding largely dependent on the voracious and growing appetite of financial institutions for new corporate securities.

QUESTIONS AND PROBLEMS

1. The investment banker is neither an investor nor a banker but is essentially a middleman whether providing the full range of services or spot services. Do you agree with this description of the functions of the investment banker? Explain, illustrating your argument with examples of the various functions performed by the investment banker.

2. Distinguish between:
   a) Private negotiation and private placement.
   b) Spread and flotation costs.
   c) Best efforts and full private negotiation.
   d) Prospectus and registration statement.
   e) Red herring prospectus and tombstone.
3. How does the way investment bankers finance themselves affect the way they carry on their business? Can you suggest changes in their financing that might allow them better to carry out their functions?
4. Consider the forces that have caused average spreads for full private negotiation to have fallen by half since 1935. Has the saving been worth it from the viewpoint of the economy as a whole?

   How much of current financing of corporations is carried on via full private negotiation?
5. In setting the terms of a direct placement, what factors determine whether the issuer or the financial institution gets the better part of the bargain?

   Aside from the cost savings of direct placement over full negotiation, what other factors may lead issuers to prefer direct placement?
6. Present a case against the requirement of competitive bidding for large public utility bond issues.
7. What is the current importance of private placement of corporate bonds? Industrial bonds? Preferred stock? Common stock?
8. What have been the principal effects of the Securities Act of 1933 and the SEC's administration thereof on the investment banking business? Select one of these effects and argue that it is not in the public interest.

SUGGESTED READINGS

CHRISTENSON, C. *Strategic Aspects of Competitive Bidding for Corporate Securities.* Cambridge, Mass.: Harvard University Press, 1965.

COHAN, A. B. *Private Placements and Public Offerings: Market Shares Since 1935.* Chapel Hill, N.C.: University of North Carolina Press, 1961.

————. *Cost of Flotation of Long-Term Corporate Debt Since 1935.* Chapel Hill, N.C.: University of North Carolina Press, 1961.

FRIEND, I. *Investment Banking and the New Issues Market—Summary Volume.* Philadelphia: University of Pennsylvania, 1965.

ROBBINS, S. M. "Competitive Bidding in the Sale of Securities," *Harvard Business Review,* September, 1949, pp. 646–64.

U.S. SECURITIES AND EXCHANGE COMMISSION, *Report of the Special Study of the Securities Markets,* Part II. Washington, D.C., 1963.

WATERMAN, W. H. *Investment Banking Functions.* Ann Arbor, Mich.: University of Michigan, 1958.

Chapter 28

THE PURCHASERS OF CORPORATE SECURITIES: THE INCREASING IMPORTANCE OF FINANCIAL INSTITUTIONS

It will come as no surprise to the careful reader of the preceding chapter that in recent years the proportion of total outstanding corporate bonds and preferred stock held by financial institutions has risen and that the proportionate holdings of individuals have declined. What may be surprising is that this trend has been in process since 1900. Obviously, then, the causes of this protracted trend involve forces quite apart from the recent shifts in flotation techniques and regulations.

Moreover, there is also a long-term trend, not as powerful but just as old, for financial institutions to hold an increasing proportion of total outstanding corporate common stock. This trend, too, has been influenced by forces more powerful and more ancient than recent changes in flotation procedures. And it may come as a shock to realize that during the 1950's—a period of stock market boom and great involvement of individuals in that boom—individuals' proportionate holdings of outstanding common stock did not increase. But neither did they decrease, as they had between 1900 and 1950. The trend toward increased institutional holdings of stock was not reversed but merely arrested; the advance resumed in the 1960's.

What are the causes of this growth in institutional appetite for corporate securities? What are the dimensions of this growth and, as a corollary, the dimensions of the decline of individuals' holdings of corporate securities? What particular financial institutions are most re-

473

sponsible for these important shifts in holders of corporate securities? Are these trends likely to be reversed or accelerated in the future? What are the implications of these trends for external corporate finance? Answers to these important questions and others form the content of this chapter.

THE INCREASING PROPORTION OF FUNDS SUPPLIED BY FINANCIAL INSTITUTIONS VIA PURCHASE OF CORPORATE BONDS AND STOCKS

Only in the last decade did reliable statistics on institutional holdings and new purchases of corporate securities become available. The historical material is provided by a masterwork of research by Raymond W. Goldsmith, *Financial Intermediaries in the American Economy since 1900.*[1] However, this provides the figures only through 1952. For the period 1952–58 we rely on Goldsmith's new study, *The Flow of Capital Funds in the Postwar Economy;* for the years since 1958, we have two continuing sources: the "flow of funds" series of the Board of Governors of the Federal Reserve System and the "sources and uses" series of the Department of Commerce.[2] For our purposes, these current statistics are most easily available and best arranged in the various annual issues of *The Investment Outlook* published by the Economics Department of the Bankers Trust Company.[3]

In this chapter, unless otherwise noted, all statistics for the years 1900–1958 are from Goldsmith's books, and those for the years since 1958 are from the various issues of the *Investment Outlook* series. The Goldsmith statistics are in terms of the portion of *outstanding* securities in institutional hands, while the more recent statistics are in terms of the volume of net new issues issued annually and the annual purchases of securities by institutions. To convert the latter statistics to the Goldsmith procedure simply requires that we add net new issues to the totals outstanding, and then add the institutional annual takings since 1958 to their totals as of 1958 and compare the two to find the new proportion of outstandings held by institutions. This procedure is quite straightforward when applied to bonds whose outstanding values are not subject to much

---

[1] Princeton: Princeton University Press, 1958.

[2] New York: Columbia University Press, 1965; the series are reported quarterly in the *Federal Reserve Bulletin* and annually (usually in October) in the *Survey of Current Business,* respectively.

[3] This annual report is available from the Bankers Trust Company at no cost to students and teachers—16 Wall Street, New York, N.Y. 10005.

market value variation,[4] but with respect to outstanding stocks the blending of the two series is more difficult, owing to the upward trend in recent years of the market values of common stock outstanding. We shall cope with this latter problem shortly. But our bond series can easily be joined.

The Role of Financial Institutions in Corporate Bond Financing

Between 1900 and 1958, financial institutions' share of corporate bonds outstanding rose from 35 percent to 95 percent. This rise was almost uninterrupted and gathered speed in the last 25 years of the period: Between 1900 and 1933 the share rose from 35 percent to 47 percent, or by one third, while in the 25 ensuing years—a shorter period—it doubled, jumping from 47 percent to 95 percent (see Table 28–1). In other words, individuals, who held two thirds of all outstanding

TABLE 28–1

SHARES OF FINANCIAL INSTITUTIONS IN DOMESTIC CORPORATE BONDS OUTSTANDING, 1900–1958

Year	Total Outstanding (Billions)	Percentage Held by Financial Institutions
1900	$ 6.9	34.5%
1912	17.5	36.2
1922	24.2	46.1
1929	39.0	51.3
1933	38.5	46.7
1939	33.5	64.6
1945	27.0	73.0
1949	39.3	89.5
1952	50.4	93.6
1958	88.7	94.6

corporate bonds in 1900, held but one twentieth of them in 1958. The absolute figures, too, are striking. In 1900, individuals held $6 billion in corporate bonds of the $9 billion outstanding; while in 1958, they held but $5 billion of the $89 billion outstanding.

But which particular financial institutions were responsible for this great secular change? The answer is life insurance companies and corporate pension funds. "Banks"[5] are the only other important institutional

---

[4] Of course, it is necessary to allow for bond retirement, but this is done for us in the annual figures which are reported "net," that is, after allowing for retirements.

[5] Including commercial banks, mutual savings banks, and personal trust departments of banks.

holders of corporate bonds, but they did not *increase* their percentage holdings of all outstanding corporate bonds between 1900 and 1958. In 1900, banks held 25 percent of all outstanding bonds, and insurance companies held 8 percent; these two institutions accounted for almost the whole of all institutional holdings. In 1958, "banks" held 19 percent of all outstanding bonds, but insurance companies held 50 percent, and corporate pension funds—nonexistent in 1900—held 21 percent. Currently, then, all other financial institutions taken together held the remainder, or 5 percent, of outstanding bonds. Obviously, in terms of current events, life insurance companies and corporate pension funds are the important institutions to examine in detail. (See Table 28–2.)

TABLE 28–2

SHARES OF PARTICULAR FINANCIAL INSTITUTIONS OF ALL DOMESTIC
CORPORATE BONDS OUTSTANDING, 1900, 1952, 1958

Institutions	1900	1952	1958
Commercial banks	9.8%	6.7%	4.0%
Mutual savings banks	6.4	4.9	4.6
Personal trust departments	8.7	9.9	10.0
Private life insurance companies ...	7.9	58.0	50.0
Pension funds	..	8.9	20.8
All other institutions	1.7	5.2	5.2
All Financial Institutions	34.5%	93.6%	94.6%

Since 1958, these trends have continued. Between 1952 and 1965, corporate bonds outstanding increased by about $40 billion, while life insurance holdings rose by $14 billion and pension fund[6] holdings by another $20 billion. Note that 85 percent of the increase in outstandings was preempted by these two sets of institutions alone. The banking group no longer is adding to its bondholdings, but its place is being more than filled by the expansion of pension funds. In fact, since 1959, pension funds' annual purchase of bonds have *exceeded* those of life insurance companies. Indeed, for 1965, it is estimated that life insurance plus pension funds institutions will have increased their bond portfolios by more than the increase in net new issues for that year![7] That is, they will have bid away some of individuals' or other institutions' holdings of corporate bonds.

---

[6] Since 1952, state and local government pension funds (for government employees) too have become important purchasers of corporate bonds.

[7] New issues for 1966 are estimated at 7.2 billion, and the increase in life insurance holdings $2.1 billion and pension fund holdings $4.0 billion, or a total of $6.1 billion.

In 1965, it is likely that the amounts of corporate bonds shown in Table 28–3 were being held by the various financial institutions.[8] Note

TABLE 28–3

HOLDINGS OF CORPORATE BONDS OUTSTANDING, 1958 AND 1965

1958 (Billions)		Institutions	1965	
			Billions	Percent of Total Outstanding
$44.5		Life insurance companies	$ 58	45%
18.5		Pension funds	39	30
	$12.5	Corporate	$21	
	6.0	State and local	18	
		Banks		
3.5		Commercial	3	2
4.1		Mutual savings	4	3
8.0		Personal trust	7	6
1.5		Fire, casualty, and miscellaneous insurance companies	2	2
1.2		Investment companies	3	2
2.7		Miscellaneous (e.g., charitable, etc.)	8	7
$84.0			$124	97%
5.0		Individual owners	4	3
$89.0		Total Bonds Outstanding	$128	100%

that 75 percent of all corporate bonds are in the portfolios of life insurance companies and pension funds. In 1952, 68 percent was in the portfolios of these two institutions. There has been little decrease in the proportion of corporate bonds owned by individuals—this has remained in recent years at a low 3 to 6 percent of the total outstanding. But clearly, there has been a shift among the institutional holders, with the result that banks hold relatively (and absolutely) less, while insurance companies and pension funds hold relatively more. There is, then, no question that the corporate bond market is dominated by these latter two sets of institutions, and increasingly so. What accounts for this development?

What Accounts for the Increasing Institutionalization of Corporate Bonds?

This is really a dual question. We must inquire why financial institutions *as a whole* have been absorbing an increasing proportion of bonds outstanding since 1900. And we must also ask why *particular* financial institutions have recently become the dominant forces within the broad

---

[8] The 1958 figures are given to show recent shifts among various institutional holders.

classification of financial institutions. Let us first consider the overall issue and then look at particular institutions.

Financial Institutions as a Whole. Fundamentally, the great growth in institutional holdings of corporate bonds stems from the simple fact that financial institutions have been growing at a far faster rate than nonfinancial corporations. When financial institutions grow, they acquire cash, which they immediately seek to "invest" in income-yielding securities such as bonds. When nonfinancial corporations grow, they acquire plant and equipment, etc., by *spending* cash, which, in part, they acquire by selling new securities such as bonds. In other words, financial institution' growth is marked by *purchase* of securities and corporation growth by *sale* of securities. Obviously, if the former grow faster than the latter, the new institutional demand for securities will outstrip the supply of corporate securities, and individuals' holdings of securities will decline as their holdings of outstanding securities are bid away or as institutions outbid them for new issues.[9] In effect, as individuals make the decision to turn over to financial institutions increasing absolute and relative amounts of their cash income, they are also deciding to hold fewer securities directly in their personal portfolios.

Between 1900 and 1950, financial institutions grew at two and a half times the rate of nonfinancial corporations; total corporate assets grew from $31 billion to $296 billion, while financial institutional assets were growing from $19 to $452 billion. Over the same period, financial institution assets as a percentage of total national assets almost doubled, rising from 12 percent to 23.5 percent. Thus, assuming that financial institutions wanted to maintain a relatively constant proportion of their total investment in corporate bonds, their demand for such bonds would outstrip new corporate issues of bonds, assuming that corporations financed a relatively constant proportion of their expansion by issuing bonds. These assumptions were realistic for the 1900–1949 period, and, as you can check in Table 28–1, institutional holding of corporate bonds swelled almost exactly two and a half times over that 50-year period, rising from 34.5 percent of the total to 89.5 percent.

Since 1950, the rate of growth of nonfinancial corporations was so spectacular that financial institutions, although they were still growing rapidly, grew at a slower rate.[10] But the proportion of bonds held by finan-

---

[9] Of course, there are forms of debt other than corporate debt—for example, home mortgage debt and government debt—for which institutions may compete with individuals, but our concern is with *corporate* securities.

[10] In fact, corporate assets doubled between 1950 and 1960 while financial institutions' assets increased by only (!) 50 percent.

cial institutions still continued to rise, albeit far more slowly than previously and in very recent years not at all. But how could they rise even
the small amount they did (89.5 percent to 97 percent) if total asset
growth was at best equal? This is an especially puzzling question because
corporations in these recent years have been financing their growth increasingly by issuing bonds. It would seem, then, that the new supply
of bonds should outstrip the institutional demand for such bonds.

The answer is that at the same time that these developments were
occurring, individuals have had strong reasons for *not* buying corporate
bonds—indeed, for reducing their bondholdings—while financial institutions have been strongly motivated to increase the *proportion* of their
portfolios that consists of corporate bonds. Moreover the fastest growing
financial institutions recently have been those, like the pension funds,
whose portfolios are heavily corporate bond oriented. To spell out the
meaning and significance of these recent developments requires that we
consider the behavior of individuals in managing their personal portfolios
as well as new developments in the field of institutional finance.

The Institutionalization of Personal Saving.   It goes without saying that financial institutions would not have grown as spectacularly as
they have since 1900, and especially in the last 25 years, if individuals
had not found it possible and desirable to increase their savings via
institutionalized facilities. Insurance companies have huge sums to invest
in corporate bonds and other securities because individuals contract for
vast quantities of insurance; banks' assets have swelled because individuals have made savings and demand deposits there; and pension
funds, the newest and fastest-growing financial institution, have become a
major factor in the institutional market for bonds because the American
citizen, wanting to provide an annuity for his retirement years, has been
contributing cash to these pension funds. In short, the individual has
increasingly provided for his safety and liquidity, and he has chosen to do
so via financial institutions rather than by measures of his own devising.

The average individual has been *able* to lay aside cash to augment his
liquidity and safety because his real income has increased so radically in
the past half century. We know that the secular average propensity to save
has been quite stable; a fairly steady 6–7 percent of rapidly rising
disposable incomes provides a rapidly rising absolute amount of personal
savings. The individual has *chosen* to direct a good portion of these
savings toward providing readily available funds for an emergency during
his working years (bank deposits), for use during his postworking years
(annuities), and for the benefit of his family after his death (insurance,

etc.). To provide for safety and liquidity in such fashion is a luxury that only the very rich were once able to afford; rising incomes have been making such luxuries increasingly possible for the mass of the people.

But it is not merely that individuals have been saving more and that institutionalized forms of saving would gain in *proportion*—the share of increasing personal savings channeled through financial institutions has increased in the last 25 years. Between 1897 and 1929, about two fifths of personal savings were made through financial institutions; since 1940, this proportion has risen from two thirds to almost four fifths and seems steady at that high level. Thus, financial institutions have grown not merely because savings have grown absolutely but also because their share of those growing amounts has risen sharply.

Let us look at the total financial savings of Americans in the years 1956–65 to see the current picture of how institutionalized these savings are. In the complete list presented in Table 28–4, noninstitutionalized savings are marked with an asterisk, and the other figures are labeled as to the financial institution involved.

During the period 1956–65, net financial savings added by individuals in an average year were $20 billion. Of this $20 billion, only $2 billion, or 10 percent, was *not* channeled through financial institutions. In other words, during the last ten-year period, 90 percent of net financial savings were made via financial institutions.[11] Thus, it is clear that the post-World War II trend toward heavy institutionalization of savings continues unabated.

Note, in particular, that individuals have been adding about $1 billion annually to their *personal* holdings of corporate bonds, and have been *reducing* their personal holdings of stock by about $2 billion a year! On the other hand, individuals channel $2 billion a year to the stock market via mutual funds—an institutional channel. It is clear that personal savings are heavily directed toward insurance and pension funds, and equally toward bank deposits; only 20 percent of personal savings in recent years has been put into securities and that largely into *government* securities or into indirect purchasing through investment companies.

It is not *impossible* for the increasingly affluent individual to provide for his own liquidity and safety by individual action and thus to avoid the financial institutions. One can keep emergency cash under the mattress, and one can set up a personal portfolio of securities and add to them annually, etc. But most individuals find it less costly and less bothersome

---

[11] Eighty-eight percent if we take *gross* financial savings as the base.

TABLE 28-4

NET ADDITIONS TO FINANCIAL SAVINGS BY INDIVIDUALS IN THE UNITED STATES, 1956-65

(Billions of Dollars)

Holdings	Institution Involved	Totals for Ten Years	Totals per Year
Currency and Deposits		203	20
Currency and Demand deposits	* and commercial banks	29	3
Time and savings deposits	Commercial and savings banks	90	9
Savings and shares	Savings and loan institutions	84	8
Securities		38	4
United States Savings bonds	*	–0	–0
Other United States governments	*	15	1.5
State and local governments	*	16	1.5
Corporate bonds and notes	*	9	1.0
Investment company shares		17	2.0
Stock	Mutual funds, etc. *	–19	–2.0
Insurance and Pension Reserves		129	13
Insurance reserves	} Insurance companies	43	4
Insured pension reserves		16	2
Noninsured pension funds	Corporation pension fund	39	4
Government insurance and pension reserves	Government pension fund	31	5
Gross financial savings		370	37
Less: Increase in individuals' debts†		–175	–17
Net Financial Savings		195	20 Annual average

† Mortgage debt increased by $125 billion (or $12.5 billion per year on the average) and consumer indebtedness by $50 billion (or $5 billion a year). Note that most of this debt is, in turn, owed to financial institutions.

SOURCES: Securities and Exchange Commission. *Statistical Releases No. 1762*, June 22, 1951; *1705*, September 20, 1960; *1964*, April 1, 1964; and *2136*, June 30, 1966.

—as well as, on the average, more fruitful in returns earned—to save via institutions. Note that a financial institution in this respect is a mere middleman: In general, it receives cash, invests it in securities, etc., and after deducting costs, adds the returns to the individual's account. The institutions provide the various benefits of pooling of assets: purchasing securities in blocs makes for lower cost, expert management can be afforded, risks can be diversified. Of course, each financial institution offers particular services and benefits to the individual, and we cannot go into detail on the various distinctions. All that needs to be noted here is that as individuals in sufficient numbers have developed newly felt needs for financial services, institutions have arisen to provide for them. The rise of pension fund arrangements and investment companies since World War II are the best recent examples.

It might be objected that individuals seem to be doing much direct purchasing of corporate securities. This is not at all true of corporate bonds, which are our current concern, and we shall see shortly that it is not even true of corporate stocks. Despite stock market activity, the great bulk of stock is owned by wealthy individuals and institutions; the average individual owns no stock, or very little, and much of what he does own is owned indirectly via investment companies or mutual funds— financial institutions. Moreover, wealthy individuals are reducing their holdings of corporate securities more than sufficiently to supply the millions of new, small stockholders with the result that we have many *more stockholders* holding in the aggregate *less stock*.

The Unattractiveness of Corporate Bonds to the Individual Investor.   Neither the wealthy individual nor the average individual has much incentive to buy corporate bonds; if he is interested in bonds at all, in almost all cases government bonds are a superior portfolio choice. In July, 1966, the wealthy individual—say, in the 40–60 percent tax bracket —could buy a first-grade tax-exempt municipal government bond yielding, with a 4.0 percent coupon, a 4 percent posttax return, while grade AAA corporates, with a 5.4 percent coupon, would yield only a 2.7 percent posttax return. It makes no sense for such an individual to buy corporates when he can get a superior yield on *at least* equally safe municipals. On the other hand, the average individual (in the 20 percent tax bracket) should buy long-term federal governments, not long-term corporate bonds, if he buys bonds at all, for the yield on the former— again in July, 1966, as an example—was 4.8 percent (or 3.85 percent after taxes), which is little less than the corporate yield of 5.4 percent (or 4.3 percent after taxes). The slight additional yield on corporates (0.4+

percent) is hardly enough to compensate the individual for the additional credit risk involved in buying corporates. After all, there is *no* credit risk in buying federal government bonds.

But in fact, the *average* individual would not be much of a demander of corporate bonds even if the yield differential were greater; it is not customary to sell such bonds singly, and they are usually in $1,000 denominations. Savings and loan deposits yield 5 percent with no brokerage fees, etc., and savings bonds currently yield 4.2 percent. Furthermore, once a man reaches the 25 percent income tax bracket, municipals become advantageous to him as well as to the really wealthy man. For example, based on the above figures, the municipal would yield 4.0 percent and the corporate bond 4.0 percent after 25 percent income taxes. The man in lower income brackets is not a buyer of bonds of any kind, except perhaps savings bonds. To the extent that corporate bonds are bought by individuals, they are bought for promise of capital gains,[12] not income possibilities; and this, again, is a wealthy man's game which is seldom worth playing in light of the tax exemptions granted by municipals. To sum up, then, individuals buy federal government or municipal government bonds, depending on their tax bracket, but seldom is it in their interest to bother with corporate bonds.

The Attractiveness of Corporate Bonds to Certain Institutions.   It is almost exclusively life insurance companies and pension funds which buy corporate bonds. We already know that these two institutions own 75 percent of all outstanding corporate bonds, with that percentage growing every year as they annually add to their portfolios more corporate bonds than are being net newly issued. Even other financial institutions, as well as individuals, are turning away from corporate bonds as a medium of investment because of their tax situation; for example, the commercial banks, which are subject to the regular 52 percent corporate income tax, increasingly favor municipals or mortgages aside from loans for income, and governments for safety and liquidity. Other banking institutions (savings institutions) have always been almost exclusively takers of residential mortgages, which yield more than corporate bonds, anyway.

Why, then, should pension funds and insurance companies be such

---

[12] Arising from falling interest rates or conversion privileges or special situations. For example, although individuals acquired only 9 percent of new bond issues in 1962, these purchases included over 50 percent of new *speculative* bonds such as subordinated or convertible debentures. See I. Friend, *Investment Banking and The New Issues Market —Summary Volume* (Philadelphia: University of Pennsylvania, 1965), p. 52.

avid takers of corporate bonds? The principal part of the answer is the tax-free status of pension funds and the privileged tax position of life insurance companies. Given no tax burden, it is clear that the yield advantage lies with corporate bonds, for they offer a higher pretax interest rate than either federal or state and local governments. It never makes sense for pension funds, and seldom for life insurance companies, to buy municipals, for the funds are already tax-exempt. And for both institutions the edge (5.4 versus 4.8) in yield of corporates over governments is worth taking, for:

1. The edge is 0.6, or 11 percent, for it is slightly (if at all) affected by taxes.
2. Where else can these institutions obtain higher yield investments? There are limits on the amounts of stock they can buy (especially insurance companies), and stocks do not have high yields today, anyway. Mortgages have higher yields, but pension funds are not yet accustomed to buying them, and insurance companies want to limit the share of mortgages in their total portfolio. Yield is critical to these institutions, for they have predictable fixed obligations to their beneficiaries to meet in future years.
3. The differential yield can be higher than 0.6 percent if lesser quality bonds are carefully chosen. For example, prominent corporations in cyclical industries pay as much as 7 percent because the credit risk involved is clearly greater than that of governments (or of American Telephone & Telegraph debentures), although they are solid investments. And as we know, such bonds can be obtained by the economical technique of direct placement, which is only possible for sizable institutional buyers.

Another way to view the continuing and almost exclusive demand for corporate bonds by these two institutions is to note that they are among the fastest-growing institutions in the nation. With so heavy a flow of funds coming to them which must be invested to meet fixed and long-term obligations, they are almost forced to turn to corporate bonds. If they exercised the whole of their huge demand or purchasing power on the governments market, they would drive prices up (and yields down) in the process, especially if the government were not borrowing much money at the time, i.e., increasing the supply of government bonds. In spreading out their demand for fixed income securities, these two institutions will necessarily buy some corporates. And these institutions are growing so fast that even if they use but a small part of the flow of new funds to them on corporate bonds, it will be important in the market for corporates, because the additions to corporate debt annually are small, relative to the additional funds flowing to these two institutions annually.

For example, it is estimated that in 1966, net new corporate bonds issued will total $10 billion, while the assets of pension funds and insurance companies will increase by over $20 billion. If these institutions place 40 percent of their funds in corporate bonds, as they tend to do, they will be taking 80 percent of all new corporate issues. And they are almost certain to buy corporate bonds because there are few alternative long-term debt investment opportunities with comparable yields. Moreover, since there is no other substantial market for corporate bonds, we can be sure that corporate issuers will make it worthwhile for these institutions to take their offerings via special arrangements (including increased yields) developed in the process of direct placement.

We already know from Table 28–3 that life insurance companies plus pension funds increased their holdings of corporate bonds from 68 percent of all bonds outstanding in 1952 to 75 percent in 1965. Let us review how this came about (see Table 28–5).

TABLE 28–5

INCREASES IN NET NEW ISSUES AND OWNERSHIP OF
CORPORATE BONDS, 1958–65

Increase in net new corporate bond issues ..	$39 billion
Increase in ownership of bonds:	
Life insurance companies	$13.5 billion
Corporate pension funds	8.5
State and local retirement funds	12.0
	$34 billion
All other	5
	$39 billion

Note that pension funds and life insurance companies increased their ownership of bonds by $34 billion over these recent years, while new issues were adding only $39 billion to the total outstanding amount of corporate bonds. In other words, these two institutions *alone* bought bonds equal in amount to 87 percent of net new issues between 1958 and 1965. This explains why these two institutions in 1965 had 75 percent of all outstanding corporate bonds in their portfolios, while they had only 70 percent in 1958.

To sum up, in 1965, these two institutions had $97 billion of the $128 billion total corporate bonds outstanding. In that last year, these institutions alone bought $10 billion of bonds, while corporations were issuing only $9 billion of bonds. Clearly, these institutions are increasing their proportions of outstanding bonds still further today, for they have a demand for corporate bonds which exceeds the fresh supply; this necessitates, of course, their buying outstanding bonds in the open market from other financial institutions and individuals.

THE INCREASED INSTITUTIONALIZATION OF CORPORATE COMMON STOCK

The rate at which financial institutions have increased their share of all outstanding common stock since 1900 has not been much slower than for corporate bonds. But the importance of their role as increasing holders of common stock is far smaller. Although the share of institutional holdings of common stock almost tripled between 1900 and 1958, rising from 7.5 percent to 20 percent, just as their share of bonds almost tripled (rising from 34.5 percent to 94.6 percent), their proportionate holdings of stock at the end of the period (20 percent in 1958) was still not as great as their proportionate holdings of bonds had been at the beginning of the period (34.5 percent in 1900). Obviously, the institutionalization of common stock is not nearly as advanced as that of bonds. However, the rate of change in this picture seems to have increased in the years since 1958; there was a 50 percent step-up on the pace of acquisition of stock by financial institutions in 1961–65 as compared with 1956–61. But in any case the absolute sums involved are large. Institutions owed $84 billion of bonds in 1958 and $83 billion in common stock; the former was 94 percent of outstanding bonds, while the latter was but 20 percent of outstanding stock.

What Accounts for the Relatively Small Institutionalization of Common Stock, 1900–1958?

1. There has been *no single outstanding institutional taker of common stock*. The holdings of common stock have been spread rather evenly among many institutions with no one of them, with the exception of personal trusts, holding a sizable percentage. And the holdings of "personal trusts"—largely managed by commercial banks—have not increased their share of total holdings since the middle 1920's. In other words, between 1900 and 1958, there was no large and growing institutional demander of stocks as life insurance companies, or even pension funds later in the period, were for bonds. It is the change in this situation in the years since 1958—the rise of investment companies and pension funds as important stock buyers and the increased interest of insurance companies as well—that seems to indicate that the institutionalization of stock is about to become more important.

TABLE 28–6

SHARES OF FINANCIAL INSTITUTIONS IN CORPORATE STOCK
OUTSTANDING—1900–1965

Institutions	1900	1922	1952	1958	1965	
Insurance companies:						
Life	0.5%	0.1%	1.3%	1.0%	1.2%	$ 9.1B.
Fire, casualty, etc.	1.0	0.6	2.2	2.0	1.6	12.4
Banks:						
Commercial	0.8	0.9	0.2	0.1	0.3	1.9
Savings institutions	0.3	0.1	0.5	0.2		
Personal trusts	4.9	11.0	12.8	9.6	8.6	67.0
Pension funds:						
Corporate	0.0	0.1	0.9	2.5	5.1	39.7
State and local	0.0	0.0	0.0	0.1	0.3	2.2
Investment companies	0.0	0.1	2.6	4.5	5.2	41.0
Total Institutional						
Holdings	7.5%	12.9%	20.5%	20.0%	22.4%	$173.3
Total Outstanding (billions)	$12.3	$57.1	$195.0	$418.0	$778	.
Total Institutional						
Holdings (billions) ,	$ 0.9	$ 7.4	$ 40.0	$ 83.6	$173.3	

Note that personal trust holdings, which are institutionally handled personal estates, dominated the list of institutional holders throughout the 1900–1958 period; they had 65 percent of all institutionally held stocks in 1900, 85 percent in 1922, 62 percent in 1952, and 48 percent in 1958 (see Table 28–6). All of the growth in institutional holdings was due to personal trusts between 1900 and 1922. Between 1922 and 1958, insurance companies, pension funds, and investment companies began to become prominent so that, by 1958, insurance companies had 15 percent of all institutional holdings, investment companies 22.5 percent, and pension funds 10 percent. In other words, one half of institutional holdings by 1958 were in these three sets of institutions.

If, as seems to be happening, these new takers of stocks continue and accelerate their perference for stocks, they will raise the total institutional holdings of stocks; for personal trusts, the dominant holder, while not dynamic, is a fairly stable holder. It now looks as if pension funds will be *the* new growth institution which will raise the share of institutional stockholdings. Investment companies will also play an important role in this. Both of these institutions have become important only in the past two decades.

2. Another reason why institutional dominance of outstanding stocks is less than that of bonds is that *the older (nonpersonal trust) institutions have had serious legal and self-imposed restrictions on the amounts of stock they could buy*—for example, insurance companies. But these limits

lately have been eased off as the economy's immunity to depression for twenty-five years and the reality of creeping inflation have made regulators realize that it is now both safer and more rewarding for insurance companies to buy stock than it was in the prewar days.[13]

3. Still another reason for the failure of financial institutions to achieve the dominating role in stocks, despite their great asset growth and the substantial dollar sums they bought, is that over the long run, *stocks, unlike bonds, do not mature, but do rise in price*. Beginning with a minority share of stocks outstanding, it takes a vast amount of buying of stocks to turn the percentage owned up; for individual holders, though doing nothing, find the outstanding market value of their shares rising. Under these conditions, institutional ability to buy up outstanding stocks of individuals is impaired with every sharp rise in stock prices. In short, financial institutions find it difficult to gain *percentagewise* even when they are increasing the amounts allotted to stock purchases, unless that increase in purchases is at least as great as the percentage rise in stock prices. If stock prices double over a period of a few years, it is hard to imagine that traditional institutions will be able to *double* their outlay on stocks in such a short period of time.

It is interesting to note that between 1922 and 1929—a period of stock market boom—the long-run trend toward slow but steady increase in institutionalization of stocks was reversed; the institutionalized percentage fell from 12.9 to 12.3 over that period. And of course, we have just experienced a similar 15-year boom in stock prices. Remember that under these circumstances, institutions can be stepping up their spending on stocks, but it will not easily affect their relative share of stocks held so long as the sharp rise in stock prices continues.

What Makes It Look as if We Are on the Verge of an Important Rise in the Share of Common Stock Owned by Institutions?

Following the analysis of the previous section, it can be shown that the institutional share of stocks will soon rise substantially because:

1. Since 1958, we have developed new important institutions with strong demands for common stocks.
2. The older institutions have stepped up their demands for stock.
3. The rate of rise in stock prices is tapering off.

---

[13] New York State now allows life insurance companies to invest as much as 5 percent of their assets in common stock.

The Rise in Institutional Takings of Stock, 1958–65.   In the period since 1958, institutions have been buying stock in amounts in excess of the total value of net new issues. Under these circumstances, there is great pressure for their percentage of total outstanding stock to rise. (See Table 28–7.)

TABLE 28–7

INCREASE IN NET NEW ISSUES AND OWNERSHIP OF
COMMON STOCK, 1958–65
(Billions of Dollars)

Increase in net new common stock issued ..	11.0
Increase in ownership of common stock:	
Life	3.0
Fire and casualty	2.0
Pension funds:	
Corporate	16.0
State and local	1.0
Investment companies	8.0
Total Institutional Increased Ownership	30.0
Residual*	−19.0
	11.0

* The residual includes reductions in individual holdings plus personal trusts.
SOURCE: *The Investment Outlook, 1966*, Banker's Trust Company, N.Y., Table 11.

Note, in particular, that corporate pension funds alone are responsible for over 50 percent of all institutional purchases of stock, and adding investment company purchases drives the percentage up to 80 percent. Here are two new and rapidly growing institutional purchasers of common stock. In 1952, these two institutions together bought $800 million of common stock when $2.4 billion were being issued; they were responsible, then, for one third of all stock purchases; in 1958–65, investment companies *alone* took off the market almost as much stock as was newly issued in those years.

Pension funds added to their portfolios $16 billion or one and one half times the amount of stock that was being added to the supply over the years 1958–65.

The Effect on Institutions' Share of Total Common Stock Outstanding, 1958–65. We know that in 1958, financial institutions held 20 percent of stock outstanding. It would seem to be simple common sense to assume that that percentage has risen in the ensuing years, since they have bought additional stock virtually equal in amount to that which has been issued since 1958.

To illustrate this matter, let us use some rounded arithmetic. In 1958, institutions held 20 percent, or $83 billion of the $418 billion outstanding market value of stock. If *stock prices had remained constant* between 1958 and 1965, institutions at year-end 1965 would have held $113 billion of outstanding stock ($83 billion plus $30 billion increase, 1958–65); and total outstanding stock would have increased from $418 billion to $429 billion, or by the $11 billion of net new issues. Institutions' share of stock in 1965 would then be $113/$429, or 26 percent—a substantial rise from the 20 percent of 1958.

But in fact, the market value of outstanding stock rose 86 percent between 1958 and 1965. How does this fact affect institutions' share of outstanding stock? This would mean that the $83 billion of 1958 holdings of institutions were worth $155 billion in 1965; this $155 billion plus the $30 billion in new acquisitions would make institutions' total holdings in 1965 sum to $185 billion. But what proportion is this of total outstanding stock in 1965? The total outstanding in 1958 was valued in the market at $418 billion; this would be worth 1.85 times as much in 1965, or $772 billion. To this total, we add the $11 billion in new issues, making the market value of all outstanding stock in 1965 approximately $783 billion. The institutions' share would be $185/$783, or 23.5 percent, or, on a somewhat more realistic calculation, 24 percent.[14] (In fact, it was 22.4 percent. See Table 28–6.)

Note that the *rise in stock prices reduces the institutional share* from 26 percent to 23 percent, or reduces their added share over the 1958–65 period to 3 percent from 6 percent. Note that between 1952 and 1958 when stock prices rose by 115 percent (faster than the 85 percent of 1958–65 over a longer period), the institutional share of stock ownership remained stable at 20 percent even though the institutions acquired stock fully equal in value to total net new issues. In addition to the inhibition of stock institutionalization via the greater stock price rise was the lesser rate of acquisition of stocks by institutions in 1952–58 as compared with 1958–65.

---

[14] Strictly speaking, we should also allow for the increased market value of the $30 billion of institutional acquisitions in recent years. Assume that the average gain was two fifths of that used for issues held as early as 1958. Then the $30 billion of acquisitions would be worth $40 billion as of 1965 (not $56 billion, which would only be the case if they had all been acquired by early 1958). Then, institutional holdings would be $155 billion plus $40 billion, or $195 billion, and total outstandings would be worth $772 billion plus $40 billion, or $812 billion. Institutional holdings in 1965, then, would be $195/$812, or 24 percent.

The Probability of Increased Institutionalization of Stock in the Future. As soon as stock prices cease to rise substantially—and can they always continue to rise at the hectic pace of the last decade?—institutions' share will rise. If prices rise not at all over the next five years, the institutional share of total stock outstanding could rise to 30 percent by 1970. If prices rose at half the rate of the 1950's in the 1960's, by 1970 institutions will hold at least *25 percent of all stock outstanding.*

Still, there is a paradox to be admitted. One of the causes of the rise in stock prices, which impairs financial institutions' efforts to increase their share, is in itself the new heavy institutional demand for common stock. Unless the *supply* of new equity issues is stepped up, some stock price rises are to be expected on this account. In other words, as long as institutions have to bid stocks away from individual owners, there will be pressures for stock prices to rise. But even with a reasonable price rise, the institutional share should rise to 25 percent by 1970.

The principal underlying forces for the rest of the 1960's will be the very great increase in demand for equities by pension funds and investment companies. It is certain that their demand alone will be more than equal to the total of all net new issues of stock. The acquisitions by all other financial institutions will necessarily dig into the holdings of individuals; thus, provided stock prices do not rise radically, the institutionalized share of stock outstanding will rise.[15] Nor should we neglect the possibility of stock price deflation.[16]

We are thus on the verge of renewed institutionalization of stocks. Institutionalization of bonds can go little further, for it is already some 97 percent; that revolution is virtually complete. But institutionalization of stock, which was 7.6 percent in 1900, 12.9 percent in 1922, and 20.5 percent in 1952, should be on the move again now and may well reach 30 percent by 1972. This would be quite in line with its long-run rate of advance. Of course, even then, in 1972, individuals would still own 70 percent of all outstanding stock.

It is important to note, for the understanding of corporate finance, that whether or not the percentage held by institutions rises, the great demand

---

[15] It has been estimated that by 1970, investment companies plus corporate pension funds will own $100 billion in common stock. This is 50 percent over their current holdings of $70 billion. It is not likely that new issues of stock between 1966 and 1970 will aggregate more than $10 billion or more than $2 billion a year. During the 1960's to date, average net new stock issues were below $2 billion per year. (Estimates from A. W. Sametz, "Financial Institutions and the Market for Equities" [unpublished manuscript].)

[16] In any case, a tripling of stock prices in the 1960's, as in the 1950's, now seems almost out of the question.

of institutions for stock now and in the future, relative to new issues added to the supply outstanding, makes the market for stocks a sellers' market from the corporate issuers' point of view. The rise of direct placement of new issues of common stock with pension funds may well become an important development over the next decade.

Individual Holdings of Common Stock.   It may seem astonishing, in view of the great stock market boom and public interest in it, that the public's personal share in that market has fallen. In fact, the *number* of individuals owning stock has increased radically since 1950, but the average individual holding has decreased in size sufficiently to have lowered the ratio of total individual holdings to total stock outstanding.

Furthermore, the undoubted increase in individual concern with stocks is largely expressed through increased holdings of shares in mutual funds, which, of course, are institutionalized holdings.

The individual today has a far larger stake in the market for stock, but this increase is due to his indirect holdings, i.e., to the increased holdings of stocks by the institutions serving the average individual. The industrial worker owns stock indirectly through his pension fund, and he may be buying shares in a mutual fund through monthly instalment purchases; occasionally, he may even buy a few shares directly for his own portfolio.

But this increased spread of individual involvement with stock is largely indirect (through institutions); and when it does involve direct ownership, large sales by *other* wealthy individuals have been sufficient to prevent such increases in the numbers of small holders of stock from increasing the share of all individuals' holdings of total stock outstanding. Apparently, the large individual holders have found it advantageous to sell their stock, taking sizable capital gains, and to invest the proceeds in tax-exempt municipal bonds or mortgage bonds, or directly in real estate, where the yields on investment are considerably greater than on common stocks.

It is true that the *number* of individuals owning stock doubled during the 1950's, rising from around six million to over twelve million and has increased by 60 percent to 20 million today.[17] Perhaps one in seven families owns stock today. But the bulk of holdings is concentrated in high-income families; for example, in 1949, families with $25,000 or

---

[17] Note that this increase in numbers finally exceeded the numbers that had owned stock at the end of the 1920's decade. Up to 1960 the percentage of total population owning stock had not yet recaptured the 8 percent proportion of 1930, owing to the sharp population increase between 1929 and 1959; by 1965 a new peak of 10 percent was set.

more income owned 50 percent of individually owned stock. In other words, while 15 percent of all families may own stock today, they are primarily rather small holdings, for 0.5 percent of all families own nearly half of the stock. Obviously, since 1949 a small amount of selling by the 0.5 percent group could account for the rise in numbers of stockholding families without there being any increase in the relative amount of stock held by individuals as a group.[18] The latest estimate is that "2 percent of stockholders with the highest incomes hold 25 percent of the shares."[19]

SUMMARY: THE PAST, CURRENT, AND PROSPECTIVE IMPORTANCE OF FINANCIAL INSTITUTIONS AS PURCHASERS OF CORPORATE SECURITIES

Financial institutions have been an important and growing source of external finance to corporations since 1900. Taking the whole period 1900–1952, they supplied about two fifths of total external finance, or one seventh of total corporate finance. But the institutions' share of external finance rose over the period from over one third in the first decade of the 1900's to one half in the early 1950's, or from one seventh of all corporate finance to one quarter in the later years.

Today, financial institutions are probably supplying two thirds of all external finance and one third of total finance of corporations. Institutions as a source specifically of long-term debt and equity—that is, as a market for corporate bonds and stocks—have increased over the long period at an even faster rate, and markedly so in recent years. In the early 1900's, institutions supplied about one fourth of long-term corporate debt and one twentieth of outside equity funds; in the late 1940's the respective fractions were over one half and one fifth. Today, we know that almost the entire bond market is institutionalized and that institutions are an increasingly important factor in the market for stocks.

It is easy to summarize the role of institutions in the bond market, for they own over 97 percent of all outstanding bonds, and they spend

---

[18] For recent estimates of numbers of shareholders, see the New York Stock Exchange *Annual Fact Book* for 1965. For that year, it is estimated that there were 20 million owners of stock in the United States. For detail on the characteristics of individual shareholders, see L. H. Kimmel, *Share Ownership in the United States* (Washington, D.C.: Brookings Institution, 1952); and J. K. Butters, L. E. Thompson, and L. L. Bollinger, *Effects of Taxation: Investment by Individuals* (Cambridge: Harvard University Press, 1953).

[19] E. B. Cox, *Trends in the Distribution of Stock Ownership* (Philadelphia: University of Pennsylvania Press, 1963), p. 197.

annually on bonds at least as much as the total value of new bonds sold. Moreover, we know that over half of all new bonds are sold directly to institutions.

In the case of stocks the evidence of institutional dominance is necessarily more indirect. There is little direct placement of stocks with institutions, and the institutions' share of total outstanding stock is probably not yet 25 percent. Still, we know that in recent years, institutional purchases of stocks annually have been larger in sum than the new stock issues added annually to the total outstanding. The rising pressures on the equity market (as well as the bond market) can be observed in the figures shown in Table 28–9.

TABLE 28–9

NET NEW ISSUES AND INCREASES IN INSTITUTIONS' HOLDINGS OF CORPORATE
SECURITIES, 1952–66
(Billions of Dollars)

	Stocks			Bonds		
	1952–56	1957–61	1962–66	1952–56	1957–61	1962–66
Net new issues..................................	10.5	11.8	3.2	22.4	25.9	36.5
Increases in institutional holdings	8.1	16.8	22.6	20.3	23.5	38.0
Insurance companies	1.7	2.3	3.6	11.8	10.3	11.6
Pension funds	3.3	8.1	13.0	8.2	10.5	18.4
Investment companies	2.6	6.1	5.5	0.2	0.3	1.6
Banks	0.5	0.3	0.5	—0.5	0.9	—0.4
State and local governments	......	......	......	0.6	1.5	6.8
Increase in individual holdings (including foreigners)	2.4	—5.0	—19.4	2.1	0.9	—1.5

In the postwar years, institutions have become increasingly important in the market for stocks. Between 1952 and 1956, they bought over $8 billion worth of stock during a period when only $10.5 billion of new issues were coming out. In effect, institutions were buying stock equal in value to over three fourths of net new issues. In 1957–61, institutional purchases were $5 billion *more* than the total of net new issues; in other words, individuals must have been *selling* stock net. Between 1962 and 1966 institutions bid away $20 billion in stock from individuals. Although institutions own less than one quarter of all outstanding stocks, they are currently of greater importance in the equity markets than that proportion would seem to indicate. Note especially that almost all of the increase in institutional takings is due to the purchases of pension funds and investment companies, and that pension funds are more important than investment companies.

By contrast, there has been little change in the market for bonds in recent years; this market is already thoroughly institutionalized. Individuals increased their holdings by about 3 percent of the amount of net new bonds issued, and this fits neatly into the pattern of institutions' ownership of over 95 percent of all outstanding bonds. The only shift in the bond area worth noting is that pension funds now are the biggest single purchaser of corporate bonds, as well as of stocks. They have replaced insurance companies as the leader here, as they did investment companies in the market for new stocks.

If the projected rates of growth for pension funds (whose assets are 40 percent in stock) and investment companies (whose assets are 90 percent in stock) follow the most conservative estimates, institutionalization of the market for stocks will increase substantially over the next decade. But it will take many decades for institutionalization of the stock markets to approach the degree of institutionalization of the bond markets. Meanwhile, however, institutions increase their weight in day-to-day stock trading, even though they are minority holders, for the vast majority of the dominant individual holdings are inactive. By 1970, institutions may have but 30 percent of all stock outstanding, but they may well account for over half of the total trading on the exchanges.

One may expect that these developments will affect corporate external finance techniques. For example, the rise of direct placement of stock with institutions rather than with old stockholders may well be around the corner. Such a development, in turn, would affect the investment banking business. Moreover, it is possible that, given such institutional demands, and possibly lower cost of equity finance, corporations may increase the extent to which they finance themselves via sales of common stock. Thus it is that developments in financial institutions may well influence the whole structure of corporate finance in the future, as they have in the past.

QUESTIONS AND PROBLEMS

1. Compare and contrast the institutionalization of the corporate bond and corporate stock markets in terms of the—
   a) Timing and extent of the trends.
   b) Causes and particular institutions involved.
   c) Prospects of further institutionalization.
   d) Effects on corporate financial patterns.

2. How do you explain the following paradoxes:
   a) While the number of shareholders has been soaring, the proportion of stock held by institutions has been rising too.
   b) In the corporate bond market noninsured pension funds buy more bonds each year than any other institutional purchaser but life in-

surance companies are the most influential force in the corporate bond market.

  c) Institutional dominance of stock market trading tends to drive stock prices up but rising stock prices retard the rise in institutions' proportionate ownership of total stock.

3. Why in the post-World War II period has personal saving become so heavily institutionalized?

    Which institutions have been the principal beneficiaries of these decisions of personal savers?

    How would corporate finance differ today if personal savings had not been increasingly institutionalized?

4. Why has the institutionalization of the corporate bond market proceed so much further than the institutionalization of the stock market.

    When, if ever, do you think the stock market will be as institutionalized as the bond market?

    Explain what recent experience has been with respect to the rate of institutionalization of the equity markets.

5. How has institutionalization of the corporate bond and stock markets affected corporate external financing techniques? What further effects do you think are likely to occur as institutionalization proceeds apace.

SUGGESTED READINGS

ANDREWS, V. L. ". . . Retirement Funds in the Financial Structure," pp. 381–531 in the Commission on Money and Credit (CMC), *Private Capital Markets*. Englewood Cliffs, N.J.: Prentice-Hall, Inc., 1964.

BRIMMER, A. *Life Insurance Companies in the Capital Markets*. Ann Arbor, Mich.: University of Michigan, 1962.

COX, E. G. *Trends in the Distribution of Stock Ownership*. Philadelphia: University of Pennsylvania, 1965.

GOLDSMITH, R. W. *Financial Intermediaries in the American Economy Since 1900*. Princeton, N.J.: Princeton University Press, 1958.

HOWELL, P. L. "Competition in the Capital Markets," *Harvard Business Review*, May–June, 1953, pp. 85–93.

McFERRIN, J. B. "The Structure of the American Capital Market," *Southern Economic Journal*, January, 1955, pp. 247–60.

MILLER, E. "Trends in Private Pension Funds," *Journal of Finance*, May, 1961, pp. 313, 327.

ROBBINS, S. *The Securities Markets—Operations and Issues*. Glencoe: The Free Press, 1966.

INDEXES

INDEX OF AUTHORS

INDEX OF SUBJECTS

This book has been set in 11 and 10 point Bodoni Book, leaded 2 points. Part numbers are in 24 point Bulmer italic; part titles and chapter numbers and titles are in 18 point Bulmer. The size of the type page is 27 by 45½ picas.